REJOICE AND SING

Melody Edition

Published by Oxford University Press
for the United Reformed Church

Oxford University Press, Walton Street, Oxford OX2 6DP
Oxford New York
Athens Auckland Bangkok Bombay
Calcutta Cape Town Dar es Salaam Delhi
Florence Hong Kong Istanbul Karachi
Kuala Lumpur Madras Madrid Melbourne
Mexico City Nairobi Paris Singapore
Taipei Tokyo Toronto
and associated companies in
Berlin Ibadan

Oxford is a trade mark of Oxford University Press

Not for Sale in the USA

ISBN 0 19 146922 X

First published 1991
Reprinted 1991, 1992 (twice), 1995

Printed in Great Britain on acid-free paper by
Richard Clay Ltd., Bungay, Suffolk

A Full Music Edition is also available

CONTENTS

PREFACE

'Hymns are the folk-song of the church militant.' Erik Routley's remark in 1952 is illustrated by the fact that the later twentieth century has been as creative a period for the writing of new hymns as any in the history of the Church. Hymns have always been particularly important to those traditions represented in the United Reformed Church, whether Congregational, Presbyterian, or Churches of Christ, for they have enabled congregations to express together their worship and praise, their wonder at the almighty power and grace of God.

In 1986 the General Assembly of the United Reformed Church agreed to publish a new main hymn-book, and appointed an Editorial Committee. The Committee now presents this book to the Church, with gratitude to all those church members who wrote in response to the preliminary lists published in REFORM. Unlike the existing hymn-books in use, *Rejoice and Sing* is not a revision of an earlier book. The presence of three different traditions in the Church also means that where versions of a hymn or the customary tune differ, no particular version or tune has an established claim. The Words Sub-committee has tried to establish the original text of each hymn, and often has preferred that text to later amended versions. The Music Sub-committee has sometimes paired tunes from different traditions and sometimes chosen completely new tunes. The Editorial Committee in general has looked at recent hymn-books and collections with the intention of presenting the best from all parts of the Church in many lands and across the centuries. The result is a freely 'catholic' selection of hymns which, in addition to Watts, Wesley, and other classic hymn-writers, includes great hymns of earlier centuries as well as contemporary hymns and some from the world Church.

From the earliest times the psalms have been an essential part of the Church's worship. The Committee has ensured that the book contains sufficient psalms for every Sunday of the liturgical year. A single section of psalms contains traditional metrical psalms from the Scottish and Irish Psalters, other metrical versions written by authors past and present, and prose psalms set for chanting using Anglican chant, psalm-tones, and Gelineau settings. Congregations therefore have the opportunity to become familiar with the great variety of ways in which psalms can be used in worship. Hymns which are based on psalms, but explicitly relate them to the Christian Gospel, are placed in the main sections of the book. There is also a section of canticles, which includes traditional canticles like the Magnificat and Te Deum and hymns based upon them, and new canticles based on New Testament passages.

There is not a section of hymns for 'times and seasons'—morning, evening, marriages, funerals, harvest, etc.—and for these reference should be made to the thematic index in the Full Music Edition. Nor is there a separate section of children's hymns. Instead the Committee has tried to ensure that in every section of the book there are hymns which can be sung by children and adults together.

The Committee has had to make some difficult decisions about the language of hymns. Some years ago the General Assembly resolved that inclusive language should be used wherever possible in the publications of the Church. The Committee has therefore avoided the use of words like 'men', 'brothers', 'sons', etc. where the reference is intended to include both sexes. Only in a handful of cases, where the original poetry would have been destroyed by any change, has this not been done. Following another Assembly ruling, however, the Committee has not attempted to remove 'he', 'his', etc. when the reference is to God.

Similar problems occur in relation to archaic language. The Committee has not attempted to eliminate all references to 'thee' and 'thou', though where it has proved possible to substitute 'you' in a way which does not jar with the original style this has been done. Words which have changed their meaning present a more difficult problem. Amendments to such words have been made as long as hymn-books have been produced, and this book is no exception.

The feature which will probably be most novel is the inclusion of prayers and responses for congregational use. In order to maintain the freedom and variety in worship which has characterized our tradition, the Committee wished to provide material which could be used in different ways. Hence the book begins with an outline order of worship, and contains a numbered sequence of prayers and ancient hymns which will be particularly useful for Communion but can be used at other times as well. There is also a section of prayer responses, and single verses which may be repeated several times. Some of these have proved popular at places like Taizé and Iona, and may be especially useful on ecumenical occasions. Confessions of faith and statements of faith, which may be used at baptisms and ordinations, appear at the end of the book.

The order of the hymns reflects the truth that our worship begins and ends with God. 'When we speak to God,' wrote P. T. Forsyth, 'it is really the God who lives in us speaking through us to Himself. His Spirit returns to Him who gave it, and returns . . . bearing our souls with Him . . . The Christian . . . prayer is the secretary of Creation's praise.' (*The Soul of Prayer*, p. 32.) The first main section therefore contains hymns of adoration for One God in Trinity.

God's love overflows in creation and redemption, and this is the theme of the second main section. It is divided into three parts, related to God the Creator, God Incarnate, and God the Life-Giver. The theme of the third main section is creation's responses to God's love. Again there are three parts. The first is concerned with the Gospel, the second with the Church's life and witness, and the third with the way the Gospel becomes effective in the world. The book concludes with a section on the unity of all creation in eternal praise. 'So identical is the praise of salvation,' wrote Henry Allon, 'that the first great song of the Christian Church on earth can hardly be distinguished from the last song of the redeemed in heaven.' (*Church Song in its relations to Church Life*.)

We gather for worship to praise God and to listen for his word. As we do so, we see only too clearly that all our words and deeds are but a feeble response to what God has done for us. In the words of Isaac Watts's doxology to the Holy Trinity (hymn no. 37):

Where reason fails, with all her powers,
there faith prevails, and love adores.

This also enables us to see his meaning when he says in another place (hymn no. 31):

None but thy wisdom knows thy might,
none but thy word can speak thy name.

The Committee hopes that this book will enable all our congregations to rejoice and sing in the eternal praise of God, to whom be glory in the Church and in Christ Jesus to all generations, for ever and ever. Amen.

David M. Thompson
(*Convener*)

INTRODUCTORY NOTE

The Prayers and Responses for Worship are preceded by an Order of Service. An Introduction to the Psalms and Canticles, and a Note on the Performance of Anglican Chant, can be found at the beginning of the Psalms and Canticles on pp. 731–733.

Refrains are printed in *italic.*

'Altd.' indicates a text which incorporates alterations to the original that appear in other hymn-books.

An asterisk (*) indicates a text which incorporates alterations to the original made or suggested by the compilers of *Rejoice and Sing*.

adpt. = adapted by
arr. = arranged by
attrib. = attributed to
cent. = century
harm. = harmonized by
para. = paraphrased by
tr. = translated by
v(v). = verse(s)

PRAYERS AND RESPONSES FOR WORSHIP

ORDER OF SERVICE

Scripture Sentences
Prayer of Approach
Confession of Sin
Assurance of Pardon
Kyrie or Gloria
Prayer for Grace or Collect

Scripture Reading
Psalm, Canticle, or Anthem (e.g. Alleluia)
Scripture Reading(s)
Sermon
Confession of Faith
Prayers of Intercession

Invitation
Offertory
Narrative of the Institution
The Thanksgiving
  Sursum Corda
  Prayer
  Sanctus
  Prayer
  Acclamation
  Prayer
The Lord's Prayer
The Peace

The Breaking of Bread
Agnus Dei
The Sharing of Bread and Wine

Prayer
Nunc Dimittis or Concluding Praise
Dismissal and Blessing
Amen

GENERAL NOTES

This Order of Service is the first one printed in the 1989 *Service Book* of the United Reformed Church. It varies at some points from that in *A Book of Services* (1980). The Kyrie precedes the Gloria, so that it may be more readily associated with the Prayer of Confession. The Acclamation appears within the Thanksgiving Prayer rather than after the Sharing of the Bread and Wine. These changes are suggested in order to encourage flexibility, and not to discourage use of the former Order.

Four items are included which were not in the former Order. Alleluias are an example of a short congregational anthem. The Agnus Dei is in the place appropriate for a communion meditation. Two new alternatives are included for use at the close of worship: the Nunc Dimittis, and a form of Concluding Praise based on an Hallel Psalm, which may have been sung by Jesus and his disciples after the Last Supper.

The opening section of this hymn-book contains most of the items in the First and Second Orders, which are for congregational use. Each has a number, following the order in which they appear in the service. Some have one or more musical settings. They are therefore conveniently available for use both in a communion service and on other occasions also.

Since there is so much variation among congregations in the number of hymns sung in worship and the points in the service at which they come, hymns have not been placed in the Outline Order. They may be included, for example, after the Prayer of Approach, after a Scripture Reading, after the Sermon, at the Offertory, and at the Conclusion of Worship. However, many of the items in the Outline Order could occasionally be in the form of a hymn: so, for example, the Prayer of Confession could be a hymn of penitence, a scripture reading might be sung as a paraphrase, the Confession of Faith might be a hymn of faith, and so on.

Psalms, Canticles, and Confessions of Faith may be found in the last three sections of the book. The Lord's Prayer and the Gloria Patri have been placed on the inside back cover for easy reference. The section of hymns on 'The Church's Life and Witness: Worship' includes a number of prayer responses (392–403) which may be used as sung responses to spoken prayers. Many other sections of the book also contain single-verse hymns, which may be used as responses to a scripture reading or the sermon, or to repeat a worship theme through the service, or in other ways. It is hoped that the availability of this material in a hymn-book will stimulate the imagination and creativity of those leading worship and of all our congregations.

1 SCRIPTURE SENTENCES

(*a*) This is the day that the Lord has made;
Let us rejoice and be glad in it.

It is good to give thanks to the Lord,
For his love endures for ever.

(*b*) Give thanks to the God of heaven,
For his love endures for ever.

The stone which the builders rejected
has become the main corner-stone.

**This is the work of the Lord;
it is wonderful in our eyes.**

2 PRAYER OF APPROACH

(*a*) **Almighty God,
to whom all hearts are open,
all desires known,
and from whom no secrets are hidden:
cleanse the thoughts of our hearts
by the inspiration of your Holy Spirit,
that we may perfectly love you,
and worthily magnify your holy Name;
through Christ our Lord. Amen.**

(*b*) **Almighty God,
infinite and eternal
in wisdom, power, and love:
we praise you for all that you are,
and for all that you do for the world.
You have shown us your truth and your love
in our Saviour Jesus Christ.
Help us by your Spirit
to worship you in spirit and in truth;
through Jesus Christ our Lord. Amen.**

3 CONFESSION OF SIN

If we say we have no sin, we deceive ourselves.
If we confess our sins, God is faithful and just
and will forgive our sins
and cleanse us from every kind of wrong.

(*a*) **Lord God most merciful,
we confess that we have sinned,
through our own fault,
and in common with others,
in thought, word, and deed,
and through what we have left undone.**

We ask to be forgiven.

**By the power of your Spirit
turn us from evil to good,
help us to forgive others,
and keep us in your ways
of righteousness and love;
through Jesus Christ our Lord. Amen.**

(*b*) **God our Father,
we have sinned against you and against one another,
in thought, word, and deed;
we have not loved you with all our heart;
we have not loved our neighbour as ourselves.
But you have kept faith with us.
Have mercy on us, forgive us our sins,
and restore us to newness of life,
through Jesus Christ our Lord. Amen.**

(*c*) I confess to God Almighty and in the presence of all God's people that I have sinned in thought, word, and deed, and I pray God Almighty to have mercy on me.

**May Almighty God have mercy on you,
pardon and deliver you from all your sins
and give you time to amend your life.**
Amen.

(*continued overleaf*)

**We confess to God Almighty
and in the presence of all his people
that we have sinned in thought, word, and deed,
and we pray God Almighty to have mercy on us.**

May Almighty God have mercy on you,
pardon and deliver you from all your sins
and give you time to amend your life.
Amen.

4 ASSURANCE OF PARDON

(*a*) In repentance and in faith, receive the promise of grace and the assurance of pardon.
Here are words you may trust,
words that merit full acceptance:
'Christ Jesus came into the world to save sinners.'
To all who turn to him he says: 'Your sins are forgiven.'
He also says: 'Follow me.'
Thanks be to God.

(*b*) 'God so loved the world
that he gave his only Son,
that everyone who has faith in him
may not perish
but have eternal life.'
To all who repent and believe,
we declare in the name of the Father,
the Son and the Holy Spirit:
God grants you
the forgiveness of your sins.
Thanks be to God.

5 KYRIES

Lord, have mercy.
Christ, have mercy.
Lord, have mercy.

Taizé Community

(*a*)

PAUL BATEMAN (1954–)

(*b*)

Taizé Community

(*c*)

6 GLORIA IN EXCELSIS

**Glory to God in the highest,
and peace to God's people on earth.**

**Lord God, heavenly King,
almighty God and Father,
we worship you, we give you thanks,
we praise you for your glory.**

**Lord Jesus Christ, only Son of the Father,
Lord God, Lamb of God,
you take away the sin of the world:
have mercy on us;
you are seated at the right hand of the Father:
receive our prayer.**

**For you alone are the Holy One,
you alone are the Lord,
you alone are the Most High,
Jesus Christ,
with the Holy Spirit,
in the glory of God the Father. Amen.**

PAUL BATEMAN (1954–)

praise you for your glo - ry. Lord Je - sus Christ, on - ly
Son of the Fa - ther, Lord God, Lamb of God, you
take a-way the sin of the world: have mer - cy on
us; you are seat - ed at the right hand of the
Fa - ther: re-ceive our prayer. For you a-lone are the
Ho - ly One, you a-lone are the Lord, you a-lone are the
Most High, Je-sus Christ, with the Ho - ly Spi - rit, in the
glo - ry of God the Fa-ther. A - - men.

7

GLORIA
(shortened)

Taizé Community

①
②
Glo - ri - a, glo - ri - a, in ex - cel - sis De - o!
Glo-ry to God, glo-ry to God, glo-ry to God in the high - est!

③
Glo - ri - a, glo - ri - a! Al - le - lu - ia, al - le - lu - ia!
Glo-ry to God, glo-ry to God! Al-le-lu-ia, al-le-lu-ia!

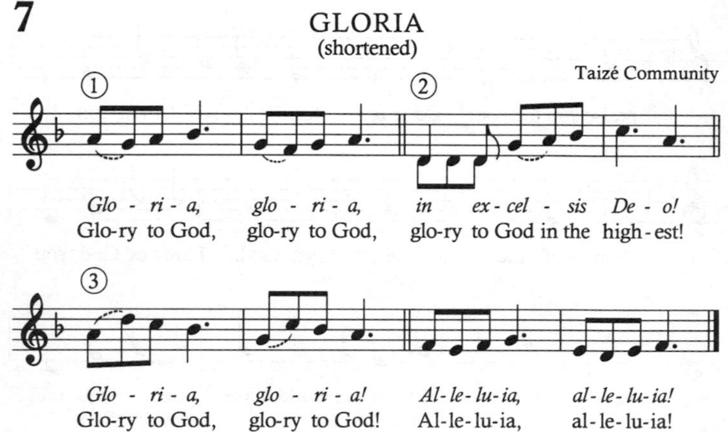

This is a three-part canon, the voices entering as indicated.

8

GLORIA
(shortened)

Source unknown, probably Peruvian

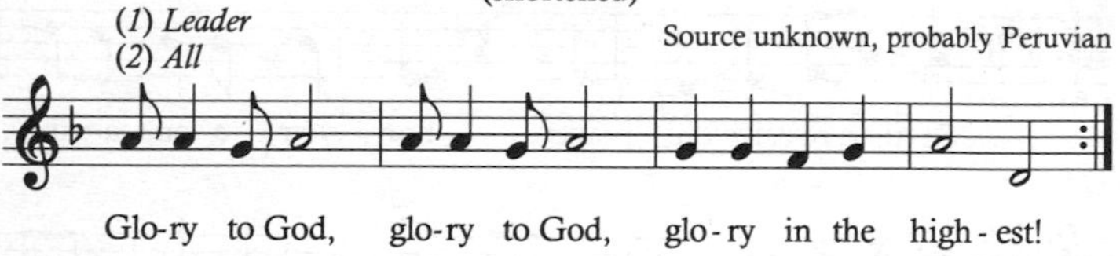
(1) Leader
(2) All
Glo-ry to God, glo-ry to God, glo - ry in the high - est!

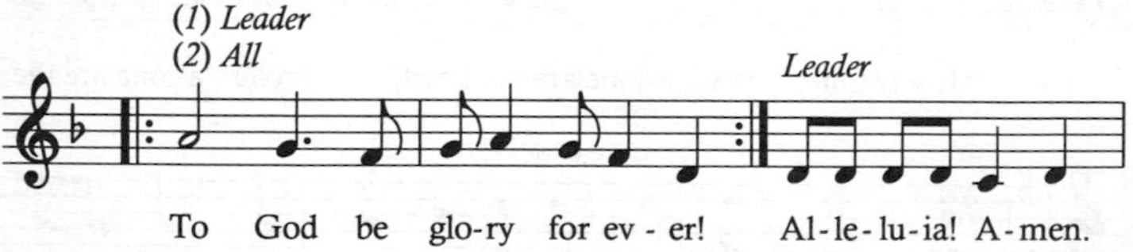
(1) Leader
(2) All
Leader
To God be glo-ry for ev - er! Al - le - lu - ia! A - men.

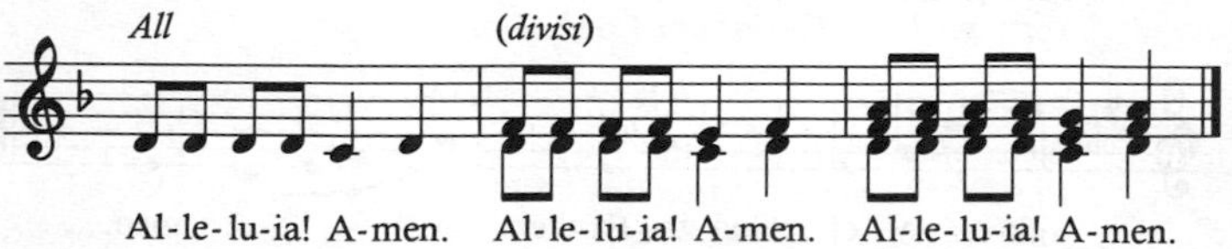
All
(divisi)
Al - le - lu - ia! A - men. Al - le - lu - ia! A - men. Al - le - lu - ia! A - men.

9 ALLELUIAS

10 OFFERTORY PRAYERS

(*a*) **Lord God, we bring to you the ordinary things of life—**
food and drink and money—
and with them we bring ourselves.
Take us, and our gifts of money, to do your work in the world.
Take this food and drink from our tables,
and feed us from your table with your love.
Accept our sacrifice of praise;
through Jesus Christ our Lord. Amen.

(*b*) **Eternal God,**
we come with these gifts
to offer the praise of our lips
and the service of our lives;
through Jesus Christ our Lord. Amen.

11 NARRATIVE OF THE INSTITUTION WITH RESPONSES

During supper Jesus poured water into a basin,
and began to wash his disciples' feet
and to wipe them with a towel.
He said: 'If I do not wash you, you have no part with me.'

By that baptism into his death
we were buried with Christ and lay dead,
so that as Christ was raised from death
we might walk in new life.

Jesus said: 'How I have longed to eat this Passover
with you before my death, for I will not eat it again
until it is fulfilled in the kingdom of God.'

Christ our Passover has been sacrificed for us.
Therefore let us keep the feast.

As they were eating, he said:
'Truly I say to you, one of you will betray me.'
And they were very sorrowful
and began to ask, 'Is it I?'

For I do not do what I want,
but I do the very thing I hate.
Who will deliver me from this body of death?

Jesus took bread, blessed and broke it, and said,
'Take, eat; this is my body.'
And he took a cup and said,
'Drink of it, all of you;
for this is my blood of the covenant,
which is poured out for the forgiveness of sins.'

Ours is not a high priest unable to sympathize
with our weaknesses,
but one who has been tested in every way.
Therefore let us boldly approach the throne of God.

He said: 'You are those who have stood by me in my trials.
I now give you the kingship which my Father gave me,
and you shall eat and drink at my table in my kingdom.'

Blessed be the coming kingdom of our father David.
Peace in heaven and glory in the highest.

12 THE THANKSGIVING

SURSUM CORDA

Lift up your hearts.
We lift them to the Lord.

Let us give thanks to the Lord our God.
It is right to give our thanks and praise.

SANCTUS

Therefore with all your people in heaven and on earth
we sing the triumphant hymn of your glory:

Holy, holy, holy Lord,
God of power and might,
heaven and earth are full of your glory.
Hosanna in the highest.

Blessed is he who comes in the name of the Lord.
Hosanna in the highest.

ACCLAMATION

Let us proclaim the mystery of faith:

Christ has died.
Christ is risen.
Christ will come again.

THE LORD'S PRAYER

THE PEACE

The peace of the Lord be always with you.
Peace be with you.

13 SANCTUS

♩ = 92

ERIK ROUTLEY (1917–82)

Ho - ly, ho - ly, ho - ly Lord, God of power and might, heaven and earth are full of your glo - ry. Ho - - san - na in the high - est. Bless - ed is he who comes in the name of the Lord. Ho - san-na in the high-est.

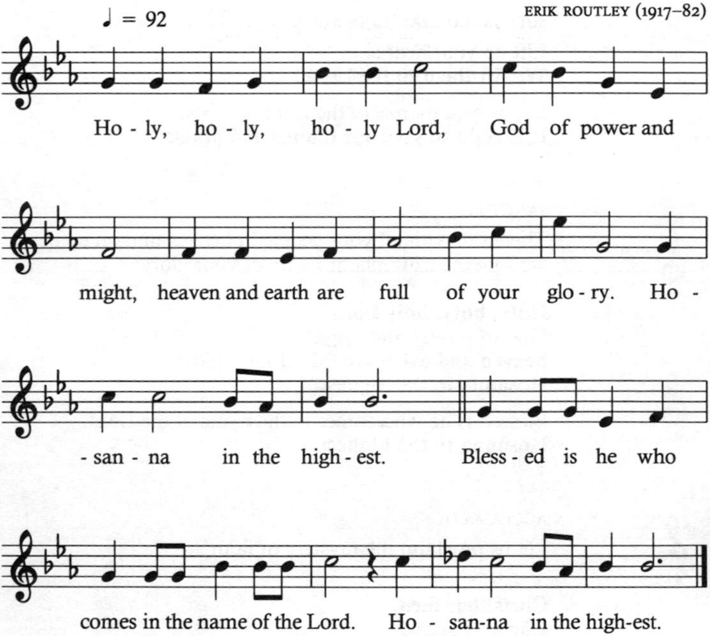

14 AGNUS DEI I

Lamb of God, you take away the sin of the world,
have mercy on us.
Lamb of God, you take away the sin of the world,
have mercy on us.
Lamb of God, you take away the sin of the world,
grant us peace.

15 AGNUS DEI II

Jesus, Lamb of God:
have mercy on us.
Jesus, bearer of our sins:
have mercy on us.
Jesus, redeemer of the world:
grant us peace.

PAUL BATEMAN (1954–)

16 BEHOLD THE LAMB OF GOD

Behold the Lamb of God who takes away the sin of the world.
Blessed are those who are called to the wedding feast of the Lamb.
Alleluia.

PAUL BATEMAN (1954–)

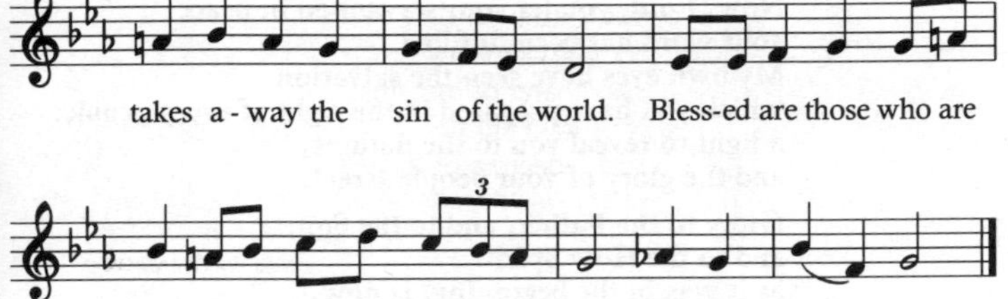

17 LORD, I AM NOT WORTHY

Lord, I am not worthy to receive you,
but only say the word and I shall be healed.

PAUL BATEMAN (1954–)

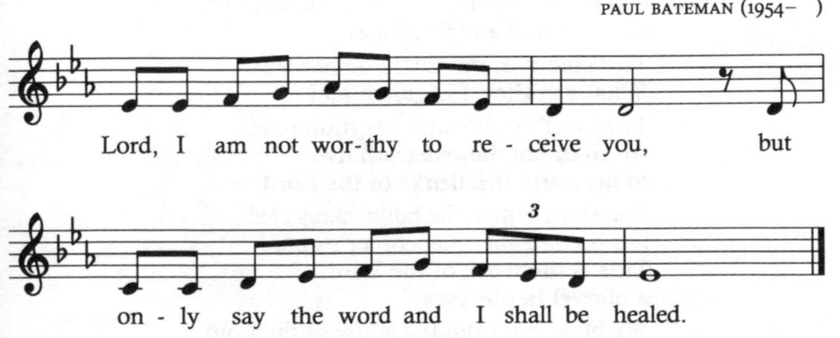

18 NUNC DIMITTIS

**Now, Lord, you let your servant go in peace:
your word has been fulfilled.
My own eyes have seen the salvation
which you have prepared in the sight of every people:
a light to reveal you to the nations,
and the glory of your people Israel.**

**Glory to the Father, and to the Son,
and to the Holy Spirit:
as it was in the beginning, is now,
and will be for ever. Amen.**

For musical settings of this canticle see no. 742.

19 CONCLUDING PRAISE

Give thanks to the Lord for he is good,
for his love endures for ever.

Let those who fear the Lord say,
his love endures for ever.

Out of the depths I called upon the Lord:
he answered and freed me.

The Lord is at my side; I do not fear.
What can they do against me?

The Lord's right hand has triumphed:
**we shall not die, we shall live
to proclaim the works of the Lord.**

The stone which the builders rejected
has become the chief corner-stone.
**This is the work of the Lord,
a marvel in our eyes.**

We bless you from the house of the Lord.
My God, I praise you.

Give thanks to the Lord for he is good,
for his love endures for ever.

20 AMENS

PERCY BUCK (1871–1947)

(*a*)

Origin unknown, perhaps Danish

(*b*)

ERIC H. THIMAN (1900–75)

(*c*)

adpt. ERIC H. THIMAN (1900–75)

(*d*)

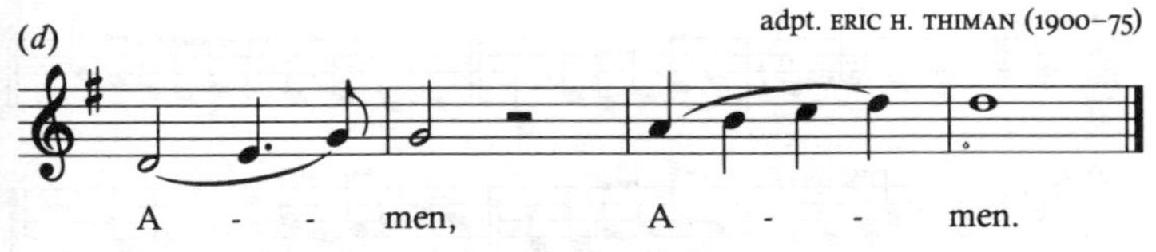

ERIC H. THIMAN (1900–75)

(*e*)

ERIC H. THIMAN (1900–75)

(*f*)

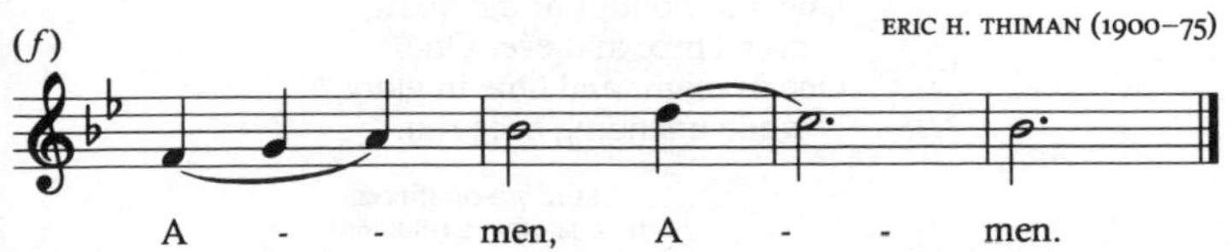

ONE GOD IN TRINITY

21 *Old Hundredth* LM

Later form of melody in the *Genevan Psalter*, 1551

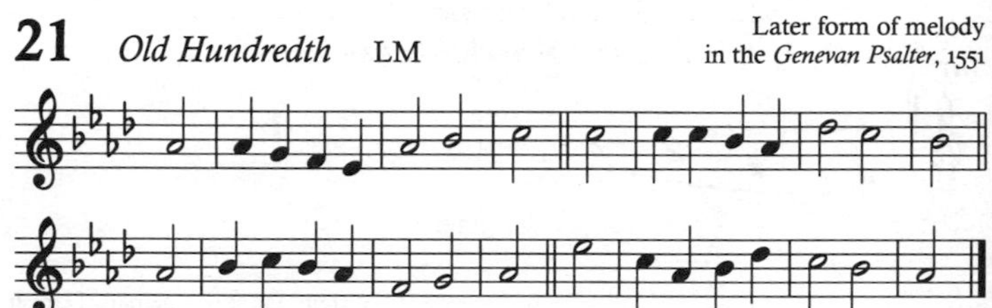

Praise God, from whom all blessings flow,
praise him, all creatures here below,
praise him above, ye heavenly host,
praise Father, Son and Holy Ghost.

THOMAS KEN (1637–1711)

22 & 23 *Grafton* 87 87 87

19th-cent. French church melody

Alternative tune: WESTMINSTER ABBEY, no. 559.

22

Laud and honour to the Father,
  laud and honour to the Son,
laud and honour to the Spirit,
  ever Three and ever One,
One in might and One in glory,
  while unending ages run.

Latin, 7th or 8th cent.
tr. J. M. NEALE (1818–66)

23

Unto God be praise and honour:
to the Father, to the Son,
to the mighty Spirit, glory—
ever Three and ever One:
power and glory in the highest
while eternal ages run.

Mediaeval Latin doxology,
tr. WILLIAM MAIR (1830–1920)
and A. W. WOTHERSPOON (1853–1936)

24 *Lasst uns erfreuen* 88 44 88 with alleluias

Melody from
Geistliche Kirchengesäng,
Cologne, 1623

Through north and south and east and west
may God's immortal Name be blest:
Alleluia, alleluia!
till everywhere beneath the sun
his kingdom comes, his will is done:
Alleluia, alleluia, alleluia, alleluia, alleluia!

PERCY DEARMER (1867–1936)
based on v. 2 of a hymn by
WILLIAM CANTON (1845–1926)

25 *Crediton* CM

THOMAS CLARK (1775–1859)

To Father, Son and Spirit blest,
the God whom we adore,
be glory, as it was, and is,
and shall be evermore.

Scottish Metrical Psalter, 1650*

26 *Christe sanctorum* 11 11 11 5

Melody from
Paris *Antiphoner*, 1681

1 Father, we praise you, now the night is over;
active and watchful, stand we all before you;
singing we offer prayer and meditation:
thus we adore you.

2 Monarch of all things, fit us for your mansions;
banish our weakness, health and wholeness sending;
bring us to heaven, where your saints united
joy without ending.

3 All-holy Father, Son and equal Spirit,
Trinity blessèd, send us your salvation;
yours is the glory, gleaming and resounding
through all creation.

attrib. GREGORY THE GREAT (*c.*540–604)
tr. PERCY DEARMER (1867–1936) altd.

27 *Sebaste* Irregular JOHN STAINER (1840–1901)

Greek, 4th cent. or earlier
tr. JOHN KEBLE (1792–1866)

28 *Halad* 55 55 55 54

ELENA G. MAQUISO, 1961

1 Father in heaven,
grant to your children
mercy and blessing,
songs never ceasing,
love to unite us,
grace to redeem us—
Father in heaven,
Father our God.

2 Jesus, Redeemer,
may we remember
your gracious passion,
your resurrection.
Worship we bring you,
praise shall we sing you—
Jesus, Redeemer,
Jesus our Lord.

3 Spirit descending
whose is the blessing,
strength for the weary,
help for the needy:
make us your temple,
born a new people—
Spirit descending,
Spirit adored.

D. T. NILES (1908–70) altd.*

29 *Father, we adore you* 66 4

TERRYE COELHO (1952–)

May also be sung as a three-part round, the voices entering as indicated.

1 Father, we adore you,
lay our lives before you:
how we love you!

2 Jesus, we adore you,
lay our lives before you:
how we love you!

3 Spirit, we adore you,
lay our lives before you;
how we love you!

TERRYE COELHO (1952–)

30 *Father, we love you* 57 95 59

DONNA ADKINS (1940–)

1 Father, we love you, we worship and adore you;

glorify your name in all the earth,
glorify your name, glorify your name,
glorify your name in all the earth.

2 Jesus, we love you, we worship and adore you;

3 Spirit, we love you, we worship and adore you;

DONNA ADKINS (1940–)

31 *Brockham* LM

JEREMIAH CLARKE (*c.*1673–1707)

The Transcendent glories of the Deity

1 God is a name my soul adores,
the almighty Three, the eternal One;
nature and grace with all their powers,
confess the Infinite Unknown.

2 Thy voice produced the seas and spheres,
bade the waves roar, the planets shine;
but nothing like thyself appears
through all these spacious works of thine.

3 Still restless nature dies and grows,
from change to change the creatures run:
thy being no succession knows,
and all thy vast designs are one.

4 A glance of thine runs through the globes,
rules the bright worlds and moves their frame;
broad sheets of light compose thy robes,
thy ministers are living flame.

5 How shall affrighted mortals dare
to sing thy glory or thy grace?
Beneath thy feet we lie afar,
and see but shadows of thy face.

6 Who can behold the blazing light?
Who can approach consuming flame?
None but thy wisdom knows thy might,
none but thy word can speak thy name.

ISAAC WATTS (1674–1748) altd.

32 *Groningen* 668 668 33 66

JOACHIM NEANDER (1650–80)

1 God is in his temple,
the Almighty Father;
round his footstool let us gather:
serve with adoration
him, the Lord most holy,
who has mercy on the lowly;
let us raise
hymns of praise
for his great salvation:
God is in his temple.

2 Christ comes to his temple:
we, his word receiving,
are made happy in believing;
now from sin delivered,
he has turned our sadness,
our deep gloom, to light
and gladness;
let us raise
hymns of praise,
for our bonds are severed:
Christ comes to his temple.

3 Come and claim your temple,
gracious Holy Spirit,
in our hearts your home inherit;
make in us your dwelling,
your high work fulfilling,
into ours your will instilling;
till we raise
hymns of praise,
beyond mortal telling,
in the eternal temple.

WILLIAM T. MATSON (1833–99) altd.

33 *Charterhouse* 11 10 11 10 DAVID EVANS (1874–1948)

1 Eternal God, your love's tremendous glory
cascades through life in overflowing grace,
to tell creation's meaning in the story
of love evolving love from time and space.

2 Eternal Son of God, uniquely precious,
in you, deserted, scorned and crucified,
God's love has fathomed sin and death's deep darkness,
and flawed humanity is glorified.

3 Eternal Spirit, with us like a mother,
embracing us in love serene and pure:
you nurture strength to follow Christ our brother,
as full-grown children, confident and sure.

4 Love's trinity, self-perfect, self-sustaining;
love which commands, enables and obeys:
you give yourself, in boundless joy, creating
one vast increasing harmony of praise.

5 We ask you now, complete your image in us;
this love of yours, our source and guide and goal.
May love in us seek love and serve love's purpose,
till we ascend with Christ and find love whole.

ALAN GAUNT (1935–)

34 *Nicaea* 11 12 12 10

J. B. DYKES (1823–76)

1 Holy, holy, holy! Lord God Almighty,
early in the morning our song shall rise to thee;
Holy, holy, holy! merciful and mighty,
God in three Persons, blessed Trinity!

2 Holy, holy, holy! All the saints adore thee,
casting down their golden crowns around the glassy sea,
cherubim and seraphim falling down before thee,
who wast and art and evermore shalt be.

3 Holy, holy, holy! Though the darkness hide thee,
though the sinful human eye thy glory may not see,
only thou art holy, there is none beside thee,
perfect in power, in love, and purity.

4 Holy, holy, holy! Lord God Almighty,
all thy works shall praise thy name, in earth, and sky, and sea;
Holy, holy, holy! merciful and mighty,
God in three Persons, blessed Trinity!

REGINALD HEBER (1783–1826)*

35 *Linnington* 66 66 88

GERALD L. BARNES (1935–)

1 God is unique and one—
Father, Sustainer, Lord!
Patterns of life were spun
by his creative Word.
Of his intention, love and care
we are with growing trust aware.

2 Love came to earth in Christ,
our common life to share;
choosing to be the least,
willing a cross to bear.
He died, he rose, that we might live
and all our love, responding, give.

3 The Holy Spirit moves
people to trace God's plan;
such inspiration proves
more than the mind can span.
Each listening heart is led to find
the will of God for humankind.

4 He shall for ever reign,
ruler of time and space;
God in the midst of life,
seen in the human face.
We give expression to our creed
by love in thought, in word and deed.

FRED KAAN (1929–)

36 *St Patrick* DLM

Irish traditional melody

1 I bind unto myself today
  the strong name of the Trinity,
by invocation of the same,
  the Three in One, and One in Three.

2 I bind this day to me for ever,
  by power of faith, Christ's incarnation;
his baptism in the Jordan river;
  his death on cross for my salvation;
his bursting from the spicèd tomb;
  his riding up the heavenly way;
his coming at the day of doom:
  I bind unto myself today.

3 I bind unto myself today
  the virtues of the starlit heaven,
the glorious sun's life-giving ray,
  the whiteness of the moon at even,
the flashing of the lightning free,
  the whirling wind's tempestuous shocks,
the stable earth, the deep salt sea,
  around the old eternal rocks.

4 I bind unto myself today
  the power of God to hold and lead,
his eye to watch, his might to stay,
  his ear to hearken to my need,
the wisdom of my God to teach,
  his hand to guide, his shield to ward,
the word of God to give me speech,
  his heavenly host to be my guard.

†5 Christ be with me, Christ within me,
  Christ behind me, Christ before me,
Christ beside me, Christ to win me,
  Christ to comfort and restore me,
Christ beneath me, Christ above me,
  Christ in quiet, Christ in danger,
Christ in hearts of all that love me,
  Christ in mouth of friend and stranger.

6 I bind unto myself the name,
  the strong name of the Trinity;
by invocation of the same,
  the Three in One, and One in Three,
of whom all nature has creation,
  eternal Father, Spirit, Word.
Praise to the Lord of my salvation:
  salvation is of Christ the Lord.

From 'St Patrick's Breastplate' (5th–7th cent. Gaelic)
sometimes attrib. ST PATRICK (*c.*370–*c.*460)
tr. CECIL FRANCES ALEXANDER (1818–95)*

† See overleaf for music.
For another version of the 'Breastplate' see 'This day God gives me' (no. 79).

Clonmacnoise 88 88 D (Trochaic) Ancient Irish melody

5. Christ be with me, Christ with-in me, Christ be - hind me, Christ be -
- fore me, Christ be - side me, Christ to win me, Christ to
com - fort and re - store me, Christ be - neath me, Christ a -
- bove me, Christ in qui - et, Christ in dan - ger, Christ in
(*Turn back for verse 6*)
hearts of all that love me, Christ in mouth of friend and stran-ger.

37 *Croft's 136th* 66 66 88

WILLIAM CROFT (1678–1727)

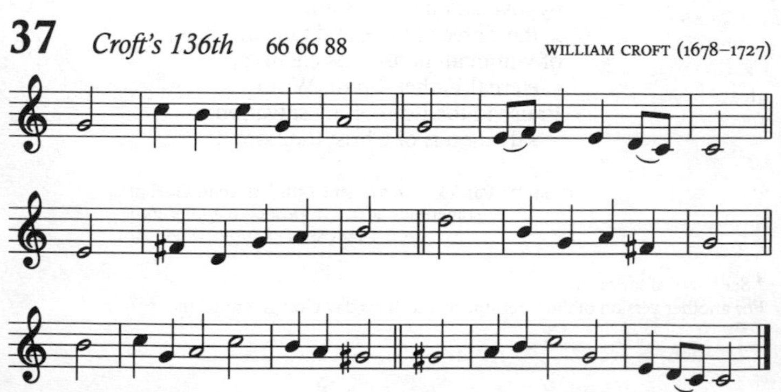

1 We give immortal praise
to God the Father's love,
for all our comforts here,
and better hopes above;
he sent his own eternal Son
to die for sins that we had done.

2 To God the Son belongs
immortal glory too,
who bought us with his blood
from everlasting woe;
and now he lives, and now he reigns,
and sees the fruit of all his pains.

3 To God the Spirit's name,
immortal worship give,
whose new-creating power
makes the dead sinner live;
his work completes the great design,
and fills the world with joy divine.

4 Almighty God, to thee
be endless honours done,
the undivided Three,
and the mysterious One;
where reason fails, with all her powers,
there faith prevails, and love adores.

ISAAC WATTS (1674–1748) altd.

38 *Moscow* 664 6664

adpt. from FELICE GIARDINI (1716–96)

1 Thou whose almighty word
chaos and darkness heard,
and took their flight,
hear us, we humbly pray,
and where the gospel day
sheds not its glorious ray,
let there be light.

2 Thou who didst come to bring
on thy redeeming wing
healing and sight,
health to the sick in mind,
sight to the inly blind,
now to all humankind
let there be light.

3 Spirit of truth and love,
life-giving, holy dove,
speed forth thy flight;
move o'er the waters' face,
bearing the lamp of grace,
and in earth's darkest place
let there be light.

4 Holy and blessed Three,
glorious Trinity,
Wisdom, Love, Might,
boundless as ocean's tide
rolling in fullest pride,
through the world, far and wide,
let there be light.

JOHN MARRIOTT (1780–1825)*

GOD'S CREATING AND REDEEMING LOVE

GOD THE CREATOR : ALL GOD'S CREATED WORKS

39 *Lasst uns erfreuen* 88 44 88 with alleluias

Melody from *Geistliche Kirchengesäng* Cologne, 1623

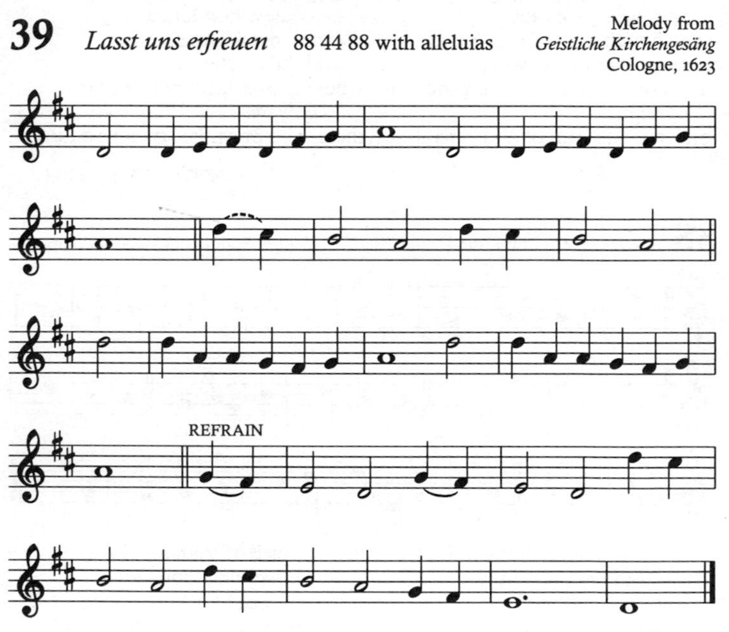

1 All creatures of our God and King,
lift up your voice and with us sing,
alleluia, alleluia!
Thou burning sun with golden beam,
thou silver moon with softer gleam:

O praise him, O praise him,
alleluia, alleluia, alleluia!

2 Thou rushing wind that art so strong,
ye clouds that sail in heaven along,
O praise him, alleluia!
Thou rising morn, in praise rejoice;
ye lights of evening, find a voice:

3 Thou flowing water, pure and clear,
make music for thy Lord to hear,
alleluia, alleluia!
Thou fire, so masterful and bright,
that givest us both warmth and light:

4 Dear mother earth, who day by day
unfoldest blessings on our way,
O praise him, alleluia!
The flowers and fruits that in thee grow,
let them his glory also show:

5 All ye that are of tender heart,
forgiving others, take your part,
O sing ye, alleluia!
Ye who long pain and sorrow bear,
praise God, and on him cast your care:

6 And thou, most kind and gentle death,
waiting to hush our latest breath,
O praise him, alleluia!
Thou leadest home the child of God,
and Christ our Lord the way has trod:

7 Let all things their creator bless,
and worship him in humbleness;
O praise him, alleluia!
Praise, praise the Father, praise the Son,
and praise the Spirit, Three in One:

W. H. DRAPER (1855–1933) altd.
based on ST FRANCIS OF ASSISI (1182–1226)

40 *St George's, Windsor* 77 77 D GEORGE J. ELVEY (1816–93)

1 Come, ye thankful people, come,
raise the song of harvest-home!
All is safely gathered in,
ere the winter storms begin:
God, our Maker, doth provide
for our wants to be supplied;
come to God's own temple, come,
raise the song of harvest-home!

2 All the world is God's own field,
fruit unto his praise to yield,
wheat and tares together sown,
unto joy or sorrow grown:
first the blade, and then the ear,
then the full corn shall appear;
grant, O harvest Lord, that we
wholesome grain and pure may be.

3 Even so, Lord, quickly come
to thy final harvest-home;
from thy field upon that day
all offences purge away:
gather thou thy people in,
free from sorrow, free from sin,
there for ever purified,
in thy glory to abide.

HENRY ALFORD (1810–71) altd.*

41 *Lucerna Laudoniae* 77 77 77

DAVID EVANS (1874–1948)

Alternative tune: HEATHLANDS, no. 575.

1 For the beauty of the earth,
for the beauty of the skies,
for the love which from our birth
over and around us lies:

Gracious God, to thee we raise
this our sacrifice of praise.

2 For the beauty of each hour
of the day and of the night,
hill and vale, and tree and flower,
sun and moon, and stars of light:

3 For the joy of ear and eye,
for the heart and mind's delight,
for the mystic harmony
linking sense to sound and sight:

4 For the joy of human love,
brother, sister, parent, child,
friends on earth, and friends above;
for all gentle thoughts and mild:

5 For each perfect gift of thine
to our race so freely given,
graces human and divine,
flowers of earth and buds of heaven:

6 For thy people, evermore
lifting holy hands above,
offering up on every shore
their pure sacrifice of love:

F. S. PIERPOINT (1835–1917) altd.*

42 *East Acklam* 84 84 888 4

FRANCIS JACKSON (1917–)

1 For the fruits of all creation,
thanks be to God;
for his gifts to every nation,
thanks be to God;
for the ploughing, sowing, reaping,
silent growth while we are sleeping,
future needs in earth's safe-keeping,
thanks be to God.

2 In the just reward of labour,
God's will is done;
in the help we give our neighbour,
God's will is done;
in our world-wide task of caring
for the hungry and despairing,
in the harvests we are sharing,
God's will is done.

3 For the harvests of the Spirit,
thanks be to God;
for the good we all inherit,
thanks be to God;
for the wonders that astound us,
for the truths that still confound us,
most of all, that love has found us,
thanks be to God.

F. PRATT GREEN (1903–)*

43

FIRST TUNE

Montrose CM

Melody from GILMOUR'S *The Psalm-singer's Assistant*, Paisley, 1790

SECOND TUNE

London New CM

Melody from the *Scottish Psalter*, 1635 as given in JOHN PLAYFORD'S *Psalms*, 1671

1 I sing the almighty power of God
that made the mountains rise,
that spread the flowing seas abroad,
and built the lofty skies.

2 I sing the wisdom that ordained
the sun to rule the day;
the moon shines full at his command,
and all the stars obey.

3 I sing the goodness of the Lord,
that filled the earth with food;
he formed the creatures with his Word,
and then pronounced them good.

4 Lord, how thy wonders are displayed
where'er I turn mine eye,
if I survey the ground I tread,
or gaze upon the sky!

5 There's not a plant or flower below
but makes thy glories known,
and clouds arise and tempests blow
by order from thy throne.

6 God's hand is my perpetual guard,
he guides me with his eye;
why should I then forget the Lord,
whose love is ever nigh?

ISAAC WATTS (1674–1748) altd.

44 *San Rocco* CM

DEREK WILLIAMS (1945–)

1 Lord of the boundless curves of space
and time's deep mystery,
to your creative might we trace
all nature's energy.

2 Your mind conceived the galaxy,
each atom's secret planned,
and every age of history
your purpose, Lord, has spanned.

3 Your Spirit gave the living cell
its hidden, vital force:
the instincts which all life impel
derive from you, their source.

4 Yours is the image humans bear,
though marred by human sin;
and yours the liberating care
again our souls to win.

5 Science explores your reason's ways,
and faith can this impart
that in the face of Christ our gaze
looks deep within your heart.

6 In Christ the human race has heard
your strong compassion plead:
he is your wisdom's perfect word,
your mercy's crowning deed.

A. F. BAYLY (1901–84)
and compilers

45 *Bunessan* 55 54 D Gaelic melody

1 Morning has broken
like the first morning,
blackbird has spoken
like the first bird.
Praise for the singing,
praise for the morning,
praise for them, springing
fresh from the Word!

2 Sweet the rain's new fall
sunlit from heaven,
like the first dewfall
on the first grass.
Praise for the sweetness
of the wet garden,
sprung in completeness
where his feet pass.

3 Mine is the sunlight;
mine is the morning,
born of the one light
Eden saw play!
Praise with elation,
praise every morning,
God's re-creation
of the new day!

ELEANOR FARJEON (1881–1965)

46 *The song of Caedmon*

DONALD SWANN (1923–)

ALL GOD'S CREATED WORKS

1 O praise him! O praise him! O praise him!
O praise him! O praise him! O praise him!
He made the heavens, he made our sky,
the sun, the moon, the stars on high;
he formed our world; his mighty hand
divided sea and land;
he moves in wind and rain and snow,
his life is in all things that grow:
O praise him! O praise him! O praise him!

2 O praise him! O praise him! O praise him!
O praise him! O praise him! O praise him!
His joy is in the eagle's flight,
the tiger's roar, the lion's might,
the lamb, the python and the whale,
the spider, ant and snail;
all things that leap and swim and fly
on land and sea and in the sky,
they praise him, they praise him, they praise him.

3 O praise him! O praise him! O praise him!
O praise him! O praise him! O praise him!
He lives his life in love and joy,
in man and woman, girl and boy;
his purpose is in me and you,
in what we are and do;
his love is in us when we sing
with every God-created thing,
and praise him, and praise him, and praise him.

ARTHUR SCHOLEY (1932–)

47 *Hanover* 10 10 11 11 (55 55 65 65)

From *A Supplement to the New Version*, 1708, probably by WILLIAM CROFT (1678–1727)

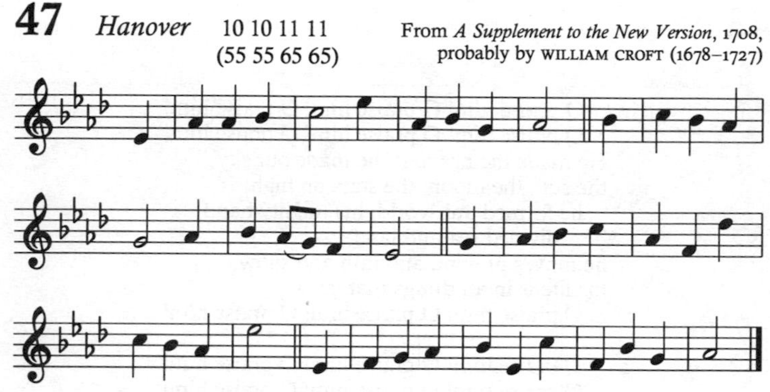

1 O worship the King,
all-glorious above;
O gratefully sing
his power and his love;
our shield and defender,
the ancient of days,
pavilioned in splendour,
and girded with praise.

2 O tell of his might,
O sing of his grace,
whose robe is the light,
whose canopy space;
his chariots of wrath
the deep thunder-clouds form;
and dark is his path
on the wings of the storm.

3 The earth with its store
of wonders untold,
Almighty, thy power
hath founded of old;
hath stablished it fast
by a changeless decree,
and round it hath cast,
like a mantle, the sea.

4 Thy bountiful care
what tongue can recite?
It breathes in the air,
it shines in the light;
it streams from the hills,
it descends to the plain,
and sweetly distils
in the dew and the rain.

5 Frail children of dust,
and feeble as frail,
in thee do we trust,
nor find thee to fail;
thy mercies how tender,
how firm to the end,
our maker, defender,
redeemer, and friend!

6 O measureless might,
ineffable love,
while angels delight
to hymn thee above,
the humbler creation,
shall struggle to raise
with true adoration
their songs to thy praise.

ROBERT GRANT (1779–1838)*
based on Psalm 104

48 *Bunessan* 55 54 D

Gaelic melody

1 Praise and thanksgiving,
Father, we offer,
for all things living
you have made good;
harvest of sown fields,
fruits of the orchard,
hay from the mown fields,
blossom and wood.

2 Lord, bless the labour
we bring to serve you,
that with our neighbour
we may be fed.
Sowing or tilling,
we would work with you;
harvesting, milling,
for daily bread.

3 Father, providing
food for your children,
your wisdom guiding
teaches us share
one with another,
so that, rejoicing,
sister and brother
may know your care.

4 Then will your blessing
reach every people;
each one confessing
your gracious hand:
when you are reigning
no one will hunger,
your love sustaining
fruitful the land.

A. F. BAYLY (1901–84) altd.

49 *Laudate Dominum* 55 55 65 65

H. J. GAUNTLETT (1805–76)

1 Sing praise to the Lord!
Praise him in the height;
rejoice in his word,
blest angels of light;
high heavens, adore him
by whom you were made,
and worship before him
in brightness arrayed.

2 Sing praise to the Lord,
all people on earth;
in tuneful accord
sing praise for new birth;
praise him who has brought you
his grace from above,
praise him who has taught you
to sing of his love.

3 Sing praise to the Lord,
all things that give sound;
each jubilant chord
re-echo around;
loud organs, his glory
forth tell in deep tone,
and, sweet harp, the story
of what he has done.

4 Sing praise to the Lord!
Thanksgiving and song
to him be outpoured
all ages along;
for love in creation,
for heaven restored,
for grace of salvation:
sing praise to the Lord!

H. W. BAKER (1821–77) altd.*

50 *Galilee* LM PHILIP ARMES (1836–1908)

1 Praise ye the Lord, 'tis good to raise
our hearts and voices in his praise;
his nature and his works invite
to make this duty our delight.

2 He formed the stars, those heavenly flames,
he counts their numbers, calls their names;
his wisdom's vast, and knows no bound,
a deep where all our thoughts are drowned.

3 Sing to the Lord, exalt him high,
who spreads his cloud all round the sky;
there he prepares the fruitful rain,
nor lets the drops descend in vain.

4 He makes the grass the hills adorn,
and clothes the smiling fields with corn;
the beasts with food his hands supply,
and the young ravens when they cry.

5 What is the creature's skill or force?
The sprightly man, the warlike horse?
The nimble wit, the active limb?
All are too mean delights for him.

6 But saints are lovely in his sight,
he views his children with delight;
he sees their hope, he knows their fear,
and looks, and loves his image there.

Psalm 147: 1, 4–5, 7–11
para. ISAAC WATTS (1674–1748) altd.

51 *Innsbruck* 776 778

German traditional melody, as set by J. S. BACH in the *St Matthew Passion*, 1727

1 The duteous day now closes,
each flower and tree reposes,
shade creeps o'er wild and wood:
let us, as night is falling,
on God our maker calling,
give thanks to him, the giver good.

2 Now all the heavenly splendour
breaks forth in starlight tender
from myriad worlds unknown;
and we, the marvel seeing,
forget our selfish being,
for joy of beauty not our own.

3 This life is our confusion,
the day is all illusion,
its brightness veils our sight;
true hope outlives our dreaming,
the sure transcends all seeming
in Christ, who is our souls' true light.

4 Awhile our mortal blindness
may miss God's loving-kindness,
and grope in faithless strife;
but when life's day is over
shall death's fair night discover
the fields of everlasting life.

VV. 1, 2, 4: ROBERT BRIDGES (1844–1930) altd.
V. 3: compilers
based on PAUL GERHARDT (1607–76)

52 *Daniel* LM Irish traditional melody

1 To God who makes all lovely things
how happy must our praises be!
Each day a new surprise he brings
to make us glad his world to see.

2 How plentiful must be the mines
from which he gives his gold away;
in March he gives us celandines,
he gives us buttercups in May.

3 He grows the wheat and never stops;
there's none can count the blades of green;
and up among the high tree-tops
as many thousand leaves are seen.

4 And when the wheat is bound in sheaves
he sends his wind among the trees,
and down come all the merry leaves
in yellow-twinkling companies.

5 On winter nights his quiet flakes
come falling, falling all the night,
and when the world next morning wakes
it finds itself all shining white.

6 He makes the sea that shines afar
with waves that dance unceasingly;
and every single little star
that twinkles in the evening sky.

7 He made the people that I meet,
the many people, great and small,
in home and school, and down the street,
and he made me to love them all.

J. M. C. CRUM (1872–1958)*

53 *Storrington* 87 87 (Iambic)

ERIC H. THIMAN (1900–75)

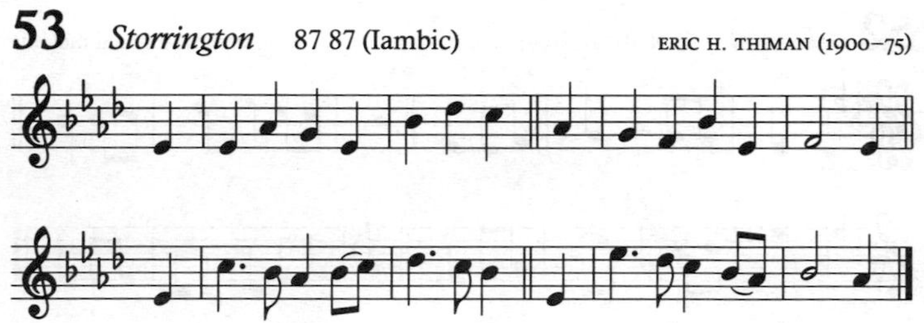

1 To thee, O Lord, our hearts we raise
   in hymns of adoration,
to thee bring sacrifice of praise
   with shouts of exultation.

2 Bright robes of gold the fields adorn,
   the hills with joy are ringing,
the valleys stand so thick with corn
   that even they are singing.

3 And now, on this our festal day,
   thy bounteous hand confessing,
before thee thankfully we lay
   the first-fruits of thy blessing.

4 By thee thy children's souls are fed
   with gifts of grace supernal;
thou who dost give us earthly bread,
   give us the bread eternal.

5 O blessèd is that land of God
   where saints abide for ever,
where golden fields spread far and broad,
   where flows the crystal river.

6 The strains of all its holy throng
   with ours today are blending;
thrice blessèd is that harvest song
   which never has an ending.

W. C. DIX (1837–98) altd.

54 *Trewen* 88 88 D (Anapaestic)

DAVID EMLYN EVANS (1843–1913)

1 A sovereign protector I have,
unseen, yet for ever at hand,
unchangeably faithful to save,
almighty to rule and command.
He smiles, and my comforts abound;
his grace as the dew shall descend,
and walls of salvation surround
the soul he delights to defend.

2 Inspirer and hearer of prayer,
thou shepherd and guardian of thine,
my all to thy covenant care
I sleeping and waking assign.
If thou art my shield and my sun,
the night is no darkness to me;
and, fast as my moments roll on,
they bring me but nearer to thee.

AUGUSTUS M. TOPLADY (1740–78) altd.*

55 *St Hugh* CM

E. J. HOPKINS (1818–1901)

1 All as God wills, who wisely heeds
to give or to withhold,
and knoweth more of all my needs
than all my prayers have told.

2 Enough that blessings undeserved
have marked my erring track;
that wheresoe'er my feet have swerved
his chastening turned me back;

3 that more and more a providence
of love is understood,
which makes the springs of time and sense
sweet with eternal good;

4 that death seems but a covered way
which opens into light,
wherein no blinded child can stray
beyond the Father's sight;

5 that all the jarring notes of life
seem blending in a psalm,
and all the angles of its strife
slow rounding into calm.

6 And so the shadows fall apart,
and so the west winds play;
and all the windows of my heart
I open to the day.

J. G. WHITTIER (1807–92)*

56 *Balmer Lawn* LM PAUL BATEMAN (1954–)

1 Creating God, your fingers trace
the bold designs of farthest space;
let sun and moon and stars and light
and what lies hidden praise your might.

2 Sustaining God, your hands uphold
earth's myst'ries known or yet untold;
let water's fragile blend with air,
enabling life, proclaim your care.

3 Redeeming God, your arms embrace
all now despised for creed or race;
let peace, descending like a dove,
make known on earth your healing love.

4 Indwelling God, your gospel claims
one family with countless names;
let every life be touched by grace
until we praise you face to face.

JEFFERY ROWTHORN (1934–)*

57

FIRST TUNE

Ballards Lane 8 33 6 GORDON HAWKINS (1911–)

SECOND TUNE

Thanet 8 33 6 JOSEPH JOWETT (1784–1856)

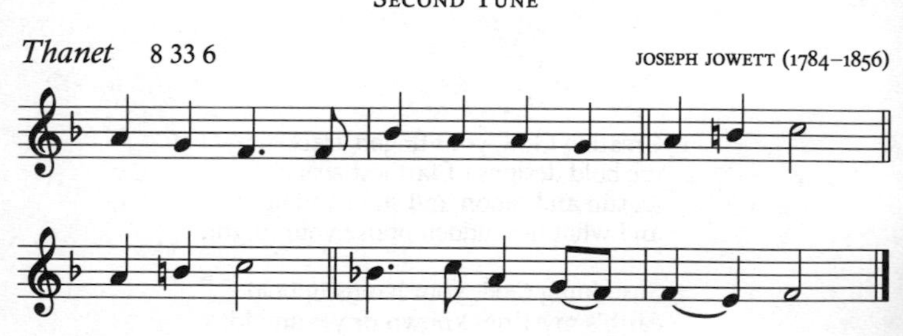

1 Ere I sleep, for every favour
this day showed
by my God,
I will bless my Saviour.

2 O my Lord, what shall I render
to thy name,
still the same,
gracious, good, and tender?

3 Visit me with thy salvation;
let thy care
now be near
round my habitation.

4 Leave me not, but ever love me;
let thy peace
be my bliss,
till thou hence remove me.

5 When at last in death I slumber,
let me rise
with the wise,
counted in their number.

JOHN CENNICK (1718–55)*

58 *Melita* 88 88 88

J. B. DYKES (1823–76)

1 Eternal Father, strong to save,
whose arm doth bind the restless wave,
who bidd'st the mighty ocean deep
its own appointed limits keep:
O hear us when we cry to thee
for those in peril on the sea.

2 O Saviour, whose almighty word
the winds and waves submissive heard,
who walkedst on the foaming deep
and calm amid its rage didst sleep:
O hear us when we cry to thee
for those in peril on the sea.

3 O Holy Spirit, who didst sweep
across the dark and formless deep
to bid its angry tumult cease,
and give, for wild confusion, peace:
O hear us when we cry to thee
for those in peril on the sea.

4 O Trinity of love and power,
sustain us all in danger's hour;
through wreck and tempest, grief and loss,
renew the triumph of the Cross:
and ever let there rise to thee
glad hymns of praise from land and sea.

WILLIAM WHITING (1825–78) altd.*

59

FIRST TUNE

Melody from the *Scottish Psalter*, 1635
as given in JOHN PLAYFORD'S *Psalms*, 1671

London New CM

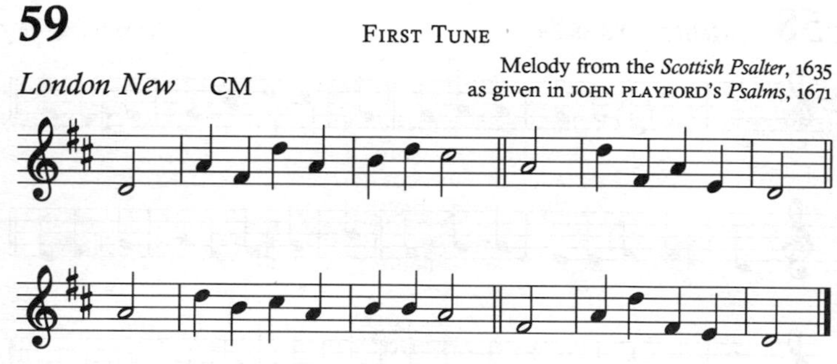

SECOND TUNE

Melody from
Hymns and Sacred Poems, Dublin 1749

Irish CM

1 God moves in a mysterious way
his wonders to perform;
he plants his footsteps in the sea,
and rides upon the storm.

2 Deep in unfathomable mines
of never-failing skill,
he treasures up his bright designs,
and works his sovereign will.

3 Ye fearful saints, fresh courage take:
the clouds ye so much dread
are big with mercy, and shall break
in blessings on your head.

4 Judge not the Lord by feeble sense,
but trust him for his grace;
behind a frowning providence
he hides a smiling face.

5 His purposes will ripen fast,
unfolding every hour;
the bud may have a bitter taste,
but sweet will be the flower.

6 Blind unbelief is sure to err,
and scan his work in vain;
God is his own interpreter,
and he will make it plain.

WILLIAM COWPER (1731–1800)

60 *Corbridge* 87 87 87 ERIK ROUTLEY (1917–82)

Alternative tune: RHUDDLAN, no. 344.

1 God who spoke in the beginning
forming rock and shaping spar,
set all life and growth in motion,
earthly world and distant star;
he who calls the earth to order
is the ground of what we are.

2 God who spoke through people, nations,
and events long past and gone,
showing still today his purpose,
speaks supremely through his Son;
he who calls the earth to order
gives his word and it is done.

3 God whose speech becomes incarnate
—Christ is servant, Christ is Lord!—
calls us to a life of service,
heart and will to action stirred;
he who uses our obedience
has the first and final word.

FRED KAAN (1929–)

61 *Abridge* CM

ISAAC SMITH (1734–1805)

1 Hast thou not known, hast thou not heard,
that firm remains on high
the everlasting throne of him
who formed the earth and sky?

2 Art thou afraid his power shall fail
when comes thy evil day?
And can an all-creating arm
grow weary or decay?

3 Supreme in wisdom as in power
the rock of ages stands;
though him thou canst not see, nor trace
the working of his hands.

4 He gives the conquest to the weak,
supports the fainting heart;
and courage in the evil hour
his heavenly aids impart.

5 Mere human power shall fast decay,
and youthful vigour cease;
but they who wait upon the Lord
in strength shall still increase.

6 They with unwearied feet shall tread
the path of life divine,
with growing ardour onward move,
with growing brightness shine.

Scottish Paraphrases, 1781
probably by WILLIAM CAMERON (1751–1811)
from Isaiah 40:28–31; based on
para. by ISAAC WATTS (1674–1748)

62 *Beechwood* 56 64

JOSIAH BOOTH (1852–1929)

1 God, who made the earth,
the air, the sky, the sea,
who gave the light its birth—
God cares for me.

2 God, who made the grass,
the flower, the fruit, the tree,
the day and night to pass—
God cares for me.

3 God, who sent his Son
to die on Calvary,
will, when life's clouds come on,
still care for me.

SARAH B. RHODES (1829–1904)*

63 *Wareham* LM

WILLIAM KNAPP (1698–1768)

1 Great God, we sing that mighty hand
by which supported still we stand;
the opening year thy mercy shows,
that mercy crowns it till it close.

2 By day, by night, at home, abroad,
still are we guarded by our God;
by his incessant bounty fed,
by his unerring counsel led.

3 With grateful hearts the past we own;
the future, all to us unknown,
we to thy guardian care commit,
and peaceful leave before thy feet.

4 In scenes exalted or depressed
thou art our joy, and thou our rest;
thy goodness all our hopes shall raise,
adored through all our changing days.

5 When death shall interrupt these songs,
and seal in silence mortal tongues,
our helper God, in whom we trust,
shall raise us glorious from our dust.

PHILIP DODDRIDGE (1702–51)*

64 *Davos* 458 457

MICHAEL BAUGHEN (1930–)

1 I lift my eyes
to the quiet hills
in the press of a busy day;
as green hills stand
in a dusty land
so God is my strength and stay.

2 I lift my eyes
to the quiet hills
to a calm that is mine to share;
secure and still
in the Father's will
and kept by the Father's care.

3 I lift my eyes
to the quiet hills
with a prayer as I turn to sleep;
by day, by night,
through the dark and light
my Shepherd will guard his sheep.

4 I lift my eyes
to the quiet hills
and my heart to the Father's throne;
in all my ways
to the end of days
the Lord will preserve his own.

TIMOTHY DUDLEY-SMITH (1926–)

65 *I love the sun* Irregular

GWEN F. SMITH

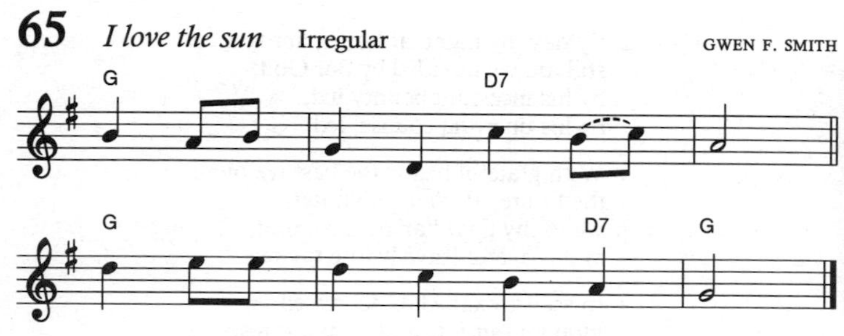

1 I love the sun,
it shines on me,
God made the sun,
and God made me.

2 I love the stars,
they twinkle on me,
God made the stars,
and God made me.

3 I love the rain,
it splashes on me,
God made the rain,
and God made me.

4 I love the wind,
it blows round me,
God made the wind,
and God made me.

5 I love the birds,
they sing to me,
God made the birds,
and God made me.

GWEN F. SMITH

66 *Wentworth* 84 84 84

F. C. MAKER (1844–1927)

1 My God, I thank thee, who hast made
the earth so bright;
so full of splendour and of joy,
of grace and light;
so many glorious things are here,
of truth and right.

2 I thank thee, Lord, that thou hast made
our joy abound;
so many gentle thoughts and deeds
enfold us round,
that in the darkest spot of earth
some love is found.

3 I thank thee more that all our joy
is touched with pain;
that shadows fall on brightest hours;
that thorns remain;
so that earth's bliss may be our guide,
and not our chain.

4 I thank thee, Lord, that thou hast kept
the best in store;
we have enough, yet not too much
to long for more—
a yearning for a deeper peace
not known before.

5 I thank thee, Lord, that here our souls,
though amply blest,
can never find, although they seek,
a perfect rest,
nor ever shall, until they lean
on Jesus' breast.

ADELAIDE A. PROCTER (1825–64) altd.*

67 *St Denio* 11 11 11 11 (Anapaestic) Welsh hymn melody

1 Immortal, invisible, God only wise,
in light inaccessible hid from our eyes,
most blessed, most glorious, the Ancient of Days,
almighty, victorious, thy great name we praise.

2 Unresting, unhasting, and silent as light,
nor wanting, nor wasting, thou rulest in might;
thy justice like mountains, high soaring above
thy clouds which are fountains of goodness and love.

3 To all life thou givest, to both great and small;
in all life thou livest, the true life of all;
we blossom and flourish as leaves on the tree,
and wither and perish—but naught changeth thee.

4 Great Father of glory: O help us to see
'tis only the splendour of light hideth thee.
And so let thy glory, Almighty, impart,
through Christ in the story, thy Christ to the heart.

W. CHALMERS SMITH (1824–1908)*

68 *Manna* 88 6 88 6

J. G. SCHICHT (1753–1823)

Alternative tune: CORNWALL, no. 318.

1 Lord God, by whom all change is wrought,
by whom new things to birth are brought,
in whom no change is known!
whate'er thou dost, whate'er thou art,
thy people still in thee have part;
still, still thou art our own.

2 Ancient of days! we dwell in thee;
out of thine own eternity
our peace and joy are wrought;
we rest in our eternal God,
and make secure and sweet abode
with thee, who changest not.

3 Spirit, who makest all things new,
thou leadest onward; we pursue
the heavenly march sublime.
'Neath thy renewing fire we glow,
and still from strength to strength we go,
from height to height we climb.

4 Darkness and dread we leave behind;
new light, new glory still we find,
new realms divine possess;
new births of grace, new raptures bring;
triumphant, the new song we sing,
the great Renewer bless.

T. H. GILL (1819–1906)

69 *Ombersley* LM

W. H. GLADSTONE (1840–91)

1 Lord of all being, throned afar,
thy glory flames from sun and star;
centre and soul of every sphere,
yet to each loving heart how near.

2 Sun of our life, thy quickening ray
sheds on our path the glow of day;
star of our hope, thy softened light
cheers the long watches of the night.

3 Our midnight is thy smile withdrawn,
our noontide is thy gracious dawn,
our rainbow arch thy mercy's sign;
all, save the clouds of sin, are thine.

4 Lord of all life, below, above,
whose light is truth, whose warmth is love,
before thy ever-blazing throne
we ask no lustre of our own.

5 Grant us thy truth to make us free,
and kindling hearts that burn for thee,
till all thy living altars claim
one holy light, one heavenly flame.

O. W. HOLMES (1809–94)

70 *Winscott* LM

S. S. WESLEY (1810–76)

1 Lord, you have searched and known my ways
and understood my thought from far;
how can I rightly sound your praise
or tell how great your wonders are?

2 Besetting me, before, behind,
upon my life your hand is laid;
caught in the compass of your mind
are all the things that you have made.

3 Such knowledge is too wonderful,
too high for me to understand—
enough that the Unsearchable
has searched my heart and held my hand.

PETER G. JARVIS (1925–)
based on Psalm 139: 1–6

71 *Salzburg* CM

J. MICHAEL HAYDN (1737–1806)

1 O God of Bethel, by whose hand
thy children still are fed;
who through this earthly pilgrimage
hast all thy people led:

2 to thee our humble vows we raise,
to thee address our prayer,
and in thy kind and faithful hands
we lay our every care.

3 Through each perplexing path of life
our wandering footsteps guide;
give us each day our daily bread,
and raiment fit provide.

4 O spread thy covering wings around,
till all our wanderings cease,
and at our Father's loved abode
our souls arrive in peace.

PHILIP DODDRIDGE (1702–51) altd.*

72 *Nun danket* 67 67 66 66

Later form of a melody
in JOHANN CRÜGER'S
Praxis Pietatis Melica, 1647

1 Now thank we all our God,
with hearts and hands and voices,
who wondrous things has done,
in whom his world rejoices;
who from our mothers' arms
has blessed us on our way
with countless gifts of love,
and still is ours today.

2 O may this bounteous God
through all our life be near us,
with ever joyful hearts
and blessed peace to cheer us;
and keep us in his grace,
and guide us when perplexed,
and free us from all ills
in this world and the next.

3 All praise and thanks to God
the Father now be given,
the Son, and him who reigns
with them in highest heaven,
the one eternal God,
whom heaven and earth adore;
for thus it was, is now,
and shall be evermore.

MARTIN RINKART (1586–1649)
tr. CATHERINE WINKWORTH (1827–78) altd.

73 *Durrow* 76 76 D

Irish traditional melody

1 O God, thou art the Father
of all that have believed:
from whom all hosts of angels
have life and power received.
O God, thou art the Maker
of all created things,
the righteous Judge of judges,
the Almighty King of kings.

2 High in the heavenly Zion
thou reignest God adored;
and in the coming glory
thou shalt be sovereign Lord.
Beyond our ken thou shinest,
the everlasting Light;
ineffable in loving,
unthinkable in might.

3 Thou to the meek and lowly
thy secrets dost unfold;
O God, thou doest all things,
all things both new and old.
I walk secure and blessed
in every clime or coast,
in Name of God the Father,
and Son, and Holy Ghost.

ST COLUMBA (521–97)
tr. DUNCAN MACGREGOR (1854–1923)

For the second part of the hymn see 'Christ is the world's Redeemer', no. 272.

74 *Lobe den Herren* 14 14 4 7 8

Later form of melody in *Stralsund Gesangbuch*, 1665
as given in *The Chorale Book for England*, 1863

1 Praise to the Lord, the Almighty, the King of creation!
O my soul, praise him, for he is thy health and salvation:
come ye who hear,
brothers and sisters, draw near,
praise him in glad adoration!

2 Praise to the Lord, who o'er all things so wondrously reigneth,
bears thee on eagle's wings, and through all troubles sustaineth:
hast thou not seen
all that is needful hath been
granted in what he ordaineth?

3 Praise to the Lord, who doth prosper thy work and defend thee!
Surely his goodness and mercy here daily attend thee:
ponder anew
all the Almighty can do,
who with his love doth befriend thee.

4 Praise to the Lord! O let all that is in me adore him!
All that hath life and breath come now with praises before him!
Let the amen
sound from his people again:
gladly for aye we adore him!

JOACHIM NEANDER (1650–80)
tr. CATHERINE WINKWORTH (1827–78) and others*
based on Psalm 103: 1–5; Psalm 150; etc.

75 *Mit Freuden zart* 87 87 887

Later form of a melody in the Bohemian Brethren's *Kirchengeseng*, Berlin, 1566

1 Sing praise to God who reigns above,
the God of all creation,
the God of power, the God of love,
the God of our salvation;
with healing balm my soul he fills,
and every faithless murmur stills:
to God all praise and glory!

2 What God's almighty power has made
that will he ever cherish,
and will, unfailing, soon and late,
with loving-kindness nourish;
and where he rules in kingly might
there all is just and all is right:
to God all praise and glory!

3 The Lord is never far away,
but, through all grief distressing,
an ever-present help and stay,
our peace, and joy, and blessing;
as with a mother's tender hand,
he leads his own, his chosen band:
to God all praise and glory!

4 O ye who name Christ's holy Name,
give God all praise and glory:
all ye who own his power, proclaim
aloud the wondrous story.
Cast each false idol from his throne,
the Lord is God, and he alone:
to God all praise and glory!

JOHANN J. SCHÜTZ (1640–90)
tr. (VV. 1, 3, 4) FRANCES E. COX (1812–97)
(V. 2) HONOR M. THWAITES (1914–)

76

FIRST TUNE

Church Triumphant LM J. W. ELLIOTT (1833–1915)

SECOND TUNE

Niagara LM ROBERT JACKSON (1840–1914)

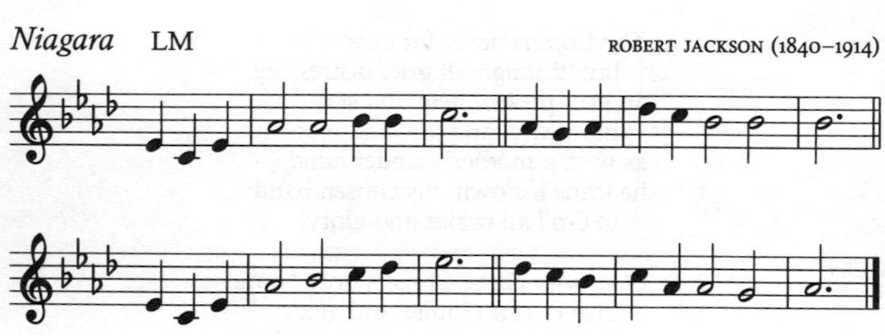

1 The Lord is King! lift up your voice
O earth, and all the heavens rejoice!
From world to world the joy shall ring,
'The Lord omnipotent is King!'

2 The Lord is King! who then shall dare
resist his will, distrust his care,
or murmur at his wise decrees,
or doubt his royal promises?

3 The Lord is King! child of the dust,
the judge of all the earth is just;
holy and true are all his ways;
let every creature speak his praise.

4 He reigns! O saints, exalt your strains;
your God is King, your Father reigns;
and he is at the Father's side,
the Man of love, the Crucified.

5 Come, make your wants, your burdens known;
Christ will present them at the throne;
this world of ours and worlds unseen:
how thin the boundary between!

6 One Lord, one empire, all secures;
he reigns, and life and death are yours;
through earth and heaven one song shall ring,
'The Lord omnipotent is King!'

JOSIAH CONDER (1789–1855) altd.*

77 *Antwerp* LM

WILLIAM SMALLWOOD (1831–97)

Alternative tune: GONFALON ROYAL, no. 136.

1 Sing to the Lord a joyful song,
   lift up your hearts, your voices raise;
to us his gracious gifts belong,
   to him our songs of love and praise.

2 For life and love, for rest and food,
   for daily help and nightly care,
sing to the Lord, for he is good,
   and praise his Name, for it is fair.

3 For strength to those who on him wait
   his truth to prove, his will to do,
praise ye our God, for he is great,
   trust in his Name, for it is true.

4 For joys untold, that from above
   cheer those who love his sweet employ,
sing to our God, for he is love,
   exalt his Name, for it is joy.

5 Sing to the Lord of heaven and earth,
   whom angels serve and saints adore,
the Father, Son, and Holy Ghost,
   to whom be praise for evermore.

J. S. B. MONSELL (1811–75)

78 *Metzler's Redhead* CM RICHARD REDHEAD (1820–1901)

1 The heaven of heavens cannot contain
the universal Lord;
yet he in humble hearts will deign
to dwell and be adored.

2 Wherever heartfelt praises rise
or sacrifice of prayer,
upon the earth or in the skies,
the heaven of God is there.

3 His presence there is spread abroad
through realms, through worlds unknown;
who seeks the mercies of his God
is ever near his throne.

W. DRENNAN (1754–1820)*

79 *Addington* 55 54 D

CYRIL V. TAYLOR (1907–91)

1 This day God gives me
strength of high heaven,
sun and moon shining,
flame in my hearth;
flashing of lightning,
wind in its swiftness,
deeps of the ocean,
firmness of earth.

2 This day God sends me
strength to sustain me,
might to uphold me,
wisdom as guide.
Your eyes are watchful,
your ears are listening,
your lips are speaking,
Friend at my side.

3 God's way is my way,
God's shield is round me,
God's host defends me,
saving from ill;
angels of heaven,
drive from me always
all that would harm me,
stand by me still.

4 Rising, I thank you,
mighty and strong one,
King of creation,
giver of rest,
firmly confessing
Threeness of Persons,
Oneness of Godhead,
Trinity blest.

JAMES QUINN (1919–)
based on 'St Patrick's Breastplate'
5th–7th cent. Gaelic

For another version of the 'Breastplate' see 'I bind unto myself today' (no. 36).

80 *Haresfield* CM

J. DYKES BOWER (1905–81)

1 Can we by searching find out God
   or formulate his ways?
Can numbers measure what he is
   or words contain his praise?

2 Although his being is too bright
   for human eyes to scan,
his meaning lights our shadowed world
   through Christ, the Son of Man.

3 Our boastfulness is turned to shame,
   our profit counts as loss,
when earthly values stand beside
   the manger and the cross.

4 We there may recognise his light,
   may kindle in its rays,
find there the source of penitence,
   the starting-point for praise.

5 There God breaks in upon our search,
   makes birth and death his own:
he speaks to us in human terms
   to make his glory known.

ELIZABETH COSNETT (1936–) altd.

81 *Martyrdom* CM

HUGH WILSON (1766–1824)
adpt. R. A. SMITH (1780–1829)

Alternative tune: KILMARNOCK, no. 487.

1 Come, let us to the Lord our God
with contrite hearts return;
our God is gracious, nor will leave
the desolate to mourn.

2 His voice commands the tempest forth,
and stills the stormy wave;
and though his arm be strong to smite,
'tis also strong to save.

3 The night of sorrow long has reigned,
the dawn shall bring us light:
God shall appear, and we shall rise
with gladness in his sight.

4 Our hearts, if God we seek to know,
shall know him, and rejoice;
his coming like the morn shall be,
like morning songs his voice.

5 As dew upon the tender herb,
diffusing fragrance round;
as showers that usher in the spring,
and cheer the thirsty ground:

6 so shall his presence bless our souls,
and shed a joyful light;
that hallowed morn shall chase away
the sorrows of the night.

Hosea 6: 1–4
para. JOHN MORISON (1750–98)
as in *Scottish Paraphrases*, 1781*

82 *Troy Court* LM

WALTER K. STANTON (1891–1978)

1 Creator of the earth and skies,
to whom the words of life belong,
grant us your truth to make us wise;
grant us your power to make us strong.

2 We have not known you: to the skies
our monuments of folly soar,
and all our self-wrought miseries
have made us trust ourselves the more.

3 We have not loved you: far and wide
the wreckage of our hatred spreads,
and evils wrought by human pride
recoil on unrepentant heads.

4 For this, our foolish confidence,
our pride of knowledge and our sin,
we come to you in penitence;
your work of grace in us begin.

5 Teach us to know and love you, Lord,
and humbly follow in your way.
Speak to us all your living word
and turn our darkness into day.

DONALD WYNN HUGHES (1911–67)*

83

First Tune

Chalfont Park 86 886 ERIK ROUTLEY (1917–82)

Second Tune

Teilo Sant 86 886 JACK P. B. DOBBS (1922–)

1 Eternal Light! Eternal Light!
How pure the soul must be,
when, placed within thy searching sight,
it shrinks not, but with calm delight
can live and look on thee.

2 The spirits that surround thy throne
may bear the burning bliss;
but that is surely theirs alone,
since they have never, never known
a fallen world like this.

3 O how shall I, whose native sphere
is dark, whose mind is dim,
before the ineffable appear,
and on my naked spirit bear
the uncreated beam?

4 There is a way for us to rise
to that sublime abode:
an offering and a sacrifice,
a Holy Spirit's energies,
an advocate with God.

5 These, these prepare us for the sight
of holiness above:
the heirs of ignorance and night
may dwell in the eternal light
through the eternal love!

THOMAS BINNEY (1798–1874) altd.

84 *Walsall* CM

W. ANCHORS' *Psalmody*, c.1721

1 'Forgive our sins as we forgive',
you taught us, Lord, to pray,
but you alone can grant us grace
to live the words we say.

2 How can your pardon reach and bless
the unforgiving heart
that broods on wrongs and will not let
old bitterness depart?

3 In blazing light your Cross reveals
the truth we dimly knew:
what trivial debts are owed to us,
how great our debt to you!

4 Lord, cleanse the depths within our souls
and bid resentment cease.
Then, bound to all in bonds of love,
our lives will spread your peace.

ROSAMOND E. HERKLOTS (1905–87)

85 *Stewardship* 11 10 11 10 (Dactylic) VALERIE RUDDLE (1932–)

1 God in his love for us lent us this planet,
gave it a purpose in time and in space:
small as a spark from the fire of creation,
cradle of life and the home of our race.

2 Thanks be to God for its bounty and beauty,
life that sustains us in body and mind:
plenty for all, if we learn how to share it,
riches undreamed-of to fathom and find.

3 Long have our human wars ruined its harvest;
long has earth bowed to the terror of force;
long have we wasted what others have need of,
poisoned the fountain of life at its source.

4 Earth is the Lord's: it is ours to enjoy it,
ours, as his stewards, to farm and defend.
From its pollution, misuse and destruction,
good Lord, deliver us, world without end!

F. PRATT GREEN (1903–)

86 *Rustington* 87 87 D

C. H. H. PARRY (1848–1918)

1 God, who stretched the spangled heavens,
infinite in time and place,
flung the suns in burning radiance
through the silent fields of space,
we your children, in your likeness,
share inventive powers with you.
Great Creator, still creating,
show us what we yet may do.

2 Proudly rise our modern cities,
stately buildings, row on row;
yet their windows, blank, unfeeling,
stare on canyoned streets below,
where the lonely drift unnoticed
in the city's ebb and flow,
lost to purpose and to meaning,
scarcely caring where they go.

3 We have ventured worlds undreamed of
since the childhood of our race;
known the ecstasy of winging
through untravelled realms of space;
probed the secrets of the atom,
yielding unimagined power,
facing us with life's destruction
or our most triumphant hour.

4 As each far horizon beckons,
may it challenge us anew,
children of creative purpose,
serving others, honouring you.
May our dreams prove rich with promise,
each endeavour, well begun.
Great Creator, give us guidance
till our goals and yours are one.

CATHERINE CAMERON (1927–)

87 *Rawthorpe* 66 66 88

PETER CUTTS (1937–)

Alternative tune: HAREWOOD, no. 190.

1 Lord, bring the day to pass
when forest, rock and hill,
the beasts, the birds, the grass,
will know your finished will:
when we attain our destiny
and nature lives in harmony.

2 Forgive our careless use
of water, ore and soil—
the plenty we abuse
supplied by others' toil:
save us from making self our creed,
turn us towards each other's need.

3 Give us, when we release
creation's secret powers,
to harness them for peace—
our children's peace and ours:
teach us the art of mastering
in servant form, which draws death's sting.

4 Creation groans, travails,
futile its present plight,
bound—till the hour it hails
God's children born of light
who enter on their true estate.
Come, Lord: new heavens and earth create.

IAN FRASER (1917–)

88 *St Nicholas* CM

Later form of a melody from HOLDROYD'S *The Spiritual Man's Companion*, 1753

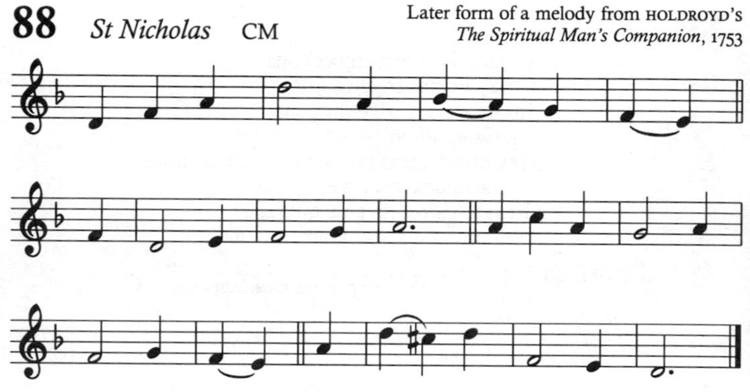

1 Out of our failure to create
a world of love and care;
out of the depths of human life
we cry to God in prayer.

2 Out of the darkness of our time,
of days for ever gone,
our souls are longing for the light,
like watchers for the dawn.

3 Out of the depths we cry to him
whose mercy ends our night.
Our human hole-and-corner ways
by him are brought to light.

4 Hope in the Lord whose timeless love
gives laughter where we wept;
the Father, who at every point
his word has given and kept.

FRED KAAN (1929–)*

89

FIRST TUNE

Harvest 98 98 (Anapaestic) GEOFFREY LAYCOCK (1927–86)

1 Now join we, to praise the creator,
our voices in worship and song;
we stand to recall with thanksgiving
that to him all seasons belong.

2 We thank you, O God, for your goodness,
for the joy and abundance of crops,
for food that is stored in our larders,
for all we can buy in the shops.

3 But also of need and starvation
we sing with concern and despair,
of skills that are used for destruction,
of land that is burnt and laid bare.

4 We cry for the plight of the hungry
while harvests are left on the field,
for orchards neglected and wasting,
for produce from markets withheld.

5 The song grows in depth and in wideness;
the earth and its people are one.
There can be no thanks without giving,
no words without deeds that are done.

6 Then teach us, O Lord of the harvest,
to be humble in all that we claim;
to share what we have with the nations,
to care for the world in your name.

FRED KAAN (1929–)

89

Second Tune

Conway 98 98 (Anapaestic) PAUL BATEMAN (1954–)

1 Now join we, to praise the creator,
our voices in worship and song;
we stand to recall with thanksgiving
that to him all seasons belong.

2 We thank you, O God, for your goodness,
for the joy and abundance of crops,
for food that is stored in our larders,
for all we can buy in the shops.

3 But also of need and starvation
we sing with concern and despair,
of skills that are used for destruction,
of land that is burnt and laid bare.

4 We cry for the plight of the hungry
while harvests are left on the field,
for orchards neglected and wasting,
for produce from markets withheld.

5 The song grows in depth and in wideness;
the earth and its people are one.
There can be no thanks without giving,
no words without deeds that are done.

6 Then teach us, O Lord of the harvest,
to be humble in all that we claim;
to share what we have with the nations,
to care for the world in your name.

FRED KAAN (1929–)

90 *O Lord, all the world belongs to you* PATRICK APPLEFORD (1925–)

Irregular

1 O Lord, all the world belongs to you
and you are always making all things new.
What is wrong you forgive,
and the new life you give
is what's turning the world upside down.

2 The world's only loving to its friends,
but your way of loving never ends,
loving enemies too;
and this loving with you
is what's turning the world upside down.

3 The world lives divided and apart,
you draw us together, and we start
in our friendship to see
that in harmony we
can be turning the world upside down.

4 The world wants the wealth to live in state,
but you show a new way to be great:
like a servant you came,
and if we do the same,
we'll be turning the world upside down.

5 O Lord, all the world belongs to you
and you are always making all things new.
What is wrong you forgive,
and the new life you give
is what's turning the world upside down.

PATRICK APPLEFORD (1925–) altd.*

91 *The hand of God* Irregular

NOEL DEXTER (1938–)

*3+3+2

1 The right hand of God is writing in our land,
writing with power and with love,
our conflicts and our fears,
our triumphs and our tears,
are recorded by the right hand of God.

2 The right hand of God is pointing in our land,
pointing the way we must go;
so clouded is the way,
so easily we stray,
but we're guided by the right hand of God.

3 The right hand of God is striking in our land,
striking out at envy, hate and greed;
our selfishness and lust,
our pride and deeds unjust,
are destroyed by the right hand of God.

4 The right hand of God is lifting in our land,
lifting the fallen one by one;
each one is known by name,
and lifted now from shame,
by the lifting of the right hand of God.

5 The right hand of God is healing in our land,
healing broken bodies, minds and souls;
so wondrous is its touch,
with love that means so much,
when we're healed by the right hand of God.

6 The right hand of God is planting in our land,
planting seeds of freedom, hope and love;
in these many-peopled lands,
let his children all join hands,
and be one with the right hand of God.

PATRICK PRESCOD, 1981, altd.

92 *Amazing grace* CM

American folk-melody
ARR. EDWIN O. EXCELL (1851–1921)

Faith's Review and Expectation

1 Amazing grace (how sweet the sound)
that saved a wretch like me!
I once was lost, but now am found,
was blind, but now I see.

2 As grace first taught my heart to fear
so grace my fears relieved;
how precious did that grace appear
the hour I first believed!

3 Through many dangers, toils and snares
I have already come;
God's grace has brought me safe thus far,
and he will lead me home.

4 The Lord has promised good to me,
his word my hope secures;
he will my shield and portion be
as long as life endures;

5 and, when this heart and flesh shall fail
and mortal life shall cease,
I shall possess within the veil
a life of joy and peace.

JOHN NEWTON (1725–1807) altd.*

93 *Stroudwater* CM

W. ANCHORS' *Psalmody*, *c.*1721

1 Begin, my tongue, some heavenly theme
  and speak some boundless thing,
the mighty works or mightier name
  of our eternal King.

2 Tell of his wondrous faithfulness,
  and sound his power abroad;
sing the sweet promise of his grace
  and the fulfilling God.

3 Engraved as in eternal brass
  the mighty promise shines;
nor can the powers of darkness rase
  those everlasting lines.

4 His very word of grace is strong
  as that which built the skies;
the voice that rolls the stars along
  speaks all the promises.

5 O might I hear thy heavenly tongue
  but whisper, 'Thou art mine';
those gentle words should raise my song
  to notes almost divine.

6 How would my leaping heart rejoice,
  and think my heaven secure!
I trust the all-creating voice,
  and faith desires no more.

ISAAC WATTS (1674–1748) altd.

94 *Duke Street* LM

Melody from BOYD'S *Psalm & Hymn Tunes*, 1793
Later attrib. JOHN HATTON (d. 1793)

God's Wonders of Creation, Providence, Redemption and Salvation

1 Give to our God immortal praise,
mercy and truth are all his ways:
wonders of grace to God belong,
repeat his mercies in your song.

2 Give to the Lord of lords renown;
the King of kings with glory crown:
his mercies ever shall endure,
when lords and kings are known no more.

3 He built the earth, he spread the sky,
and fixed the starry lights on high:
wonders of grace to God belong,
repeat his mercies in your song.

4 He fills the sun with morning light,
he bids the moon direct the night:
his mercies ever shall endure
when suns and moons shall shine no more.

5 He sent his Son with power to save
from guilt and darkness and the grave:
wonders of grace to God belong,
repeat his mercies in your song.

6 Through this vain world he guides our feet,
and leads us to his mercy-seat;
his mercies ever shall endure,
when this vain world shall be no more.

Psalm 136: 1–9, (16, 24)
para. ISAAC WATTS (1674–1748) altd.

95 *Blaenwern* 87 87 D

W. P. ROWLANDS (1860–1937)

1 God is love: let heaven adore him;
God is love: let earth rejoice;
let creation sing before him,
and exalt him with one voice.
He who laid the earth's foundation,
he who spread the heavens above,
he who breathes through all creation,
he is love, eternal love.

2 God is love, and is enfolding
all the world in one embrace;
his unfailing grasp is holding
every child of every race;
and when human hearts are breaking
under sorrow's iron rod,
that same sorrow, that same aching
wrings with pain the heart of God.

3 God is love: and though with blindness
sin afflicts and clouds the will,
God's eternal loving-kindness
holds us fast and guides us still.
Sin and death and hell shall never
o'er us final triumph gain;
God is love, so Love for ever
o'er the universe must reign.

TIMOTHY REES (1874–1939)*

96 *Faithfulness*

W. M. RUNYAN (1870–1957)

11 10 11 10 (Dactylic) with refrain

1 Great is thy faithfulness, O God my Father,
there is no shadow of turning with thee;
thou changest not, thy compassions, they fail not;
as thou hast been thou for ever wilt be.

Great is thy faithfulness, great is thy faithfulness,
morning by morning new mercies I see;
all I have needed thy hand hath provided,
great is thy faithfulness, Lord, unto me.

2 Summer and winter, and springtime and harvest,
sun, moon and stars in their courses above,
join with all nature in manifold witness
to thy great faithfulness, mercy and love.

3 Pardon for sin and a peace that endureth,
thine own dear presence to cheer and to guide;
strength for today and bright hope for tomorrow,
blessings all mine, with ten thousand beside!

T. O. CHISHOLM (1866–1960)

97

First Tune

Gwalchmai 74 74 D

JOSEPH DAVID JONES (1827–70)

Second Tune

Redland 74 74 D

MALCOLM ARCHER (1952–)

1 King of glory, King of peace,
I will love thee;
and, that love may never cease,
I will move thee.
Thou hast granted my request,
thou hast heard me,
thou didst note my working breast,
thou hast spared me.

2 Wherefore with my utmost art
I will sing thee,
and the cream of all my heart
I will bring thee.
Though my sins against me cried,
thou didst clear me;
and alone, when they replied,
thou didst hear me.

3 Seven whole days, not one in seven,
I will praise thee;
in my heart, though not in heaven,
I can raise thee.
Small it is, in this poor sort
to enrol thee;
ev'n eternity's too short
to extol thee.

GEORGE HERBERT (1593–1633)

98 *Austria* 87 87 D FRANZ JOSEF HAYDN (1732–1809)

1 Mighty God, while angels bless thee,
  may a mortal sing thy name?
Lord of earth as well as heaven,
  thou art every creature's theme.
Lord of every land and nation,
  Ancient of eternal Days,
sounded through the wide creation
  be thy just and faithful praise.

2 For the grandeur of thy nature,
  grand beyond a seraph's thought;
for created works of power,
  works with skill and kindness wrought;
for thy providence that governs
  through thine empire's wide domain,
wings an angel, guides a sparrow,
  blessèd be thy gentle reign.

3 But thy rich, thy free redemption,
  dark through brightness all along—
thought is poor and poor expression—
  who dare sing that awesome song?
Brightness of the Father's glory,
  shall thy praise unuttered lie?
Break, my tongue, such guilty silence,
  sing the Lord who came to die.

4 From the highest throne of glory,
   to the cross of deepest woe,
all to ransom guilty captives,
   flow, my praise, for ever flow!
Go, return, immortal Saviour,
   leave thy footstool, take thy throne;
thence return and reign for ever,
   be the kingdom all thine own!

ROBERT ROBINSON (1735–90) altd.*

99 *Emma* 77 77

PAUL LEDDINGTON WRIGHT (1951–)

1 Morning glory, starlit sky,
   soaring music, scholar's truth,
flight of swallows, autumn leaves,
   memory's treasure, grace of youth:

2 open are the gifts of God,
   gifts of love to mind and sense;
hidden is love's agony,
   love's endeavour, love's expense.

3 Love that gives, gives evermore,
   gives with zeal, with eager hands,
spares not, keeps not, all outpours,
   ventures all, its all expends.

4 Drained is love in making full,
   bound in setting others free,
poor in making many rich,
   weak in giving power to be.

5 Therefore he who shows us God
   helpless hangs upon the tree;
and the nails and crown of thorns
   tell us what God's love must be.

6 Here is God, no monarch he,
   throned in easy state to reign;
here is God, whose arms of love
   aching, spent, the world sustain.

W. HUBERT VANSTONE (1923–)*

100 *Eisenach* LM

JOHANN SCHEIN (1586–1630)

1 O love of God, how strong and true,
eternal and yet ever new;
uncomprehended and unbought,
beyond all knowledge and all thought!

2 O love of God, how deep and great,
far deeper than our deepest hate;
self-fed, self-kindled like the light,
changeless, eternal, infinite.

3 O wide, embracing, wondrous love,
we read you in the sky above;
we read you in the earth below,
in seas that swell and streams that flow.

4 We read you best in him who came
to bear for us the cross of shame,
sent by the Father from on high,
our life to live, our death to die.

5 We read your power to bless and save
ev'n in the darkness of the grave;
still more in resurrection light
we read the fullness of your might.

6 O love of God, our shield and stay
through all the perils of our way;
eternal love, in you we rest,
for ever safe, for ever blest.

H. BONAR (1808–89) altd.

101 *Stracathro* CM CHARLES HUTCHESON (1792–1860)

The Beauty of God

1 O matchless beauty of our God
so ancient and so new,
kindle in us your fire of love,
fall on us as the dew!

2 How late we came to love you, Lord,
how strong the hold of sin!
Your beauty speaks from all that is,
your likeness pleads within.

3 You called and cried, yet we were deaf;
our stubborn wills you bent;
you shed your fragrance, and we caught
a moment of its scent.

4 You blazed and sparkled, yet our hearts
to lesser glories turned;
your radiance touched us far from home,
your beauty in us burned!

5 And should our faith grow weak and fall,
tried in the wilderness,
let beauty blossom out of ash,
and streams of water bless!

6 O matchless beauty of our God
so ancient and so new,
enfold in us your fire of love,
anoint us with your dew!

COLIN THOMPSON (1945–)
based on ST AUGUSTINE (354–430), *Confessions*

102 *Llanfair* 77 77 with alleluias

Probably by R. WILLIAMS (*c.* 1781–1821)

1 Praise the Lord, his glories show,
Alleluia!
saints within his courts below,
Alleluia!
angels round his throne above,
Alleluia!
all that see and share his love.
Alleluia!

2 Earth to heaven, and heaven to earth,
tell his wonders, sing his worth;
age to age and shore to shore,
praise him, praise him evermore!

3 Praise the Lord, his mercies trace;
praise his providence and grace,
all that he for us has done,
all he sends us through his Son.

4 Strings and voices, hands and hearts,
in the concert play your parts;
all that breathe, your Lord adore,
praise him, praise him evermore!

H. F. LYTE (1793–1847) altd.

103

First Tune

Chorus Angelorum CM

ARTHUR SOMERVELL (1863–1937)

1 Praise to the Holiest in the height,
and in the depth be praise,
in all his words most wonderful,
most sure in all his ways.

2 O loving wisdom of our God!
When all was sin and shame,
a second Adam to the fight
and to the rescue came.

3 O wisest love! that flesh and blood,
which did in Adam fail,
should strive afresh against the foe,
should strive and should prevail;

4 and that a higher gift than grace
should flesh and blood refine:
God's presence and his very self
and essence all divine.

5 O generous love! that he who smote
in man for man the foe,
the double agony in man
for man should undergo;

6 and in the garden secretly,
and on the cross on high,
should teach his brethren, and inspire
to suffer and to die.

7 Praise to the Holiest in the height,
and in the depth be praise,
in all his words most wonderful,
most sure in all his ways.

J. H. NEWMAN (1801–90) altd.*

103

SECOND TUNE

Gerontius CM J. B. DYKES (1823–76)

1 Praise to the Holiest in the height,
and in the depth be praise,
in all his words most wonderful,
most sure in all his ways.

2 O loving wisdom of our God!
When all was sin and shame,
a second Adam to the fight
and to the rescue came.

3 O wisest love! that flesh and
blood,
which did in Adam fail,
should strive afresh against the foe,
should strive and should prevail;

4 and that a higher gift than grace
should flesh and blood refine:
God's presence and his very self
and essence all divine.

5 O generous love! that he who smote
in man for man the foe,
the double agony in man
for man should undergo;

6 and in the garden secretly,
and on the cross on high,
should teach his brethren, and
inspire
to suffer and to die.

7 Praise to the Holiest in the height,
and in the depth be praise,
in all his words most wonderful,
most sure in all his ways.

J. H. NEWMAN (1801–90) altd.*

104

Praise, my soul 87 87 87 JOHN GOSS (1800–80)

Alternative tune: REGENT SQUARE, no. 319.

1 Praise, my soul, the King of heaven;
to his feet thy tribute bring;
ransomed, healed, restored, forgiven,
who like me his praise should sing?
Praise him! praise him!
praise the everlasting King!

2 Praise him for his grace and favour
to his people in distress;
praise him still the same for ever,
slow to chide, and swift to bless:
Praise him! praise him!
glorious in his faithfulness!

3 Father-like he tends and spares us;
well our feeble frame he knows;
in his hands he gently bears us,
rescues us from all our foes:
Praise him! praise him!
widely as his mercy flows!

4 Frail as summer's flower we flourish,
blows the wind and it is gone,
but while mortals rise and perish
God endures unchanging on.
Praise him! praise him!
praise the high Eternal One!

5 Angels, help us to adore him,
ye behold him face to face;
sun and moon, bow down before him,
dwellers all in time and space:
Praise him! praise him!
praise with us the God of grace!

H. F. LYTE (1793–1847) altd.
based on Psalm 103

105 *Thailand* 56 56

ELISHA A. HOFFMAN (1839–1929)

1 The great love of God
  is revealed in the Son,
who came to this earth
  to redeem every one.

2 That love, like a stream
  flowing clear to the sea,
makes clean every heart
  that from sin would be free.

3 It binds the whole world,
  every barrier it breaks,
the hills it lays low,
  and the mountains it shakes.

4 It's yours, it is ours,
  O how lavishly given!
the pearl of great price,
  and the treasure of heaven!

D. T. NILES (1908–70)

106 *University* CM

Melody from JOHN RANDALL'S
Psalm and Hymn Tunes, 1794
Probably by CHARLES COLLIGNON (1725–85)

1 Thy ceaseless, unexhausted love,
unmerited and free,
delights our evil to remove,
and help our misery.

2 Thou waitest to be gracious still;
thou dost with sinners bear,
that, saved, we may thy goodness feel,
and all thy grace declare.

3 Thy goodness and thy truth to me,
to every soul, abound,
a vast, unfathomable sea,
where all our thoughts are drowned.

4 Its streams the whole creation reach,
so plenteous is the store,
enough for all, enough for each,
enough for evermore.

5 Faithful, O Lord, thy mercies are,
a rock that cannot move;
a thousand promises declare
thy constancy of love.

6 Throughout the universe it reigns,
unalterably sure;
and while the truth of God remains
the goodness must endure.

CHARLES WESLEY (1707–88)

107 *Rhosymedre* 66 66 888

JOHN DAVID EDWARDS (1805–85)

1 The love of God comes close
  where stands an open door
to let the stranger in,
  to mingle rich and poor.
The love of God is here to stay;
embracing those who walk his way,
the love of God is here to stay.

2 The peace of God comes close
  to those caught in the storm,
forgoing lives of ease
  to ease the lives forlorn.
The peace of God is here to stay;
embracing those who walk his way,
the peace of God is here to stay.

3 The joy of God comes close
  where faith encounters fears,
where heights and depths of life
  are found through smiles and tears.
The joy of God is here to stay;
embracing those who walk his way,
the joy of God is here to stay.

4 The grace of God comes close
  to those whose grace is spent,
when hearts are tired or sore
  and hope is bruised and bent.
The grace of God is here to stay;
embracing those who walk his way,
the grace of God is here to stay.

5 The Son of God comes close
  where people praise his name,
where bread and wine are blest
  and shared as when he came.
The Son of God is here to stay;
embracing those who walk his way,
the Son of God is here to stay.

JOHN BELL (1949–)
and GRAHAM MAULE (1958–)

108 *Som Stranden*

LARS ÅKE LUNDBERG (1935–)

11 10 11 10 with refrain

1 The love of God is broad like beach and meadow,
wide as the wind, and an eternal home.
God leaves us free to seek him or reject him,
he gives us room to answer Yes or No.

The love of God is broad like beach and meadow,
wide as the wind, and an eternal home.

2 We long for freedom where our truest being
is given hope and courage to unfold.
We seek in freedom space and scope for dreaming,
and look for ground where trees and plants can grow.

3 But there are walls that keep us all divided;
we fence each other in with hate and war.
Fear is the bricks and mortar of our prison,
our pride of self the prison coat we wear.

4 O judge us, Lord, and in your judgement free us,
and set our feet in freedom's open space;
take us as far as your compassion wanders
among the children of the human race.

ANDERS FROSTENSON (1906–)
tr. FRED KAAN (1929–)

109 *Belgrave* CM

WILLIAM HORSLEY (1774–1858)

Gratitude

1 When all thy mercies, O my God,
my rising soul surveys,
transported with the view, I'm lost
in wonder, love and praise.

2 Unnumbered comforts to my soul
thy tender care bestowed,
before my infant heart conceived
from whom these comforts flowed.

3 When worn with sickness, oft hast thou
with health renewed my face;
and, when in sins and sorrows sunk,
revived my soul with grace.

4 Ten thousand thousand precious gifts
my daily thanks employ;
nor is the least a cheerful heart,
that tastes those gifts with joy.

5 Through every moment of my life
thy goodness I'll pursue;
and after death, in distant worlds,
the glorious theme renew.

6 Through all eternity to thee
a joyful song I'll raise;
for O! eternity's too short
to utter all thy praise.

signed 'c' in *The Spectator*, 9 Aug. 1712
attrib. JOSEPH ADDISON (1672–1719)*

110 *All kinds of light* 5 88 55

CARYL MICKLEM (1925–)

1 Father, we thank you.
For the light that shines all the day;
for the bright sky you have given,
most like your heaven;
Father, we thank you.

2 Father, we thank you.
For the lamps that lighten the way;
for human skill's exploration
of your creation;
Father, we thank you.

3 Father, we thank you.
For the friends who brighten our play;
for your command to call others
sisters and brothers;
Father, we thank you.

4 Father, we thank you.
For your love in Jesus today,
giving us hope for tomorrow
through joy and sorrow;
Father, we thank you.

CARYL MICKLEM (1925–)

111 *Echternach* 10 10 10 10

CARYL MICKLEM (1925–)

1 In praise of God meet duty and delight,
angels and creatures, flesh and spirit bless'd;
in praise is earth transfigured by the sound
and sight of heaven's everlasting feast.

2 In praise the artist and the craftsman meet,
inspired, obedient, patient, practical;
in praise join instrument and voice and sound
to make one music for the Lord of all.

3 The desert is refreshed by songs of praise,
relaxed the frown of pride, the stress of grief;
in praise forgotten all our human spite;
in praise the burdened heart finds sure relief.

4 No skill of ours, no music made on earth,
no mortal song could scale the height of heaven;
yet stands that cross, through grace ineffable
an instrument of praise to sinners given.

5 So, confident and festive, let us sing
of wisdom, power and mercy there made known;
the song of Moses and the Lamb is ours,
through Christ raised up to life in God alone.

ERIK ROUTLEY (1917–82)*

112

First Tune

Caerlaverock 6 444 6 CARYL MICKLEM (1925–)

Second Tune

Emley Moor 6 444 6 PETER CUTTS (1937–)

1 Joy wings to God our song,
for all life holds
to stir the heart,
to light the mind
and make our spirit strong.

2 Joy wings our grateful hymn,
for home and friends
and all the love
that fills our cup
of gladness to the brim.

3 Joy wings to God our praise,
for wisdom's wealth,
our heritage
from every age,
to guide us in his ways.

4 Joy wings to God our prayer.
All gifts we need
of courage, faith,
forgiveness, peace,
are offered by his care.

5 Joy wings our heart and voice
to give ourselves
to Christ who died
and, risen, lives
that we may all rejoice.

A. F. BAYLY (1901–84)

113 *Jubilate* CM extended, with refrain JOSEPH BARNBY (1838–96)

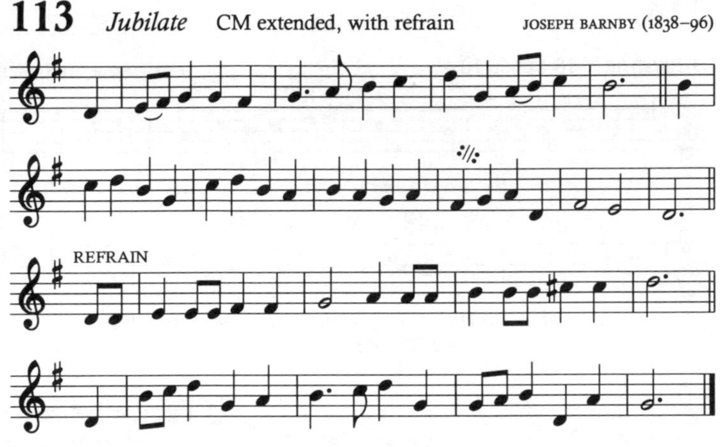

1 Let all God's people join in one
  to lift the heart and voice,
the Lord hath done great things for us,
  and therefore we rejoice:

For the harvest of bygone ages,
  in the hope of the coming days,
go into his gates with thankfulness
  and into his courts with praise.

2 We with our ears have heard the tale,
  the tale apostles told,
what wonders God for them and us
  did in the time of old:

3 They sowed the seed and watered it
  in sorrow and in care;
but God alone the increase gave
  and made it blossom fair:

4 All praise to him whose bounty crowns
  with flowers and fruit the year;
God is our hope and strength today,
  therefore we will not fear:

A. C. AINGER (1841–1919)*

114

FIRST TUNE

Augustine 10 4 6666 10 4 ERIK ROUTLEY (1917–82)

Let all the world in ev - 'ry_ cor - ner sing 'My

God and King!' 1. The heav'ns are not too high, his
2. The Church with psalms must shout, no

praise may thi - ther fly: the earth is not too low, his prai-ses_
door can keep them out: but, a - bove all, the heart must bear the_

SECOND TUNE

Luckington 10 4 6666 10 4 BASIL HARWOOD (1859–1949)

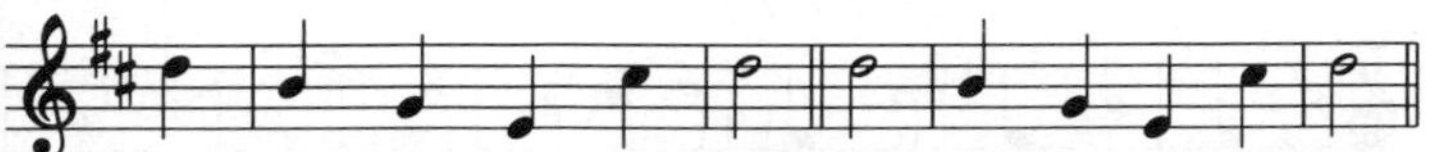

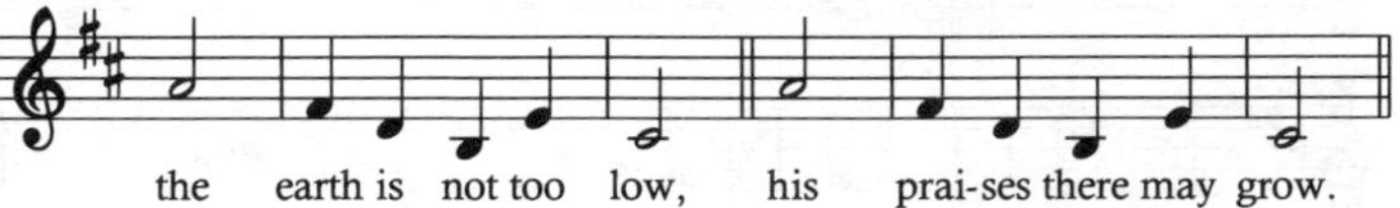

Antiphon

Let all the world in every corner sing
'My God and King!'

The heavens are not too high,
his praise may thither fly:
the earth is not too low,
his praises there may grow.

Let all the world in every corner sing
'My God and King!'

The Church with psalms must shout,
no door can keep them out:
but, above all, the heart
must bear the longest part.

Let all the world in every corner sing
'My God and King!'

GEORGE HERBERT (1593–1633)

The words are printed here as in the author's original poem, for which the tune AUGUSTINE was composed. When this hymn is sung to LUCKINGTON the antiphon, which precedes and follows the first verse, is repeated before the second.

115 *St Bartholomew* LM

HENRY DUNCALF (d. 1762)
from W. RILEY'S *Parochial Harmony*, 1762

The Greatness of God

1 My God, my king, thy various praise
shall fill the remnant of my days;
thy grace employ my humble tongue,
till death and glory raise the song.

2 The wings of every hour shall bear
some thankful tribute to thine ear,
and every setting sun shall see
new works of duty done for thee.

3 Thy truth and justice I'll proclaim;
thy bounty flows, an endless stream;
thy mercy swift; thine anger slow,
but dreadful to the stubborn foe.

4 Thy works with sovereign glory shine
and speak thy majesty divine:
while peoples round the earth proclaim
the sound and honour of thy name.

5 Let distant times and nations raise
the long succession of thy praise;
and unborn ages make my song
the joy and labour of their tongue.

6 But who can speak thy wondrous deeds?
Thy greatness all our thoughts exceeds;
vast and unsearchable thy ways,
vast and immortal be thy praise.

ISAAC WATTS (1674–1748)*
based on Psalm 145: 1–10 (20)

116 *Laus Deo* 87 87 (Trochaic)

Composed or adapted by
RICHARD REDHEAD (1820–1901)

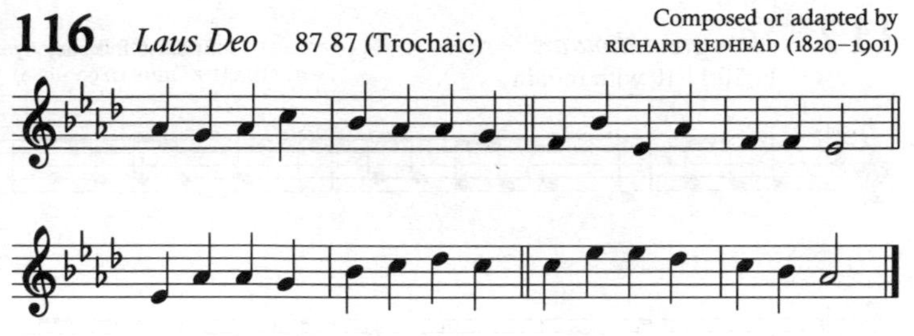

1 Praise the Lord, ye heavens adore him;
praise him, angels in the height;
sun and moon, bow down before him,
praise him, all ye stars and light.

2 Praise the Lord, for he hath spoken;
worlds his mighty voice obeyed;
laws, that never shall be broken,
for their guidance he hath made.

3 Praise the Lord, for he is glorious;
never shall his promise fail;
God hath made his saints victorious;
sin and death shall not prevail.

4 Praise the God of our salvation;
hosts on high, his power proclaim;
heaven and earth, and all creation,
laud and magnify his name.

Anon.
in *Foundling Hospital Collection*, 1796/1801, altd.
based on Psalm 148: 1–6, 14

117 *How great thou art*

11 10 11 10 with refrain

Swedish folk melody
arr. STUART K. HINE (1899–1989)

1 O Lord my God, when I in awesome wonder
consider all the works thy hand hath made,
I see the stars, I hear the mighty thunder,
thy power throughout the universe displayed:

Then sings my soul, my Saviour God, to thee,
How great thou art, how great thou art!
Then sings my soul, my Saviour God, to thee,
How great thou art, how great thou art!

2 When through the woods and forest glades I wander,
and hear the birds sing sweetly in the trees;
when I look down from lofty mountain grandeur,
and hear the brook, and feel the gentle breeze;

3 But when I think that God, his Son not sparing,
sent him to die—I scarce can take it in
that on the cross, our burden gladly bearing,
he bled and died to take away our sin;

4 When Christ shall come with shout of acclamation
and take me home—what joy shall fill my heart!
Then shall I bow in humble adoration,
and there proclaim: My God, how great thou art!

Russian hymn
tr. STUART K. HINE (1899–1989) altd.

118 *Leoni* 66 84 D

Hebrew melody
noted by THOMAS OLIVERS (1725–99)

1 Praise to the living God!
All praise be to his name,
who was, and is, and is to be,
for aye the same!
The one eternal God
ere aught that now appears:
the First, the Last, beyond all thought
his timeless years!

2 Formless, all lovely forms
declare his loveliness;
holy, no holiness of earth
can his express.
Lo, he is Lord of all!
Creation speaks his praise,
and everywhere, above, below,
his will obeys.

3 His Spirit floweth free,
high surging where it will;
in prophet's word he spoke of old,
he speaketh still.
Established is his law,
and changeless it shall stand,
deep written on the human heart,
on sea, on land.

4 Eternal life hath he
implanted in the soul,
his love shall be our strength and stay,
while ages roll.
Praise to the living God!
all praise be to his name,
who was, and is, and is to be,
for aye the same!

from the *Hebrew Yigdal*, *c.*13th cent.
tr. MAX LANDSBERG (1845–1928)
NEWTON MANN (1836–1926)
and WILLIAM C. GANNETT (1840–1923)*

119 *Old Hundredth* LM

Later form of melody
in the *Genevan Psalter*, 1551

1 Sing to the Lord with joyful voice;
let every land his name adore;
the farthest isles shall send the noise
across the ocean to the shore.

2 Nations, attend before his throne
with solemn fear, with sacred joy;
know that the Lord is God alone;
he can create, and he destroy.

3 His sovereign power, without our aid,
made us, and formed our mortal frame;
and when like wandering sheep we strayed,
he brought us to his fold again.

4 We'll crowd thy gates with thankful songs,
high as the heavens our voices raise;
and earth with her ten thousand tongues
shall fill thy courts with sounding praise.

5 Wide as the world is thy command,
vast as eternity thy love,
firm as a rock thy truth must stand
when rolling years shall cease to move.

Psalm 100
para. ISAAC WATTS (1674–1748) altd.*

120 *Ruth* 65 65 D

SAMUEL SMITH (1821–1917)

1 Summer suns are glowing
over land and sea;
happy light is flowing,
bountiful and free.
Everything rejoices
in the mellow rays;
all earth's thousand voices
swell the psalm of praise.

2 God's free mercy streameth
over all the world,
and his banner gleameth,
everywhere unfurled.
Broad and deep and glorious,
as the heaven above,
shines in might victorious
his eternal love.

3 Lord, upon our blindness
thy pure radiance pour;
for thy loving-kindness
make us love thee more.
And, when clouds are drifting
dark across our sky,
then, the veil uplifting,
Father, be thou nigh.

4 We will never doubt thee,
though thou veil thy light;
life is dark without thee;
death with thee is bright.
Light of light, shine o'er us
on our pilgrim way;
go thou still before us,
to the endless day.

W. W. HOW (1823–97)

121 *Leoni* 66 84 D

Hebrew melody
noted by THOMAS OLIVERS (1725–99)

1 The God of Abraham praise
who reigns enthroned above;
Ancient of everlasting Days,
and God of love:
Jehovah, great I AM,
by earth and heaven confest;
I bow and bless the sacred name
for ever blest.

2 The God of Abraham praise,
at whose supreme command
from earth I rise and seek the joys
at his right hand:
I all on earth forsake,
its wisdom, fame and power;
and him my only portion make,
my shield and tower.

3 He by himself hath sworn,
I on his oath depend;
I shall, on eagles' wings upborne,
to heaven ascend:
I shall behold his face,
I shall his power adore,
and sing the wonders of his grace
for evermore.

4 The God who reigns on high
the great archangels sing,
and 'Holy, holy, holy,' cry,
'Almighty King!
who wast, and art the same,
and evermore shalt be;
Jehovah, Father, great I AM!
we worship thee!'

5 Before the Saviour's face
the ransomed nations bow;
o'erwhelmed at his almighty grace,
for ever new.
He shows his prints of love,
they kindle to a flame,
and sound through all the worlds above
the slaughtered Lamb.

6 The whole triumphant host
give thanks to God on high:
'Hail, Father, Son, and Holy Ghost',
they ever cry;
Hail, Abraham's God and mine!
(I join the heavenly lays),
all might and majesty are thine,
and endless praise.

THOMAS OLIVERS (1725–99)
para. from the *Hebrew Yigdal*, *c.*13th cent.
and Revelation 4 and 5

122 *Song 20* SM

ORLANDO GIBBONS (1583–1625)

The Life of Universal Praise

1 The universe to God
in silence sings its praise,
to echo Love's divine abyss
through all its silent ways.

2 And all created hosts,
the angels, stars and sun
give praise to God in solemn dance;
as when all time began.

3 The earth, the air, the sea
and every living thing
praise Christ, the uncreated, born
to be creation's king.

4 Christ's spirit makes us one,
and, built in Christ, we find
humanity, the beating heart
and image of God's mind.

5 The Spirit's pulsing life
shall find us, lost in night,
and in the peace of love and praise
shall lead us in the light.

DAVID FOX (1956–)

123 *Genesis* Irregular GRAHAM WESTCOTT (1947–)

1 Think of a world without any flowers,
  think of a wood without any trees,
think of a sky without any sunshine,
  think of the air without any breeze:
we thank you, Lord, for flowers and trees and sunshine;
we thank you, Lord, and praise your holy name.

2 Think of a world without any people,
  think of a street with no-one living there,
think of a town without any houses,
  no-one to love and nobody to care:
we thank you, Lord, for families and friendships;
we thank you, Lord, and praise your holy name.

3 Think of a world without any worship,
  think of a God without his only Son,
think of a cross without a resurrection
  only a grave and not a victory won:
we thank you, Lord, for showing us our Saviour;
we thank you, Lord, and praise your holy name.

4 Thanks to our Lord for being here among us,
  thanks be to him for sharing all we do,
thanks for our church and all the love we find here,
  thanks for this place and all its promise true:
we thank you, Lord, for life in all its richness;
we thank you, Lord, and praise your holy name.

BUNTY NEWPORT (1927–) and children from
Emmanuel Junior Church, Cambridge, 1966

124 *Wir pflügen* 76 76 D 66 84 J. A. P. SCHULZ (1747–1800)

1 We plough the fields, and scatter
the good seed on the land,
but it is fed and watered
by God's almighty hand;
he sends the snow in winter,
the warmth to swell the grain,
the breezes and the sunshine,
and soft refreshing rain:

All good gifts around us
are sent from heaven above;
then thank the Lord, O thank the Lord,
for all his love.

2 He only is the maker
of all things near and far;
he paints the wayside flower;
he lights the evening star;
the winds and waves obey him,
by him the birds are fed;
much more to us, his children,
he gives our daily bread:

3 We thank you then, O Father,
for all things bright and good,
the seed-time and the harvest,
our life, our health, our food.
No gifts have we to offer
for all your love imparts,
but that which you most welcome,
our humble, thankful hearts:

MATTHIAS CLAUDIUS (1740–1815)
tr. JANE CAMPBELL (1817–78)*

125 *Darwall* 66 66 44 44 JOHN DARWALL (1731–89)

1 Ye holy angels bright
who wait at God's right hand,
or through the realms of light
fly at your Lord's command,
assist our song,
or else the theme
too high doth seem
for mortal tongue.

2 Ye blessed souls at rest,
who see your Saviour's face,
whose glory, ev'n the least,
is far above our grace:
God's praises sound,
as in his sight
with sweet delight
ye do abound.

3 Ye saints who toil below,
adore your heavenly King,
and onward as ye go
some joyful anthem sing;
take what he gives
and praise him still,
through good and ill,
who ever lives.

4 My soul, bear thou thy part,
triumph in God above;
and with a well-tuned heart
sing thou the songs of love.
Thou art his own,
whose precious blood
shed for thy good
his love made known.

5 Let all creation sing
and join the marvellous throng
who crowns of glory bring
and raise the Lamb's new song.
Let all our days
till life shall end,
whate'er he send
be filled with praise.

RICHARD BAXTER (1615–91) altd.*
V. 3: J. H. GURNEY (1802–62)

126 *Veni Immanuel* LM with refrain

Melody from a 15th-century processional

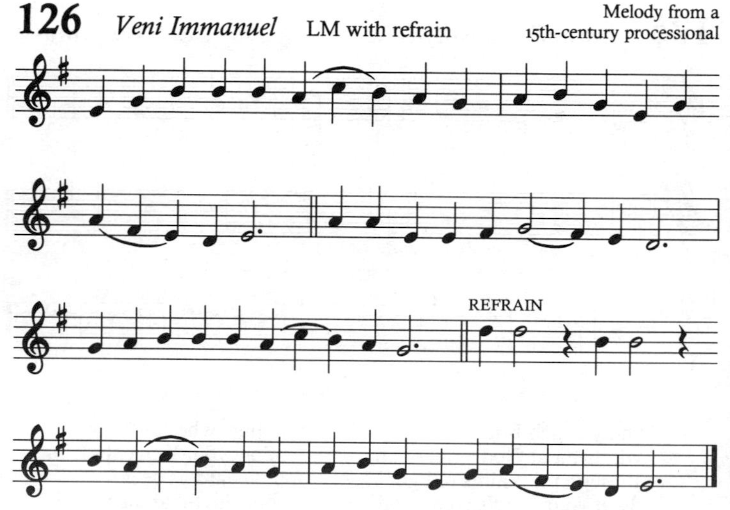

1 O come, O come, Immanuel,
and ransom captive Israel,
that mourns in lonely exile here
until the Son of God appear:

Rejoice! Rejoice!
Immanuel shall come to thee, O Israel.

2 O come, thou Wisdom from above
who ord'rest all things through thy love;
to us the path of knowledge show
and teach us in her ways to go:

3 O come, O come, thou Lord of might,
who to thy tribes, on Sinai's height,
in ancient times didst give the law
in cloud, and majesty, and awe:

4 O come, thou Rod of Jesse, free
thine own from Satan's tyranny;
from depths of hell thy people save,
and give them vict'ry o'er the grave:

5 O come, thou Key of David, come,
and open wide our heavenly home;
make safe the way that leads on high,
and close the path to misery:

6 O come, thou Dayspring, come and cheer
our spirits by thine advent here;
disperse the gloomy clouds of night,
and death's dark shadows put to flight:

7 O come, Desire of nations, bring
all peoples to their Saviour King;
thou Corner-stone, who makest one,
complete in us thy work begun:

†(8) O come, O come, Immanuel,
and ransom captive Israel,
that mourns in lonely exile here
until the Son of God appear:

Latin, 18th cent. (or earlier)
based on Antiphons from 9th cent. (or earlier)
tr. J. M. NEALE (1818–66) and others; altd.*

†Optional. The original seven 'Great O' Antiphons, on which this hymn is based, were sung, one each day, on seven days before Christmas, ending with the antiphon corresponding to v. 1 (*O come, O come, Immanuel*) on 23 December. That verse is now traditionally sung first; but if desired it may be sung at the end of the hymn as well as, or instead of, at the beginning.

127 *Crüger* 76 76 D

adpt. W. H. MONK (1823–89)
from a chorale by
JOHANN CRÜGER (1598–1662)

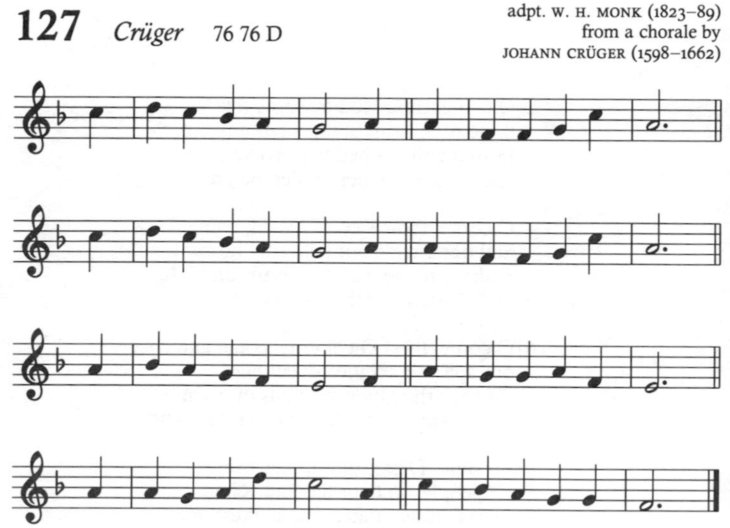

1 Hail to the Lord's Anointed,
great David's greater Son!
Hail, in the time appointed,
his reign on earth begun!
He comes to break oppression,
to set the captive free,
to take away transgression,
and rule in equity.

2 He comes with succour speedy
to those who suffer wrong;
to help the poor and needy,
and bid the weak be strong;
to give them songs for sighing,
their darkness turn to light,
whose souls, condemned and dying,
were precious in his sight.

3 He shall come down like showers
upon the fruitful earth;
and love, joy, hope, like flowers,
spring in his path to birth:
before him on the mountains,
shall peace the herald go,
and righteousness in fountains
from hill to valley flow.

4 Kings shall fall down before him,
and gold and incense bring;
and nations shall adore him,
his praise all people sing;
for he shall have dominion
o'er river, sea, and shore,
far as the eagle's pinion
or dove's light wing can soar.

5 O'er every foe victorious,
he on his throne shall rest;
from age to age more glorious,
all-blessing and all-blest:
the tide of time shall never
his covenant remove;
his name shall stand for ever;
that name to us is Love.

Psalm 72
para. JAMES MONTGOMERY (1771–1854)

128 *St Stephen (Newington)* CM

WILLIAM JONES (1726–1800)

1 The Lord will come and not be slow,
his footsteps cannot err;
before him righteousness shall go,
his royal harbinger.

2 Mercy and truth that long were missed,
now joyfully are met;
sweet peace and righteousness have kissed,
and hand in hand are set.

3 Surely to such as do him fear
salvation is at hand;
and glory shall ere long appear
to dwell within our land.

4 Rise, God, judge thou the earth in might,
this wicked earth redress;
for thou art he who shall by right
the nations all possess.

5 The nations all whom thou hast made
shall come, and all shall frame
to bow them low before thee, Lord,
and glorify thy name.

6 For great thou art, and wonders great
by thy strong hand are done;
thou in thine everlasting seat
remainest God alone.

from Psalms 82, 85, 86
para. JOHN MILTON (1608–74) altd.

129 *Dundee (French)* CM

Scottish Psalter, 1615

1 The race that long in darkness pined
  have seen a glorious light;
the people dwell in day, who dwelt
  in death's surrounding night.

2 To hail thee, Sun of Righteousness,
  the gathering nations come,
rejoicing as when reapers bear
  their harvest treasures home.

3 To us a child of hope is born,
  to us a Son is given;
him shall the tribes of earth obey,
  him all the hosts of heaven.

4 His name shall be the Prince of Peace,
  for evermore adored,
the Wonderful, the Counsellor,
  the great and mighty Lord.

5 His power increasing still shall spread,
  his reign no end shall know;
justice shall guard his throne above,
  and peace abound below.

from Isaiah 9: 2–3*a*, 6, 7
para. JOHN MORISON (1750–98) altd.

130 *Glasgow* CM

Melody from T. MOORE's *Psalm-singer's Pocket Companion*, Glasgow, *c.*1756

1 Behold the mountain of the Lord
in latter days shall rise
on mountain tops, above the hills,
and draw the wondering eyes.

2 To this the joyful nations round,
all tribes and tongues, shall flow;
up to the hill of God, they'll say,
and to his house we'll go.

3 The beam that shines from Zion hill
shall lighten every land;
the King who reigns in Salem's towers
shall all the world command.

4 Among the nations he shall judge;
his judgements truth shall guide;
his sceptre shall protect the just,
and quell the sinner's pride.

5 No strife shall rage, nor hostile feuds
disturb those peaceful years;
to ploughshares nations beat their swords,
to pruning hooks their spears.

6 No longer hosts encountering hosts
shall crowds of slain deplore;
they hang the trumpet in the hall,
and study war no more.

7 Come then, O come, from every land,
to worship at his shrine;
and, walking in the light of God,
with holy beauties shine.

Scottish Paraphrases, 1781 altd.*
from Isaiah 2: 2–5

131 *Blackbird Leys* 10 10 10 10

PETER CUTTS (1937–)

1 The voice of God goes out to all the world;
his glory speaks across the universe.
The Great King's herald cries from star to star:
'With power, with justice, he will walk his way'.

2 The Lord has said: 'Receive my messenger,
my promise to the world, my pledge made flesh,
a lamp to every nation, light from light:
With power, with justice, he will walk his way'.

3 The broken reed he will not trample down,
nor set his heel upon the dying flame.
He binds the wounds, and health is in his hand:
With power, with justice, he will walk his way.

4 Anointed with the Spirit and with power,
he comes to crown with comfort all the weak,
to show the face of justice to the poor:
With power, with justice, he will walk his way.

5 His touch will bless the eyes that darkness held,
the lame shall run, the halting tongue shall sing,
and prisoners laugh in light and liberty:
With power, with justice, he will walk his way.

LUKE CONNAUGHTON (1917–79)

132 *Wachet auf* 898 D 664 448

Melody by PHILIPP NICOLAI (1556–1608)
adpt. J. S. BACH (1685–1750)

CHRIST'S COMING

1 Wake, O wake! with tidings thrilling
the watchmen all the air are filling,
'Arise, Jerusalem, arise!'
Midnight strikes! no more delaying,
'The hour has come!', we hear them saying.
'Where are you all, you virgins wise?
The Bridegroom comes in sight,
raise high your torches bright!'
Alleluia!
The wedding song
swells loud and strong:
go forth and join the festal throng.

2 Zion hears the watchmen shouting,
her heart leaps up with joy undoubting,
she stands and waits with eager eye.
See her Friend from heaven descending,
adorned with truth and grace unending!
Her light burns clear, her star climbs high.
Now come, our precious crown,
Lord Jesus, God's own Son!
Alleluia!
Let us prepare
to follow there,
where in your supper we may share.

3 Every soul in you rejoices;
from earth and from angelic voices
be glory given to you alone!
Now the gates of pearl receive us,
your presence never more shall leave us,
we stand with angels round your throne.
Earth cannot give below
the bliss that you bestow.
Alleluia!
Grant us to raise,
to length of days,
the triumph-chorus of your praise.

PHILIPP NICOLAI (1556–1608)
tr. F. C. BURKITT (1864–1935) altd.*

133 *Venice* SM

WILLIAM AMPS (1824–1910)

Alternative tune: ST GEORGE, no. 429.

1 How beauteous are their feet
who stand on Zion's hill!
who bring salvation on their tongues,
and words of peace reveal.

2 How charming is their voice!
How sweet the tidings are!—
'Zion, behold thy Saviour-King;
he reigns and triumphs here.'

3 How happy are our ears
that hear this joyful sound!
which kings and prophets waited for,
and sought, but never found.

4 How blessèd are our eyes
that see this heavenly light!
Prophets and kings desired it long,
but died without the sight.

5 The watchers join their voice,
and tuneful notes employ;
Jerusalem breaks forth in songs,
and deserts learn the joy.

6 The Lord makes bare his arm,
through all the earth abroad;
let every nation now behold
their Saviour and their God.

ISAAC WATTS (1674–1748)*

134 *Solemnis haec festivitas* LM Melody from Paris *Gradual*, 1685

1 On Jordan's bank the Baptist's cry
announces that the Lord is nigh;
come then and hearken, for he brings
glad tidings from the King of kings.

2 Then cleansed be every breast from sin;
make straight the way for God within;
and in each heart prepare a home
where such a mighty guest may come.

3 For thou art our salvation, Lord,
our refuge and our great reward;
without thy grace we waste away
like flowers that wither and decay.

4 To heal the sick stretch out thy hand,
and bid the fallen sinner stand;
shine forth, and let thy light restore
earth's own true loveliness once more.

5 All praise, eternal Son, to thee
whose advent sets thy people free,
whom, with the Father, we adore,
and Spirit blest, for evermore.

CHARLES COFFIN (1676–1749)
tr. JOHN CHANDLER (1806–76) altd.*

135

First Tune

Nativity CM

H. LAHEE (1826–1912)

1 Joy to the world, the Lord is come!
Let earth receive her King;
let every heart prepare him room,
and heaven and nature sing.

2 Joy to the world, the Saviour reigns!
Let all their songs employ;
while fields and floods, rocks, hills and plains
repeat the sounding joy.

3 No more let thorns infest the ground,
or sins and sorrows grow;
wherever pain and death are found
he makes his blessings flow.

4 He rules the world with truth and grace,
and makes the nations prove
the glories of his righteousness
and wonders of his love.

ISAAC WATTS (1674–1748) altd.*
based on Psalm 98

CHRIST'S COMING

Second Tune

Antioch CM extended From W. HOLFORD'S *Voce di Melodia*, *c.*1834

136 *Gonfalon Royal* LM

PERCY BUCK (1871–1947)

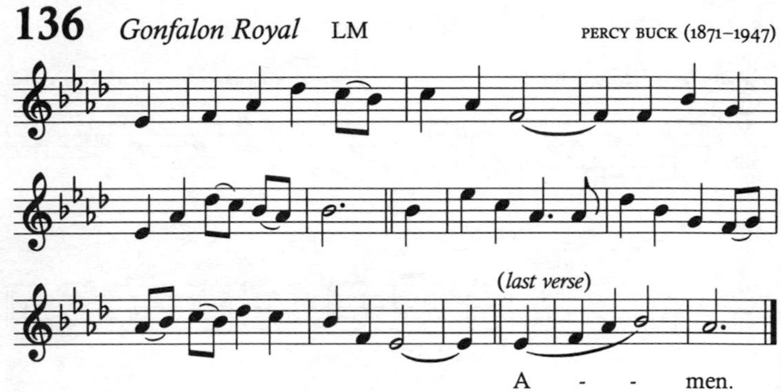

1 And art thou come with us to dwell,
our prince, our guide, our love, our Lord?
And is thy name Immanuel,
God present with his world restored?

2 The heart is glad for thee: it knows
none now shall bid it err or mourn,
and o'er its desert breaks the rose
in triumph o'er the grieving thorn.

3 Thou bringest all again; with thee
is light, is space, is breadth, and room
for each thing fair, beloved and free,
to have its hour of life and bloom.

4 Each heart's deep instinct, unconfessed;
each lowly wish, each daring claim;
all, all that life hath long repressed,
unfolds, undreading blight or blame.

5 Thy reign eternal will not cease;
thy years are sure and glad, and slow,
within thy mighty world of peace
the humblest flower hath leave to blow.

6 The world is glad for thee; the heart
is glad for thee, and all is well
and fixed, and sure, because thou art,
whose name is called Immanuel.
(Amen.)

DORA GREENWELL (1821–82)

137 *Bristol* CM

Melody from
THOMAS RAVENSCROFT'S *Psalmes*, 1621

1 Hark, the glad sound! The Saviour comes,
the Saviour promised long:
let every heart prepare a throne,
and every voice a song.

2 He comes, the prisoners to release
in Satan's bondage held;
the gates of brass before him burst,
the iron fetters yield.

3 He comes, from ignorance and doubt
to clear the inward sight;
and on the darkness of the blind
to pour celestial light.

4 He comes, the broken heart to bind,
the wounded soul to cure,
and with the treasures of his grace
to enrich the humble poor.

5 Our glad hosannas, Prince of Peace,
thy welcome shall proclaim;
and heaven's eternal arches ring
with thy beloved name.

PHILIP DODDRIDGE (1702–51) altd.*

138 *Corinth (Tantum ergo)*

87 87 D

Melody from SAMUEL WEBBE'S *An Essay on the Church Plain Chant*, 1782

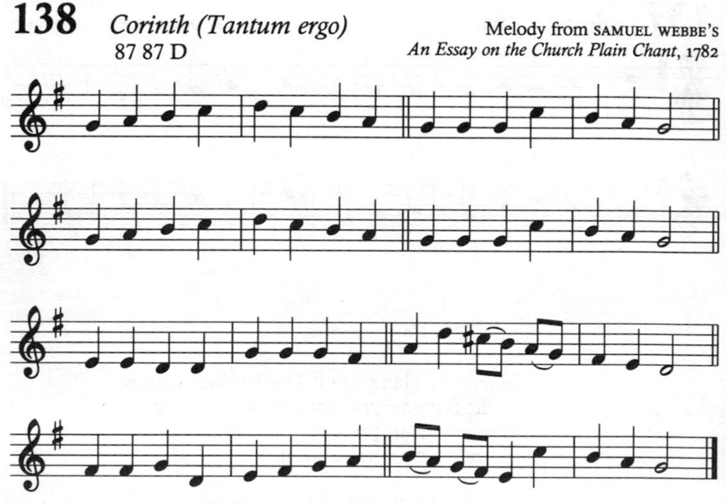

1 Come, thou long-expected Jesus,
   born to set thy people free;
from our fears and sins release us;
   let us find our rest in thee.
Israel's strength and consolation,
   hope of all the earth thou art;
dear Desire of every nation,
   joy of every longing heart.

2 Born thy people to deliver;
   born a child, and yet a King;
born to reign in us for ever;
   now thy gracious kingdom bring.
By thine own eternal Spirit
   rule in all our hearts alone;
by thine all-sufficient merit
   raise us to thy glorious throne.

CHARLES WESLEY (1707–88)

139 *Gabriel's Message* 10 10 12 7 3 Basque traditional carol melody

1 The Angel Gabriel from heaven came,
his wings as drifted snow, his eyes as flame;
'All Hail', said he, 'thou lowly maiden Mary,
most highly favoured lady.'
Gloria!

2 'For known a blessed Mother thou shalt be,
all generations laud and honour thee,
thy Son shall be Immanuel, by seers foretold;
most highly favoured lady.'
Gloria!

3 Then gentle Mary meekly bowed her head,
'To me be as it pleaseth God', she said,
'my soul shall laud and magnify his holy name':
most highly favoured lady.
Gloria!

4 Of her, Immanuel the Christ was born
in Bethlehem, all on a Christmas morn,
and Christian folk throughout the world will ever say
'Most highly favoured lady'.
Gloria!

Basque Carol
para. S. BARING-GOULD (1834–1924)

140 *Passion Chorale* 76 76 D

HANS LEO HASSLER (1562–1612)

1 O Lord, how shall I meet you,
how welcome you aright?
Your people long to greet you,
my hope, my heart's delight!
O kindle, Lord most holy,
a lamp within my breast,
to do in spirit lowly
all that may please you best.

2 Love caused your incarnation,
love brought you down to me;
your thirst for my salvation
procured my liberty:
O love beyond all telling,
that led you to embrace
in love all love excelling
our lost and fallen race.

3 A heavenly hope you give me,
a treasure safe on high,
that will not fail nor leave me
as earthly riches fly.
My heart shall bloom for ever
with joyful praises new,
and from your name shall never
withhold the honour due.

PAUL GERHARDT (1607–76)
tr. CATHERINE WINKWORTH (1827–78) altd.*

141 *Make way* Irregular

GRAHAM KENDRICK (1950–)

1 Make way, make way, for Christ the King
in splendour arrives.
Fling wide the gates and welcome him
into your lives.

Make way! Make way
for the King of kings, King of kings!
Make way! Make way
and let his kingdom in.

2 He comes the broken hearts to heal,
the prisoners to free;
the deaf shall hear, the lame shall dance,
the blind shall see.

3 And those who mourn with heavy hearts,
who weep and sigh,
with laughter, joy and royal crown
he'll beautify.

4 We call you now to worship him
as Lord of all,
to have no other gods but him;
their thrones must fall.

GRAHAM KENDRICK (1950–)*

142 *Chartres* 77 77 76 76

Old French Noël

1 Now tell us, gentle Mary,
what did Gabriel say to you?
Now tell us of the tidings
that he brought to Galilee.
'He told me I was favoured,
that I would be the one
God chose to be the mother
of Jesus, his own Son.'

2 Now tell us, gentle Mary,
of the birth of Christ that morn.
Now tell us of Christ Jesus,
where it was that he was born.
'Not in a palace glorious,
not in a silken bed,
but in a stable humble
did Jesus lay his head.'

(part of) French carol, 15th cent.
tr. W. B. LINDSAY; arr. RUTH HELLER*

143 *Bonn* 8 33 6 D

J. G. EBELING (1637–76)

1 All my heart this night rejoices,
as I hear,
far and near,
sweetest angel voices;
'Christ is born!', their choirs are singing,
till the air,
everywhere,
now with joy is ringing.

2 Hark! a voice from yonder manger,
soft and sweet,
does entreat:
'Flee from woe and danger;
come, O come: from all that grieves you
you are freed;
all you need
I will surely give you'.

3 Come, then, let us hasten yonder;
here let all,
great and small,
kneel in awe and wonder;
love him who with love is yearning;
hail the star
that from far
bright with hope is burning.

4 Thee, O Lord, with heed I'll cherish,
live to thee,
and with thee
dying, shall not perish,
but shall dwell with thee for ever
far on high,
in the joy
that can alter never.

PAUL GERHARDT (1607–76)
tr. CATHERINE WINKWORTH (1827–78) altd.*

144 *Noel* DCM

English traditional melody
extended and adpt.
ARTHUR SULLIVAN (1842–1900)

1 It came upon the midnight clear,
that glorious song of old,
from angels bending near the earth
to touch their harps of gold:
'Glory to God! On earth be peace,
from heaven's all-gracious King';
the world in solemn stillness lay
to hear the angels sing.

2 Still through the cloven skies they come,
with peaceful wings unfurled,
and still their heavenly music floats
o'er all the weary world:
above its sad and lowly plains
they bend on hovering wing,
and ever o'er its Babel sounds
the blessed angels sing.

3 Yet with the woes of sin and strife
the world has suffered long,
beneath the angel-strain have rolled
two thousand years of wrong;
and we, at bitter war, hear not
the love-song which they bring:
O hush the noise and end the strife,
to hear the angels sing.

4 For lo! the days are hastening on,
by prophet bards foretold,
when with the ever-circling years
comes round the age of gold;
when peace shall over all the earth
its ancient splendours fling,
and all the world give back the song
which now the angels sing.

E. H. SEARS (1810–76) altd.*

145 *Forest Green*

8686 7686 Irregular (or DCM*)

English traditional melody

*With [music notation] in b. 3 of third stave.

CHRIST'S BIRTH

1 O little town of Bethlehem,
how still we see thee lie!
Above thy deep and dreamless sleep
the silent stars go by:
yet in thy dark streets shineth
the everlasting Light;
the hopes and fears of all the years
are met in thee tonight.

2 O morning stars, together
proclaim the holy birth,
and praises sing to God the King,
goodwill and peace on earth.
For Christ is born of Mary;
and gathered all above,
while mortals sleep, the angels keep
their watch of wondering love.

3 How silently, how silently,
the wondrous gift is given!
So God imparts to human hearts
the blessings of his heaven:
no ear may hear his coming;
but in this world of sin,
where meek souls will receive him, still
the dear Christ enters in.

4 O Holy Child of Bethlehem,
descend to us, we pray;
cast out our sin, and enter in,
be born in us today.
We hear the Christmas angels
the great glad tidings tell:
O come to us, abide with us,
our Lord, Immanuel.

PHILLIPS BROOKS (1835–93)

146

FIRST TUNE

Cradle song 11 11 11 11 (Anapaestic) W. J. KIRKPATRICK (1838–1921)

SECOND TUNE

Normandy 11 11 11 11 (Anapaestic) Basque carol

1 Away in a manger, no crib for a bed,
the little Lord Jesus laid down his sweet head.
The stars in the bright sky looked down where he lay,
the little Lord Jesus asleep on the hay.

2 Be near me, Lord Jesus; I ask you to stay
close by me for ever, and love me, I pray.
Bless all the world's children in your tender care,
and fit us for heaven to live with you there.

v. 1: Anon., *c.*1885
v. 2: Anon., *c.*1892*

147 *Stille Nacht* Irregular

F. X. GRUBER (1787–1863)

1 Silent night, holy night:
sleeps the world; hid from sight,
Mary and Joseph in stable bare
watch o'er the Child beloved and fair,
sleeping in heavenly rest,
sleeping in heavenly rest.

2 Silent night, holy night:
shepherds first saw the light,
heard resounding clear and long,
far and near the angel-song,
'Christ the Redeemer is here,
Christ the Redeemer is here'.

3 Silent night, holy night:
Son of God, O how bright
love is smiling from your face
with the dawn of redeeming grace,
Jesus, Lord, at your birth,
Jesus, Lord, at your birth.

JOSEPH MOHR (1792–1848)
tr. STOPFORD A. BROOKE (1832–1916) altd.*

148 *In der Wiegen* Irregular

Melody from CORNER'S *Geistliche Nachtigall*, 1649

1 He smiles within his cradle,
a Babe with face so bright
it beams most like a mirror
against a blaze of light:
this Babe so burning bright.

2 This Babe we now declare to you
is Jesus Christ our Lord;
he brings both peace and joyfulness:
haste, haste with one accord
to feast with Christ our Lord.

3 And who would rock the cradle
wherein this Infant lies,
must rock with easy motion
and watch with humble eyes,
like Mary pure and wise.

4 O Jesus, dearest Babe of all,
and dearest Babe of mine,
thy love is great, thy limbs are small.
O flood this heart of mine
with overflow from thine!

Austrian Carol, 1649 (? D. G. CORNER, 1587–1648)
tr. ROBERT GRAVES (1895–1985)*

149 *Infant holy* 447D 4444 77

Polish carol

1 Infant holy,
infant lowly,
for his bed a cattle stall;
oxen lowing,
little knowing
Christ the Babe is Lord of all.
Swift are winging
angels singing,
nowells ringing,
tidings bringing:
Christ the Babe is Lord of all;
Christ the Babe is Lord of all.

2 Flocks are sleeping,
shepherds keeping
vigil till the morning new
see the glory,
hear the story,
tidings of a gospel true.
Thus rejoicing,
free from sorrow,
praises voicing,
greet the morrow:
Christ the Babe is born for you!
Christ the Babe is born for you!

Polish traditional carol (13th cent.?)
tr. EDITH M. G. REED (1885–1933)*

150 *Bunessan* 55 54 D Gaelic melody

1 Child in the manger,
infant of Mary;
outcast and stranger,
Ruler of all:
Child who inherits
all our transgressions,
all our demerits
on him will fall.

2 Once the most holy
Child of salvation
gentle and lowly
lived here below;
now as our glorious
mighty Redeemer,
see him victorious
over the foe.

3 Prophets foretold him,
infant of wonder;
angels behold him
high on his throne;
worthy our Saviour
of all their praises;
happy for ever
are all his own.

MARY MACDONALD (1789–1872)
tr. L. MACBEAN (1853–1931)*

151 *Calypso carol* Irregular MICHAEL PERRY (1942–)

1 See him lying on a bed of straw,
draughty stable with an open door,
Mary cradling the child she bore;
 the Prince of Glory is his name:

O now carry me to Bethlehem
to see the Lord of love again,
just as poor as was the stable then,
 the Prince of Glory when he came.

2 Star of silver, sweep across the skies,
show where Jesus in the manger lies;
shepherds, swiftly from your stupor rise
 to see the Saviour of the world:

3 Angels, sing again the song you sang,
God's great glory and redeeming plan;
sing that Bethlem's little baby can
 be the Saviour of us all:

4 Mine are riches from your poverty;
from your innocence, eternity,
mine, forgiveness by your death for me;
 Child of sorrow for my joy:

MICHAEL PERRY (1942–)*

152 *Cheshunt* 57 10 D

RICHARD H. JACQUET (1947–)

1 Ring a bell for peace,
for the babe born on this night,
ring a bell through the country and the town;
ring a bell for peace,
come and see the wondrous light,
ring a bell, ring it merry up and down.

2 Blow a horn for joy,
for the babe born in the hay,
blow a horn through the country and the town;
blow a horn for joy,
come and hear what people say,
blow a horn, blow it merry up and down.

3 Play a flute for hope,
for the babe now fast asleep,
play a flute through the country and the town;
play a flute for hope,
see the shepherds leave their sheep,
play a flute, play it merry up and down.

4 Beat the drum for faith,
for the babe born 'neath the star,
beat the drum through the country and the town;
beat the drum for faith,
come and play where'er you are,
beat the drum, beat it merry up and down.

MARIAN COLLIHOLE (1933–)

153 *Sussex Carol* 88 88 88

English traditional melody

1 On Christmas night all Christians sing, } (*twice*)
to hear the news the angels bring,
news of great joy, news of great mirth,
news of our merciful King's birth.

2 Then why should we on earth be so sad, } (*etc.*)
since our Redeemer made us glad,
when from our sin he set us free,
all for to gain our liberty.

3 When sin departs before his grace,
then life and health come in its place;
heaven and earth with joy may sing,
all for to see the new-born King.

4 All out of darkness we have light,
which made the angels sing this night;
'Glory to God, on earth be peace,
goodwill to all shall never cease.'

English Traditional*

154 *Vom Himmel hoch* LM

Melody attrib.
MARTIN LUTHER (1483–1546)

The Angel's Message

1 From heaven above to earth I come
to bear good news to everyone;
glad tidings of great joy I bring,
of which I now will say and sing:

2 To you this night is born a child
of Mary, chosen mother mild;
this new-born babe of lowly birth,
shall be the joy of all the earth.

3 This is the Christ who far on high
has heard your sad and bitter cry;
himself will your salvation be;
himself from sin will make you free.

The Children's Welcome

4 Welcome to earth, most noble guest,
through whom this sinful world is blest!
you come to share our sorrow here;
what can we give you, Lord, most dear?

5 Were earth a thousand times as fair,
and set with gold and jewels rare,
it still would seem too poor to be
a cradle for your purity.

6 Ah, dearest Jesus, holy child,
make here your bed, soft, undefiled,
within my heart, and I will keep
a quiet chamber for your sleep.

7 My heart for very joy must leap;
my lips no more can silence keep;
I too must sing with joyful tongue
that sweetest ancient cradle song:

8 'Glory to God in highest heaven,
for he to us his Son has given!'
while angels sing with holy mirth
a glad new year to all the earth.

MARTIN LUTHER (1483–1546)
tr. CATHERINE WINKWORTH (1827–78) altd.*

155 *Winchester Old* CM

Melody from ESTE'S *Whole Booke of Psalmes*, 1592

1 While shepherds watched their flocks by night,
all seated on the ground,
the angel of the Lord came down,
and glory shone around.

2 'Fear not,' said he (for mighty dread
had seized their troubled mind),
'glad tidings of great joy I bring
to you and all mankind.

3 'To you in David's town this day
is born of David's line
a Saviour, who is Christ the Lord;
and this shall be the sign:

4 'the heavenly Babe you there shall find
to human view displayed,
all meanly wrapped in swathing-bands,
and in a manger laid.'

5 Thus spake the seraph; and forthwith
appeared a shining throng
of angels, praising God, who thus
addressed their joyful song:

6 'All glory be to God on high,
and to the world be peace!
Goodwill henceforth from heaven to earth
begin and never cease!'

Luke 2: 8–14
para. N. TATE (1652–1715) altd.*

156 *Quem pastores laudavere* 888 7

German carol melody, 14th cent.

1 Shepherds came, their praises bringing,
who had heard the angels singing,
'Far from you be fear unruly,
Christ is King of Glory born.'

2 Sages, whom a star had guided,
incense, gold and myrrh provided,
made their sacrifices duly
to the King of Glory born.

3 Jesus, born the King of Heaven,
Christ to us through Mary given,
for your praise and honour truly
be resounding glory done.

Latin, 14th cent.
tr. GEORGE B. CAIRD (1917–84)*

157 *Humility* 77 77 with refrain

JOHN GOSS (1800–80)

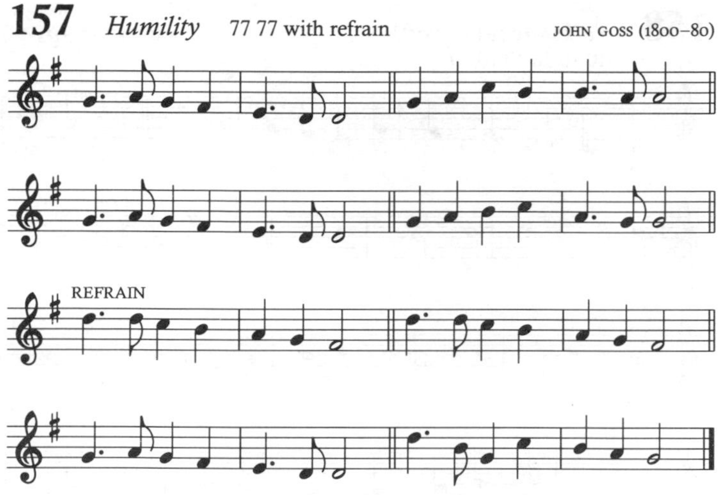

1 See! in yonder manger low
born for us on earth below,
see! the tender Lamb appears
promised from eternal years:

Hail, thou ever-blessed morn!
Hail, redemption's happy dawn!
Sing through all Jerusalem,
'Christ is born in Bethlehem!'

2 Lo! within a stable lies
he who built the starry skies,
he who, throned in height sublime,
sits amid the cherubim:

3 Say, ye holy shepherds, say,
what your joyful news today;
wherefore have ye left your sheep
on the lonely mountain steep?

4 'As we watched at dead of night,
lo, we saw a wondrous light:
angels, singing "Peace on earth",
told us of the Saviour's birth':

5 Sacred Infant, all Divine,
what a tender love was thine,
thus to come from highest bliss
down to such a world as this!

EDWARD CASWALL (1814–78) altd.

158 *Yorkshire (Stockport)*

10 10 10 10 10 10

J. WAINWRIGHT (1723–68)

1 Christians, awake, salute the happy morn,
whereon the Saviour of the world was born.
Rise to adore the mystery of love
which hosts of angels chanted from above;
with them the joyful tidings first begun
of God incarnate and the Virgin's Son.

2 Then to the watchful shepherds it was told,
who heard the angelic herald's voice—'Behold!
I bring good tidings of a Saviour's birth
to you and all the nations upon earth.
This day hath God fulfilled his promised word,
this day is born a Saviour, Christ the Lord'.

3 He spake, and straightway the celestial choir
in hymns of joy unknown before conspire.
The praises of redeeming love they sang
and heaven's whole orb with hallelujahs rang.
God's highest glory was their anthem still,
peace upon earth, from each to each good will.

4 Then Bethl'em straight th'enlightened shepherds sought
to see the wonder God for us had wrought.
They saw their Saviour as the angel said,
the swaddled infant in the manger laid.
They to their flocks and praising God return
with joyful hearts that did within them burn.

5 Like Mary let us ponder in our mind
God's wondrous love in saving humankind.
Trace we the babe who has retrieved our loss
from his poor manger to his bitter cross.
Follow we him who has our cause maintained
and earth's first heavenly state shall be regained.

6 Then may we hope, th' angelic thrones among,
to sing, redeemed, a glad triumphal song.
He that was born upon this joyful day
around us all his glory shall display;
saved by his love, incessant we shall sing
eternal praise to heaven's almighty King.

JOHN BYROM (1692–1763) altd.*

159 *Mendelssohn*
77 77 D with refrain

FELIX MENDELSSOHN (1809–47)
adpt. WILLIAM H. CUMMINGS (1831–1915)

1 Hark! the herald angels sing
Glory to the new-born King,
peace on earth, and mercy mild,
God and sinners reconciled.
Joyful, all ye nations, rise;
join the triumph of the skies,
with the angelic host proclaim,
Christ is born in Bethlehem :

Hark! the herald angels sing
Glory to the new-born King.

2 Christ by highest heaven adored,
Christ the everlasting Lord,
late in time behold him come,
offspring of a virgin's womb:
veiled in flesh the Godhead see;
hail the incarnate Deity,
pleased as man with us to dwell,
Jesus, our Immanuel:

3 Hail the heaven-born Prince of peace!
Hail the Sun of righteousness!
Light and life to all he brings,
risen with healing in his wings:
mild he lays his glory by,
born that we no more may die,
born to raise the things of earth,
born to give us second birth:

CHARLES WESLEY (1707–88) altd.*

160 *Adeste fideles* Irregular

Melody from MS of *c.*1745
Possibly by JOHN F. WADE (*c.*1711–86)

1 O come, all ye faithful,
joyful and triumphant,
O come ye, O come ye to Bethlehem:
come and behold him
born the King of angels:

O come, let us adore him,
O come, let us adore him,
O come, let us adore him,
Christ the Lord.

2 God of God,
Light of light,
lo, he abhors not the virgin's womb;
very God,
begotten, not created:

3 See how the shepherds,
summoned to his cradle,
leaving their flocks, draw nigh to gaze;
we too will thither
bend our joyful footsteps:

4 Lo, star-led chieftains,
magi, Christ adoring,
offer him incense, gold and myrrh;
we to the Christ-child
bring our hearts' oblations:

5 Sing, choirs of angels,
sing in exultation,
sing, all ye citizens of heaven above,
'Glory to God
in the highest':

6 Yea, Lord, we greet thee,
born this happy morning,
Jesus, to thee be glory given;
Word of the Father,
now in flesh appearing:

Latin, 18th cent., possibly JOHN F. WADE (*c.*1711–86)
tr. FREDERICK OAKELEY (1802–80) altd.

161 *In dulci jubilo* 66 7778 55

German carol melody, 14th cent.

1 Good Christians all, rejoice
with heart and soul and voice;
give good heed to what we say:
Jesus Christ is born today,
ox and ass before him bow,
and he is in the manger now;
Christ is born today,
Christ is born today.

2 Good Christians all, rejoice
with heart and soul and voice;
now you hear of endless bliss,
Jesus Christ was born for this:
he has opened heaven's door,
and you are blest for evermore;
Christ was born for this,
Christ was born for this.

3 Good Christians all, rejoice
with heart and soul and voice;
now you need not fear the grave:
Jesus Christ was born to save,
calls you one and calls you all,
to gain his everlasting hall;
Christ was born to save,
Christ was born to save.

J. M. NEALE (1818–66) altd.*

CHRISTINA ROSSETTI (1830–94) altd.

163 *Iris* 87 87 (Trochaic) with refrain

Flemish or French carol melody

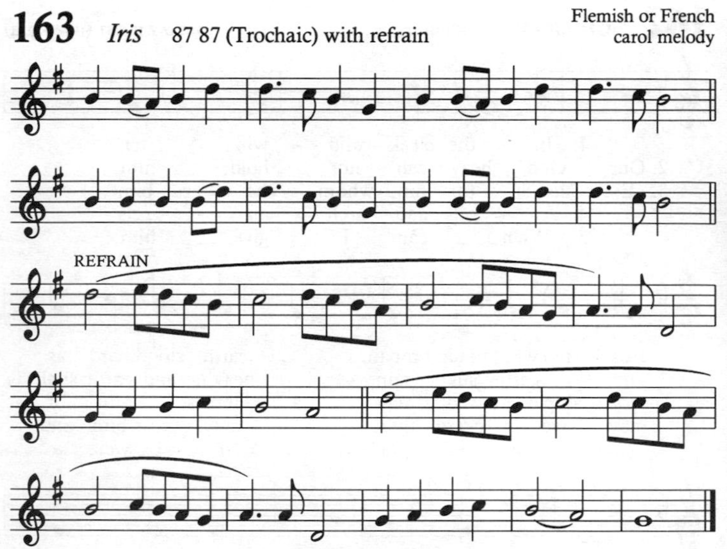

1 Angels from the realms of glory,
   wing your flight o'er all the earth;
ye who sang creation's story,
   now proclaim Messiah's birth:
      Gloria in excelsis Deo!
      Gloria in excelsis Deo!

2 Shepherds, in the field abiding,
   watching o'er your flocks by night:
God with you is now residing,
   yonder shines the Infant Light:

3 Sages, leave your contemplations,
   brighter visions beam afar;
seek the great Desire of Nations;
   ye have seen his natal star:

4 Saints, before the altar bending,
   watching long in hope and fear,
suddenly the Lord, descending,
   in his temple shall appear:

JAMES MONTGOMERY (1771–1854)*

164 *Go tell it on the mountain*

76 76 with refrain

North American Spiritual

Go tell it on the mountain,
over the hills and ev'rywhere:
go tell it on the mountain
that Jesus Christ is born.

1 While shepherds kept their watching
o'er silent flocks by night,
behold, throughout the heavens
there shone a holy light:

2 The shepherds feared and trembled
when, lo, above the earth
rang out the angel chorus
that hailed our Saviour's birth:

3 Down in a lonely manger
the humble Christ was born;
and God sent us salvation
that blessed Christmas morn:

Refrain: Traditional Spiritual
Verses: J. W. WORK (1872–1925) altd.

165 *Olwen* 668 668 Ter. Welsh carol

1 O deued pob Cristion
i Fethlem yr awrhon,
i weled mor dirion yw'n Duw;
O ddyfnder rhyfeddod!
fe drefnodd y Duwdod
dragwyddol gyfamod i fyw!
Daeth Brenin yr hollfyd
i oedfa ein hadfyd,
er symud ein penyd a'n pwn;
heb le yn y llety,
heb aelwyd, heb wely,
Nadolig fel hynny gadd hwn!

Rhown glod i'r Mab bychan,
ar liniau Mair wiwlan—
daeth Duwdod mewn Baban i'n byd!
Ei ras, O derbyniwn,
ei haeddiant cyhoeddwn,
a throsto ef gweithiwn i gyd.

2 Tywysog tangnefedd
wna'n daear o'r diwedd
yn aelwyd gyfannedd i fyw;
ni fegir cenfigen,
na chynnwrf, na chynnen—
dan goron bydd diben ein Duw.
Yn frodyr i'n gilydd,
drigolion y gwledydd,
cawn rodio yn hafddydd y nef;
ein disgwyl yn Salem,
i ganu yr anthem
ddechreuwyd ym Methlem,
mae ef.

Seiliedig ar hen garol Gymraig

1 The poor and the humble
and all those who stumble
come hastening, and feel not afraid;
for Jesus, our Treasure,
with love past all measure,
in lowly poor manger was laid.
Though wise men who found him
laid rich gifts around him,
yet oxen they gave him their hay:
and Jesus in beauty
accepted their duty:
contented in manger he lay.

Then haste we to show him
the praises we owe him;
our service he ne'er can despise;
whose love still is able
to show us that stable,
where softly in manger he lies.

2 The Christ Child will lead us,
the Good Shepherd feed us
and with us abide till his day.
Then hatred he'll banish;
then sorrow will vanish,
and death and despair flee away.
And he shall reign ever,
and nothing shall sever
from us the great love of our King;
his peace and his pity
shall bless his fair city;
his praises we ever shall sing;

Based on a traditional Welsh carol
V. 1: tr. KATHARINE E. ROBERTS (1877–1962)*
V. 2: tr. W. T. PENNAR DAVIES (1911–)

166 *Celebrations* 11 14 with refrain

VALERIE COLLISON (1933–)

Come and join the celebration,
it's a very special day;
come and share our jubilation,
there's a new King born today!

1 See the shepherds hurry down to Bethlehem,
gaze in wonder at the Son of God who lay before them:

2 Wise men journey, led to worship by a star,
kneel in homage, bringing precious gifts from lands afar; So:

3 'God is with us': round the world the message bring,
he is with us; 'Welcome' all the bells on earth are pealing:

VALERIE COLLISON (1933–)

167 *Irby* 87 87 77

H. J. GAUNTLETT (1805–76)

1 Once in royal David's city
stood a lowly cattle shed,
where a mother laid her baby
in a manger for his bed:
Mary was that mother mild,
Jesus Christ her little child.

2 He came down to earth from heaven,
who is God and Lord of all;
and his shelter was a stable,
and his cradle was a stall:
with the poor, and mean, and lowly
lived on earth our Saviour holy.

3 And he is our childhood's pattern,
day by day like us he grew;
he was little, weak and helpless,
tears and smiles like us he knew;
and he feeleth for our sadness,
and he shareth in our gladness.

4 Not in that poor lowly stable,
with the oxen standing by,
we shall see him, but in heaven,
set at God's right hand on high;
for he leads his people on
to the place where he is gone.

CECIL FRANCES ALEXANDER (1818–95)*

168 *Zu Bethlehem geboren* 76 76 46

German carol melody

1 To us in Bethlem city
was born a little Son;
in him all gentle graces
were gathered into one,
O joy! glad joy!
were gathered into one.

2 And all our love and fortune
lie in his mighty hands;
our sorrows, joys and failures,
he sees and understands,
O joy! glad joy!
he sees and understands.

3 O Shepherd, ever near us,
we'll go where you will lead;
no matter where the pasture,
with you at hand to feed,
O joy! glad joy!
with you at hand to feed.

4 No grief shall part us from you,
however sharp the edge;
we'll serve, and do your bidding;
O take our hearts in pledge!
O joy! glad joy!
take now our hearts in pledge.

PERCY DEARMER (1867–1936) altd.*
para. from the *Kölner Psalter*, 1638

169 *Puer nobis* 76 77 Irregular German carol melody

1 Unto us a boy is born!
King of all creation,
came he to a world forlorn,
the Lord of every nation.

2 Christ from heaven descending low
comes, on earth a stranger;
ox and ass their Owner know,
becradled in the manger.

3 Herod then with fear was filled:
'A prince', he said, 'in Jewry!';
all the little boys he killed
at Bethlem in his fury.

4 Now may Mary's son, who came
so long ago to love us,
lead us all with hearts aflame
unto the joys above us.

5 Omega and Alpha he!
Let the organ thunder,
while the choir with peals of glee
doth rend the air asunder.

German carol, 15th cent.
tr. (v. 1 & 3–5) PERCY DEARMER (1867–1936)
(v. 2) G. R. WOODWARD (1848–1934)

170 *Greensleeves* 87 87 68 67

English melody, pre-1642

1 What child is this, who, laid to rest,
on Mary's lap is sleeping?
whom angels greet with anthems sweet,
while shepherds watch are keeping?
This, this is Christ the King,
whom shepherds worship and angels sing;
haste, haste to bring him praise,
the Babe, the son of Mary.

2 Why lies he in so poor a place
where ox and ass are feeding?
Come have no fear: for sinners here
the silent Word is pleading.
Nails, spear shall pierce him through,
the cross be borne for me, for you:
hail, hail the Saviour comes,
the Babe, the son of Mary.

3 So bring him incense, gold and myrrh,
all tongues and peoples own him,
the King of kings salvation brings,
let every heart enthrone him.
Raise, raise your song on high
while Mary sings a lullaby,
joy, joy, for Christ is born,
the Babe, the son of Mary.

W. C. DIX (1837–98) altd.*

171 *This endris nyght* CM

English carol, 15th cent.

1 Behold the great Creator makes
himself a house of clay,
a robe of human flesh he takes
which he will wear for aye.

2 Hark, hark, the wise Eternal Word
like a weak infant cries!
See in a servant's form the Lord
as God in cradle lies.

3 This wonder struck the world amazed,
it shook the starry frame;
squadrons of angels stood and gazed,
then down in troops they came.

4 This day prepares his day of doom;
his mercy now is nigh;
the mighty God of love is come,
the dayspring from on high!

5 Join then, all hearts that are not stone,
and all our voices prove,
to celebrate this Holy One,
the God of peace and love.

THOMAS PESTEL (*c.*1584–1659) altd.*

172 *This endris nyght* CM English carol, 15th cent.

1 From east to west, from shore to shore,
let earth awake and sing
the holy child whom Mary bore,
the Christ, the Lord, the King!

2 For lo! The world's Creator wears
the fashion of a slave:
our human flesh our Maker bears,
our fallen race to save.

3 He shrank not from the oxen's stall,
nor scorned the manger-bed;
and he, whose bounty feedeth all,
at Mary's breast was fed.

4 While angel choirs sang joyously
above the midnight field;
to shepherds poor the Lord most high,
great Shepherd, was revealed.

5 All glory be to God above,
and on the earth be peace
to all who long to taste his love,
till time itself shall cease.

CAELIUS SEDULIUS *c.*450
tr. JOHN ELLERTON (1826–93) altd.*

173 *Henley* CM

PHOCION HENLEY (1728–64)

1 The maker of the sun and moon,
the maker of our earth,
lo! late in time, a fairer boon,
himself is brought to birth.

2 How blest was all creation then,
when God so gave increase;
and Christ, to heal our hearts of sin
brought righteousness and peace.

3 No star in all the heights of heaven
but burned to see him go;
yet unto earth alone was given
his human form to know.

4 His human form, by earth denied,
took death for human sin;
his endless love, through faith descried,
still lives the world to win.

5 O perfect love, outpassing sight,
O light beyond our ken,
come down through all the world tonight,
and heal our hearts again!

LAURENCE HOUSMAN (1865–1959)*

174 *Ottery St Mary* 87 87 (Trochaic) HENRY G. LEY (1887–1962)

1 Where is this stupendous stranger?
Prophets, shepherds, kings advise:
lead me to my Master's manger,
show me where my Saviour lies.

2 O most mighty, O most holy,
far beyond the seraph's thought,
are you then so mean and lowly
as unheeded prophets taught?

3 O the magnitude of meekness,
worth from worth immortal sprung:
O the strength of infant weakness,
if eternal is so young.

4 God all-bounteous, all-creative,
whom no ills from good dissuade,
is incarnate, and a native
of the very world he made.

CHRISTOPHER SMART (1722–71)*

175 *Es ist ein' Ros' entsprungen*

76 76 676

German carol melody

1 Lo, how a rose is growing,
a bloom of finest grace;
the prophets had foretold it:
a branch of Jesse's race
would bear one perfect flower
here in the cold of winter
and darkest midnight hour.

2 The rose of which I'm singing,
Isaiah had foretold.
He came to us through Mary
who sheltered him from cold.
Through God's eternal will
this child to us was given
at midnight calm and still.

3 The shepherds heard the story
the angels sang that night:
how Christ was born of Mary;
he was the Son of light.
To Bethlehem they ran
to find him in the manger
as angel heralds sang.

4 This flower, so small and tender,
with fragrance fills the air;
his brightness ends the darkness
that kept the earth in fear.
True God and yet true man,
he came to save his people
from earth's dark night of sin.

5 O Saviour, Child of Mary,
who felt all human woe;
O Saviour, King of glory,
who triumphed o'er our foe:
bring us at length, we pray,
to the bright courts of heaven
and into endless day.

German, 15th cent.
tr. GRACIA GRINDAL (1943–)

176 *St Cecilia* 66 66

L. G. HAYNE (1836–83)

1 God from on high has heard;
   let sighs and sorrows cease;
the skies unfold, and lo!
   descends the gift of peace.

2 Hark! On the midnight air
   celestial voices swell;
the hosts of heaven proclaim
   God comes on earth to dwell.

3 Haste with the shepherds; see
   the mystery of grace:
a manger-bed, a child,
   is all the eye can trace.

4 Is this the eternal Son,
   who on the starry throne
before the worlds began
   was with the Father one?

5 Yes, faith can pierce the cloud
   which shrouds his glory now,
and hail him God and Lord,
   to whom all creatures bow.

6 O Child! Your silence speaks,
   and bids us not refuse
to bear what flesh would shun,
   to spurn what flesh would choose.

7 Fill us with holy love
   and heal our earthly pride;
born in each lowly heart,
   for ever there abide.

CHARLES COFFIN (1676–1749)
tr. J. R. WOODFORD (1820–85) altd.

177 *Once there came to earth* 55 88 5 J. F. SHEPHERD (1871–1963)

1 Once there came to earth
a child of lowly birth;
far from home the tiny stranger
lay contented in a manger,
Jesus came to earth.

2 Little Jesus grew,
joy and grief he knew,
when he reached his manhood glorious,
over sin he lived victorious,
strong in love he grew.

3 Then himself he gave,
all the world to save:
sin and strife and hatred slew him,
only those who loved him knew him,
Jesus strong to save.

4 Jesus still can bind
in love all humankind.
To the manger humbly kneeling,
still they come for help and healing,
weary humankind!

5 Now let people sing,
'Praise to God we bring.
"Peace on earth", we hail the blessing
sent from heaven for our possessing,
Jesus, Saviour, King!'

DOROTHY ANGUS (1891–1979)*

178 *Scarlet Ribbons* 87 87 D

English traditional melody

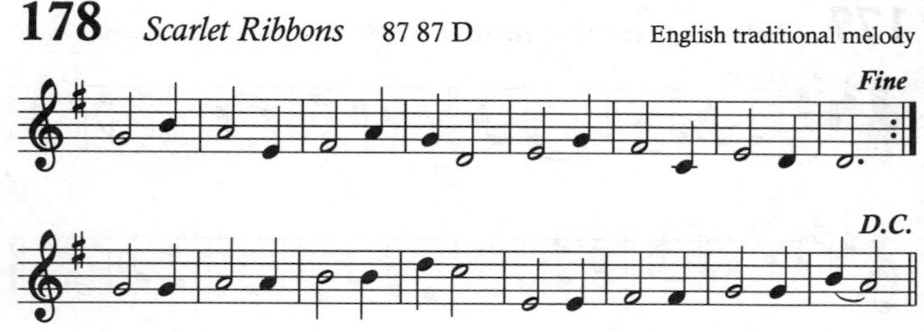

1 Who would think that what was needed
 to transform and save the earth
might not be a plan or army
 proud in purpose, proved in worth?
Who would think, despite derision,
 that a child should lead the way?
God surprises earth with heaven,
 coming here on Christmas Day.

2 Shepherds watch and wise men wonder,
 monarchs scorn and angels sing;
such a place as none would reckon
 hosts a holy, helpless thing;
stabled beasts and passing strangers
 watch a baby laid in hay:
God surprises earth with heaven,
 coming here on Christmas Day.

3 Centuries of skill and science
 span the past from which we move,
yet experience questions whether
 with such progress we improve.
In our search for sense and meaning,
 lest our hopes and humour fray,
God surprises earth with heaven,
 coming here on Christmas Day.

JOHN BELL (1949–)
and GRAHAM MAULE (1958–)*

179 *Sharon* 87 87 (Trochaic)

WILLIAM BOYCE (1711–79)

1 God and Father, we adore thee
for the Son, thine image bright,
in whom all thy holy nature
dawned on our once hopeless night.

2 Far from thee our footsteps wandered
on dark paths of sin and shame;
but our midnight turned to morning,
when the Lord of glory came.

3 Word Incarnate, God revealing,
longed-for while dim ages ran,
Love Divine, we bow before thee,
Son of God and Son of Man.

4 Let our life be new created,
ever-living Lord, in thee,
till we wake with thy pure likeness,
when thy face in heaven we see;

5 where the saints of all the ages,
where the martyrs, glorified,
clouds and darkness far beneath them,
in unending day abide.

6 God and Father, now we bless thee
for the Son, thine image bright,
in whom all thy holy nature
dawns on our adoring sight.

v. 1: attrib. J. N. DARBY (1800–82)
vv. 2–5 & adaptation of v. 6: HUGH FALCONER (1859–1931)*

180 *Incarnation* 64 64 66 64

JOHN BELL (1949–)

1 Before the world began
one Word was there;
grounded in God he was,
rooted in care;
by him all things were made;
in him was love displayed,
through him God spoke and said
'I am for you'.

2 Life found in him its source,
Death found its end;
Light found in him its course,
Darkness its friend;
for neither death nor doubt
nor darkness can put out
the glow of God, the shout
'I am for you'.

3 The Word was in the world
which from him came;
unrecognised was he,
unknown by name;
one with all humankind,
with the unloved aligned,
convincing sight and mind
'I am for you'.

4 All who received the Word,
by God were blessed,
sisters and brothers they
of earth's fond guest.
So did the Word of Grace
proclaim in time and space,
and with a human face,
'I am for you'.

JOHN BELL (1949–)
and GRAHAM MAULE (1958–)

181 *Divinum mysterium* 87 87 877

Late form of a plainsong melody
as given in *Piae Cantiones*, 1582

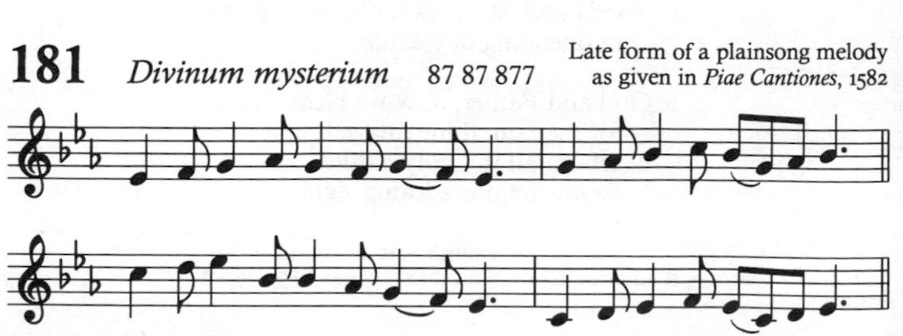

1 Of the Father's love begotten
ere the worlds began to be,
he is Alpha and Omega,
he the source, the ending he,
of the things that are, that have been,
and that future years shall see:
evermore and evermore.

2 By his word was all created;
he commanded and 'twas done;
earth and sky and boundless ocean,
universe of Three in One,
all that sees the moon's soft radiance,
all that breathes beneath the sun:
evermore and evermore.

3 O that birth for ever blessed,
when the Virgin, full of grace,
by the Spirit's power conceiving
bore the Saviour of our race;
and the babe, the world's Redeemer
first revealed his sacred face:
evermore and evermore!

4 This is he whom seers in old time
chanted of with one accord,
whom the voices of the prophets
promised in their faithful word:
now he shines, the long-expected;
let creation praise its Lord:
evermore and evermore.

5 Let the heights of heaven adore him;
angel hosts, his praises sing;
powers, dominions, bow before him,
and extol our God and King;
let no tongue on earth be silent,
every voice in concert sing:
evermore and evermore.

PRUDENTIUS (348–c.413)
tr. J. M. NEALE (1818–66)
and H. W. BAKER (1821–77) altd.*

182 *Wie schön leuchtet* 887 D 8448 PHILIPP NICOLAI (1556–1608)

1 How brightly beams the morning star!
What sudden radiance from afar
now cheers us with its shining!
Brightness of God, that breaks our night
and fills the darkened souls with light
who once for truth were pining!
Your word, Jesus,
inly feeds us,
rightly leads us,
life bestowing.
Praise, O praise such love o'erflowing!

2 Through you alone can we be blest;
then deep be on our hearts impressed
the love that you have borne us;
so make us ready to fulfil
with burning zeal your holy will,
though some may vex or scorn us.
Saviour, let us
never lose you;
for we choose you,
thirst to know you;
all we are and have we owe you!

3 All praise to him who came to save,
who conquered death and burst the grave;
each day new praise is sounding
to him the Lamb who once was slain,
the friend whom none shall trust in vain,
whose grace is still abounding;
sing, you people,
tell the story
of his glory,
till his praises
flood with light earth's darkest places!

JOHANN SCHLEGEL (1721–93)
'Wie herrlich strahlt der Morgenstern'
based on 'Wie schön leuchtet der Morgenstern'
by PHILIPP NICOLAI (1556–1608);
tr. CATHERINE WINKWORTH (1827–78) altd.*

183

FIRST TUNE

Jesmian 11 10 11 10 (Dactylic) GEORGE THALBEN-BALL (1896–1987)

SECOND TUNE

Epiphany Hymn 11 10 11 10 (Dactylic) J. F. THRUPP (1827–67)

CHRIST'S EPIPHANY

1 Brightest and best of the Sons of the Morning,
dawn on our darkness, and lend us thine aid,
star of the east, the horizon adorning,
guide where our infant Redeemer is laid!

2 Cold on his cradle the dewdrops are shining,
low lies his head with the beasts of the stall;
angels adore him, in slumber reclining,
Maker, and Monarch, and Saviour of all.

3 Say, shall we yield him, in costly devotion,
odours of Edom and offerings divine;
gems of the mountain, and pearls of the ocean,
myrrh from the forest, or gold from the mine?

4 Vainly we offer each ample oblation,
vainly with gifts would his favour secure;
richer by far is the heart's adoration,
dearer to God are the prayers of the poor.

5 Brightest and best of the Sons of the Morning,
dawn on our darkness, and lend us thine aid,
star of the east, the horizon adorning,
guide where our infant Redeemer is laid!

REGINALD HEBER (1783–1826)

184 *Dix* 77 77 77

Adapted from a chorale by CONRAD KOCHER (1786–1872)

1 As with gladness men of old
did the guiding star behold,
as with joy they hailed its light,
leading onward, beaming bright;
so, most gracious Lord, may we
evermore be led to thee.

2 As with joyful steps they sped,
Saviour, to thy lowly bed,
there to bend the knee before
thee whom heaven and earth adore;
so may we with willing feet
ever seek thy mercy-seat.

3 As they offered gifts most rare
at thy cradle plain and bare;
so may we with holy joy,
pure, and free from sin's alloy,
all our costliest treasures bring,
Christ, to thee, our heavenly King.

4 Holy Jesus, every day
keep us in the narrow way;
and, when earthly things are past,
bring our ransomed souls at last
where they need no star to guide,
where no clouds thy glory hide.

5 In the heavenly country bright
need they no created light;
thou its light, its joy, its crown,
thou its sun which goes not down;
there for ever may we sing
alleluias to our King.

W. C. DIX (1837–98) altd.*

185 *Glenfinlas* 65 65

K. G. FINLAY (1882–1974)

1 Wise men seeking Jesus
travelled from afar,
guided on their journey
by a beauteous star.

2 But if we desire him,
he is close at hand;
for our native country
is our Holy Land.

3 Prayerful souls may find him
by our quiet lakes,
meet him on our hillsides
when the morning breaks.

4 In our fertile cornfields
while the sheaves are bound,
in our busy markets,
Jesus may be found.

5 Fishermen talk with him
by the great north sea,
as the first disciples
did in Galilee.

6 Every town and village
in our land might be
made by Jesus' presence
like sweet Bethany.

7 He is more than near us,
if we love him well;
for he seeks us, ever
in our hearts to dwell.

J. T. EAST (1860–1937) altd.*

186 *Ryburn* 88 88 88

NORMAN COCKER (1889–1953)

Wise Men and Shepherds

1 Lord, when the wise men came from far,
led to thy cradle by a star,
then did the shepherds too rejoice,
instructed by thy angel's voice,
blest were the wisemen in their skill,
and shepherds in their harmless will.

2 Wisemen in tracing nature's laws
ascend unto the highest cause,
shepherds with humble fearfulness
walk safely, though their light be less:
though wisemen better know the way,
it seems no honest heart can stray.

3 There is no merit in the wise
but love, (the shepherds' sacrifice).
Wisemen, all ways of knowledge past,
to shepherds' wonder come at last;
to know, can only wonder breed,
and not to know, is wonder's seed.

4 A wiseman at the altar bows
and offers up his studied vows
and is received; may not the tears,
which spring too from a shepherd's fears,
and sighs upon his frailty spent,
though not distinct, be eloquent?

5 'Tis true, the object sanctifies
all passions which within us rise,
but since no creature comprehends
the cause of causes, end of ends,
he who himself vouchsafes to know
best pleases his creator so.

6 When then our sorrows we apply
to our own wants and poverty,
when we look up in all distress
and our own misery confess,
sending both thanks and prayers above,
then, though we do not know, we love.

SIDNEY GODOLPHIN (1610–43)*

187 *Was lebet, was schwebet*

12 10 12 10

Melody from the *Rheinhardt MS*, Üttingen, 1754

1 Worship the Lord in the beauty of holiness,
bow down before him, his glory proclaim:
gold of obedience and incense of lowliness
bring and adore him, the Lord is his name.

2 Low at his feet lay thy burden of carefulness,
high on his heart he will bear it for thee,
comfort thy sorrows and answer thy prayerfulness,
guiding thy steps as may best for thee be.

3 Fear not to enter his courts in the slenderness
of the poor wealth thou would'st reckon as thine:
truth in its beauty and love in its tenderness,
these are the offerings to lay on his shrine.

4 These, though we bring them in trembling and fearfulness,
he will accept for the name that is dear:
mornings of joy give for evenings of tearfulness,
trust for our trembling and hope for our fear.

5 Worship the Lord in the beauty of holiness,
bow down before him, his glory proclaim:
gold of obedience and incense of lowliness
bring and adore him, the Lord is his name.

J. S. B. MONSELL (1811–75)

188 *Mary's child* 4 3 6 D

GEOFFREY AINGER (1925–)

1 Born in the night,
Mary's child,
a long way from your home:
coming in need,
Mary's child,
born in a borrowed room.

2 Clear shining Light,
Mary's child,
your face lights up our way;
light of the world,
Mary's child,
dawn on our darkened day.

3 Truth of our life,
Mary's child,
you tell us God is good;
prove it is true,
Mary's child,
go to your cross of wood.

4 Hope of the world,
Mary's child,
you're coming soon to reign;
King of the earth,
Mary's child,
walk in our streets again.

GEOFFREY AINGER (1925–)

189 *Ely* LM

THOMAS TURTON (1780–1864)

1 Why, Herod, so unpitying,
so fearful of the new-born king?
He seeks no mortal sovereignty
who reigns as God eternally.

2 The magi, travelling so far,
preceded by his natal star,
have sought, with gifts, the helpless mite,
and humbly greet the Light of Light.

3 Baptized for us, the Holy One,
the Lamb of God, proclaimed by John,
still comes to cleanse our guilt today,
and take the whole world's sin away.

4 Faith springs to being at the sign
of water which is poured as wine;
and all his glory and our good
are in the shedding of his blood.

5 Now, Christ, your glory is unfurled
across the nations of the world;
in humble love, revealed as Lord,
you reign, eternally adored.

CAELIUS SEDULIUS *c.*450
tr. ALAN GAUNT (1935–)

190 *Harewood* 66 66 88

S. S. WESLEY (1810–76)

1 Let earth and heaven combine,
 and joyfully agree,
to praise in songs divine
 the incarnate Deity,
our God, contracted to a span,
incomprehensibly made man.

2 He laid his glory by,
 he wrapped him in our clay;
unmarked by human eye,
 the latent Godhead lay;
infant of days he here became,
and bore the mild Immanuel's name.

3 Unsearchable the love
 that has the Saviour brought;
the grace is far above
 the power of human thought:
suffice for us that God, we know,
our God, is manifest below.

4 He deigns in flesh to appear,
 widest extremes to join;
to bring our baseness near,
 and make us all divine:
and we the life of God shall know,
for God is manifest below.

5 Made perfect first in love,
 and sanctified by grace,
we shall from earth remove,
 and see his glorious face:
his love shall then be fully showed,
and we shall all be lost in God.

CHARLES WESLEY (1707–88) altd.*

191 *Salzburg* 77 77 D

JAKOB HINTZE (1622–1702)

1 Songs of thankfulness and praise
Jesus, Lord, to you we raise,
manifested by the star
to the wise men from afar.
Branch of royal David's stem
in your birth at Bethlehem:
praise to you, the ever-blest
God in flesh made manifest.

2 Manifest at Jordan's stream,
Prophet, Priest and King supreme,
and at Cana, wedding-guest,
in your Godhead manifest;
manifest in power divine,
changing water into wine:
praise to you, the ever-blest,
God in flesh made manifest.

3 Manifest in making whole
failing limbs and fainting soul,
manifest in healing pain,
ending Satan's bitter reign;
manifest in gracious will
ever bringing good from ill:
praise to you, the ever-blest,
God in flesh made manifest.

4 Grant us grace to see you, Lord,
mirrored in your holy word;
may we seek to know your will,
all your purposes fulfil;
then, transformed, your glory see
at your great Epiphany,
when you are by all confessed
God in flesh made manifest.

CHRISTOPHER WORDSWORTH (1807–85)
and compilers

192 *Margaret* Irregular

T. R. MATTHEWS (1826–1910)

1 Thou didst leave thy throne
and thy kingly crown
when thou camest to earth for me,
but in Bethlehem's home
there was found no room
for thy holy nativity:
O come to my heart, Lord Jesus!
There is room in my heart for thee.

2 Heaven's arches rang
when the angels sang,
to proclaim thy royal degree;
but of lowly birth
cam'st thou, Lord, on earth,
and in great humility:
O come to my heart, Lord Jesus!
There is room in my heart for thee.

3 The foxes found rest,
and the bird its nest,
in the shade of the forest tree;
but thy rest was found
on the stony ground
in the deserts of Galilee:
O come to my heart, Lord Jesus!
There is room in my heart for thee.

4 Thou camest, O Lord,
with the living word
that should set thy people free;
but, with mocking scorn,
and with crown of thorn,
they bore thee to Calvary:
O come to my heart, Lord Jesus!
Thy cross is my only plea.

5 When heav'n's arches ring,
and her glad choirs sing,
at thy coming to victory,
let thy voice call me home,
saying, 'Yet there is room,
there is room at my side for thee!'
And my heart shall rejoice, Lord Jesus,
when thou comest and callest for me.

EMILY E. S. ELLIOTT (1836–97) altd.*

193 *Kent (Devonshire or Invitation)* LM

J. F. LAMPE (1703–51)

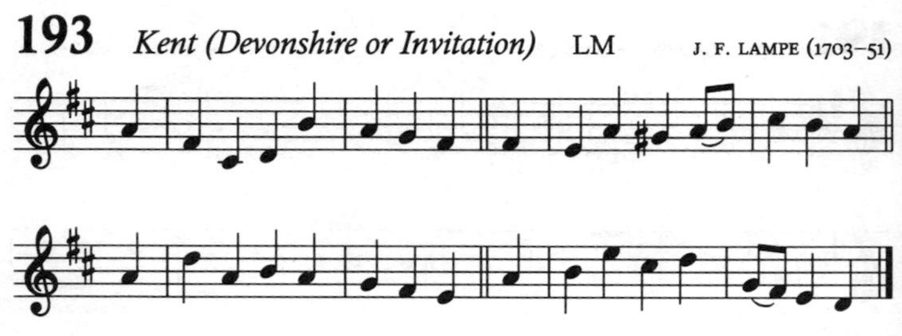

1 Thou Son of God and Son of Man,
beloved, adored Immanuel;
who didst, before all time began,
in glory with thy Father dwell:

2 we sing thy love, who didst in time
for us humanity assume;
to answer for the sinner's crime,
to suffer in the sinner's room.

3 The ransomed Church thy glory sings;
the hosts of heaven thy will obey;
and, Lord of lords and King of kings,
we celebrate thy blessed sway.

4 A servant's form didst thou sustain;
and with delight the law obey;
and then endure amazing pain,
whilst all our sorrows on thee lay.

5 Blest Saviour! We are wholly thine;
so freely loved, so dearly bought,
our souls to thee would we resign,
to thee subject our every thought.

JOHN RYLAND (1753–1825)

194 *St Charles* 66 66 88

CARYL MICKLEM (1925–)

1 Behold a little child
laid in a manger bed;
the wintry blasts blow wild
around his infant head.
But who is this, so lowly laid?
The Lord by whom the worlds were made.

2 The hands that all things made
an earthly craft pursue;
where Joseph plies his trade,
there Jesus labours too,
that weary ones in him may rest,
and faithful toil through him be blest.

3 Christ, Master Carpenter,
we come rough-hewn to thee;
at last, through wood and nails,
thou mad'st us whole and free.
In this thy world remake us, planned
to truer beauty of thine hand.

VV. 1 & 2 W. W. HOW (1823–97) altd.
V. 3 DONALD MCILHAGGA (1933–)

195 *Shaker tune* Irregular Adapted by SYDNEY CARTER (1915–)

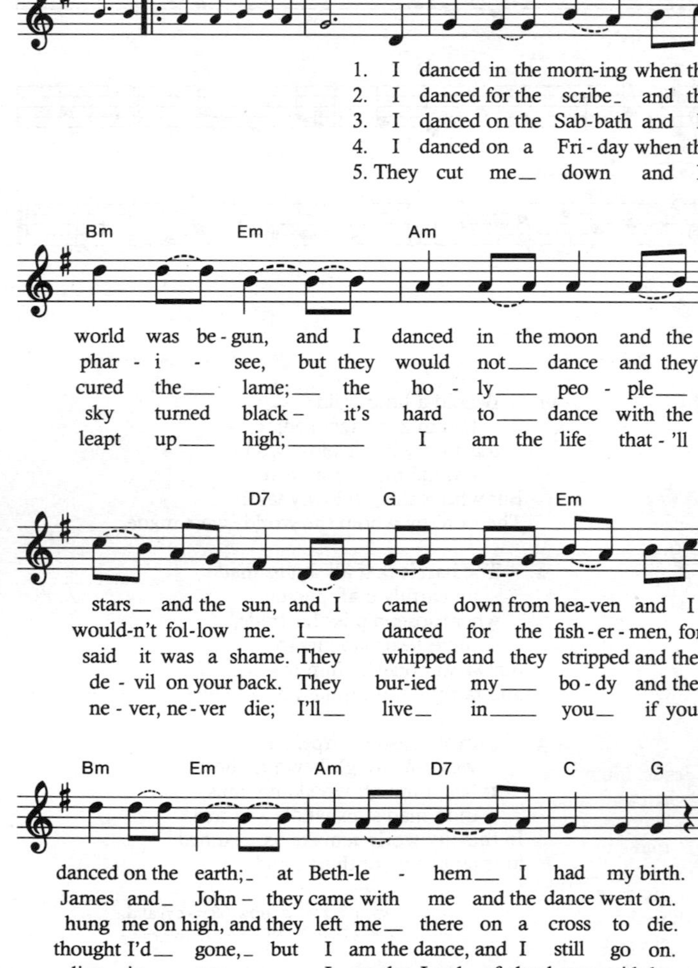

196 *Petersfield* 77 77

WILLIAM H. HARRIS (1883–1973)

1 Jesus, humble was your birth
when you came from heaven to earth;
every day, in all we do,
make us humble, Lord, like you.

2 Jesus, strong to help and heal,
showing that your love is real;
every day, in all we do,
make us strong and kind like you.

3 Jesus, when you were betrayed
still you trusted God and prayed;
every day, in all we do,
help us trust and pray like you.

4 Jesus, risen from the dead,
with us always, as you said;
every day, in all we do,
help us live and love like you.

PATRICK APPLEFORD (1925–) altd.

197 *Au clair de la lune* 65 65 D

French traditional melody

1 Jesus' hands were kind hands, doing good to all,
healing pain and sickness, blessing children small,
washing tired feet and saving those who fall.
Jesus' hands were kind hands, doing good to all.

2 Take my hands, Lord Jesus, let them work for you.
Make them strong and gentle, kind in all I do.
Let me watch you, Jesus, till I'm gentle too;
till my hands are kind hands, quick to work for you.

MARGARET CROPPER (1886–1980)

198 *Surrey (Carey's)* 88 88 88

HENRY CAREY (1687–1743)

1 A stranger once did bless the earth
who never caused a heart to mourn,
whose very voice gave sorrow mirth—
and how did earth his worth return?
It spurned him from its lowliest lot,
the meanest station owned him not.

2 An outcast thrown in sorrow's way,
a fugitive that knew no sin,
yet in lone places forced to stray—
and none would take the stranger in.
Yet peace, though much himself he mourned,
was all to others he returned.

3 His presence was a peace to all,
he bade the sorrowful rejoice.
Pain turned to pleasure at his call,
health lived and issued from his voice;
he healed the sick, and sent abroad
the dumb rejoicing in the Lord.

4 The blind met daylight in his eye,
the joys of everlasting day;
the sick found health in his reply;
the cripple threw his crutch away.
Yet he with troubles did remain,
and suffered poverty and pain.

5 Though without sin, he suffered more
from fools and scoffers standing by
than ever sinners did before,
and, scourged and mocked, made no reply;
in peace on thorns, in faith forgiven,
Christ offers us the hope of heaven.

JOHN CLARE (1793–1864) altd.
and compilers

199 *Yisu ne Kaha* Irregular

Urdu melody

1 Jesus the Lord says, I am the bread,
the bread of life for the world am I.
The bread of life for the world am I,
the bread of life for the world am I.
Jesus the Lord says, I am the bread,
the bread of life for the world am I.

2 Jesus the Lord says, I am the vine,
the true and fruitful vine am I.

3 Jesus the Lord says, I am the way,
the true and living way am I.

4 Jesus the Lord says, I am the light,
the one true light of the world am I.

5 Jesus the Lord says, I am the life,
the resurrection and the life am I.

vv. 1, 3–5: Anon.
tr. from Urdu C. D. MONAHAN (1906–57) altd.*
v. 2: compilers

200 or Hanover 47

FIRST TUNE

Tetherdown 55 55 65 65

GERALD L. BARNES (1935–)

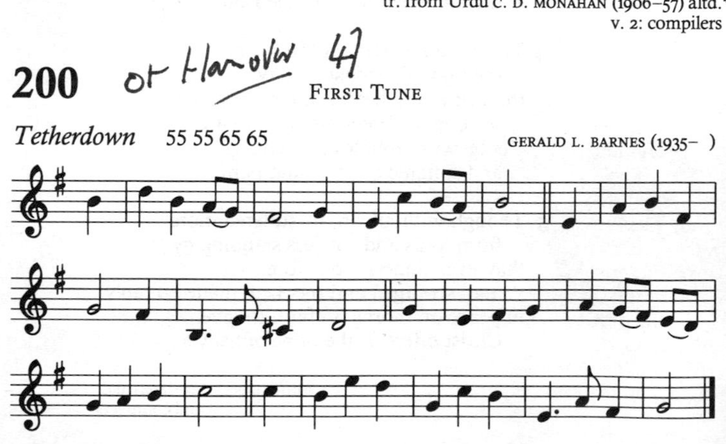

SECOND TUNE

Out Skerries 55 55 65 65 PAUL BATEMAN (1954–)

1 The kingdom of God
is justice and joy,
for Jesus restores
what sin would destroy;
God's power and glory
in Jesus we know,
and here and hereafter
the kingdom shall grow.

2 The kingdom of God
is mercy and grace,
the prisoners are freed,
the sinners find place,
the outcast are welcomed
God's banquet to share,
and hope is awakened
in place of despair.

3 The kingdom of God
is challenge and choice,
believe the good news,
repent and rejoice!
His love for us sinners
brought Christ to his cross,
our crisis of judgement
for gain or for loss.

4 God's kingdom is come,
the gift and the goal,
in Jesus begun,
in heaven made whole;
the heirs of the kingdom
shall answer his call,
and all things cry 'Glory!'
to God all in all.

BRYN A. REES (1911–83)*

201 *Kingsfold* DCM

English traditional melody

1 O sing a song of Bethlehem,
of shepherds watching there,
and of the news that came to them
from angels in the air:
the light that shone on Bethlehem
fills all the world today;
of Jesus' birth and peace on earth
the angels sing alway.

2 O sing a song of Galilee,
of lake and woods and hill,
of him who walked upon the sea,
and bade its waves be still:
for though, like waves on Galilee,
dark seas of trouble roll,
when faith has heard the Master's word,
peace falls upon the soul.

3 O sing a song of Calvary,
its glory and dismay;
of him who hung upon the tree,
and took our sins away:
for he who died on Calvary
is risen from the grave,
and Christ our Lord, by heaven adored,
is mighty now to save.

L. F. BENSON (1855–1930)*

202 *Lawes' Psalm XLVII* 66 66 88

HENRY LAWES (1596–1662)

1 Son of the Lord most high
who gave the worlds their birth,
he came to live and die
the Son of Man on earth;
in Bethlem's stable born was he,
and humbly bred in Galilee.

2 Born in so low estate,
schooled in a workman's trade,
not with the high and great
his home the Highest made;
but, labouring by his comrades' side,
life's common lot he glorified.

3 Then, when his hour was come,
he heard his Father's call;
and, leaving friends and home,
he gave himself for all,
glad news to bring, the lost to find,
to heal the sick, the lame, the blind.

4 Toiling by night and day,
and often burdened sore,
where hearts in bondage lay,
himself their burden bore;
till, scorned by them he died to save,
himself in death, as life, he gave.

5 O lowly majesty,
lofty in lowliness!
Blest Saviour, who am I
to share thy blessedness?
Yet thou hast called me, even me,
Servant divine, to follow thee.

G. W. BRIGGS (1875–1959) altd.*

203 *Venice* SM

WILLIAM AMPS (1824–1910)

1 How good, Lord, to be here!
Your glory fills the night;
your face and garments, like the sun,
shine with unborrowed light.

2 How good, Lord, to be here,
your beauty to behold,
where Moses and Elijah stand,
your messengers of old!

3 Fulfiller of the past,
promise of things to be,
we hail your body glorified,
and our redemption see.

4 Before we taste of death,
we see your kingdom come;
we long to hold the vision bright,
and make this hill our home.

5 How good, Lord, to be here!
Yet we may not remain;
but since you bid us leave the mount
come with us to the plain.

J. ARMITAGE ROBINSON (1858–1933) altd.

204 *Deus tuorum militum* LM

French church melody
from the *Grenoble Antiphoner*, 1753

1 O vision blest of heavenly light,
which meets the three disciples' sight,
when on the holy mount they see
their Lord's transfigured majesty.

2 More bright than day his raiment shone;
the Father's voice proclaimed the Son
belov'd before the worlds were made,
for us in mortal flesh arrayed.

3 And with him there on either hand
both Moses and Elijah stand,
to show how Christ, to those who see,
fulfils both law and prophecy.

4 O Light from light, by love inclined,
Jesus, redeemer of mankind,
accept thy people's prayer and praise
which on the mount to thee they raise.

5 Be with us, Lord, as we descend
to walk with thee to journey's end,
that through thy cross we too may rise,
to share thy life and claim the prize.

6 To thee, O Father; Christ, to thee,
let praise and endless glory be,
whom with the Spirit we adore,
one Lord, one God, for evermore.

GEORGE B. TIMMS (1910–)*
based on a 15th-cent. Latin hymn

205 *Breslau* LM

Modern form of melody from
As Hymnodus Sacer, Leipzig, 1625

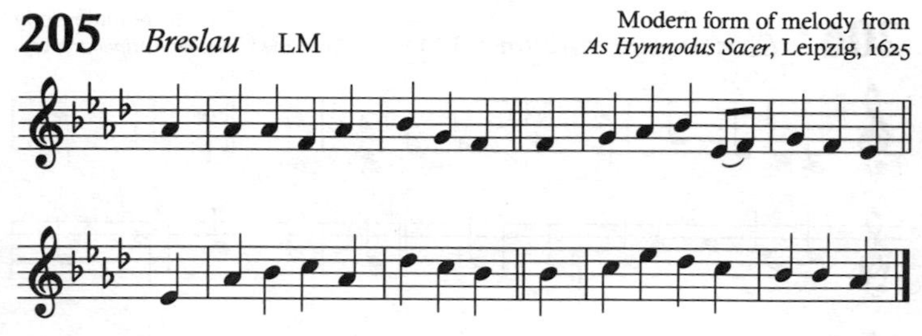

1 My dear Redeemer and my Lord,
I read my duty in thy word;
but in thy life the law appears
drawn out in living characters.

2 Such was thy truth, and such thy zeal,
such deference to thy Father's will,
such love, and meekness so divine,
I would transcribe and make them mine.

3 Cold mountains and the midnight air
witnessed the fervour of thy prayer;
the desert thy temptations knew,
thy conflict and thy victory too.

4 Be thou my pattern, make me bear
more of thy gracious image here;
then God, the judge, shall own my name
amongst the followers of the Lamb.

ISAAC WATTS (1674–1748)

206 *Manchester* CM ROBERT WAINWRIGHT (1748–82)

1 With joy we meditate the grace
of our High Priest above;
his heart is made of tenderness,
it overflows with love.

2 Touched by a sympathy within,
he knows our feeble frame;
he knows what sore temptations mean,
for he has felt the same.

3 But spotless, innocent, and pure
the great Redeemer stood,
while Satan's fiery darts he bore,
and did resist to blood.

4 He, in the days of feeble flesh,
poured out his cries and tears;
and in his measure feels afresh
what every member bears.

5 He'll never quench the smoking flax,
but raise it to a flame;
the bruisèd reed he never breaks,
nor scorns the meanest name.

6 Then let our humble faith address
his mercy and his power;
we shall obtain delivering grace
in the distressing hour.

ISAAC WATTS (1674–1748) altd.

207 *Love unknown* 66 66 4 44 4

JOHN IRELAND (1879–1962)

1 My song is love unknown,
my Saviour's love to me,
love to the loveless shown,
that they might lovely be.
O who am I
that for my sake
my Lord should take
frail flesh, and die?

2 He came from his blest throne,
salvation to bestow;
but men made strange, and none
the longed-for Christ would know.
But O, my friend,
my friend indeed,
who at my need
his life did spend!

3 Sometimes they strew his way,
and his sweet praises sing;
resounding all the day
hosannas to their King.
Then 'Crucify'
is all their breath,
and for his death
they thirst and cry.

4 Why, what hath my Lord done?
What makes this rage and spite?
He made the lame to run,
he gave the blind their sight.
Sweet injuries!
Yet they at these
themselves displease,
and 'gainst him rise.

5 They rise, and needs will have
my dear Lord made away;
a murderer they save,
the Prince of Life they slay.
Yet cheerful he
to suffering goes,
that he his foes
from thence might free.

6 In life, no house, no home
my Lord on earth might have;
in death, no friendly tomb
but what a stranger gave.
What may I say?
Heaven was his home;
but mine the tomb
wherein he lay.

7 Here might I stay and sing
no story so divine;
never was love, dear King,
never was grief like thine.
This is my friend,
in whose sweet praise
I all my days
could gladly spend.

SAMUEL CROSSMAN (1624–84)

208 *St Theodulph* 76 76 D

Later form of a melody by MELCHIOR TESCHNER (1584–1635)

1 All glory, laud, and honour
to thee, Redeemer, King,
to whom the lips of children
made sweet hosannas ring!
Thou art the King of Israel,
thou David's royal Son,
who in the Lord's name comest,
the King and Blessed One.

2 The company of angels
are praising thee on high,
and mortal flesh and all things
created make reply.
The people of the Hebrews
with palms before thee went;
our praise and prayer and anthems
before thee we present.

3 To thee before thy Passion
they sang their hymns of praise;
to thee now high exalted
our melody we raise.
Thou didst accept their praises;
accept the prayers we bring,
who in all good delightest,
thou good and gracious King.

4 All glory, laud, and honour
to thee, Redeemer, King,
to whom the lips of children
made sweet hosannas ring!

THEODULPH OF ORLEANS (d. 821)
tr. J. M. NEALE (1818–66)*

209 *Winchester New* LM

Adpt. from a melody in *Musikalisches Hand-Buch*, Hamburg, 1690
arr. W. H. HAVERGAL (1793–1870)

1 Ride on! ride on in majesty!
Hark, all the tribes hosanna cry;
thine humble beast pursues his road
with palms and scattered garments strowed.

2 Ride on! ride on in majesty!
In lowly pomp ride on to die;
O Christ, thy triumphs now begin
o'er captive death and conquered sin.

3 Ride on! ride on in majesty!
Thy last and fiercest strife is nigh;
the Father, on his sapphire throne,
expects his own anointed Son.

4 Ride on! ride on in majesty!
In lowly pomp ride on to die;
bow thy meek head to mortal pain,
then take, O God, thy power and reign.

H. H. MILMAN (1791–1868)

210 *Shanty* Irregular

Traditional

* ♪ here and so on throughout verse 4 only, to accommodate the words.

1 We have a king who rides a donkey,
we have a king who rides a donkey,
we have a king who rides a donkey,
and his name is Jesus.

Jesus the king is risen,
Jesus the king is risen,
Jesus the king is risen,
early in the morning.

2 Trees are waving a royal welcome
for the king called Jesus.

3 We have a king who cares for people,
and his name is Jesus.

4 A loaf and a cup upon the table,
bread-and-wine is Jesus.

5 We have a king with a bowl and towel,
Servant-king is Jesus.

6 What shall we do with our life this morning?
Give it up in service!

FRED KAAN (1929–)

211 *Farley Castle* 10 10 10 10

HENRY LAWES (1596–1662)

1 Draw nigh to thy Jerusalem, O Lord,
thy faithful people cry with one accord:
ride on in triumph; Lord, behold we lay
our passions, lusts, and proud wills in thy way.

2 Thy road is ready; and thy paths, made straight,
with longing expectation now await
their consecration by thy beauteous feet,
and silently thy promised advent greet.

3 Hosanna! welcome to our hearts; for here
thou hast a temple, thy delight and care;
thy care and thy delight, but full of sin;
how long shall thieves and robbers dwell therein?

4 Enter and chase them forth, and cleanse the floor;
o'erthrow them all, that they may never more
profane with traffic vile that holy place,
where thou hast chosen, Lord, to set thy face.

5 And then, if our stiff tongues shall faithlessly
be mute in praises of thy deity,
the very temple stones shall loud repeat
Hosanna! and thy glorious footsteps greet.

Variant from JEREMY TAYLOR (1613–67)
(first appeared in *Leeds Hymn Book*, 1853) altd.*

212 *Bangor* CM

WILLIAM TANS'UR (*c.*1700–83)

1 Alone you once went forth, O Lord,
in sacrifice to die;
does not your sorrow touch the hearts
of people passing by?

2 Our sins, not yours, you bore then, Lord:
make us your sorrow feel,
till through our pity and our shame
Love answers love's appeal.

3 This was earth's darkest hour, but you
did light and life restore;
then let us give all praise to you
who live for evermore.

4 Grant us with you to suffer, Lord,
that, as we share this hour,
your cross may bring us to your joy
and resurrection power.

PETER ABELARD (1079–1142)
tr. F. BLAND TUCKER (1895–1984) altd.

213 *Binney's* 86 886

ERIC H. THIMAN (1900–75)

1 Jesus, in dark Gethsemane,
in anguish and dismay,
keeping your watch alone you weep
with your disciples fast asleep.
Keep us awake, we pray.

2 Your only consolation there
—God's answer to your prayer—
the strength to rise and make your way
through deeper gloom to Calvary,
to fathom our despair.

3 There, at your grief's extremity
in friendless agony,
heaven descended into hell
because in you God loved so well
guilty humanity.

4 Now, through your tears and deep distress,
your grief and loneliness,
faith contemplates God's heart and knows
the anguish love still undergoes,
to heal our wretchedness.

5 When we must shoulder our own cross,
Lord, join our will to yours;
though flesh is weak, help us to cling
to your nailed hands and, trusting, sing
the triumph of your cause.

6 Keep us awake, Lord, strong in faith
and let your Spirit's breath
strengthen our voices in your praise
through all time's hurtful, hopeful days,
and through the void of death.

ALAN GAUNT (1935–)

214 *Hallgrim* 65 65 (Iambic) LAWRENCE F. BARTLETT (1933-)

1 Before the cock crew twice—
dread hour of trial—
the Apostle uttered thrice
his dark denial.

2 And then the Saviour turned,
on Peter gazing—
a look divine, that yearned
with love amazing.

3 Swiftly to Peter's face
the shame came leaping;
he had denied such grace,
and went forth weeping.

4 Lord Jesus, look on me,
your kind face turning;
my soul with agony
of sin is burning.

5 The way is long, I find
my weak steps falling;
O turn, to my dark mind
your grace recalling.

6 Oft, oft with weeping eyes
I gaze to heaven;
then, at your look, arise
restored, forgiven.

HALLGRIM PJETURSSON (1614–74)
tr. C. V. PILCHER (1879–1961) altd.

215 *Herzliebster Jesu* 11 11 11 5

Later form of a melody by JOHANN CRÜGER (1598–1662)

1 Ah, holy Jesus, how hast thou offended,
that we to judge thee have in hate pretended:
by foes derided, by thine own rejected,
O most afflicted?

2 Who was the guilty? Who brought this upon thee?
Alas, my treason, Jesus, hath undone thee.
'Twas I, Lord Jesus, I it was denied thee:
I crucified thee.

3 Lo, the good Shepherd for the sheep is offered:
the slave hath sinned, and yet the Son hath suffered:
for our atonement, while we nothing heeded,
God interceded.

4 For me, kind Jesus, was thy incarnation,
thy mortal sorrow, and thy life's oblation;
thy death of anguish and thy bitter passion,
for my salvation.

5 Therefore, kind Jesus, since I cannot pay thee,
I do adore thee, and will ever pray thee,
think on thy pity and thy love unswerving,
not my deserving.

ROBERT BRIDGES (1844–1930) altd.*
based on JOHANN HEERMAN (1585–1647)

216 *Solemnis haec festivitas* LM

Melody from
Paris *Gradual*, 1685

1 As royal banners are unfurled
 the cross displays its mystery:
the maker of our flesh, in flesh,
 impaled and hanging helplessly.

2 Already deeply wounded: see
 his side now riven by a spear,
and all our sins are swept away
 by blood and water flowing here.

3 See everything the prophets wrote
 fulfilled in its totality,
and tell the nations of the world
 our God is reigning from the tree.

4 This tree, ablaze with royal light
   and with the blood-red robe it wears,
is hallowed and embellished by
   the weight of holiness it bears.

5 Stretched like a balance here, his arms
   have gauged the price of wickedness;
but, hanging here, his love outweighs
   Hell's unforgiving bitterness.

6 The Saviour, victim, sacrifice
   is, through his dying, glorified;
his life is overcome by death
   and leaps up, sweeping death aside.

7 We hail the cross, faith's one true hope:
   God's passion set in time and space,
by which our guilt is blotted out,
   engulfed in such stupendous grace!

ALAN GAUNT (1935–)
from a Mediaeval Latin hymn;
VV. 1–6: VENANTIUS FORTUNATUS (*c.*530–609);
V. 7: Anon., *c.*10th cent.

217 *Rockingham* LM

Melody adpt.
EDWARD MILLER (1735–1807)

Alternative tune: LLEF, no. 369.

Crucifixion to the World by the Cross of Christ (Gal. 6: 14)

1 When I survey the wondrous Cross,
  on which the Prince of glory died,
my richest gain I count but loss,
  and pour contempt on all my pride.

2 Forbid it, Lord, that I should boast,
  save in the death of Christ my God;
all the vain things that charm me most,
  I sacrifice them to his blood.

3 See from his head, his hands, his feet,
  sorrow and love flow mingled down;
did e'er such love and sorrow meet,
  or thorns compose so rich a crown?

4 His dying crimson, like a robe,
  spreads o'er his body on the tree;
then am I dead to all the globe,
  and all the globe is dead to me.

5 Were the whole realm of nature mine,
  that were a present far too small;
love so amazing, so divine,
  demands my soul, my life, my all.

ISAAC WATTS (1674–1748)

218 *Canterbury* 77 77

Simplified from *Song 13*
ORLANDO GIBBONS (1583–1625)

1 When my love to God grows weak,
when for deeper faith I seek,
then in thought I go to thee,
Garden of Gethsemane.

2 There I walk amid the shades,
while the lingering twilight fades;
see that suffering, friendless one,
weeping, praying there alone.

3 When my will to love grows weak,
when for stronger faith I seek,
Hill of Calvary, I go
to thy scenes of fear and woe.

4 There behold his agony,
suffered on the bitter tree;
see his anguish, see his faith,
Love triumphant still in death.

5 Then to life I turn again,
learning all the worth of pain,
learning all the might that lies
in a full self-sacrifice;

6 and I praise with firmer faith
Christ, who vanquished pain and death;
and to Christ enthroned above
raise my song of selfless love.

J. R. WREFORD (1800–81)
altd. SAMUEL LONGFELLOW (1819–92)*

219 *Tugwood* LM NICHOLAS GATTY (1874–1946)

Christ Crucify'd; the Wisdom and Power of God

1 Nature with open volume stands,
to spread her maker's praise abroad;
and every labour of his hands
shows something worthy of a God.

2 But in the grace that rescued us,
his brightest form of glory shines;
'tis fairest drawn upon the cross
in precious blood, and crimson lines.

3 Here his whole name appears complete:
nor wit can guess, nor reason prove,
which of the letters best is writ,
the Power, the Wisdom, or the Love.

4 O the sweet wonders of that cross
where Christ my Saviour loved, and died!
Her noblest life my spirit draws
from his dear wounds, and bleeding side.

5 I would for ever speak his name
in sounds to mortal ears unknown,
with angels join to praise the Lamb,
and worship at his Father's throne.

ISAAC WATTS (1674–1748) altd.

220 *Passion Chorale* 76 76 D

HANS LEO HASSLER (1562–1612)

1 O sacred head, sore wounded,
with grief and shame weighed down;
O royal head, surrounded
with thorns, thy only crown;
O Lord of life and glory:
what bliss till now was thine!
I read the wondrous story,
I joy to call thee mine.

2 What thou, my Lord, hast suffered,
was all for sinner's gain;
mine, mine was the transgression,
but thine the deadly pain.
By this, thy bitter passion,
Good Shepherd, think on me;
vouchsafe to me compassion,
unworthy though I be.

3 For this thy dying sorrow,
O Jesus, dearest friend,
what language shall I borrow
to thank thee without end?
O make me thine for ever,
and, should I fainting be,
Lord, let me never, never
outlive my love to thee.

4 Be near when I am dying,
and show thy cross to me
that I, for succour flying,
may rest my eyes on thee.
My Lord, thy grace receiving,
let faith my fears dispel,
that I may die believing,
and in thee, Lord, die well.

PAUL GERHARDT (1607–76)
tr. J. W. ALEXANDER (1804–59),
H. W. BAKER (1821–77), and others*

221 *Third Mode Melody* DCM

THOMAS TALLIS (*c.*1505–85)

Alternative tune: KINGSFOLD, no. 201.

1 To mock your reign, O dearest Lord,
they made a crown of thorns,
set you with taunts along that road
from which no one returns.
They could not know, as we do now,
how glorious is that crown,
that thorns would flower upon your brow,
your sorrows heal our own.

2 In mock acclaim, O gracious Lord,
they snatched a purple cloak,
your passion turned, for all they cared,
into a soldier's joke.
They could not know, as we do now,
that though we merit blame
your robe of mercy you will throw
around our naked shame.

3 A sceptred reed, O patient Lord,
they thrust into your hand,
and acted out their grim charade
to its appointed end.
They could not know, as we do now,
though empires rise and fall,
your kingdom shall not cease to grow
till love embraces all.

F. PRATT GREEN (1903–) altd.*

222 *Springdale* CM

ERIK ROUTLEY (1917–82)

1 O dearest Lord, thy sacred head
with thorns was pierced for me;
now pour thy blessing on my head,
that I may think for thee.

2 O dearest Lord, thy sacred hands
with nails were pierced for me;
now pour thy blessing on my hands,
that they may work for thee.

3 O dearest Lord, thy sacred feet
with nails were pierced for me;
now pour thy blessing on my feet,
that they may follow thee.

4 O dearest Lord, thy sacred heart
with spear was pierced for me;
now pour thy spirit in my heart,
that I may live for thee.

H. E. HARDY (1869–1946) altd.*

223 *Horsley* CM

WILLIAM HORSLEY (1774–1858)

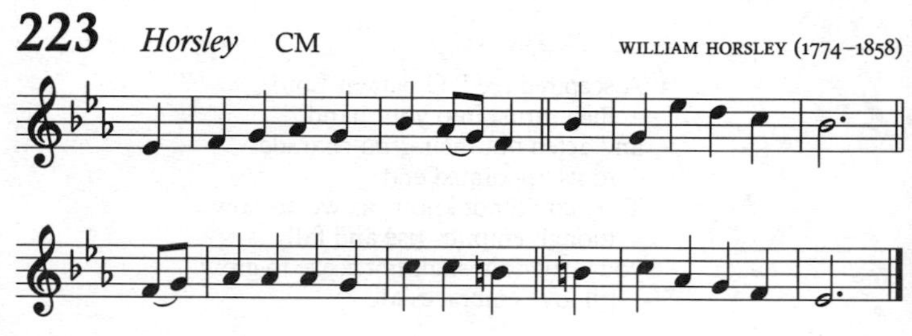

1 There is a green hill far away,
outside a city wall,
where the dear Lord was crucified,
who died to save us all.

2 We may not know, we cannot tell,
what pains he had to bear,
but we believe it was for us
he hung and suffered there.

3 He died that we might be forgiven,
he died to make us good,
that we might go at last to heaven,
saved by his precious blood.

4 O dearly, dearly has he loved,
and we must love him too,
and trust in his redeeming blood,
and try his works to do.

CECIL FRANCES ALEXANDER (1818–95)

224 *All for Jesus* 87 87 (Trochaic) JOHN STAINER (1840–1901)

1 In the cross of Christ I glory,
towering o'er the wrecks of time;
all the light of sacred story
gathers round its head sublime.

2 When the woes of life o'ertake me,
hopes deceive, and fears annoy,
never shall the cross forsake me:
lo! it glows with peace and joy.

3 When the sun of bliss is beaming
light and love upon my way,
from the cross the radiance streaming
adds more lustre to the day.

4 Bane and blessing, pain and pleasure,
by the cross are sanctified;
peace is there that knows no measure,
joys that through all time abide.

JOHN BOWRING (1792–1872)

225 *Shrub End* 76 76

PETER CUTTS (1937–)

1 Here hangs a man discarded,
a scarecrow hoisted high,
a nonsense pointing nowhere
to all who hurry by.

2 Can such a clown of sorrows
still bring a useful word
where faith and love seem phantoms
and every hope absurd?

3 Can he give help or comfort
to lives by comfort bound,
when drums of dazzling progress
give strangely hollow sound?

4 Life emptied of all meaning,
drained out in bleak distress,
can share in broken silence
my deepest emptiness;

5 and love that freely entered
the pit of life's despair
can name our hidden darkness
and suffer with us there.

6 Lord, if you now are risen
help all who long for light
to hold the hand of promise
and walk into the night.

BRIAN WREN (1936–)

226 *Sebastian* 7 88 7 87 87

Melody from J. A. FREYLINGHAUSEN'S *Gesangbuch*, 1714

1 'It is finished!' Christ has known
all the life of our wayfaring,
human joys and sorrows sharing,
making human needs his own.
Lord, in us your life renewing,
lead us where your feet have trod,
till, the way of truth pursuing,
human souls find rest in God.

2 'It is finished!' Christ is slain
on the altar of creation,
offering for a world's salvation
sacrifice of love and pain.
Lord, your love through pain revealing,
purge our passions, scourge our vice,
till upon the tree of healing
self is slain in sacrifice.

3 'It is finished!' Christ our King
wins the victor's crown of glory;
sun and stars recite his story,
floods and fields his triumph sing.
Lord, whose praise the world is telling,
Lord, to whom all power is given,
by your death hell's armies quelling,
bring your saints to reign in heaven!

GABRIEL GILLETT (1873–1948)*

227 *Were you there?*

American folk hymn melody

1 Were you there when they crucified my Lord?
Were you there when they crucified my Lord?
Oh, sometimes it causes me to tremble, tremble, tremble;
Were you there when they crucified my Lord?

2 Were you there when they nailed him to the tree?

3 Were you there when they pierced him in the side?

4 Were you there when the sun refused to shine?

5 Were you there when they laid him in the tomb?

6 Were you there when God raised him from the dead?

American folk hymn

228 *Pange lingua* 87 87 87

Plainsong melody
(Sarum form), mode iii

Alternative tune: PICARDY, no. 457.

1 Here proclaim the glorious battle
  and the deadly conflict fought;
celebrate the cross, the glory,
  and the noble triumph wrought,
as the world's redeemer conquered
  through the sacrifice he brought.

2 Since the work of our salvation
  made for this necessity
that the manifold deceiver
  be destroyed on Calvary,
so, from wounds the foe inflicted,
  flows the certain remedy.

3 Cross of faith, among all others
  none so noble, none so great;
not another in the forest
  bears such leaves, or flowers or fruit;
wood and nails become so precious,
  bearing such a precious weight.

4 Towering tree, now bend your branches,
  let compassion, reaching wide,
soften all your normal hardness
  as your nature is belied;
holding there the King of heaven,
  gently tend him, crucified.

5 Praise to the eternal Father,
  praise to the eternal Son,
praise to the eternal Spirit,
  honour to the Three in One;
praise the love that has redeemed us;
  publish all God's grace has done.

VENANTIUS FORTUNATUS (*c.*530–609)
tr. ALAN GAUNT (1935–)

229 *Bow Brickhill* LM SYDNEY H. NICHOLSON (1875–1947)

Alternative tune: BRESLAU, no. 358.

1 We sing the praise of him who died,
of him who died upon the cross;
the sinner's hope though all deride,
for this we count the world but loss.

2 Inscribed upon the cross we see
in shining letters, 'God is Love';
he bears our sins upon the tree;
he brings us mercy from above.

3 The cross! it takes our guilt away;
it holds the fainting spirit up;
it cheers with hope the gloomy day,
and sweetens every bitter cup.

4 It makes the coward spirit brave,
and nerves the feeble arm for fight;
it takes the terror from the grave,
and gilds the bed of death with light;

5 the balm of life, the cure of woe,
the measure and the pledge of love,
the sinners' refuge here below,
the angels' theme in heaven above.

THOMAS KELLY (1769–1855) altd.

230 *King's Langley* CM

Traditional May-Day carol melody

1 The glory of our King was seen
when he came riding by,
and people ran and waved and sang:
'Hosanna, King most high!'.

2 The glory of our King was seen
when, with his arms stretched wide
to show his love to everyone,
our King was crucified.

3 The glory of our King was seen
on the first Easter day,
when Christ rose up, set free from death,
to love, to guide, to stay.

MARGARET CROPPER (1886–1980)*

231 *Sursum corda* 10 10 10 10

ALFRED M. SMITH (1879–1971)

Your body in the tomb, your soul in hell,
and with the dying thief in paradise,
enthroned as God, in holy Trinity:
Christ, filling all things, ever unconfined.

Anon.
Adapted from the Orthodox Liturgy

232 *Easter Hymn* 77 77 with alleluias

Adpt. from a melody in
Lyra Davidica, 1708

Al - le - lu - ia!

Al - le - lu - ia!

Al - le - lu - ia!

Al - le - lu - ia!

1 Christ the Lord is risen today,
Alleluia!
let creation join to say:
Alleluia!
raise your joys and triumphs high,
Alleluia!
sing, ye heavens; thou earth, reply:
Alleluia!

2 Love's redeeming work is done,
fought the fight, the battle won;
lo! our sun's eclipse is o'er;
lo! he sets in blood no more.

3 Vain the stone, the watch, the seal;
Christ hath burst the gates of hell:
death in vain forbids his rise;
Christ hath opened paradise.

4 Lives again our glorious King;
where, O death, is now thy sting?
Dying once, he all doth save;
where's thy vict'ry, boasting grave?

5 Soar we now where Christ hath led,
following our exalted Head;
made like him, like him we rise:
ours the cross, the grave, the skies.

6 Hail the Lord of earth and heaven!
Praise to thee by both be given:
thee we greet triumphant now,
hail, the Resurrection Thou!

CHARLES WESLEY (1707–88) altd.*

233 *Würtemberg* 77 77 with alleluia

Hundert Arien, 1694
arr. W. H. MONK (1823–89)

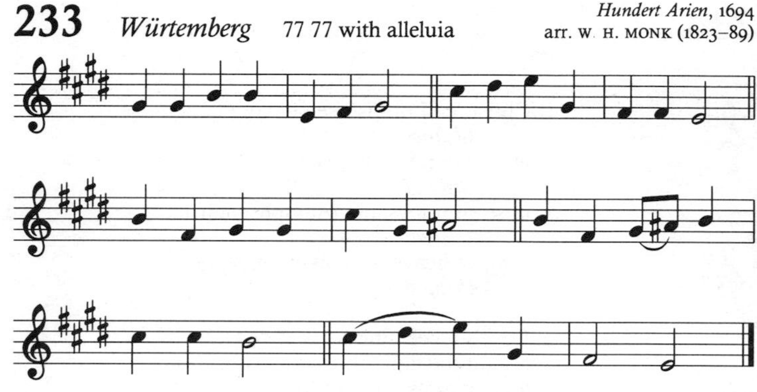

1 Christ the Lord is risen again;
Christ has broken every chain;
hark! the angels shout for joy,
singing evermore on high:
Alleluia!

2 He who gave for us his life,
who for us endured the strife,
is our Paschal Lamb today;
we too sing for joy, and say:
Alleluia!

3 He who bore all pain and loss
comfortless upon the cross,
lives in glory now on high,
pleads for us, and hears our cry:
Alleluia!

4 He whose path no records tell,
who descended into hell,
who the strong man armed has bound,
now in highest heaven is crowned:
Alleluia!

5 He who slumbered in the grave
is exalted now to save;
now through Christendom it rings
that the Lamb is King of kings:
Alleluia!

6 Christ our Paschal Lamb indeed,
Christ, today your people feed;
take our sins and guilt away,
that our song may be alway:
Alleluia!

MICHAEL WEISSE (*c.*1480–1534)
tr. CATHERINE WINKWORTH (1827–78) altd.

For the allusion to 'the strong man' in v. 4, compare Mark 3: 27.

234 *Alleluia* Irregular

DON FISHEL (1950–)

Alleluia, alleluia,
give thanks to the risen Lord,
alleluia, alleluia,
give praise to his name.

1 Jesus is Lord of all the earth;
he is the King of creation:

2 Spread the good news o'er all the earth;
Jesus has died and has risen:

3 We have been crucified with Christ;
now we shall live for ever:

4 Come, let us praise the living God,
joyfully sing to our Saviour:

DON FISHEL (1950–)

235 *Christ lag in Todesbanden*

87 87 787 with alleluia

Melody from WALTHER'S *Gesangbuchlein*, 1524
adpt. MARTIN LUTHER (1483–1546)

1 Christ Jesus lay in death's strong bands
for our offences given;
but now at God's right hand he stands
and brings us life from heaven:
wherefore let us joyful be,
and sing to God right thankfully
our songs of Alleluia:
Alleluia!

2 It was a strange and awesome strife
when life and death contended;
the victory remained with life,
the rule of death was ended:
stripped of power, no more he reigns,
an empty form alone remains;
his sting is gone for ever:
Alleluia!

3 So let us keep the festival,
our Lord himself invites us;
Christ is the Lamb, the joy of all,
the sun that warms and lights us.
Through the glory of his grace
all darkness must today give place,
the night of sin is ended:
Alleluia!

4 Then let us feast this holy day
on the true bread of heaven.
The word of grace has purged away
the old and wicked leaven.
Christ alone our souls can feed,
he is our meat and drink indeed,
faith lives upon no other:
Alleluia!

MARTIN LUTHER (1483–1546)
tr. RICHARD MASSIE (1800–87) altd

236 *Ave virgo virginum*

76 76 D (Trochaic)

Melody from HORN's *Gesangbuch*, 1544 (rhythm slightly altered)

1 Come, ye faithful, raise the strain
of triumphant gladness;
God has brought his Israel
into joy from sadness,
loosed from Pharaoh's bitter yoke
Jacob's sons and daughters,
led them with their feet dry-shod
through the Red Sea waters.

2 See the spring of souls today;
Christ has burst his prison,
and from three days' sleep in death
as a sun has risen;
all the winter of our sins,
long and dark, is flying
from his light, to whom we give
laud and praise undying.

3 Now the queen of seasons, bright
with the day of splendour,
with the royal feast of feasts
comes its joy to render;
comes to glad Jerusalem,
who with true affection
welcomes in unwearied strains
Jesu's resurrection.

4 Neither could the keys of death,
nor the tomb's dark portal,
nor the wrappings, nor the stone,
hold thee as a mortal;
but today amidst thy friends
thou dost stand, bestowing
thine own peace, which evermore
passes human knowing.

JOHN OF DAMASCUS (d. *c.*750)
tr. J. M. NEALE (1818–66) altd.*

237 *Addington* 55 54 D CYRIL V. TAYLOR (1907–91)

1 God came in Jesus,
human life sharing;
gave his life for us,
suffered and died;
then, Resurrection!
death could not hold him;
by love's perfection
death was defied.

2 Then, as they waited,
all of a sudden,
strong and elated,
freed of all cares;
with no misgiving,
joyful apostles
knew that his living
Spirit was theirs.

3 So let us greet his
coming among us;
let us still meet his
love with delight;
through resurrection
joyfully taking
love's new direction
flooded with light.

4 He will be coming,
mighty and glorious,
universe humming
loud in acclaim;
through resurrection
all of creation
brought to perfection,
praising his name.

ALAN GAUNT (1935–)

238 *Vulpius* 888 with alleluias MELCHIOR VULPIUS (*c.*1570–1615)

1 Good Christians all, rejoice and sing!
Now is the triumph of our King!
To all the world glad news we bring:

Alleluia! Alleluia! Alleluia!

2 The Lord of Life is risen for aye;
bring flowers of song to strew his way;
let all the world rejoice and say:

3 Praise we in songs of victory
that Love, that Life which cannot die,
and sing with hearts uplifted high:

4 Your name we bless, O risen Lord,
and sing today with one accord
the life laid down, the Life restored:

C. A. ALINGTON (1872–1955) altd.

239

First Tune

Mowsley 78 78 4 CYRIL V. TAYLOR (1907–91)

Second Tune

St Albinus 78 78 4 H. J. GAUNTLETT (1805–76)

1 Jesus lives! Thy terrors now
can, O death, no more appal us;
Jesus lives! By this we know
thou, O grave, canst not enthral us:
Alleluia!

2 Jesus lives! For us he died;
hence may we, to Jesus living,
pure in heart and act abide,
praise to him and glory giving:
Alleluia!

3 Jesus lives! Our hearts know well
naught from us his love shall sever;
life, nor death, nor powers of hell
part us now from Christ for ever:
Alleluia!

4 Jesus lives! Henceforth is death
entrance-gate of life immortal;
this shall calm our trembling breath,
when we pass its gloomy portal:
Alleluia!

5 Jesus lives! To him the throne
over all the world is given;
may we go where he is gone,
live and reign with him in heaven:
Alleluia!

C. F. GELLERT (1715–69)
tr. FRANCES E. COX (1812–97) altd.*

240

First Tune

Evelyns 65 65 D W. H. MONK (1823–89)

Second Tune

King's Weston 65 65 D R. VAUGHAN WILLIAMS (1872–1958)

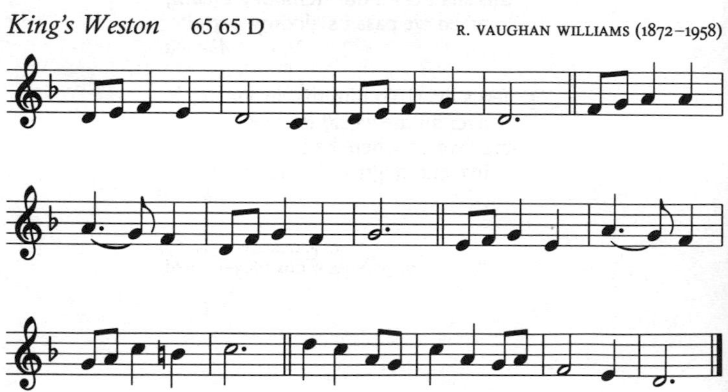

1 Jesus, Lord, Redeemer,
once for sinners slain,
crucified in weakness,
raised in power to reign,
dwelling with the Father,
endless in your days,
unto you be glory,
honour, blessing, praise.

2 Faithful ones communing
towards the close of day,
desolate and weary,
met you in the way.
So, when sun is setting,
come to us and show
all the truth, and in us
make our hearts to glow.

3 In the upper chamber,
where the ten, in fear,
gathered sad and troubled,
there you did appear.
Present with us now, Lord,
bid our sorrows cease;
breathing on us, Saviour,
say, 'I give you peace.'

PATRICK M. KIRKLAND (1857–1943)*

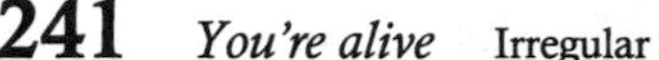

241 *You're alive* Irregular

GRAHAM KENDRICK (1950–)

1. Led like a lamb to the slaugh-ter in si - lence and shame,
2. At break of dawn poor Ma - ry, still weep-ing, she came,
3. At the right hand of the Fa - ther now seat - ed on high,

there on your back you car-ried a world of vio-lence and pain,
when through her grief she heard your voice now speak-ing her name:
you have be - gun your e-ter - nal_ reign of jus - tice and joy;

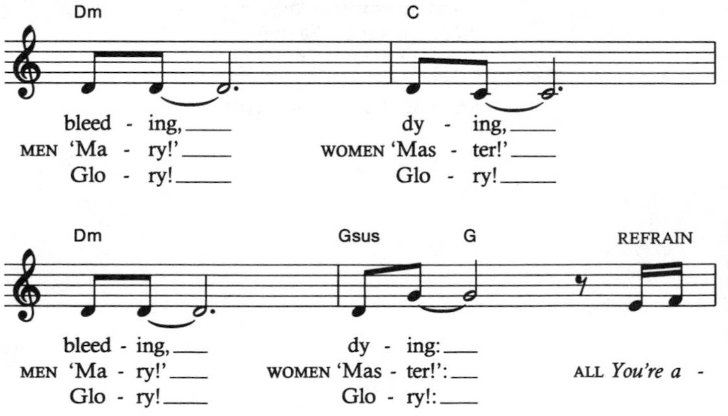

C Bb/C C Bb/C F C F C F C Dm F/G
- live, you're a- live, you have ri- sen! Al-le-lu-ia! And the
C Bb/C C Bb/C F C F C F C Dm F/G
power and the glo - ry is giv- en, Al-le- lu- ia! Je-sus, to
1,2
C Bb/C F C C Bb/C F C
you!
3
C Bb/C F C
you!

242 *Wetherby* CM

S. S. WESLEY (1810–76)

1 Ye humble souls that seek the Lord,
chase all your fears away;
and bow with rapture down to see
the place where Jesus lay.

2 Thus low the Lord of life was brought,
such wonders love can do;
thus cold in death that bosom lay,
which throbbed and bled for you.

3 Then raise your eyes and tune your songs;
the Saviour lives again:
not all the bolts and bars of death
the conqueror could detain.

4 High o'er the angelic bands he rears
his once dishonoured head;
and through unnumbered years he reigns,
who dwelt among the dead.

PHILIP DODDRIDGE (1702–51) altd.

243 *Noël nouvelet* 11 11 10 11 French melody

1 Now the green blade rises from the buried grain,
wheat that in the dark earth many days has lain;
Love lives again, that with the dead has been:
Love is come again, like wheat that springs up green.

2 In the grave they laid him, Love whom we had slain,
thinking that he never would awake again,
laid in the earth like grain that sleeps unseen:
Love is come again, like wheat that springs up green.

3 Forth he came at Easter, like the risen grain,
he that for the three days in the grave had lain,
quick from the dead my risen Lord is seen:
Love is come again, like wheat that springs up green.

4 When our hearts are wintry, grieving, or in pain,
then your touch can call us back to life again,
fields of our hearts that dead and bare have been:
Love is come again, like wheat that springs up green.

J. M. C. CRUM (1872–1958) altd.*

244 *O filii et filiae* 888 with alleluia French carol melody

Part I

1 O sons and daughters let us sing!
The King of heaven, the glorious King
o'er death today rose triumphing:
Alleluia!

2 On that first morning of the week,
before the day began to break,
the Marys went their Lord to seek:
Alleluia!

3 A young man bade their sorrow flee,
for thus he spake unto the three:
'Your Lord is gone to Galilee':
Alleluia!

4 Then for that first and best of days
to God your hearts and voices raise
in laud and jubilee and praise:
Alleluia!

5 And thus with all the Church unite,
as evermore is just and right,
in glory to the King of Light:
Alleluia!

Part II

1 O sons and daughters let us sing!
The King of heaven, the glorious King
o'er death today rose triumphing:
Alleluia!

7 That night the apostles met in fear;
amidst them came their Lord most dear
and said,'My peace be on all here':
Alleluia!

8 When Thomas first the tidings heard
he doubted if it were the Lord
until he came and spoke the word:
Alleluia!

9 'My piercèd side, O Thomas, see;
behold my hands and feet:' said he,
'not faithless but believing be':
Alleluia!

10 No longer Thomas then denied;
he saw the feet, the hands, the side;
'You are my Lord and God', he cried:
Alleluia!

11 How blest are they who have not seen,
and yet whose faith has constant been,
for they eternal life shall win:
Alleluia!

JEAN TISSERAND (d. 1494)
tr. J. M. NEALE (1818–66) and others, altd.

245 *Christus ist erstanden* 78 88 88

Old German carol melody as given in the *Trier Gesangbuch*, 1871

1 Round the earth a message runs:
Awake, awake, you drowsy ones!
Now leaps the sap in every stem
to chant the winter's requiem.
No more of sloth and dullness sing:
sing love, sing joy, for Christ is King!

2 Round the earth a message runs:
Arise, arise, you doleful ones!
Cast off your chains, you captives all
who long have lain in sorrow's thrall.
No more of grief and anguish sing:
sing love, sing joy, for Christ is King!

3 Round the earth a message runs:
For shame, for shame, you brawling ones!
You shall more true adventure find
in friendliness of heart and mind.
No more of hate and envy sing:
sing love, sing joy, for Christ is King!

4 Round the earth a message runs:
Rejoice, rejoice, you happy ones!
Now fall the gods of wrath and pain,
now comes your Prince of joy to reign;
to him your brave allegiance sing:
sing love, sing joy, for Christ is King.

'JAN STRUTHER' (1901–53)

246 *Komm, Seele* 76 76 D

J. W. FRANCK (1644–*c.*1710)

1 The day of resurrection!
earth, tell it out abroad;
the passover of gladness,
the passover of God!
From death to life eternal,
from earth unto the sky,
our Christ has brought us over
with hymns of victory.

2 Our hearts be pure from evil,
that we may see aright
the Lord in rays eternal
of resurrection light;
and, listening to his accents,
may hear, so calm and plain,
his own 'All hail!' and hearing
may raise the victor strain.

3 Now let the heavens be joyful,
and earth her song begin;
the round world keep high triumph,
and all that is therein:
let all things seen and unseen
their notes of gladness blend,
for Christ the Lord is risen,
our joy that has no end.

JOHN OF DAMASCUS, (d. *c.*750)
tr. J. M. NEALE (1818–66) altd.

247 *Maccabaeus* 10 11 11 11 with refrain G. F. HANDEL (1685–1759)

Version I

1 Thine be the glory, risen, conquering Son,
endless is the victory thou o'er death hast won;
angels in bright raiment rolled the stone away,
kept the folded grave-clothes where thy body lay.

Thine be the glory, risen, conquering Son,
endless is the victory thou o'er death hast won.

2 Lo, Jesus meets us, risen from the tomb;
lovingly he greets us, scatters fear and gloom;
let the Church with gladness hymns of triumph sing,
for her Lord now liveth, death hath lost its sting:

3 No more we doubt thee, glorious Prince of Life;
life is naught without thee: aid us in our strife;
make us more than conquerors through thy deathless love;
bring us safe through Jordan to thy home above:

EDMOND BUDRY (1854–1932)
tr. R. B. HOYLE (1875–1939)

Version II

1 Yours is the glory, resurrected one;
yours the final victory, God's eternal Son.
Now the angel greets you, sweeping through death's night;
moves the stone that guards you, floods the grave with light.

Yours is the glory, resurrected one;
yours the final victory, God's eternal Son.

2 See his appearing, with the wounds he bore;
see your Saviour living: see, and doubt no more!
Enter into gladness, people of the King;
let delight be endless: Christ is triumphing!

3 Fear flies before him! He whom we adore,
once death's helpless victim, lives for evermore.
Prince of Peace: our victory, life and strength are here,
flooding us with glory; no, we shall not fear.

EDMOND BUDRY (1854–1932)
tr. ALAN GAUNT (1935–)

248 *Vruechten* 67 67 with refrain 17th-cent. Dutch melody

1 This joyful Eastertide
away with sin and sorrow!
My Love, the Crucified,
has sprung to life this morrow.

Had Christ, that once was slain,
ne'er burst his three-days' prison,
our faith had been in vain;
but now is Christ arisen, arisen, arisen,
arisen!

2 Death's flood has lost its chill,
since Jesus crossed the river;
lover of souls, from ill
my passing soul deliver.

G. R. WOODWARD (1848–1934) altd.*

249 *Dryden Place* 76 76 D with refrain CARYL MICKLEM (1925–)

1 Too early for the blackbird,
too early for the lark,
a group of grieving women
set out into the dark.
Their hearts were full of sadness,
their faces full of gloom;
the faithful friends of Jesus
were going to his tomb.

Chase, chase your gloom and grief away
and welcome hope instead,
for Jesus Christ is ris'n today
and death itself is dead.

2 Two days before, on Friday
they'd seen their Master die;
they'd watched the Roman soldiers,
they'd heard the parting cry.
The Sabbath day was over,
so now, at break of day,
they hurried to the garden
in which his body lay.

3 With anxious hearts they noticed
the stone was rolled away,
they looked inside and, trembling,
they heard an angel say
'He is not here, he's living!';
so back they went to tell
to Peter and the others
the tale we hear as well.

4 Wherever people seek him
the story is the same;
he meets us by the roadside,
he calls us by our name.
His 'Peace be with you' calms us,
his 'Go and tell' inspires;
'For I am with you always'
puts paid to all our fears.

CARYL MICKLEM (1925–)

250 *Victory* 888 with alleluia

adpt. W. H. MONK (1823–89)
from a Magnificat by PALESTRINA, 1591

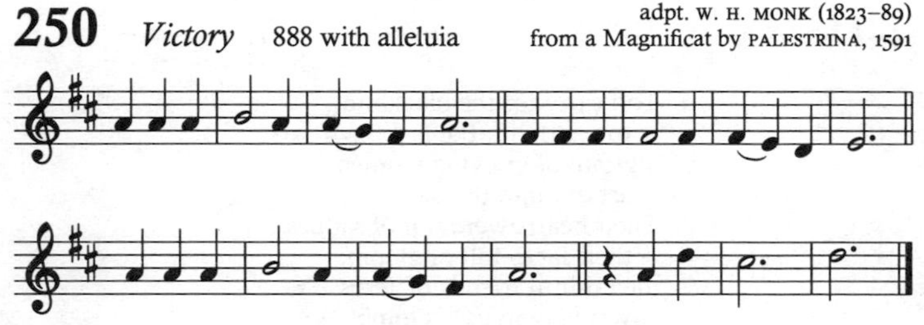

Alternative tune: VULPIUS, no. 571.

1 The strife is o'er, the battle done;
now is the Victor's triumph won;
O let the song of praise be sung:
Alleluia!

2 Death's mightiest powers have done their worst,
but Christ their legions has dispersed;
let shouts of praise and joy outburst:
Alleluia!

3 On the third day he rose again
glorious in majesty to reign;
O let us swell the joyful strain:
Alleluia!

4 He broke the ancient chains of hell;
the bars from heaven's high portals fell;
let hymns of praise his triumph tell:
Alleluia!

5 Lord, by the stripes which wounded thee,
from death's dread sting thy servants free,
that we may live, and sing to thee:
Alleluia!

Latin, 17th cent.
tr. FRANCIS POTT (1832–1909) altd.*

251 *Hilariter* 88 89

Melody from *Geistliche Kirchengesäng*,
Cologne, 1623

1 When Easter to the dark world came
bright flowers glowed like scarlet flame:

At Eastertide, at Eastertide,
O glad was the world at Eastertide.

2 When Mary in the garden walked,
and with her risen Master talked:

3 When John and Peter in their gloom
met angels at the empty tomb:

4 When ten disciples met in fear,
then 'Peace,' said Jesus, 'I am here':

5 When Thomas could not understand,
then Jesus stretched his wounded hand:

6 And friend to friend in wonder said:
'The Lord is risen from the dead!':

7 This Eastertide with joyful voice
we'll sing 'The Lord is King! Rejoice!':

At Eastertide, at Eastertide,
O sing, all the world, for Eastertide.

W. H. HAMILTON (1886–1958)*
(v. 4: compilers)

252 *Ascension* 77 77 with alleluias

W. H. MONK (1823–89)

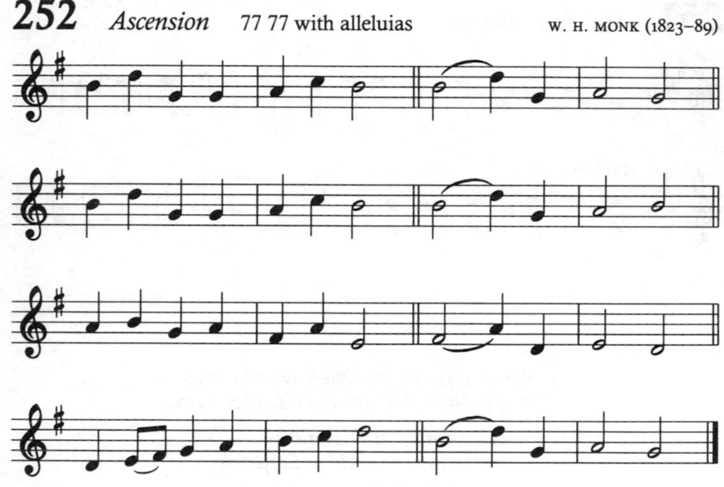

1 Hail the day that sees him rise,
Alleluia!
taken from our wondering eyes!
Alleluia!
Christ, awhile to mortals given,
Alleluia!
reascends his native heaven.
Alleluia!

2 There the glorious triumph waits:
lift your heads, eternal gates;
Christ has conquered death and sin;
let the King of glory in!

3 Though returning to his throne,
still he calls the world his own;
him though highest heaven receives,
still he loves the world he leaves.

4 See! he lifts his hands above;
see! he shows the prints of love;
hark! his gracious lips bestow
blessings on his Church below.

5 Still for us he intercedes,
his prevailing death he pleads;
near himself prepares our place,
first-fruits of our human race.

6 There we shall with thee remain,
partners of thine endless reign;
there thy face unclouded see,
find our heaven of heavens in thee.

CHARLES WESLEY (1707–88) altd.*

253 *Darwall* 66 66 44 44

JOHN DARWALL (1731–89)

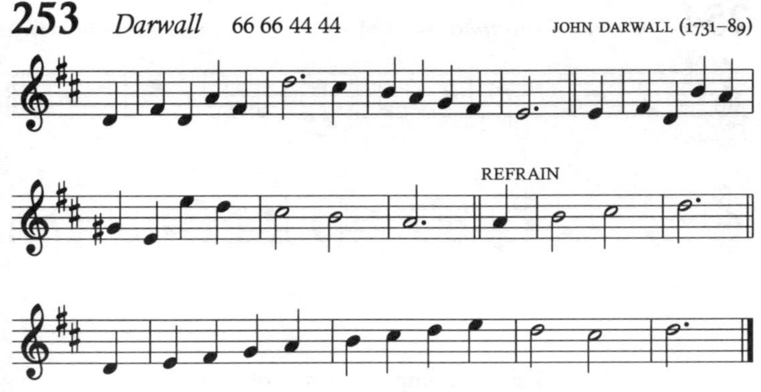

1 God is gone up on high,
with a triumphant noise;
the clarions of the sky
proclaim the angelic joys:

Join all on earth, rejoice and sing;
glory ascribe to glory's King.

2 God in the flesh below,
for us he reigns above;
let all the nations know
our Saviour's conquering love:

3 All power to our great Lord
is by the Father given;
by angel hosts adored,
he reigns supreme in heaven:

4 High on his holy seat
he bears the righteous sway;
his foes beneath his feet
shall sink and die away:

5 till all the earth, renewed
in righteousness divine,
with all the hosts of God
in one great chorus join:

CHARLES WESLEY (1707–88)*

254 *Church Triumphant* LM J. W. ELLIOTT (1833–1915)

1 Sing we triumphant hymns of praise,
new hymns to heaven exulting raise:
Christ, by a road before untrod,
ascendeth to the throne of God.

2 O grant that we may thither tend,
and with unwearied hearts ascend
toward thy kingdom's throne, where thou,
our great high priest, art seated now.

3 Be thou our joy and strong defence,
who art our future recompense:
so shall the light which springs from thee
be ours through all eternity.

4 O risen Christ, ascended Lord,
all praise to thee let earth accord,
who art, while endless ages run,
with Father and with Spirit one.

THE VENERABLE BEDE (673–735)
tr. BENJAMIN WEBB (1819–85) altd.

255 *Holy Well* DCM English traditional melody

1 To God with heart and cheerful voice
a triumph song we sing;
and with true thankful hearts rejoice
in our almighty King;
yea, to his glory we record,
who were but dust and clay,
what honour he did us afford
on his ascending day.

2 Each door and everlasting gate
to him hath lifted been;
and in a glorious wise thereat
our King is entered in;
whom if to follow we regard,
with ease we safely may,
for he hath all the means prepared
and made an open way.

3 Then follow, follow on apace,
and let us not forgo
our Captain, till we win the place
that he hath scaled unto.
And for his honour, let our voice
a shout so hearty make,
the heavens may at our mirth rejoice,
and earth and hell may shake.

GEORGE WITHER (1588–1667)

256 *Bristol* CM

Melody from
THOMAS RAVENSCROFT'S *Psalmes*, 1621

1 The golden gates are lifted up,
the doors are open wide;
the King of Glory is gone in
unto his Father's side.

2 Thou art gone in before us, Lord,
to make for us a place,
that we may be where now thou art
and look upon God's face.

3 And ever on our earthly path
a gleam of glory lies;
a light still breaks behind the cloud
that veiled thee from our eyes.

4 Lift up our hearts, lift up our minds,
and let thy grace be given,
that, while we journey here below,
our treasure be in heaven;

5 that where thou art at God's right hand,
our hope, our love may be;
dwell thou in us, that we may dwell
for evermore in thee.

CECIL FRANCES ALEXANDER (1818–95)*

257 *St Magnus* CM Probably by JEREMIAH CLARKE (*c.*1673–1707)

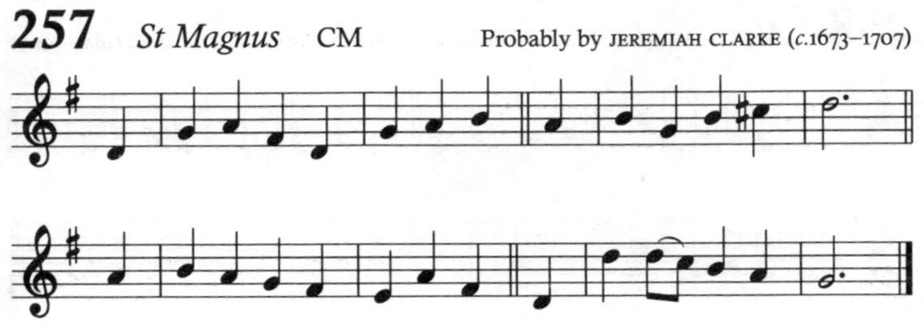

1 The head that once was crowned with thorns
is crowned with glory now:
a royal diadem adorns
the mighty victor's brow.

2 The highest place that heaven affords
is his, is his by right:
the King of kings, and Lord of lords,
and heaven's eternal light,

3 the joy of all who dwell above,
the joy of all below,
to whom he manifests his love,
and grants his name to know.

4 To them the cross, with all its shame,
with all its grace, is given;
their name an everlasting name,
their joy the joy of heaven.

5 They suffer with their Lord below;
they reign with him above;
their profit and their joy to know
the mystery of his love.

6 The cross he bore is life and health,
though shame and death to him;
his people's hope, his people's wealth,
their everlasting theme.

THOMAS KELLY (1769–1855)

258 *Aberystwyth* 77 77 D

JOSEPH PARRY (1841–1903)

1 Saviour, who exalted high
in thy Father's majesty,
yet vouchsaf'st thyself to show
to thy faithful flock below;
Saviour, though this earthly shroud
now my mortal vision cloud,
still thy presence let me see:
manifest thyself to me.

2 Son of God, to thee I cry;
by the holy mystery
of thy dwelling here on earth,
by thy pure and holy birth,
by thy griefs, to us unknown,
by thy spirit's parting groan;
Lord, thy presence let me see:
manifest thyself to me.

3 Prince of life, to thee I cry;
by thy glorious majesty,
by thy triumph o'er the grave,
strong to conquer, strong to save,
by the thralls of death unchained,
by the prize of life regained;
Lord, thy presence let me see:
manifest thyself to me.

4 Lord of glory, God most high,
Man exalted to the sky,
with thy love my being fill,
prompt me to perform thy will;
so may'st thou, my Saviour, come,
make this wayward heart thy home;
then thy presence I shall see
manifest, my Lord, in me.

RICHARD MANT (1776–1848) altd.*

259 *Eisenach* LM

JOHANN SCHEIN (1586–1630)

1 Where high the heavenly temple stands,
the house of God not made with hands,
a great High Priest our nature wears,
the Saviour of the world appears.

2 He who for us as surety stood
and poured on earth his precious blood,
pursues in heaven his plan of grace,
the Saviour of the human race.

3 Though now ascended up on high,
he bends on earth a brother's eye;
partaker of the human name,
he knows the frailty of our frame.

4 Our fellow-sufferer yet retains
a fellow-feeling of our pains,
and still remembers in the skies
his tears, his agonies and cries.

5 In every pang that rends the heart
the Man of Sorrows has a part;
he sympathises with our grief,
and to the sufferer sends relief.

6 With boldness, therefore, at the throne
let us make all our sorrows known;
and ask the aid of heavenly power
to help us in the evil hour.

Hebrews 4: 14–16,
para. MICHAEL BRUCE (1746–67)
or possibly JOHN LOGAN (1748–88)
in *Scottish Paraphrases*, 1781*

260 *Truro* LM

Melody from T. WILLIAMS's *Psalmodia Evangelica*, 1789

1 Christ is alive! Let Christians sing.
The cross stands empty to the sky.
Let streets and homes with praises ring.
Love, drowned in death, shall never die!

2 Christ is alive! No longer bound
to distant years in Palestine,
but saving, healing, here and now,
and touching every place and time.

3 Not throned afar, remotely high,
untouched, unmoved by human pains,
but daily, in the midst of life,
our Saviour in the Godhead reigns.

4 In every insult, rift and war
where colour, scorn or wealth divide,
Christ suffers still, yet loves the more,
and lives where even hope has died.

5 Christ is alive, and comes to bring
good news to this and every age,
till earth and sky and ocean ring
with joy, with justice, love and praise!

BRIAN WREN (1936–)

261 *Evelyns* 65 65 D

W. H. MONK (1823–89)

1 At the Name of Jesus
every knee shall bow,
every tongue confess him
King of glory now.
'Tis the Father's pleasure
we should call him Lord,
who from the beginning
was the mighty Word.

2 Humbled for a season,
to receive a Name
from the lips of sinners
unto whom he came,
he became a witness,
faithful to the last,
and returned victorious
when from death he passed.

3 In your hearts enthrone him;
there let him make new
all that is not holy,
all that is not true.
He is God the Saviour,
he is Christ the Lord,
ever to be worshipped,
trusted and adored.

4 When this same Lord Jesus
shall appear again
in his Father's glory,
there with him to reign,
then may we adore him,
all before him bow,
as our hearts confess him
King of glory now.

CAROLINE M. NOEL (1817–77)*

262 *Diademata* DSM

GEORGE J. ELVEY (1816–93)

1 Crown him with many crowns,
the Lamb upon his throne;
hark! how the heavenly anthem drowns
all music but its own.
Awake, my soul, and sing
of him who died for thee,
and hail him as thy chosen King
through all eternity.

2 Crown him the Son of God,
before the worlds began:
and ye, who tread where he hath trod,
crown him the Son of Man;
who every grief hath known
that wrings the human breast,
and takes and bears them for his own,
that all in him may rest.

3 Crown him the Lord of life,
who triumphed o'er the grave,
and rose victorious in the strife
for those he came to save:
his glories now we sing
who died, and rose on high;
who died eternal life to bring,
and lives that death may die.

4 Crown him, the Lord of Love!
Behold his hands and side,
rich wounds, yet visible above
in beauty glorified.
All hail, Redeemer, hail!
for thou hast died for me:
thy praise shall never, never fail
throughout eternity.

MATTHEW BRIDGES (1800–94) (vv. 1, 4) altd.
GODFREY THRING (1823–1903) (vv. 2, 3)

263 *Barnwell* LM with alleluias PAUL BATEMAN (1954–)

1 Glorious the day when Christ was born
to wear the crown that Caesars scorn,
Alleluia! Alleluia!
whose life and death that love reveal
which all hearts need and need to feel.
Alleluia! Alleluia!

2 Glorious the day when Christ arose,
the surest Friend of all his foes;
who for the sake of those he grieves
transcends the world he never leaves.

3 Glorious the days of gospel grace,
when Christ restores the fallen race;
when doubters kneel and waverers stand,
and faith achieves what reason planned.

4 Glorious the day when Christ fulfils
what self rejects yet feebly wills;
when that strong Light puts out the sun
and all is ended, all begun.

F. PRATT GREEN (1903–)*

264 *He is Lord*

Anon.

1 He is Lord, he is Lord;
he is risen from the dead, and he is Lord;
every knee shall bow, every tongue confess
that Jesus Christ is Lord.

2 He is love, he is love;
he has shown us by his cross that he is love;
all his people sing with one voice of joy
that Jesus Christ is love.

3 He is life, he is life;
he has died to set us free and he is life;
and he calls us all to live evermore,
for Jesus Christ is life.

4 He is Lord, he is Lord;
he is risen from the dead, and he is Lord;
every knee shall bow, every tongue confess
that Jesus Christ is Lord.

Anon.

265 *Londonderry Air* Irish traditional melody
11 10 11 10 11 10 11 12

CHRIST'S REIGN

1 I cannot tell why he, whom angels worship,
should set his love upon the human race,
or why, as Shepherd, he should seek the wanderers,
to bring them back within the fold of grace.
But this I know, that he was born of Mary,
when Bethlehem's manger was his only home,
and that he lived at Nazareth and laboured,
and so the Saviour, Saviour of the world, is come.

2 I cannot tell how silently he suffered,
as with his peace he graced this place of tears,
or how his heart upon the cross was broken,
the crown of pain to three and thirty years.
But this I know, he heals the broken-hearted,
and stays our sin, and calms our lurking fear,
and lifts the burden from the heavy-laden,
for yet the Saviour, Saviour of the world, is here.

3 I cannot tell how he will win the nations,
how he will claim his earthly heritage,
how satisfy the needs and aspirations
of East and West, of sinner and of sage.
But this I know, all flesh shall see his glory,
and he shall reap the harvest he has sown,
and some glad day his sun shall shine in splendour
when he the Saviour, Saviour of the world, is known.

4 I cannot tell how all the lands shall worship
when, at his bidding, every storm is stilled,
or who can say how great the jubilation
when all the hearts on earth with love are filled.
But this I know, the skies will thrill with rapture,
and myriad, myriad human voices sing,
and earth to heaven, and heaven to earth, will answer:
At last the Saviour, Saviour of the world, is King!

W. Y. FULLERTON (1857–1932)*

266 *Lux vera* 10 6 10 6 J. B. DYKES (1823–76)

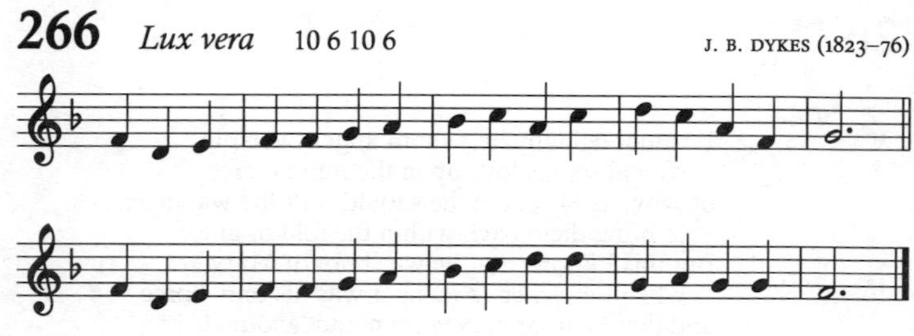

1 Eye hath not seen thy glory; thou alone
the path of light hast trod;
and in thy kingdom, on the Father's throne,
thou reignest, Son of God.

2 Yet thou abidest with us, King of kings,
thy loveliness we see;
and through the hallowed veil of earthly things
communion hold with thee.

3 Thou livest in us: from the tomb of earth,
to heaven with thee we rise;
and through the gateway of our second birth
behold the eternal prize.

4 The door of heaven is open: Jesus, Lord,
the crown is on thy brow;
by the immortal hosts of light adored
in glory dwellest thou.

E. W. EDDIS (1825–1905)*

267 *Haresfield* CM

J. DYKES BOWER (1905–81)

1 Immortal love for ever full,
for ever flowing free,
for ever shared, for ever whole,
a never-ebbing sea!

2 Our outward lips confess the name,
all other names above;
love only knoweth whence it came
and comprehendeth love.

3 We may not climb the heavenly steeps
to bring the Lord Christ down;
in vain we search the lowest deeps,
for him no depths can drown.

4 But warm, sweet, tender, even yet
a present help is he;
and faith has still its Olivet,
and love its Galilee.

5 The healing of his seamless dress
is by our beds of pain;
we touch him in life's throng and press,
and we are whole again.

6 O Lord and Master of us all,
whate'er our name or sign,
we own thy sway, we hear thy call,
we test our lives by thine.

J. G. WHITTIER (1807–92)

268 *Jesus is Lord*

DAVID MANSELL (1936–)

11 12 11 12 with refrain

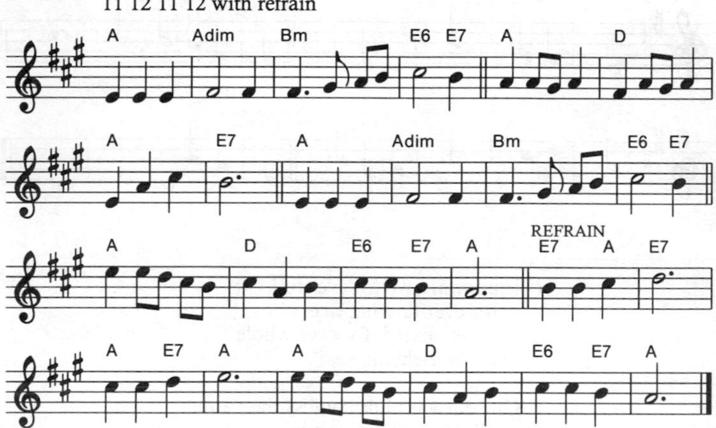

1 Jesus is Lord! Creation's voice proclaims it,
for by his power
each tree and flower
was planned and made.
Jesus is Lord! The universe declares it—
sun, moon and stars in heaven cry: 'Jesus is Lord!'

Jesus is Lord, Jesus is Lord!
Praise him with Alleluias,
for Jesus is Lord!

2 Jesus is Lord! Yet from his throne eternal
in flesh he came
to die in pain
on Calvary's tree.
Jesus is Lord! From him all life proceeding,
he gave his life a ransom thus setting us free.

3 Jesus is Lord! O'er sin the mighty conqueror,
from death he rose
and all his foes
shall own his name.
Jesus is Lord! God sends his Holy Spirit
showing by works of power that Jesus is Lord.

DAVID MANSELL (1936–)*

269 *Warrington* LM

RALPH HARRISON (1748–1810)

Alternative tune: GALILEE, no. 50.

1 Jesus shall reign where'er the sun
does his successive journeys run;
his kingdom stretch from shore to shore,
till moons shall wax and wane no more.

2 For him shall endless prayer be made,
and praises throng to crown his head;
his name like sweet perfume shall rise
with every morning sacrifice.

3 People and realms of every tongue
dwell on his love with sweetest song;
and infant voices shall proclaim
their early blessings on his name.

4 Blessings abound where'er he reigns;
the prisoners leap to lose their chains,
the weary find eternal rest,
and all who suffer want are blest.

5 Let every creature rise and bring
peculiar honours to our King;
angels descend with songs again,
and earth repeat the loud Amen.

Psalm 72: 12–19
para. ISAAC WATTS (1674–1748) altd.

In verse 5 line 2, 'peculiar' means 'appropriate'.

270 *Lindeman* 87 87 887 L. M. LINDEMAN (1812–87)

Alternative tune: LUTHER'S HYMN, no. 484.

1 Lord Christ, when first you came to earth,
upon a cross they bound you,
and mocked your saving kingship's worth
by thorns with which they crowned you:
and still our wrongs may weave you now
new thorns to pierce that steady brow,
and robe of sorrow round you.

2 New advent of the love of Christ,
shall we again refuse you,
till in the night of hate and war
we perish as we lose you?
From old unfaith our souls release
to seek the kingdom of your peace,
by which alone we choose you.

3 O wounded hands of Jesus, build
in us your new creation;
our pride is dust, our boasting stilled,
we wait your revelation.
O love that triumphs over loss,
we bring our hearts before your cross,
to finish your salvation.

W. RUSSELL BOWIE (1882–1969) altd.*

271 *You are the King of Glory*

Words and music by
MAVIS FORD, 1978

272

FIRST TUNE

Moville 76 76 D

Irish traditional melody

SECOND TUNE

Stokesay Castle 76 76 D

ERIC H. THIMAN (1900–75)

1 Christ is the world's Redeemer,
the lover of the pure,
the fount of heavenly wisdom,
our trust and hope secure;
the armour of his soldiers,
the Lord of earth and sky;
our health while we are living,
our life when we shall die.

2 Christ has our host surrounded
with clouds of martyrs bright,
who wave their palms in triumph,
and fire us for the fight.
For Christ the cross ascended
to save a world undone,
and, suffering for the sinful,
our full redemption won.

3 Down in the realm of darkness
he lay a captive bound,
but at the hour appointed
he rose, a Victor crowned;
and now, to heaven ascended,
he sits upon the throne,
in glorious dominion,
his Father's and his own.

4 Glory to God the Father,
the unbegotten One;
all honour be to Jesus,
his sole-begotten Son;
and to the Holy Spirit—
the perfect Trinity.
Let all the worlds give answer,
'Amen—so let it be!'

ST COLUMBA (521–97)
tr. DUNCAN MACGREGOR (1854–1923) altd.

For the first part of this hymn see 'O God, thou art the Father,' no. 73.

273 *St Elisabeth (Ascalon)* Irregular

Silesian melody

1 Fairest Lord Jesus,
Lord of all creation,
Son of God and Mary's son;
you will I cherish,
you will I honour,
you are my soul's delight and crown.

2 Fair are the flowers,
fairer still the human race
in all the freshness of youth arrayed;
yet is their beauty
fading and fleeting;
Lord Jesus, yours will never fade.

3 Fair is the moonlight,
fairer still the sunshine,
fair is the shimmering, starry sky;
Jesus shines brighter,
Jesus shines clearer
than all the heavenly host on high.

4 Jesus, all beauty,
heavenly and earthly,
in you is wondrously found to be;
none can be nearer,
fairer or dearer,
than you, my Saviour, are to me.

5 When I am dying,
still on you relying,
suffer me not from your arms to fall;
at my last hour,
come in your power,
Lord Jesus, be my all in all.

Anon. (German, 1677) altd.
tr. LILIAN STEVENSON (1870–1960) and others*

274 *Theodoric* 666 66 with refrain

German, 1360, arr. adpt.
from GUSTAV HOLST (1874–1934)

1 God is love, his the care
tending each, everywhere.
God is love—all is there!
Jesus came to show him,
that we all might know him:

Sing aloud, loud, loud,
Sing aloud, loud, loud,
God is good,
God is truth,
God is beauty: praise him!

2 Jesus came, lived and died
for our sake, crucified,
rose again, glorified:
he was born to save us
by the truth he gave us:

3 None can see God above;
Jesus shows how to love;
thus may we Godward move,
joined as sisters, brothers,
finding him in others:

4 To our Lord praise we sing—
light and life, friend and King
coming down love to bring,
pattern for our duty,
showing God in beauty:

PERCY DEARMER (1867–1936)*

275 *Wellington Square* DCM

GUY WARRACK (1900–86)

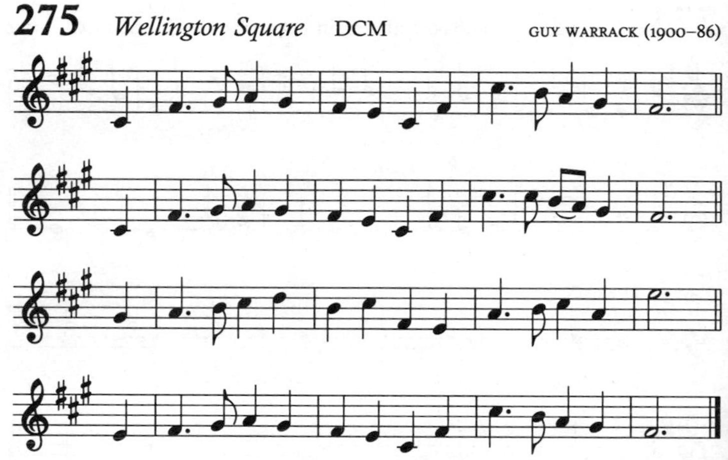

1 God's glory fills the universe,
the heavens proclaim his power;
but small and weak the Word made flesh,
and dark and brief his hour!
The mystery sought through ages past
is born with human face;
the treasure of eternal love
dwells with the human race.

2 His words and signs of healing power
are wonders to the poor;
blind eyes, cold hearts protest and scheme
till love stands judged by law.
Let peace and mercy weep apart,
and justice, truth, take flight
when God's own Word to silence falls
and darkness veils the Light.

3 Uplifted on the Cross, Christ bears
our shame in his disgrace,
his outstretched arms enfold us all,
and heaven and earth embrace.
For Love will know the darkest depths,
and taste our bitterest pain
to prove himself their vanquisher,
and spring from buried grain.

4 The Lord ascends, and death bows down
to his triumphant name.
The Spirit stirs our sleeping faith
in wind and tongue of flame.
Christ strengthens us, calls us to live
as children of the day,
to shine where shadows still oppress,
to walk his risen way.

COLIN THOMPSON (1945–)

276 *His name is wonderful*

AUDREY MIEIR (1916–)

277

FIRST TUNE

Stracathro CM

CHARLES HUTCHESON (1792–1860)

SECOND TUNE

St Peter CM

A. R. REINAGLE (1799–1877)

1 How sweet the name of Jesus sounds
in a believer's ear:
it soothes our sorrows, heals our wounds,
and drives away our fear.

2 It makes the wounded spirit whole,
and calms the troubled breast;
'tis manna to the hungry soul,
and to the weary rest.

3 Dear Name! the rock on which I build,
my shield and hiding-place,
my never-failing treasury, filled
with boundless stores of grace:

4 Jesus, my Shepherd and my Friend,
my Prophet, Priest, and King,
my Lord, my Life, my Way, my End,
accept the praise I bring.

5 Weak is the effort of my heart,
and cold my warmest thought;
but when I see thee as thou art,
I'll praise thee as I ought.

6 Till then I would thy love proclaim
with every fleeting breath;
and may the music of thy Name
refresh my soul in death.

JOHN NEWTON (1725–1807)*

278 *Church Triumphant* LM

J. W. ELLIOTT (1833–1915)

1 I know that my Redeemer lives—
what comfort this assurance gives!
He lives, who once lived on the earth,
who through his death now brings new birth.

2 He lives, triumphant from the grave;
what joy, eternally to save!
He lives to bless me with his love,
to plead for me in heaven above.

3 He lives to help in time of need;
what gifts, my hungry soul to feed!
He lives, and grants me daily breath
and leads me on to conquer death.

4 He lives, my wise and constant friend,
what kindness guards me to the end!
He lives, and while he lives I'll sing
Jesus, my Prophet, Priest and King.

5 He lives: all glory to his name!
What love, unchangeably the same!
What joy the blest assurance gives.
I know that my Redeemer lives!

SAMUEL MEDLEY (1738–99) altd.*

279 *I will sing* Irregular

MAX DYER, 1974

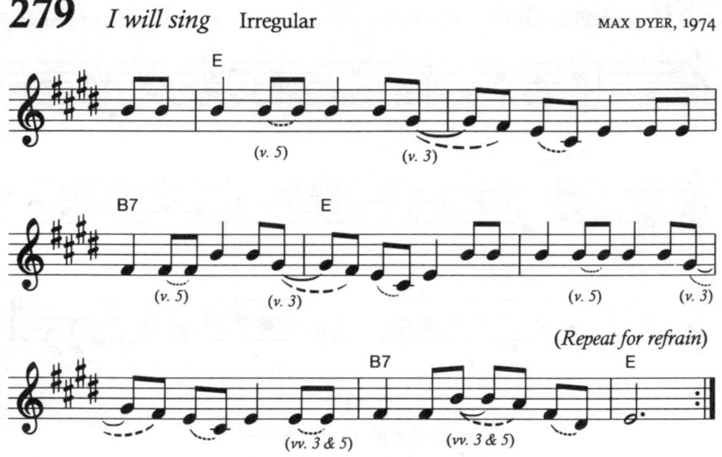

1 I will sing, I will sing a song unto the Lord, (*3 times*)
alleluia, glory to the Lord:

Allelu, alleluia, glory to the Lord,
allelu, alleluia, glory to the Lord,
allelu, alleluia, glory to the Lord,
alleluia, glory to the Lord.

2 We will come, we will come as one before the Lord. (*etc.*)
Alleluia, glory to the Lord:

3 If the Son, if the Son shall make you free,
you shall be free indeed:

4 They that sow, they that sow in tears shall reap in joy.
Alleluia, glory to the Lord:

5 Every knee shall bow and every tongue confess
that Jesus Christ is Lord:

6 In his name, in his name we have the victory.
Alleluia, glory to the Lord.

MAX DYER, 1974

280 *Croft's 136th* 66 66 88 WILLIAM CROFT (1678–1727)

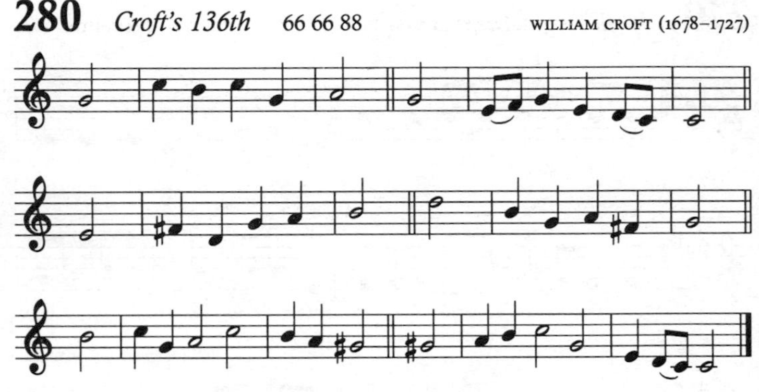

1 Join all the glorious names
of wisdom, love and power,
that ever mortals knew,
that angels ever bore.
All are too mean to speak his worth,
too mean to set my *Saviour* forth.

2 Great *Prophet* of my God,
my tongue would bless thy name;
by thee the joyful news
of our salvation came:
the joyful news of sins forgiven,
of hell subdued and peace with heaven.

3 Jesus, my great *High-Priest*,
offered his blood and died:
my guilty conscience seeks
no sacrifice beside;
his powerful blood did once atone,
and now it pleads before the throne.

4 My dear almighty *Lord*,
my *Conqueror* and my *King*,
thy sceptre and thy sword,
thy reigning grace I sing.
Thine is the power: behold I sit
in willing bonds before thy feet.

5 Now let my soul arise
and tread the tempter down;
my *Captain* leads me forth
to conquest and a crown.
A feeble saint shall win the day,
though death and hell obstruct the way.

6 Should all the hosts of death
and powers of hell unknown
put their most dreadful forms
of rage and mischief on,
I shall be safe, for *Christ* displays
superior power, and guardian-grace.

ISAAC WATTS (1674–1748)

281 *King of kings*

Anon.

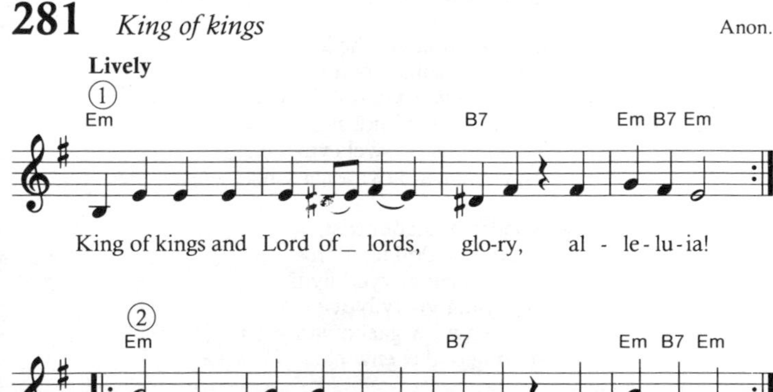

May be sung as a two-part round, the voices entering as indicated.
The first half is repeated before the second voice enters.

282 *Rhosymedre* 66 66 888

JOHN D. EDWARDS (1805–85)

1 O nefol addfwyn Oen
  sy'n llawer gwell na'r byd!
A lluoedd maith y nef
  yn rhedeg arno'u bryd;
dy ddawn a'th ras a'th gariad drud
sy'n llanw'r nef, yn llanw'r byd. (*twice*)

2 O ffynnon fawr o hedd!
  O anchwiliadwy fôr,
sy'n cynnwys ynddo'i hun
  ryw annherfynol stôr!
Ti biau'r clod—wel cymer ef,
trwy'r ddaear lawr a nef y nef. (*etc.*)

3 Noddfa pechadur trist,
  dan bob drylliedig friw
a phwys euogrwydd llym,
  yn unig yw fy Nuw;
'does enw i'w gael o dan y nef
yn unig ond ei enw ef.

4 Ymgrymed pawb i lawr
  i enw'r addfwyn Oen;
yr enw mwyaf mawr
  erioed a glywyd sôn:
y clod, y mawl, y parch a'r bri
fo byth i enw'n Harglwydd ni.

WILLIAM WILLIAMS, Pantycelyn (1717–91)

1 Most gentle, heavenly Lamb
whom hosts of heaven adore,
with them we set our hearts
on loving you the more;
your costly love, your gifts and grace,
fill all the bounds of time and space. (*twice*)

2 You are the source of peace,
you the uncharted sea
where we may search and find
a rich infinity:
all praise belongs to you, our Lord,
throughout the earth and heaven adored. (*etc.*)

3 You are the sinner's hope
when loaded down with guilt;
our confidence to rise
on God alone is built.
No other name can bear our loss
but that of Jesus on the Cross.

4 Let everyone rejoice
and sing the Lamb's new song,
that gentle Lamb, to whom
all joy and praise belong;
we celebrate with all above
the Saviour's new great name of Love.

tr. ENID A. EVANS (1926–)
and STEPHEN ORCHARD (1942–)

283 *O amor quam ecstaticus (Coutances)* LM

French church melody
from Rouen *Antiphoner,* 1728

Alternative tune: EISENACH NO. 100

1 O love, how deep, how broad, how high!
It fills the heart with ecstasy,
that God, the Son of God, should take
our mortal form, for mortals' sake.

2 He sent no angel to our race,
of higher or of lower place,
but wore the robe of human frame
himself, and to this lost world came.

3 For us he was baptized and bore
his holy fast, and hungered sore;
for us temptation sharp he knew,
for us the tempter overthrew.

4 For us he prayed, for us he taught,
for us his daily works he wrought,
by words and signs and actions thus
still seeking not himself, but us.

5 For us to wicked hands betrayed,
scourged, mocked, in purple robe arrayed,
he bore the shameful cross and death,
for us at length gave up his breath.

6 For us he rose from death again;
for us he went on high to reign;
for us he sent his Spirit here
to guide, to strengthen, and to cheer.

7 To him whose boundless love has won
salvation for us through his Son,
to God the Father, glory be,
both now and through eternity.

attrib. THOMAS À KEMPIS (*c.*1379–1471)
tr. BENJAMIN WEBB (1819–85) altd.*

284 *Truro* LM

Melody from T. WILLIAMS's *Psalmodia Evangelica,* 1789

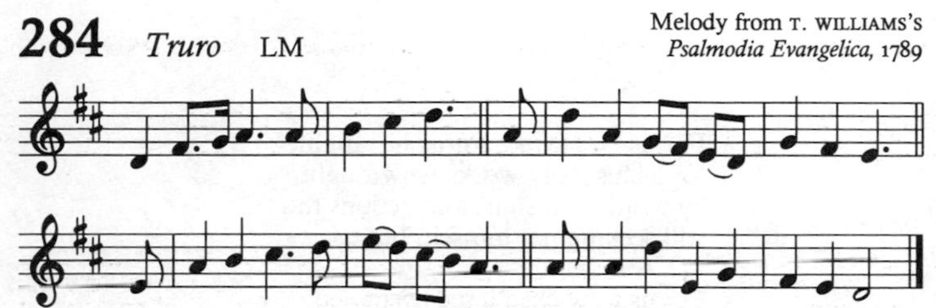

1 Now to the Lord a noble song,
awake, my soul; awake, my tongue;
hosanna to the Eternal Name,
and all his boundless love proclaim!

2 See where it shines in Jesus' face,
the brightest image of his grace;
God, in the person of his Son,
has all his mightiest works outdone.

3 The spacious earth and ocean's flood
proclaim the wise, the powerful God;
and thy rich glories from afar
sparkle in every rolling star.

4 But in his looks a glory stands,
the noblest labour of thy hands;
the radiant lustre of his eyes
outshines the wonders of the skies.

5 Grace is a sweet, a charming theme;
my thoughts rejoice at Jesus' name:
ye angels, dwell upon the sound;
ye heavens, reflect it to the ground!

ISAAC WATTS (1674–1748) altd.*

285 *University* CM

Melody from JOHN RANDALL's *Psalm and Hymn Tunes,* 1794
Probably by CHARLES COLLIGNON (1725–85)

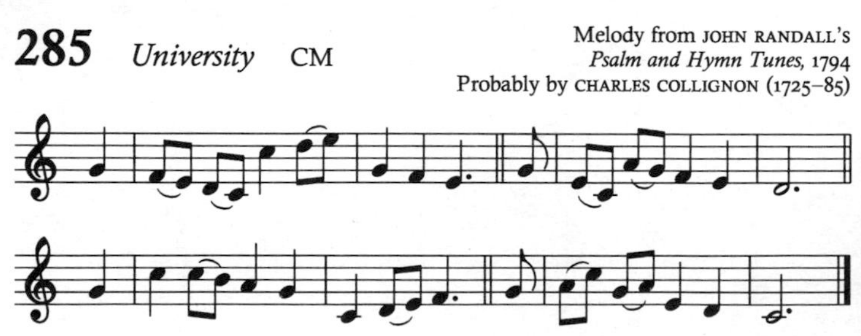

Alternative tune: RICHMOND, no. 376

1 O for a thousand tongues to sing
my great Redeemer's praise,
the glories of my God and King,
the triumphs of his grace.

2 Jesus, the name that charms our fears,
   that bids our sorrows cease;
'tis music in the sinner's ears,
   'tis life and health and peace.

3 He breaks the power of cancelled sin,
   he sets the prisoner free;
his blood can make the foulest clean,
   his blood availed for me.

4 He speaks, and listening to his voice
   new life the dead receive;
the mournful, broken hearts rejoice,
   the humble poor believe.

5 Hear him, ye deaf; his praise, ye dumb,
   your loosened tongues employ;
ye blind, behold your Saviour come;
   and leap, ye lame, for joy!

6 My gracious Master and my God,
   assist me to proclaim,
to spread through all the earth abroad
   the honours of thy name.

CHARLES WESLEY (1707–88)

286 *Rejoice in the Lord always*

Traditional

from Philippians 4: 4

May be sung as a two-part round, the voices entering as indicated.
The first half is repeated before the second voice enters.

287 *Deus tuorum militum* LM

French church melody
from the *Grenoble Antiphoner,* 1753

1 The light of morning sheds its rays
the sky reverberates with praise,
the earth responds with joyful cries,
with lamentations hell replies;

2 because the undisputed king
has shattered death and, triumphing,
treads down the evil that remains
to free the wretched from their chains.

3 He, though his tomb was sealed and barred
and soldiers kept a constant guard,
takes pride of place in majesty
and leaps from death to victory.

4 The groans of hell are set at rest
and all its agonies redressed,
because the Lord, though left for dead,
is risen, as the angel said.

5 Jesus, our triumph and delight,
your Easter ends the soul's dark night,
restores the heart's integrity
and keeps us to eternity.

6 Jesus, at one with us, you died:
at one with God, now glorified;
one with the Spirit evermore;
one Trinity whom we adore.

Latin (possibly 4th or 5th cent.)
tr. ALAN GAUNT (1935–)*

288 *Conquest* 86 86 88

DONALD S. BARROWS (1877–1951)

1 Thou art the everlasting Word,
the Father's only Son;
God manifestly seen and heard,
and heaven's Beloved One:

Worthy, O Lamb of God, art thou
that every knee to thee should bow.

2 True image of the infinite,
whose essence is concealed;
brightness of uncreated light;
the heart of God revealed:

3 But the high mysteries of thy name
an angel's grasp transcend;
the Father only—glorious claim—
the Son can comprehend:

4 Throughout the universe of bliss,
the centre thou, and Sun;
the eternal theme of praise is this,
to heaven's Beloved One:

JOSIAH CONDER (1789–1855)

289 *To God be the glory*

11 11 11 11 with refrain

W. H. DOANE (1832–1915)

1 To God be the glory, great things he has done!
So loved hc thc world that he gave us his Son,
who yielded his life in atonement for sin,
and opened the life-gate that all may go in.

Praise the Lord! Praise the Lord! Let the earth hear his voice!
Praise the Lord! Praise the Lord! Let the people rejoice!
O come to the Father, through Jesus the Son;
and give him the glory—great things he has done!

2 O perfect redemption, the purchase of blood,
to every believer the promise of God!
And every offender who truly believes,
that moment from Jesus a pardon receives:

3 Great things he has taught us, great things he has done,
and great our rejoicing through Jesus the Son;
but purer and higher and greater will be
the wonder, the beauty, when Jesus we see:

FANNY CROSBY (1820–1915) altd.

290 *Birstal* LM

ACCEPTED WIDDOP (*c*.1750–1801)

Alternative tune: GALILEE, no. 50.

Christ's Humiliation and Exaltation
Revelation 5: 12

1 What equal honours shall we bring
to thee, O Lord our God, the Lamb,
when all the notes that angels sing
are far inferior to thy name?

2 Worthy is he that once was slain,
the Prince of Peace that groaned and died;
worthy to rise and live and reign
at his almighty Father's side.

3 Power and dominion are his due
who stood condemned at Pilate's bar;
wisdom belongs to Jesus, too,
though he was charged with madness here.

4 All riches are his native right,
yet he sustained amazing loss;
to him ascribe eternal might,
who left his weakness on the cross.

5 Honour immortal must be paid,
instead of scandal and of scorn;
while glory shines around his head,
and a bright crown without a thorn.

6 Blessings for ever on the Lamb,
who bore the curse for sinners then;
let angels sound his sacred name,
and every creature say, Amen.

ISAAC WATTS (1674–1748)*

291 *Oriel* 87 87 87

From CASPAR ETT'S *Cantica Sacra,* 1840
adpt. W. H. MONK (1823–89)

1 To the name of our salvation
praise and honour let us pay,
which for many a generation
hid in God's foreknowledge lay,
but with holy exultation
we may sing aloud today.

2 Jesus is the name we treasure:
name beyond what words can tell;
name of gladness, name of pleasure,
ear and heart delighting well;
name of sweetness passing measure,
saving us from sin and hell:

3 name that calls for adoration,
name that speaks of victory,
name for grateful meditation
in the vale of misery,
name for loving veneration
by the citizens on high:

4 name by hard-won right exalted
over every other name,
which, when we were sore assaulted,
put the enemy to shame:
strength to them that else had halted,
sight to blind, and health to lame.

5 Therefore, Jesus, we adore you,
your most blessed Name revere,
and in humble love implore you
so to write it in us here
that we stand at last before you
and among your saints appear.

Latin, 15th cent.
tr. J. M. NEALE (1816–66) and others*

292 *Laudes Domini* 66 6 D

JOSEPH BARNBY (1838–96)

1 When morning gilds the skies,
my heart awaking cries
May Jesus Christ be praised!
Alike at work and prayer
to him I would repair:
May Jesus Christ be praised!

2 When sleep her balm denies,
my silent spirit sighs:
May Jesus Christ be praised!
When evil thoughts molest,
with this I shield my breast:
May Jesus Christ be praised!

3 Does sadness fill my mind?
A solace here I find:
May Jesus Christ be praised!
Or fades my earthly bliss?
My comfort still is this:
May Jesus Christ be praised!

4 Let earth's wide circle round
in joyful notes resound:
May Jesus Christ be praised!
Let air and sea and sky
from depth to height reply:
May Jesus Christ be praised!

5 Be this, while life is mine,
my canticle divine:
May Jesus Christ be praised!
Be this the eternal song
through all the ages long:
May Jesus Christ be praised!

Anon. German hymn, early 19th cent.
tr. EDWARD CASWALL (1814–78) altd.

293 *Laudate Dominum* 55 55 65 65 C. H. H. PARRY (1848–1918)

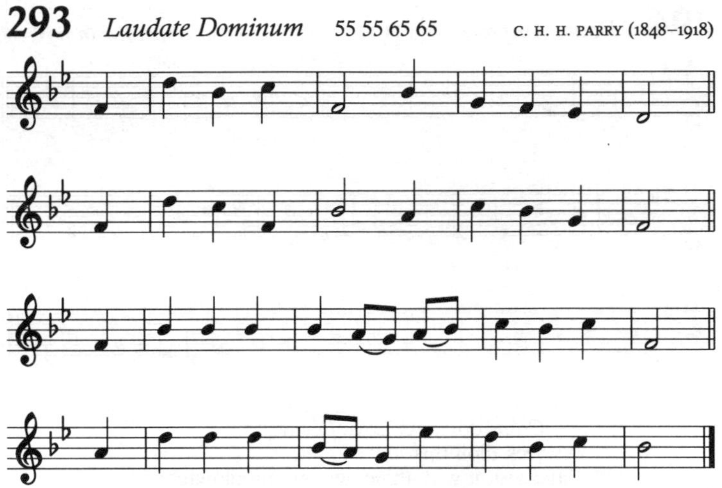

1 Ye servants of God,
your Master proclaim,
and publish abroad
his wonderful name;
the name all-victorious
of Jesus extol;
his kingdom is glorious
and rules over all.

2 God ruleth on high,
almighty to save;
and still he is nigh,
his presence we have;
the great congregation
his triumph shall sing,
ascribing salvation
to Jesus our King.

3 Salvation to God,
who sits on the throne!
let all cry aloud,
and honour the Son;
the praises of Jesus
the angels proclaim,
fall down on their faces,
and worship the Lamb.

4 Then let us adore,
and give him his right,
all glory and power,
all wisdom and might,
all honour and blessing,
with angels above,
and thanks never ceasing,
and infinite love.

CHARLES WESLEY (1707–88)

294 *Down Ampney* 66 11 D R. VAUGHAN WILLIAMS (1872–1958)

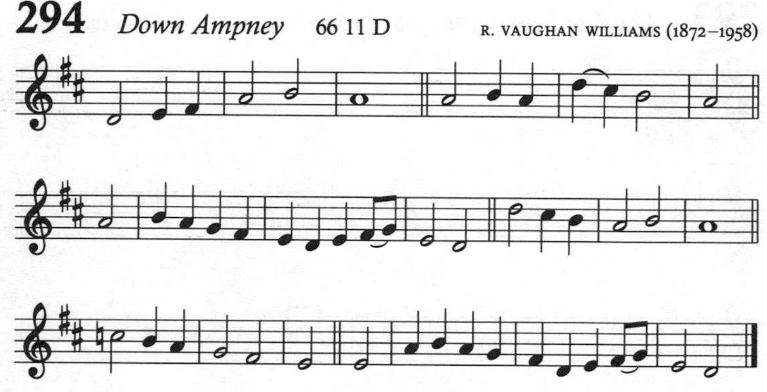

1 Come down, O Love Divine,
seek thou this soul of mine,
and visit it with thine own ardour glowing;
O Comforter, draw near,
within my heart appear,
and kindle it, thy holy flame bestowing.

2 O let it freely burn,
till earthly passions turn
to dust and ashes in its heat consuming;
and let thy glorious light
shine ever on my sight,
and clothe me round, the while my path illuming.

3 Let holy charity
mine outward vesture be,
and lowliness become mine inner clothing;
true lowliness of heart,
which takes the humbler part,
and o'er its own shortcomings weeps with loathing.

4 And so the yearning strong
with which the soul will long,
shall far outpass the power of human telling;
for none can guess its grace,
till he become the place
wherein the Holy Spirit makes his dwelling.

BIANCO DA SIENA (d. 1434)
tr. R. F. LITTLEDALE (1833–90)

295

FIRST TUNE

Veni Spiritus SM JOHN STAINER (1840–1901)

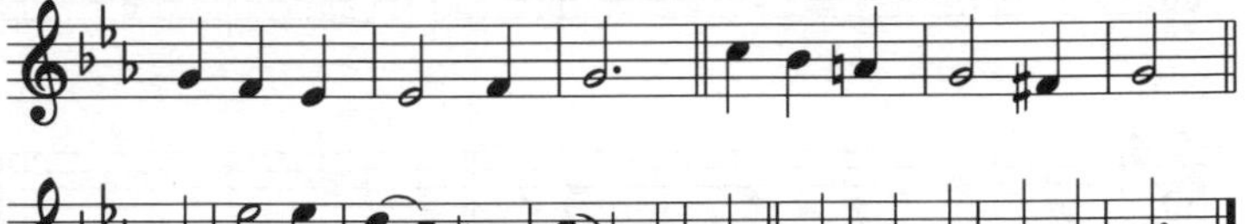

SECOND TUNE

Yattendon No. 46 SM H. E. WOOLDRIDGE (1845–1917)

1 Breathe on me, breath of God,
fill me with life anew,
that I may love what thou dost love,
and do what thou wouldst do.

2 Breathe on me, breath of God,
until my heart is pure,
until with thee I will one will
to do and to endure.

3 Breathe on me, breath of God,
till I am wholly thine,
until this earthly part of me
glows with thy fire divine.

4 Breathe on me, breath of God;
so shall I never die,
but live with thee the perfect life
of thine eternity.

EDWIN HATCH (1835–89) altd.

296 *Corrour Bothy* 66 84

CARYL MICKLEM (1925–)

1 O King, enthroned on high,
thou Comforter divine,
blest Spirit of all truth, be nigh
and make us thine.

2 Thou art the source of life,
thou art our treasure-store;
give us thy peace, and end our strife
for evermore.

3 Descend, O heavenly dove,
abide with us alway;
and in the fullness of thy love
cleanse us, we pray.

Greek, 8th cent.
tr. JOHN BROWNLIE (1857–1925)

297 *Veni Sancte Spiritus* 77 7 D

SAMUEL WEBBE (1740–1816)

1 Come, thou Holy Spirit, come,
and from thy celestial home
  thine unclouded light impart;
come, sustainer of the poor;
all good gifts are from thy store;
  come, illumine every heart.

2 Thou of comforters the best,
thou the soul's most welcome guest,
  sweet refreshment here below;
who in toil art rest complete,
tempered coolness in the heat,
  solace in the midst of woe:

3 O most blessèd light divine,
shine within these hearts of thine,
  and our inmost being fill;
where thou art not, we have naught,
nothing good in deed or thought,
  nothing free from taint of ill.

4 Heal our wounds; our strength renew;
on our dryness pour thy dew;
  wash the taint of guilt away:
bend the stubborn heart and will;
melt the frozen, warm the chill;
  guide the steps that go astray.

5 On the faithful, who adore
and confess thee, evermore
  in thy sevenfold gifts descend;
give them virtue's sure reward,
give them thy salvation, Lord,
  give them joys that never end.

13th cent., possibly STEPHEN LANGTON (d. 1228)
tr. EDWARD CASWALL (1814–78)
and others; altd.*

298 *Drakes Broughton* 87 87 (Trochaic) EDWARD ELGAR (1857–1934)

1 Holy Spirit, come, confirm us
in the truth that Christ makes known;
we have faith and understanding
through your helping gifts alone.

2 Holy Spirit, come, console us,
come as Advocate to plead;
loving Spirit from the Father,
grant in Christ the help we need.

3 Holy Spirit, come, renew us,
come yourself to make us live;
holy through your loving presence,
holy through the gifts you give.

4 Holy Spirit, come, possess us,
you the love of Three in One,
holy Spirit of the Father,
holy Spirit of the Son.

BRIAN FOLEY (1919–)

299 *Manchester* CM

ROBERT WAINWRIGHT (1748–82)

1 Come, Holy Spirit, heavenly Dove,
with all thy quickening powers;
kindle a flame of sacred love
in these cold hearts of ours.

2 In vain we tune our formal songs,
in vain we strive to rise;
hosannas languish on our tongues,
and our devotion dies.

3 And shall we then for ever be
in this poor dying state?
our love so faint, so cold to thee,
and thine to us so great!

4 Come, Holy Spirit, heavenly Dove,
with all thy quickening powers;
come, shed abroad the Saviour's love,
and that shall kindle ours.

ISAAC WATTS (1674–1748) altd.*

300 *Sursum corda* 10 10 10 10 ALFRED M. SMITH (1879–1971)

1 Eternal Spirit of the living Christ,
  I know not how to ask or what to say;
I only know my need, as deep as life,
  and only you can teach me how to pray.

2 Come, pray in me the prayer I need this day;
  help me to see your purpose and your will,
where I have failed, what I have done amiss;
  held in forgiving love, let me be still.

3 Come with the strength I lack, bring vision clear
  of human need; O give me eyes to see
fulfilment of my life in love outpoured:
  my life in you, O Christ; your love in me.

F. VON CHRISTIERSON (1900–)

301 *Buckland* 77 77

L. G. HAYNE (1836–83)

1 Holy Spirit, truth divine,
dawn upon this soul of mine;
Word of God, and inward light,
wake my spirit, clear my sight.

2 Holy Spirit, love divine,
reign within this heart of mine;
be my law, and I shall be
firmly bound, for ever free.

3 Holy Spirit, power divine,
fill and nerve this will of mine;
by thee may I strongly live,
bravely bear, and nobly strive.

4 Holy Spirit, peace divine,
still this restless heart of mine;
speak to calm this tossing sea
stayed in thy tranquillity.

5 Holy Spirit, joy divine,
gladden thou this heart of mine;
in the desert ways I sing:
'Spring, O Well, for ever spring!'

SAMUEL LONGFELLOW (1819–92)*

302 *Spiritus Vitae* 98 98 MARY J. HAMMOND (1878–1964)

1 O breath of life, come sweeping through us,
revive your Church with life and power;
O Breath of life, come, cleanse, renew us,
and fit your Church to meet this hour.

2 O Wind of God, come, bend us, break us,
till humbly we confess our need;
then in your tenderness remake us,
revive, restore; for this we plead.

3 O Breath of love, come, breathe within us
renewing thought and will and heart;
come, love of Christ, afresh to win us,
revive your Church in every part.

BESSIE PORTER HEAD (1850–1936) altd.

303 *Ayrshire* CM

K. G. FINLAY (1882–1974)

1 Spirit divine, attend our prayers,
and make this house your home;
descend with all your gracious powers;
O come, great Spirit, come!

2 Come as the light: to us reveal
our emptiness and woe,
and lead us in those paths of life
where all the righteous go.

3 Come as the fire; and purge our hearts
like sacrificial flame;
let our whole life an offering be
to our Redeemer's name.

4 Come as the dove; and spread your wings,
the wings of peaceful love;
and let your Church on earth become
blest as the Church above.

5 Come as the wind, with rushing sound
and Pentecostal grace,
that all of woman born may see
the glory of your face.

6 Spirit divine, attend our prayers;
make this lost world your home;
descend with all your gracious powers;
O come, great Spirit, come!

ANDREW REED (1787–1862) altd.

304 *Deben* 76 86 86 86

GORDON HAWKINS (1911–)

1 Spirit of God within me,
possess my human frame;
fan the dull embers of my heart,
stir up the living flame.
Strive till that image Adam lost,
new minted and restored,
in shining splendour brightly bears
the likeness of the Lord.

2 Spirit of truth within me,
possess my thought and mind;
lighten anew the inward eye
by Satan rendered blind;
shine on the words that wisdom speaks,
and grant me power to see
the truth made known to all in Christ,
and in that truth be free.

3 Spirit of love within me,
possess my hands and heart;
break through the bonds of self-concern
that seeks to stand apart;
grant me the love that suffers long,
that hopes, believes and bears,
the love fulfilled in sacrifice
that cares as Jesus cares.

4 Spirit of life within me,
possess this life of mine;
come as the wind of heaven's breath,
come as the fire divine!
Spirit of Christ, the living Lord,
reign in this house of clay,
till from its dust with Christ I rise
to everlasting day.

TIMOTHY DUDLEY-SMITH (1926–)

305 *Sheldonian* 10 10 10 10

CYRIL V. TAYLOR (1907–91)

1 Spirit of God, descend upon my heart;
wean it from earth; through all its pulses move;
stoop to my weakness, mighty as thou art,
and make me love thee as I ought to love.

2 I ask no dream, no prophet-ecstasies,
no sudden rending of the veil of clay,
no angel-visitant, no opening skies;
but take the dimness of my soul away.

3 Hast thou not bid me love thee, God and King—
all, all thine own: soul, heart, and strength, and mind?
I see thy cross—there teach my heart to cling:
O let me seek thee, and O let me find!

4 Teach me to feel that thou art always nigh;
teach me the struggles of the soul to bear,
to check the rising doubt, the rebel sigh;
teach me the patience of unanswered prayer.

5 Teach me to love thee as thine angels love,
one holy passion filling all my frame—
the baptism of the heaven-descended Dove,
my heart an altar, and thy love the flame.

GEORGE CROLY (1780–1860)

306 *David's Harp* 88 88 88 ROBERT KING (*fl.*1676–1728)

1 Spirit of flame, whose living glow
was known to prophet, saint and seer,
where faith is cold thy fire bestow,
where love is distant draw thou near!
Apostles ventured in thy power;
so fill us in this present hour.

2 Spirit of peace, for healing grace
a parched world waits in dry despair;
break through the clouds that hide thy face,
for hope unconquered knows thee there:
humble our pride and come as guest,
most hidden and most manifest.

3 Spirit of truth, thy blinding light
must needs be tempered to our eyes;
yet dawn upon our darkened sight
with freedom as our dearest prize:
with torch of truth held high above,
help us to cast out fear by love.

4 Spirit of love, all souls are thine,
redeemed and claimed by love unpriced;
O seeking love, do thou incline
our hearts to love and follow Christ;
Love that is stronger than our fears,
uplift our hearts through coming years.

A. H. DRIVER (1897–1968)*

307 *Shepherd's pipes* DCM

ANNABETH MCCLELLAND GAY (1925–)

1 Though gifts of knowledge and of tongues
I should in full possess;
though I should suffer for a cause,
and shine at selflessness;
though I had mountain-moving faith,
or gave with all my will,
my life would all be wasted breath
if I were loveless still.

2 True love is patient, kind and brave—
no envy there, or pride,
no touchiness, no evil glee
when others slip or slide.
Love always takes a pure delight
in truth, in people's best:
it trusts, endures, forgives and hopes,
and overlooks the rest.

3 Our anxious gazings at the glass
no certain future see;
yet, growing up, we leave behind
the child we used to be.
Complete in Christ, we'll fully know
and face to face be known:
so faith and hope will find in love
their everlasting crown.

CARYL MICKLEM (1925–)
based on 1 Corinthians 13

308 & 309

Spirit of the living God 75 75 44 75 DANIEL IVERSON (1890–1972)

308

1 Spirit of the living God,
fall afresh on me.
Spirit of the living God,
fall afresh on me.
Melt me! Mould me!
Fill me! Use me!
Spirit of the living God,
fall afresh on me.

DANIEL IVERSON (1890–1972)

309

1 Spirit of the living God,
move among us all;
make us one in heart and mind,
make us one in love;
humble, caring,
selfless, sharing—
Spirit of the living God,
fill our lives with love!

MICHAEL BAUGHEN (1930–)

310 *Charity* 777 5

JOHN STAINER (1840–1901)

1 Gracious Spirit, Holy Ghost,
taught by thee, we covet most,
of thy gifts at Pentecost,
holy, heavenly love.

2 Faith that mountains could remove,
tongues of earth or heaven above,
knowledge, all things, empty prove
if I have no love.

3 Though I as a martyr bleed,
give my goods the poor to feed,
all is vain, if love I need;
therefore give me love.

4 Love is kind, and suffers long;
love is meek, and thinks no wrong,
love than death itself more strong;
therefore give us love.

5 Prophecy will fade away,
melting in the light of day;
love will ever with us stay;
therefore give us love.

6 Faith and hope and love we see,
joining hand in hand, agree;
but the greatest of the three,
and the best, is love.

CHRISTOPHER WORDSWORTH (1807–85) altd.
based on 1 Corinthians 13

311 *Soll's sein* DCM CORNER'S *Geistliche Nachtigall*, 1649

1 The Spirit of the Lord revealed
his will to saints of old;
their heart and mind and lips unsealed,
his glory to unfold.
Amid the gloom of ancient night
they hailed the dawning Word,
and in the coming of the light
proclaimed the coming Lord.

2 The prophets passed; at length there came,
to sojourn and abide,
the Word incarnate, to whose name
the prophets testified;
and he, the twilight overpast,
himself the Light of light,
a man with us, revealed at last
the Father to our sight.

3 Eternal Spirit, who dost speak
to mind and conscience still,
that we, in this our day, may seek
to do our Father's will,
to us the word of life impart,
of Christ, the living way;
give us the quiet humble heart
to hear and to obey.

G. W. BRIGGS (1875–1959)*

312 *Kilmarnock* CM

NEIL DOUGALL (1776–1862)

1 Come, Spirit, all our hearts inspire;
let us thine influence prove,
source of the old prophetic fire,
fountain of life and love.

2 Come Spirit now, for moved by thee
the prophets wrote and spoke;
unlock the truth, thyself the key,
unseal the sacred book.

3 Expand thy wings, life-giving dove,
brood o'er our nature's night;
on our disordered spirits move,
and let there now be light.

4 God, through himself, we then shall know,
if thou within us shine,
and sound, with all thy saints below,
the depths of love divine.

CHARLES WESLEY (1707–88) altd.*

313 *Jena* 88 88 88 MELCHIOR VULPIUS (*c.*1570–1615)

1 Spirit of truth, essential God,
 who didst thine ancient saints inspire,
shed in their hearts thy love abroad,
 and touch their hallowed lips with fire:
our God from all eternity,
world without end we worship thee.

2 Still we believe, almighty Lord,
 whose presence fills both earth and heaven,
the meaning of the written word
 is by thy inspiration given;
thou only dost thyself explain,
the secret mind of God make plain.

3 Come then, divine Interpreter,
 the Scriptures to our hearts apply;
and, taught by thee, we God revere,
 him in three Persons magnify,
in each the triune God adore,
who was, and is, for evermore.

CHARLES WESLEY (1707–88)*

314

First Tune

Bread of life 64 64 ERIC H. THIMAN (1900–75)

Second Tune

Haymarket 64 64 D PAUL BATEMAN (1954–)

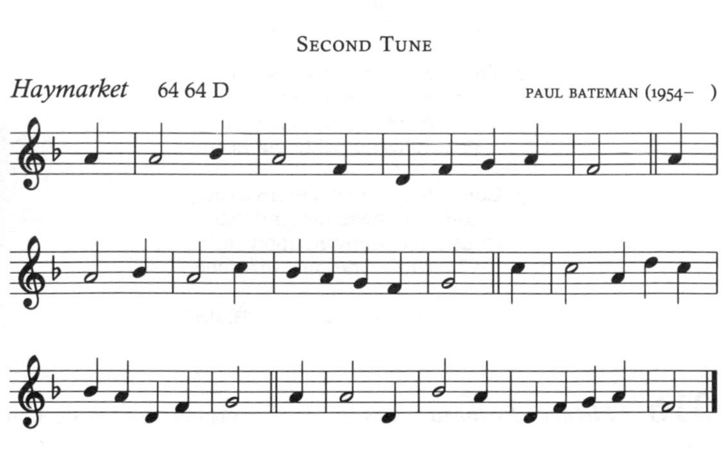

1 Break thou the bread of life,
dear Lord, to me,
as thou didst break the loaves
beside the sea;

beyond the sacred page
I seek thee, Lord,
my spirit longs for thee,
O living Word.

2 Bless thou the truth, dear Lord,
to me, to me,
as thou didst bless the bread
by Galilee;

then shall all bondage cease,
all fetters fall,
and I shall find my peace,
my all in all.

MARY A. LATHBURY (1841–1913)

315 *Mahon* 87 87 (Trochaic) C. EDGAR KNOWLES (1887–1973)

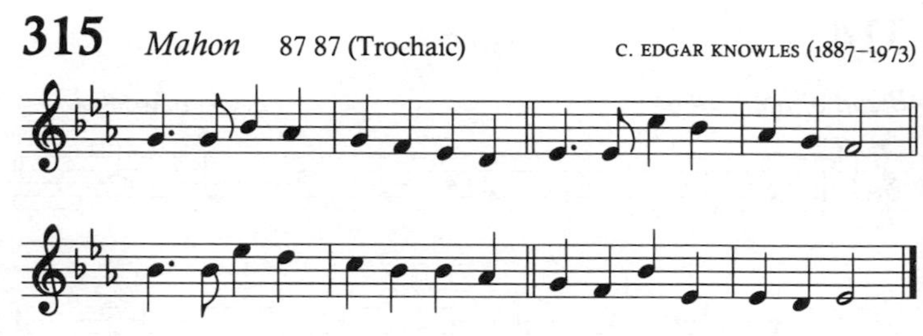

1 Come, thou everlasting Spirit,
bring to every thankful mind
all the Saviour's dying merit,
all his suffering for mankind.

2 True Recorder of his passion,
now the living faith impart,
now reveal his great salvation,
preach his gospel to our heart.

3 Come, thou witness of his dying;
come, Remembrancer divine;
let us feel thy power, applying
Christ to every soul, and mine.

CHARLES WESLEY (1707–88) altd.

316 *Metzler's Redhead* CM RICHARD REDHEAD (1820–1901)

1 Lord, I have made thy word my choice,
my lasting heritage;
there shall my noblest powers rejoice,
my warmest thoughts engage.

2 I'll read the histories of thy love,
  and keep thy laws in sight;
while through thy promises I rove,
  with ever fresh delight.

3 'Tis a broad land of wealth unknown,
  where springs of life arise,
seeds of immortal bliss are sown,
  and hidden glory lies.

4 The best relief that mourners have;
  it makes our sorrows blest;
our fairest hope beyond the grave,
  and our eternal rest.

ISAAC WATTS (1674–1748)

317 *Ravenshaw* 66 66 (Trochaic)

Adpt. W. H. MONK (1823–89)
from a melody in M. WEISSE'S
Ein Neu Gesengbuchlen, 1531

1 Lord, thy word abideth,
and our footsteps guideth;
who its truth believeth
light and joy receiveth.

2 When our foes are near us,
then thy word doth cheer us;
word of consolation,
message of salvation.

3 When the storms are o'er us,
and dark clouds before us,
then its light directeth
and our way protecteth.

4 Who can tell the pleasure,
who recount the treasure,
by thy word imparted
to the simple-hearted?—

5 word of mercy, giving
succour to the living;
word of life, supplying
comfort to the dying.

6 O that we, discerning
its most holy learning,
Lord, may love and fear thee,
evermore be near thee.

H. W. BAKER (1821–77)

318 *Cornwall* 88 6 88 6

S. S. WESLEY (1810–76)

Alternative tune: MANNA, no. 68.

1 Not far beyond the sea, nor high
above the heavens, but very nigh
  your voice, O God, is heard.
For each new step of faith we take
you have more truth and light to break
  forth from your holy word.

2 The babes in Christ your scriptures feed
with milk sufficient for their need,
  the nurture of the Lord.
Beneath life's burden and its heat
the fully grown find stronger meat
  in your unfailing word.

3 Rooted and grounded in your love,
with saints on earth and saints above
  we join in full accord
to grasp the breadth, length, depth and height,
the crucified and risen might
  of Christ, the incarnate Word.

4 Help us to press toward that mark,
and, though our vision now is dark,
  to live by what we see;
so, when we see you face to face,
your truth and light our dwelling-place
  for evermore shall be.

GEORGE CAIRD (1917–84)*

319 *Regent Square* 87 87 87 HENRY SMART (1813–79)

1 Thanks to God whose Word was spoken
in the deed that made the earth.
His the voice that called a nation,
his the fires that tried her worth.
God has spoken:
praise him for his open word.

2 Thanks to God whose Word incarnate
human flesh has glorified,
who by life and death and rising
grace abundant has supplied.
God has spoken:
praise him for his open word.

3 Thanks to God whose word was written
in the Bible's sacred page,
record of the revelation
showing God to every age.
God has spoken:
praise him for his open word.

4 Thanks to God whose word is published
in the tongues of every race,
see its glory undiminished
by the change of time or place.
God has spoken:
praise him for his open word.

5 Thanks to God whose word is answered
by the Spirit's voice within.
Here we drink of joy unmeasured,
life redeemed from death and sin.
God is speaking:
praise him for his open word.

R. T. BROOKS (1918–85) altd.

320 *Cromer* LM

J. AMBROSE LLOYD (1815–74)

1 The heavens declare thy glory, Lord,
in every star thy wisdom shines;
but when our eyes behold thy word,
we read thy name in fairer lines.

2 The rolling sun, the changing light,
and night and day, thy power confess;
but the blest volume thou hast writ
reveals thy justice and thy grace.

3 Sun, moon and stars convey thy praise
round the whole earth, and never stand;
so when thy truth began its race,
it touched and glanced on every land.

4 Nor shall thy spreading gospel rest
till through the world thy truth has run;
till Christ has all the nations blessed,
that see the light or feel the sun.

5 Great Sun of Righteousness, arise,
bless the dark world with heavenly light:
thy gospel makes the simple wise;
thy laws are pure, thy judgements right.

6 Thy noblest wonders here we view,
in souls renewed, and sins forgiven;
Lord, cleanse my sins, my soul renew,
and make thy word my guide to heaven.

ISAAC WATTS (1674–1748)

321 *Capel* CM English traditional carol melody

1 Your words to me are life and health;
put strength into my soul;
enable, guide, and teach my heart
to reach its perfect goal.

2 Your words to me are light and truth;
from day to day I know
their wisdom, passing human thought,
as in their truth I grow.

3 Your words to me are full of joy,
of beauty, peace and grace;
from them I learn your perfect will,
through them I see your face.

4 Your words are perfected in one,
yourself, the living Word;
print your own image in my heart
in clearest lines, my Lord.

G. CURRIE MARTIN (1865–1937)*

322 *Salve festa dies* Irregular R. VAUGHAN WILLIAMS (1872–1958)

Latin, *c.*14th cent.; based on a hymn by
VENANTIUS FORTUNATUS (*c.*530–609)
tr. GABRIEL GILLETT (1873–1948)*

323 *Sutton Courtenay* 55 5 11

ERIK ROUTLEY (1917–82)

1 Away with our fears,
our troubles and tears:
the Spirit is come,
the witness of Jesus returned to his home.

2 Our Advocate there
by his blood and his prayer
the gift has obtained,
for us he has prayed, and the Comforter gained.

3 Our glorified Head
his Spirit has shed,
with his people to stay,
and never again will he take him away.

4 Our heavenly Guide
with us shall abide,
his comforts impart,
and set up his kingdom of love in the heart.

5 The heart that believes
his kingdom receives,
his power and his peace,
his life, and his joy's everlasting increase.

CHARLES WESLEY (1707–88) altd.

324 *Everton* 87 87 D

HENRY SMART (1813–79)

1 Holy Spirit, ever dwelling
in the glorious realms of light;
Holy Spirit, ever brooding
o'er a world of gloom and night;
Holy Spirit, ever forming
in the Church the mind of Christ;
thee we praise with endless worship
for thy fruit and gifts unpriced.

2 Holy Spirit, ever working
through the Church's ministry;
quick'ning, strength'ning, and absolving,
setting captive sinners free;
Holy Spirit, ever binding
age to age, and soul to soul,
in a fellowship unending—
thee we worship and extol.

TIMOTHY REES (1874–1939)

325 *Beweley* 66 66

CYRIL V. TAYLOR (1907–91)

Alternative tune: ECCLES, no. 449.

1 Into a world of dark,
waste and disordered space,
he came, a wind that moved
across the waters' face.

2 The Spirit in the wild
breathed, and a world began.
From shapelessness came form,
from nothingness, a plan.

3 Light in the darkness grew;
land in the water stood;
and space and time became
a beauty that was good.

4 Into a world of doubt,
through doors we closed, he came,
the breath of God in power
like wind and roaring flame.

5 From empty wastes of death
on love's disordered grief
light in the darkness blazed
and kindled new belief.

6 Still, with creative power,
God's Spirit comes to give
a pattern of new life—
our worlds begin to live.

ANN PHILLIPS (1930–) and compilers

326 *Omni die* 87 87 (Trochaic)

Melody from CORNER'S *Gesangbuch*, 1631
arr. W. S. ROCKSTRO (1823–95)

1 Loving Spirit, loving Spirit,
you have chosen me to be—
you have drawn me to your wonder,
you have set your sign on me.

2 Like a mother, you enfold me,
hold my life within your own,
feed me with your very body,
form me of your flesh and bone.

3 Like a father, you protect me,
teach me the discerning eye,
hoist me up upon your shoulder,
let me see the world from high.

4 Friend and lover, in your closeness
I am known and held and blest:
in your promise is my comfort,
in your presence I may rest.

5 Loving Spirit, loving Spirit,
you have chosen me to be—
you have drawn me to your wonder,
you have set your sign on me.

SHIRLEY ERENA MURRAY (1931–)

327 *Sussex Carol* 88 88 88 English traditional melody

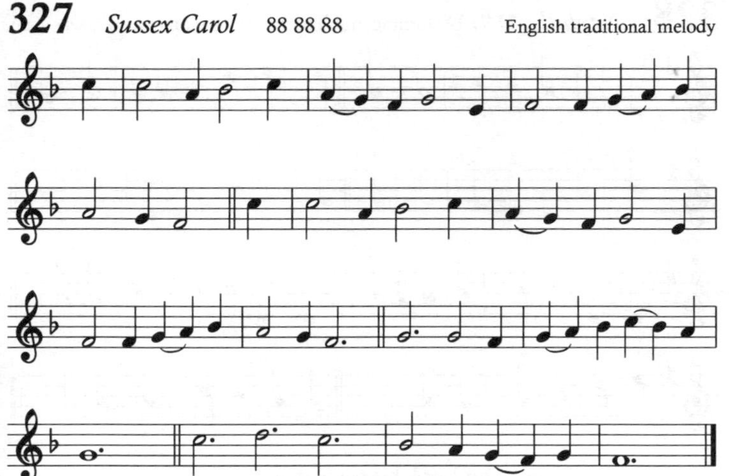

1 O God, your love's undying flame
   was seen in desert bush ablaze,
when Moses learned your secret name,
   the Lord of past and future days;
Lord, we would learn what you require,
and burn for you with living fire.

2 O Lord of fire, your love a flame
   that longed to set the earth ablaze:
to bring the Kingdom's joy you came
   and freed us, trapped in earth-bound ways;
Lord, we would share your love's desire,
and burn for you with living fire.

3 O Holy Spirit, tongues of flame
   that set the new-born Church ablaze;
to each believer then you came,
   and lives were filled with power and praise;
O Spirit, come, our lives inspire
to burn for you with living fire.

BASIL E. BRIDGE (1927–)*
(Exodus 3: 2, Luke 12: 49, Acts 2: 3)

328 *Naphill* 77 77 D (Iambic and Trochaic) HAROLD DARKE (1888–1976)

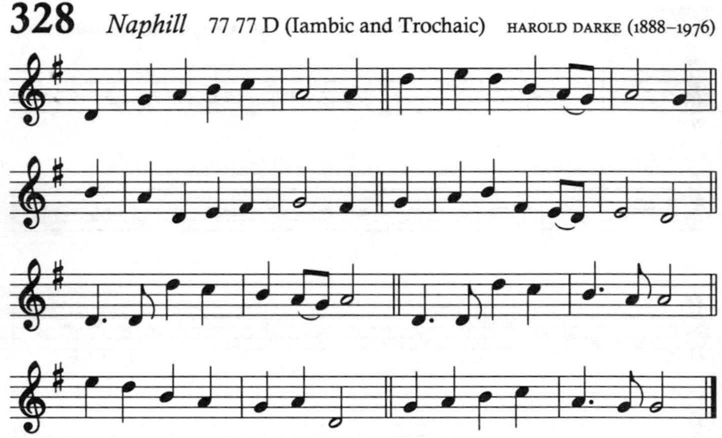

1 Our Lord, his passion ended,
has gloriously ascended,
yet though from him divided,
he leaves us not unguided;
  all his benefits to crown
  he has sent his spirit down,
  burning like a flame of fire,
  his disciples to inspire.

2 God's Spirit is directing;
no more they sit expecting;
but forth to all the nation
they go with exultation;
  that which God in them has wrought
  fills their life and soul and thought,
  so their witness now can do
  work as great in others too.

3 O Lord of every nation,
fill us with inspiration!
We know our own unfitness,
yet would for you bear witness.
  By your Spirit now we raise
  to the heavenly Father praise:
  Holy Spirit, Father, Son,
  make us know you, ever one.

F. C. BURKITT (1864–1935) altd.*

329 *Lauds* 77 77

JOHN WILSON (1905–92)

1 There's a spirit in the air,
telling Christians everywhere:
'Praise the love that Christ revealed,
living, working in our world.'

2 Lose your shyness, find your tongue,
tell the world what God has done:
God in Christ has come to stay.
Live tomorrow's life today.

3 When believers break the bread,
when a hungry child is fed,
praise the love that Christ revealed,
living, working in our world.

4 Still the Spirit gives us light,
seeing wrong and setting right:
God in Christ has come to stay.
Live tomorrow's life today.

5 When a stranger's not alone,
where the homeless find a home,
praise the love that Christ revealed,
living, working in our world.

6 May the Spirit fill our praise,
guide our thoughts and change our ways:
God in Christ has come to stay.
Live tomorrow's life today.

7 There's a Spirit in the air,
calling people everywhere:
'Praise the love that Christ revealed,
living, working in our world.'

BRIAN WREN (1936–)

330

FIRST TUNE

Wicklow 86 84 Irish traditional melody (slightly adapted)

SECOND TUNE

St Cuthbert 86 84 J. B. DYKES (1823–76)

1 Our blest Redeemer, ere he breathed
his tender, last farewell,
a guide, a Comforter, bequeathed
with us to dwell.

2 He came in semblance of a dove,
with sheltering wings outspread,
the holy balm of peace and love
on earth to shed.

3 He came in tongues of living flame
to teach, convince, subdue;
all-powerful as the wind he came,
as viewless too.

4 He came sweet influence to impart,
a gracious, willing guest,
while he can find one humble heart
wherein to rest.

5 Spirit of purity and grace,
our weakness pitying see;
O make our hearts thy dwelling-place,
and worthier thee.

HARRIET AUBER (1773–1862)

CREATION'S RESPONSE TO GOD'S LOVE

THE GOSPEL : THE NEED FOR GOD

331 *Coburg (Aus tiefer Noth)* 87 87 887 — German hymn melody, 16th cent.

1 Out of the depths I cry to thee
with voice of lamentation;
Lord, turn a gracious ear to me,
and hear my supplication.
If thou shouldst be extreme to mark
each secret sin and misdeed dark,
O who could stand before thee?

2 To wash away the scarlet stain,
grace, grace alone availeth;
our works, alas! are all in vain;
and ev'n the best life faileth.
For none can glory in thy sight,
all must alike confess thy might,
and live alone by mercy.

3 Therefore my trust is in the Lord,
and not in mine own merit;
on him my soul shall rest, his word
upholds my fainting spirit.
His promised mercy is my fort,
my comfort and my sure support;
I wait for it with patience.

4 What though I wait the whole dark night,
until the dawn appeareth,
my heart still trusteth in his might;
it doubteth not, nor feareth.
So let us all, made new in heart,
born of the Spirit, do our part,
and wait till God appeareth.

5 Although our sin is great indeed,
God's mercies far exceed it;
his hand can give the help we need,
however much we need it.
He is the Shepherd of the sheep
who doth his Israel guard and keep,
and shall from sin redeem us.

MARTIN LUTHER (1483–1546)
tr. RICHARD MASSIE (1800–87)*

332 *Aberystwyth* 77 77 D

JOSEPH PARRY (1841–1903)

1 Jesus, lover of my soul,
   let me to thy bosom fly,
while the nearer waters roll,
   while the tempest still is high.
Hide me, O my Saviour, hide,
   till the storm of life is past;
safe into the haven guide,
   O receive my soul at last!

2 Other refuge have I none,
   hangs my helpless soul on thee;
leave, ah leave me not alone,
   still support and comfort me.
All my trust on thee is stayed,
   all my help from thee I bring;
cover my defenceless head
   with the shadow of thy wing.

3 Thou, O Christ, art all I want;
   more than all in thee I find;
raise the fallen, cheer the faint,
   heal the sick, and lead the blind.
Just and holy is thy name,
   I am all unrighteousness;
false and full of sin I am,
   thou art full of truth and grace.

4 Plenteous grace with thee is found,
grace to cover all my sin;
let the healing streams abound,
make and keep me pure within.
Thou of life the fountain art,
freely let me take of thee;
spring thou up within my heart,
rise to all eternity.

CHARLES WESLEY (1707–88)

333 *Lawes' Psalm XXXII* 66 66

HENRY LAWES (1596–1662)

1 My spirit longs for thee
within my troubled breast,
though I unworthy be
of so divine a guest.

2 Of so divine a guest
unworthy though I be,
yet has my heart no rest
unless it come from thee.

3 Unless it come from thee
in vain I look around;
in all that I can see
no rest is to be found.

4 No rest is to be found
but in thy blessèd love;
O let my wish be crowned,
and send it from above!

JOHN BYROM (1692–1763) altd.

334 *Dun Aluinn* 65 65 65 75 Irish traditional melody

1 Walking in a garden
at the close of day,
Adam tried to hide him
when he heard God say:
'Why are you so frightened,
why are you afraid?
You have brought the winter in,
made the flowers fade.'

2 Walking in a garden
where the Lord had gone,
three of the disciples,
Peter, James and John;
they were very weary,
could not keep awake,
while the Lord was kneeling there,
praying for their sake.

3 Walking in a garden
at the break of day,
Mary asked the gardener
where the body lay;
but he turned towards her,
smiled at her and said:
'Mary, spring is here to stay,
only death is dead.'

HILARY GREENWOOD (1929–)

335 *Albano* CM

VINCENT NOVELLO (1781–1861)

1 Heal us, Immanuel! Hear our prayer;
we wait to feel thy touch;
deep-wounded souls to thee repair,
and, Saviour, we are such.

2 Our faith is feeble, we confess;
we faintly trust thy word;
but wilt thou pity us the less?
Wilt thou forsake us, Lord?

3 Remember him who once applied
with trembling for relief:
'Lord, I believe!' with tears he cried,
'O help my unbelief!'

4 She, too, who touched thee in the press,
and healing virtue stole,
was answered: 'Daughter, go in peace,
thy faith has made thee whole'.

5 Concealed amid the gathering throng,
she would have shunned thy view
and, though her faith was firm and strong,
had strong misgivings too.

6 Like her, with hopes and fears we come
to touch thee, if we may;
O send us not despairing home,
send none unhealed away!

WILLIAM COWPER (1731–1800)*

336 *Eventide* 10 10 10 10

W. H. MONK (1823–89)

1 Abide with me; fast falls the eventide;
the darkness deepens; Lord, with me abide,
when other helpers fail, and comforts flee,
help of the helpless, O abide with me.

2 Swift to its close ebbs out life's little day;
earth's joys grow dim, its glories pass away;
change and decay in all around I see;
O thou who changest not, abide with me.

3 I need thy presence every passing hour;
what but thy grace can foil the tempter's power?
Who like thyself my guide and stay can be?
Through cloud and sunshine, O abide with me.

4 I fear no foe, with thee at hand to bless;
ills have no weight, and tears no bitterness.
Where is death's sting? where, grave, thy victory?
I triumph still, if thou abide with me.

5 Hold thou thy cross before my closing eyes;
shine through the gloom, and point me to the skies;
heaven's morning breaks, and earth's vain shadows flee;
in life, in death, O Lord, abide with me.

H. F. LYTE (1793–1847)

337 *Bedford* CM

WILLIAM WEALE (1696–1727)

1 O lift us up, strong Son of God;
restore our fallen race;
we who have marred your image shall
regain it through your grace.

2 The subtle serpent of our sin
ensnares our helpless feet;
the lifted serpent of your health
can make our souls complete.

3 And you, who came into the world
to take our human frame,
did not condemn our fallen state,
but took away our shame.

4 Your law is holy, just and good;
but still we fail to do
all that your gracious words require
to keep us close to you.

5 So lift us up, strong Son of God,
restore your fallen race;
we who have lost your image shall
regain it through your grace.

CYRIL G. HAMBLY (1931–)

338 *Zu meinem Herrn* 11 10 11 10 J. G. SCHICHT (1753–1823)

1 Stay with us, God, as longed-for peace eludes us;
stay with us if our health is undermined;
when no good comes and faithless hope deludes us,
when terror reigns and grief is unconfined.

2 When consequence on consequence of evil
brings dreadful judgement on the human race,
stay with us, God, through torment and upheaval,
defeat despair with your persistent grace.

3 Yet grant no easy answer, no conclusion
with which we might shrug off love's agony;
bring us with Christ through grief and disillusion,
fast-bound by faith to love's integrity.

4 Work out in us your love's determination
to bear your children's guilt and wickedness,
to harrow hell and harvest resurrection,
to forge creation's joy from wretchedness.

ALAN GAUNT (1935–)
after Jeremiah 8: 18–9: 3

339 *Abingdon* 88 88 88 ERIK ROUTLEY (1917–82)

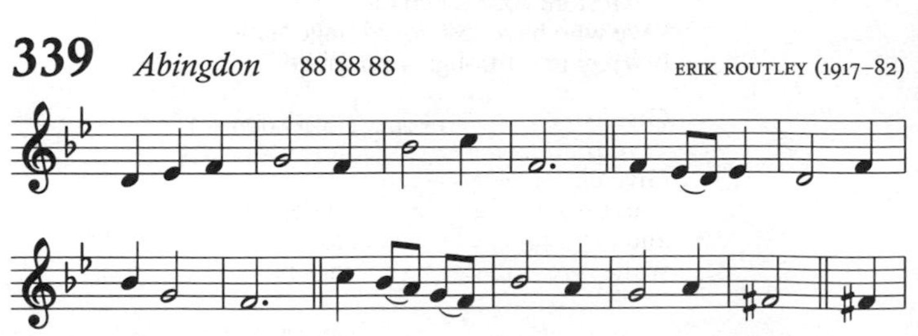

THE NEED FOR GOD

1 Great God, your love has called us here
as we, by love, for love were made.
Your living likeness still we bear,
though marred, dishonoured, disobeyed.
We come, with all our heart and mind
your call to hear, your love to find.

2 We come with self-inflicted pains
of broken trust and chosen wrong,
half-free, half-bound by inner chains,
by social forces swept along,
by powers and systems close confined
yet seeking hope for humankind.

3 Great God, in Christ you call our name
and then receive us as your own
not through some merit, right or claim
but by your gracious love alone.
We strain to glimpse your mercy-seat
and find you kneeling at our feet.

4 Then take the towel, and break the bread,
and humble us, and call us friends.
Suffer and serve till all are fed,
and show how grandly love intends
to work till all creation sings,
to fill all worlds, to crown all things.

5 Great God, in Christ you set us free
your life to live, your joy to share.
Give us your Spirit's liberty
to turn from guilt and dull despair
and offer all that faith can do
while love is making all things new.

BRIAN WREN (1936–)

340 *Lightcliffe* 10 10 10 10 10

PAUL BATEMAN (1954–)

1 I have no bucket, and the well is deep.
My thirst is endless, and my throat is dry.
I ask you, stranger, silent at my side,
can words refresh my longings if you speak?
I have no bucket, and the well is deep.

2 Can love unbar the strongrooms of the mind
and scour the tombs and warrens underground
for toys and treasures lost, or never found,
for all I cannot name, yet ache to find?
I have no bucket, and the well is deep.

3 Who are you, strange yet friendly at my side,
and can you see and judge, yet understand
my hidden self, and heal with wounded hands?
Are you the path, the gateway and the guide,
the keys, the living water, and the light?

4 Come break the rock, and bid the rivers flow
from deep unending wells of joy and worth,
for tears, for drinking, drowning and new birth,
and I shall find and give myself, and know
the keys, the living water, and the light.

BRIAN WREN (1936–)

341 *O amor quam ecstaticus (Coutances)* LM

French church melody
from Rouen *Antiphoner,* 1728

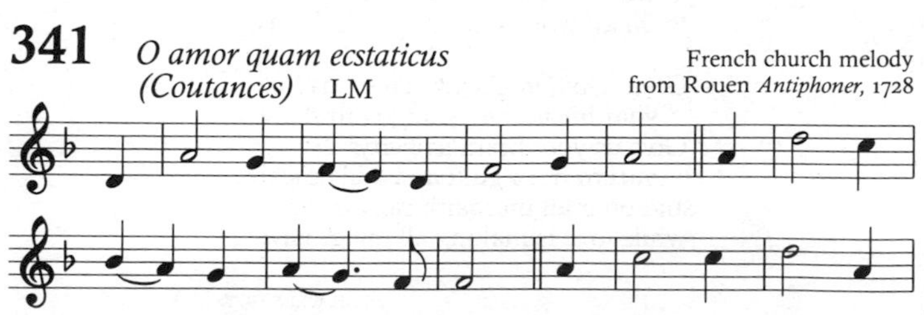

1 Our hunger cries from plenty, Lord:
for bread which does not turn to stone;
for peace the world can never give;
for truth unreached, for love unknown.

2 'Let all who hunger come to me!'
Christ's bread is life, his word is true;
our lives are grounded in that love
which is creating all things new.

3 Enlarge the boundaries of our love,
O life of God, so freely given,
till all whom hunger breaks are whole
through Christ, the broken bread of heaven.

COLIN THOMPSON (1945–)

342 *Holborn* 10 10 10 10

ERIC H. THIMAN (1900–75)

1 People draw near to God in their distress,
pleading for help and begging peace and bread,
rescue from guilt and sickness, nearly dead.
Christian or not, all come in helplessness.

2 People draw near to God in his distress,
find him rejected, homeless, without bread,
burdened with sin and weakness, nearly dead.
Christians stand with God in his wretchedness.

3 And God draws near to people in distress,
feeding their souls and bodies with his bread;
Christian or not, for both he's hanging dead,
forgiving, from the cross, their wickedness.

DIETRICH BONHOEFFER (1906–45)
tr. ALAN GAUNT (1935–)

343 *Fortunatus New* 87 87 77

CARL F. SCHALK (1929–)

1 When, O God, our faith is tested
and our hope is undermined;
when our love of living shrivels
and we feel bereft and drained,
then we turn to you and cry
for your answer to our 'why?'.

2 With emotions taut to breaking,
hearts with hurt and havoc frayed,
reason by remorse diminished,
souls distraught as if betrayed,
God of bleakness and abyss,
why have you forsaken us?

3 As we question and accuse you,
out of depths of being tried,
could it be, God! that in weakness
you yourself are crucified?
Are you with us in our grief?
Help us in our unbelief!

FRED KAAN (1929–)

344 *Rhuddlan* 87 87 87

Welsh traditional melody

1 God of grace and God of glory,
on thy people pour thy power;
crown thine ancient Church's story;
bring her bud to glorious flower.
Grant us wisdom,
grant us courage,
for the facing of this hour.

2 Lo! the hosts of evil round us
scorn thy Christ, assail his ways!
From the fears that long have bound us,
free our hearts to faith and praise.
Grant us wisdom,
grant us courage,
for the living of these days.

3 Cure thy children's warring madness;
bend our pride to thy control;
shame our wanton, selfish gladness,
rich in things and poor in soul.
Grant us wisdom,
grant us courage,
lest we miss thy kingdom's goal.

4 Save us from weak resignation
to the evils we deplore;
let the gift of thy salvation
be our glory evermore.
Grant us wisdom,
grant us courage,
serving thee whom we adore.

H. E. FOSDICK (1878–1969) altd.

345 *Cwm Rhondda*

87 87 47 extended

JOHN HUGHES (Pontypridd) (1873–1932)

1 Arglwydd, arwain drwy'r anialwch
fi, bererin gwael ei wedd;
nad oes ynof nerth na bywyd,
fel yn gorwedd yn y bedd;
Hollalluog
ydyw'r un a'm cwyd i'r lan.

2 Agor y ffynhonnau melys
sydd yn tarddu o'r Graig i maes;
'r hyd yr anial mawr canlyned
afon iachawdwriaeth gras:
rho im' hynny—
dim i mi ond dy fwynhau.

3 Pan fwy'n myned trwy'r Iorddonen,
angau creulon yn ei rym,
aethost trywddi gynt dy hunan,
pam yr ofnaf bellach ddim?
Buddogoliaeth!
Gwna im' weiddi yn y llif.

WILLIAM WILLIAMS, Pantycelyn (1717–91)

1 Guide me, O thou great Jehovah,
pilgrim through this barren land;
I am weak, but thou art mighty,
hold me with thy powerful hand:
bread of heaven,
feed me now and evermore.

2 Open thou the crystal fountain
whence the healing stream doth flow;
let the fiery, cloudy pillar
lead me all my journey through:
strong deliverer,
be thou still my strength and shield.

3 When I tread the verge of Jordan,
bid my anxious fears subside;
death of death, and hell's destruction,
land me safe on Canaan's side:
songs of praises,
I will ever give to thee.

v. 1 tr. PETER WILLIAMS (1722–96) altd.
vv. 2–3 tr. WILLIAM WILLIAMS
(or JOHN WILLIAMS, 1754–1828) altd.

346 *King's Lynn* 76 76 D

English traditional melody

Alternative tune: LLANGLOFFAN, no. 604.

1 O God of earth and altar,
bow down and hear our cry,
our earthly rulers falter,
our people drift and die;
the walls of gold entomb us,
the swords of scorn divide,
take not thy thunder from us,
but take away our pride.

2 From all that terror teaches,
from lies of tongue and pen,
from all the easy speeches
that comfort cruel men,
from sale and profanation
of honour and the sword,
from sleep and from damnation,
deliver us, good Lord!

3 Tie in a living tether
the prince and priest and thrall,
bind all our lives together,
smite us and save us all;
in ire and exultation
aflame with faith, and free,
lift up a living nation,
a single sword to thee.

G. K. CHESTERTON (1874–1936)

347 *Be still* 87 87 (Iambic)

JOHN BELL (1949–)

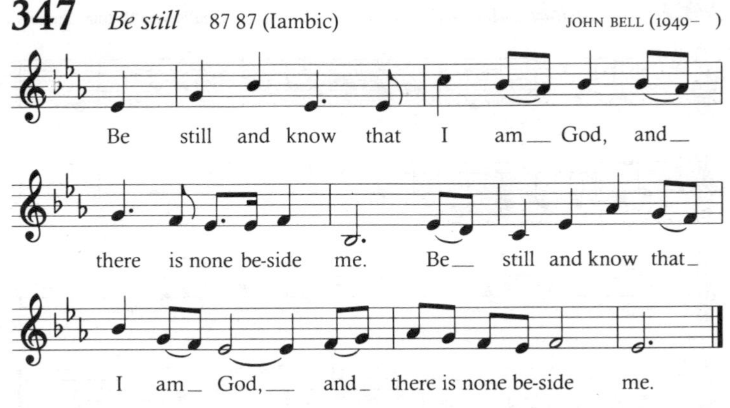

Psalm 46: 10 and Isaiah 45: 6
adpt. Iona Community, 1988

348 *Savannah* 77 77

Melody from MS *Choralbuch*, Herrnhut, *c.*1740, as given in J. WESLEY'S *Foundery Collection*, 1742

Alternative tune: CANTERBURY (SONG 13), no. 218.

1 Hark, my soul! it is the Lord:
'tis thy Saviour, hear his word;
Jesus speaks, and speaks to thee,
'Say, poor sinner, lov'st thou me?

2 'I delivered thee when bound,
and, when bleeding, healed thy wound;
sought thee wandering, set thee right,
turned thy darkness into light.

3 'Can a woman's tender care
cease toward the child she bare?
Yes, she may forgetful be,
yet will I remember thee.

4 'Mine is an unchanging love,
higher than the heights above,
deeper than the depths beneath,
free and faithful, strong as death.

5 'Thou shalt see my glory soon,
when the work of grace is done;
partner of my throne shalt be;
say, poor sinner, lov'st thou me?'

6 Lord, it is my chief complaint,
that my love is weak and faint;
yet I love thee, and adore;
O for grace to love thee more!

WILLIAM COWPER (1731–1800)

349 *Kingsfold* DCM

English traditional melody

1 I heard the voice of Jesus say,
'Come unto me and rest;
lay down, O weary one, lay down
your head upon my breast.'
I came to Jesus as I was,
forlorn and faint and sad;
I found in him a resting-place,
and he has made me glad.

2 I heard the voice of Jesus say,
'Behold, I freely give
the living water; thirsty one,
stoop down, and drink, and live.'
I came to Jesus, and I drank
of that life-giving stream;
my thirst was quenched, my soul revived,
and now I live in him.

3 I heard the voice of Jesus say,
'I am this dark world's light;
look unto me, your morn shall rise,
and all your day be bright.'
I looked to Jesus, and I found
in him my star, my sun;
and in that light of life I'll walk,
till travelling days are done.

H. BONAR (1808–89) altd.*

350 *Catherine* 77 77

RICHARD CONNOLLY (1927–)

1 God my Father, loving me,
gave his Son my friend to be:
gave his Son my form to take,
and to suffer for my sake.

2 Jesus still remains the same
as in days of old he came:
as my brother by my side
still he seeks my steps to guide.

3 How can I repay your love,
Lord of all the hosts above?
What have I, a child, to bring
unto you, my heavenly King?

4 I have but myself to give:
let me to your glory live
let me follow day by day
where you guide me in the way.

G. W. BRIGGS (1875–1959) altd.*

351 *St Magnus* CM

Probably by JEREMIAH CLARKE (*c.*1673–1707)

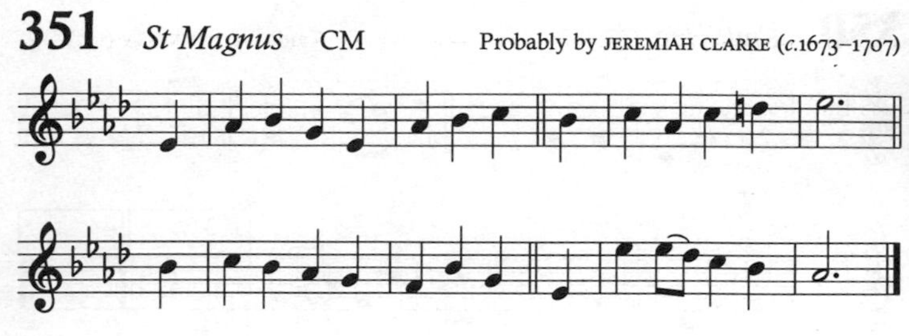

1 Father of Jesus Christ, my Lord,
my Saviour, and my Head,
I trust in thee, whose powerful word
hath raised him from the dead.

2 It was for my offence he died,
he rose again for me,
fully and freely justified,
that I might live to thee.

3 Faith in thy power thou seest I have,
for thou this faith hast wrought;
dead souls thou callest from the grave,
and speakest worlds from naught.

4 In hope, against all human hope,
self-desperate, I believe;
thy quickening word shall raise me up,
thou shalt thy Spirit give.

5 Faith, mighty faith, the promise sees,
and looks to that alone,
laughs at impossibilities,
and cries: 'It shall be done!'

CHARLES WESLEY (1707–88)*

352 *Come, my Way* 77 77

ALEXANDER BRENT SMITH (1889–1950)

1 Come my Way, my Truth, my Life:
such a Way, as gives us breath:
such a Truth, as ends all strife:
such a Life, as killeth death.

2 Come, my Light, my Feast, my Strength:
such a Light, as shows a feast:
such a Feast, as mends in length:
such a Strength, as makes his guest.

3 Come, my Joy, my Love, my Heart:
such a Joy, as none can move:
such a Love, as none can part:
such a Heart, as joys in love.

GEORGE HERBERT (1593–1633)

'mends in length' in v. 2 line 3 means 'gets better and better as it goes on' (see John 2: 10).

353 *Sussex* 87 87 (Trochaic)

English traditional melody
adpt. R. VAUGHAN WILLIAMS (1872–1958)

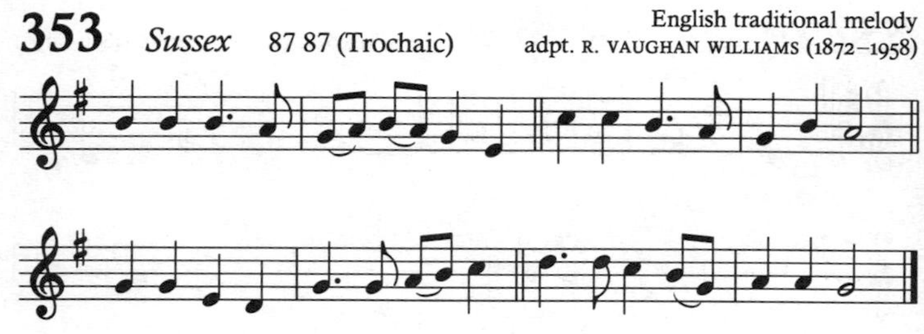

1 There's a wideness in God's mercy
like the wideness of the sea;
there's a kindness in his justice
which is more than liberty.

2 There is plentiful redemption
in the blood that has been shed;
there is joy for all the members
in the sorrows of the Head.

3 There is grace enough for thousands
of new worlds as great as this;
there is room for fresh creations
in the Lord's unfathomed bliss.

4 For the love of God is broader
than the measures of our mind;
and the heart of the Eternal
is most wonderfully kind.

5 But we make his love too narrow
by false limits of our own;
and we magnify his strictness
with a zeal he will not own.

6 If our love were but more simple
we should take him at his word;
and our lives would be illumined
by the glory of the Lord.

F. W. FABER (1814–63) altd.*

354 *Sunset* 98 98

G. G. STOCKS (1877–1960)

1 Come, living God, when least expected,
when minds are dull and hearts are cold,
through sharpening word and warm affection
revealing truth as yet untold.

2 Break from the tomb in which we hide you
to speak again in startling ways;
break through the words in which we bind you
to resurrect our lifeless praise.

3 Come now, as once you came to Moses
within the bush alive with flame;
or to Elijah on the mountain,
by silence pressing home your claim.

4 So, let our minds be sharp to read you
in sight or sound or printed page,
and let us greet you in our neighbours,
in ardent youth or mellow age.

5 Then, through our gloom, your Son will meet us
as vivid truth and living Lord,
exploding doubt and disillusion
to scatter hope and joy abroad.

6 And we will share his radiant brightness,
and, blazing through the dread of night,
illuminate by love and reason,
for those in darkness, faith's delight.

ALAN GAUNT (1935–)

355 *Cross of Jesus* 87 87 (Trochaic) JOHN STAINER (1840–1901)

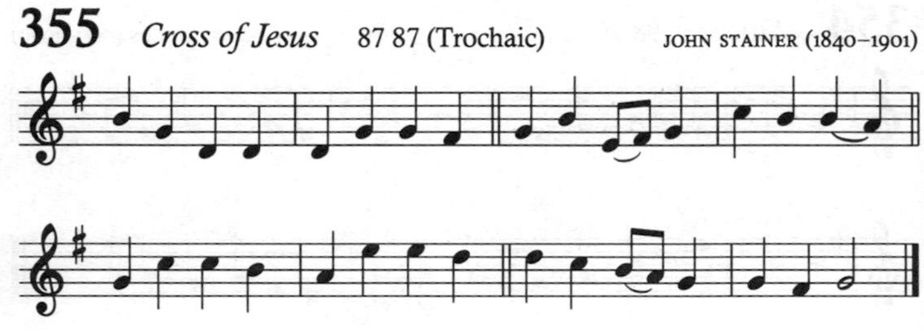

1 Jesus calls us! O'er the tumult
of our life's wild, restless sea,
day by day his voice is sounding,
saying, 'Christian, follow me':

2 as, of old, apostles heard it
by the Galilean lake,
turned from home, and toil, and kindred,
leaving all for his dear sake.

3 Jesus calls us from the worship
of the vain world's golden store,
from each idol that would keep us,
saying, 'Christian, love me more'.

4 In our joys and in our sorrows,
days of toil and hours of ease,
still he calls, in cares and pleasures,
'Christian, love me more than these.'

5 Jesus calls us! By your mercies,
Saviour, make us hear your call,
give our hearts to your obedience,
serve and love you best of all.

CECIL FRANCES ALEXANDER (1818–95) altd.*

356 *Nun danket all* CM

Praxis Pietatis Melica, 1647

1 O Jesus, King most wonderful,
thou conqueror renowned,
thou sweetness most ineffable,
in whom all joys are found!

2 Jesus, the very thought of thee
with sweetness fills the breast;
but sweeter far thy face to see,
and in thy presence rest.

3 O hope of every contrite heart,
O joy of all the meek,
to those who fall how kind thou art,
how good to those who seek!

4 But what to those who find? Ah, this
nor tongue nor pen can show;
the love of Jesus, what it is
none but his loved ones know.

5 When once thou visitest the heart
then truth begins to shine,
then earthly vanities depart,
then kindles love divine.

6 Thee may our tongues for ever bless,
thee may we love alone,
and ever in our lives express
the image of thine own.

7 Jesus, our only joy be thou,
as thou our prize wilt be;
Jesus, be thou our glory now,
and through eternity.

Latin, 12th cent.
tr. EDWARD CASWALL (1814–78) altd.

357 *All Souls* 10 10 10 10 J. YOAKLEY (1860–1932)

1 My God, I love thee; not that my poor love
may win me entrance to thy heaven above,
nor yet that strangers to thy love must know
the bitterness of everlasting woe.

2 But, Jesus, I am thine and thou art mine;
clasped in the safety of thine arms divine,
who on the cruel cross for me hast borne
the nails, the spear, and cold unpitying scorn.

3 No thought can fathom, and no tongue express
thy griefs, thy toils, thine anguish measureless,
thy death, O Lamb of God, the undefiled;
and all for me, thy wayward, sinful child.

4 How can I choose but love thee, God's dear Son,
O Jesus, loveliest and most loving one!
Were there no heav'n to gain, no hell to flee,
for what thou art alone I must love thee.

5 Not for the hope of glory or reward,
but even as thyself hast loved me, Lord,
I love thee, and will love thee and adore,
who art my King, my God, for evermore.

17th-cent. Latin, based on a 16th-cent. Spanish poem
tr. E. H. BICKERSTETH (1825–1906)*

358 *Breslau* LM

Modern form of melody
from *As Hymnodus Sacer*, Leipzig, 1625

1 Lord, I was blind: I could not see
in your marred visage any grace;
but now the beauty of your face
in radiant vision dawns on me.

2 Lord, I was deaf: I could not hear
the thrilling music of your voice;
but now I hear you and rejoice,
and all your uttered words are dear.

3 Lord, I was dumb: I could not speak
the grace and glory of your name;
but now, as touched with living flame,
my eager lips the silence break.

4 Lord, I was dead: I could not stir
my lifeless soul to come to you;
but now restored, my life made new,
I rise from sin's dark sepulchre.

5 Lord, you have made the blind to see,
the deaf to hear, the dumb to speak,
the dead to live; and now I break
the chains of my captivity.

WILLIAM T. MATSON (1833–99) altd.*

359 *Festus* LM

Adpt. from FREYLINGHAUSEN'S *Gesangbuch*, 1704

1 O happy day that fixed my choice
on thee my Saviour and my God:
well may this glowing heart rejoice,
and tell its raptures all abroad.

2 O happy bond, that seals my vows
to him who merits all my love:
let cheerful anthems fill his house,
while to that sacred shrine I move.

3 'Tis done, the great transaction's done;
I am my Lord's, and he is mine;
he drew me, and I followed on,
charmed to confess the voice divine.

4 Now rest, my long-divided heart,
fixed on this blissful centre, rest;
with ashes who would grudge to part,
when called on angels' bread to feast?

5 High heaven, that heard the solemn vow,
that vow renewed shall daily hear;
till in life's latest hour I bow,
and bless in death a bond so dear.

PHILIP DODDRIDGE (1702–51) altd.

In verse 4 the author may have been thinking of Psalm 102: 9 and Psalm 78: 25.

360 *Ebenezer* 87 87 D

T. J. WILLIAMS (1869–1944)

1 Come, thou fount of every blessing;
tune my heart to sing thy grace:
streams of mercy, never ceasing,
call for songs of loudest praise.
Teach me some melodious measure,
sung by flaming tongues above;
on the mountain-top I'll treasure
signs of God's unchanging love.

2 Here I place mine Ebenezer:
'Hither, by thy help, I'm come';
and I hope, by thy good pleasure,
safely to arrive at home.
Jesus sought me when a stranger
wandering from the fold of God;
he, to rescue me from danger,
interposed his precious blood.

3 O to grace how great a debtor
daily I'm constrained to be!
Let that grace, Lord, like a fetter
bind my wandering heart to thee.
Prone to wander, Lord, I feel it,
prone to leave the God I love;
take my heart, O take and seal it,
seal it from thy courts above.

ROBERT ROBINSON (1735–90) altd.*

361 *Quedgeley* 76 76 (Trochaic) J. DYKES BOWER (1905–81)

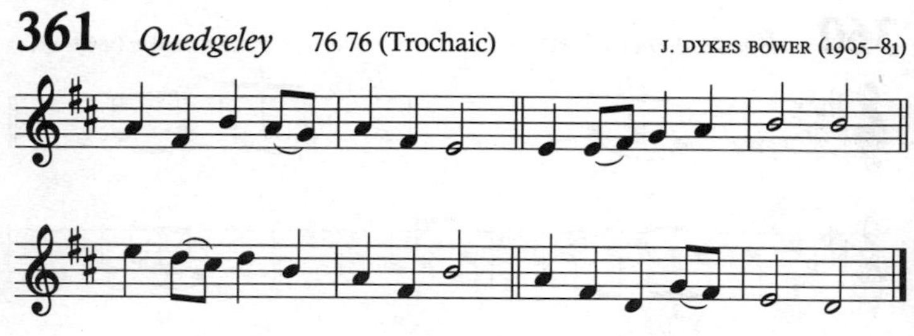

1 Come, Lord, to our souls come down,
through the gospel speaking;
let your words, your cross and crown,
lighten all our seeking.

2 Drive out darkness from the heart,
banish pride and blindness;
plant in every inward part
truthfulness and kindness.

3 Eyes be open, spirits stirred,
minds new truth receiving;
lead us, Lord, by your own Word;
strengthen our believing.

H. C. A. GAUNT (1902–83)*

362 *Wych Cross* 88 88 88

ERIK ROUTLEY (1917–82)

1 Lord Jesus, in the days of old
  two walked with thee in waning light;
and love's blind instinct made them bold
  to crave thy presence through the night.
As night descends, we too would pray,
O leave us not at close of day.

2 Did not their hearts within them burn?
  and though their Lord they failed to know,
did not their spirits in them yearn?
  They could not let the Stranger go.
Much more must we who know thee pray,
O leave us not at close of day.

3 Day is far spent, and night is nigh;
  stay with us, Saviour, through the night;
talk with us, touch us tenderly,
  lead us to peace, to rest, to light;
dispel our darkness with thy face,
radiant with resurrection grace.

4 Nor this night only, blessed Lord,
  we, every day and every hour,
would walk with thee Emmaus-ward
  to hear thy voice of love and power;
and every night would by thy side
look, listen, and be satisfied.

J. A. NOBLE (1844–96)*

363 *Southwell* SM

Melody from DAMON'S *The Psalmes of David*, 1579 (altd.)

1 Lord Jesus, think on me
and purge away my sin;
from earthbound passions set me free,
and make me pure within.

2 Lord Jesus, think on me
with care and woe oppressed;
let me your loving servant be,
and taste your promised rest.

3 Lord Jesus, think on me,
amid the bitter strife;
through all my pain and misery
become my health and life.

4 Lord Jesus, think on me,
nor let me go astray;
through darkness and perplexity
point out the heavenly way.

5 Lord Jesus, think on me,
when tempests round me roll,
when onward comes the enemy,
O Saviour, guard my soul.

6 Lord Jesus, think on me,
that, when the flood is past,
I may the eternal brightness see,
and share your joy at last.

SYNESIUS OF CYRENE (*c.*375–430)
tr. A. W. CHATFIELD (1808–96) altd.*

364 *Saffron Walden* 888 6 A. H. BROWN (1830–1926)

1 Just as I am, without one plea
but that thy blood was shed for me,
and that thou bidst me come to thee,
O Lamb of God, I come.

2 Just as I am, though tossed about
with many a conflict, many a doubt,
fightings and fears within, without,
O Lamb of God, I come.

3 Just as I am, poor, wretched, blind;
sight, riches, healing of the mind,
yea, all I need, in thee to find,
O Lamb of God, I come.

4 Just as I am, thou wilt receive,
wilt welcome, pardon, cleanse, relieve,
because thy promise I believe,
O Lamb of God, I come.

5 Just as I am, thy love unknown
has broken every barrier down;
now to be thine, yea, thine alone,
O Lamb of God, I come.

6 Just as I am, of that free love
the breadth, length, depth and height to prove,
here for a season, then above,
O Lamb of God, I come.

CHARLOTTE ELLIOTT (1789–1871)

365 *Petra* 77 77 77

RICHARD REDHEAD (1820–1901)
using the shape of a Spanish *Tantum Ergo*

A Living and Dying Prayer for the
Holiest Believer in the World

1 Rock of ages, cleft for me,
let me hide myself in thee;
let the water and the blood,
from thy riven side which flowed,
be of sin the double cure,
cleanse me from its guilt and power.

2 Not the labours of my hands
can fulfil thy law's demands;
could my zeal no respite know,
could my tears for ever flow,
all for sin could not atone;
thou must save, and thou alone.

3 Nothing in my hand I bring;
simply to thy cross I cling;
naked, come to thee for dress;
helpless, look to thee for grace;
foul, I to the fountain fly;
wash me, Saviour, or I die.

4 While I draw this fleeting breath,
when mine eyes shall close in death,
when I soar through tracts unknown,
see thee on thy judgement-throne;
Rock of ages, cleft for me,
let me hide myself in thee.

AUGUSTUS M. TOPLADY (1740–78) altd.

366 *Abingdon* 88 88 88

ERIK ROUTLEY (1917–82)

Free Grace

1 And can it be that I should gain
an interest in the Saviour's blood?
Died he for me, who caused his pain;
for me, who him to death pursued?
Amazing love! How can it be
that thou, my God, shouldst die for me?

2 'Tis mystery all: the Immortal dies!
Who can explore his strange design?
In vain the first-born seraph tries
to sound the depths of love divine.
'Tis mercy all! Let earth adore,
let angel-minds enquire no more.

3 He left his Father's throne above—
so free, so infinite his grace—
emptied himself of all but love,
and bled for Adam's helpless race.
'Tis mercy all, immense and free;
for, O my God, it found out me!

4 Long my imprisoned spirit lay
fast bound in sin and nature's night;
thine eye diffused a quickening ray—
I woke, the dungeon flamed with light,
my chains fell off, my heart was free,
I rose, went forth, and followed thee.

5 No condemnation now I dread;
Jesus, and all in him, is mine!
Alive in him, my living Head,
and clothed in righteousness divine,
bold I approach the eternal throne,
and claim the crown, through Christ, my own.

CHARLES WESLEY (1707–88)

367 *Helvetia* Irregular Swiss folk-tune

1 I want to walk with Jesus Christ
all the days I live of this life on earth,
to give to him complete control
of body and of soul:

Follow him, follow him, yield your life to him,
he has conquered death, he is King of kings.
Accept the joy which he gives to those
who yield their lives to him.

2 I want to learn to speak to him,
to pray to him, confess my sin,
to open my life and let him in,
for joy will then be mine:

3 I want to learn to read his word,
for this is how I know the way,
to live my life as pleases him,
in holiness and joy:

4 I want to learn to speak of him;
my life must show that he lives in me,
my deeds, my thoughts, my words must speak
of all his love for me:

5 O holy Spirit of the Lord,
enter now into this heart of mine,
take full control of my selfish will
and make me wholly thine:

C. SIMMONDS, 1964*

368 *Quest* 10 10 10 6 BERNARD S. MASSEY (1927–)

1 I sought the Lord, and afterward I knew
he moved my soul to seek him, seeking me;
it was not I that found, O Saviour true;
no, I was found by thee.

2 Thou didst reach forth thy hand and mine enfold;
I walked and sank not on the storm-vexed sea;
'twas not so much that love on thee took hold
as thou, dear Lord, on me.

3 I find, I walk, I love, but O the whole
of love is but my answer, Lord, to thee!
For thou wast long beforehand with my soul;
thou always lovedst me.

Anon. (*c.*1880)*

369 *Llef* LM

G. H. JONES (1849–1919)

1 No more, my God, I boast no more
of all the duties I have done;
I quit the hopes I held before,
to trust the merits of your Son.

2 Now, for the love I bear his name,
what was my gain I count my loss;
my former pride I call my shame,
and nail my glory to his cross.

3 Yes, and I must and will esteem
all things but loss for Jesus' sake;
O may my soul be found in him,
and of his righteousness partake.

4 The best obedience of my hands
dares not appear before your throne;
but faith can answer your demands
by pleading what my Lord has done.

ISAAC WATTS (1674–1748)*

370 *From strength to strength* DSM

E. W. NAYLOR (1867–1934)

1 Soldiers of Christ! arise,
and put your armour on,
strong in the strength which God supplies
through his eternal Son;
strong in the Lord of hosts,
and in his mighty power;
who in the strength of Jesus trusts
is more than conqueror.

2 Stand, then, in his great might,
with all his strength endued;
and take, to arm you for the fight,
the panoply of God.
To keep your armour bright
attend with constant care,
still walking in your Captain's sight,
and watching unto prayer.

3 From strength to strength go on;
wrestle, and fight, and pray;
tread all the powers of darkness down,
and win the well-fought day,—
that, having all things done,
and all your conflicts passed,
ye may o'ercome through Christ alone,
and stand complete at last.

CHARLES WESLEY (1707–88) altd.

371 *St Bees* 77 77

J. B. DYKES (1823–76)

1 Take my life, and let it be
consecrated, Lord, to thee;
take my moments and my days,
let them flow in ceaseless praise.

2 Take my hands, and let them move
at the impulse of thy love;
take my feet, and let them be
swift and beautiful for thee.

3 Take my voice, and let me sing
always, only, for my King;
take my lips, and let them be
filled with messages from thee.

4 Take my silver and my gold,
not a mite would I withhold;
take my intellect, and use
every power as thou shalt choose.

5 Take my will, and make it thine;
it shall be no longer mine;
take my heart, it is thine own;
it shall be thy royal throne.

6 Take my love, my Lord, I pour
at thy feet its treasure-store;
take myself, and I will be
ever, only, all for thee.

FRANCES RIDLEY HAVERGAL (1836–79)

372 *Cornwall* 88 6 88 6

S. S. WESLEY (1810–76)

1 O love divine, how sweet thou art!
When shall I find my longing heart
all taken up by thee?
I thirst, I faint, and die to prove
the greatness of redeeming love,
the love of Christ to me.

2 Stronger his love than death or hell,
its riches are unsearchable;
the angels in their light
desire in vain its depths to see,
they cannot reach the mystery,
the length, the breadth, and height.

3 God only knows the love of God;
O that it now were shed abroad
in this poor stony heart!
For love I sigh, for love I pine;
this only portion, Lord, be mine,
be mine this better part!

CHARLES WESLEY (1707–88)*

373 *Living Lord* 4 55 3 888 3

PATRICK APPLEFORD (1925–)

1 Lord Jesus Christ,
you have come to us,
you are one with us,
Mary's Son—
cleansing our souls from all their sin,
pouring your love and goodness in;
Jesus, our love for you we sing,
living Lord.

2 Lord Jesus Christ,
now and every day
teach us how to pray,
Son of God.
You have commanded us to do
this, in remembrance, Lord, of you;
into our lives your power breaks through,
living Lord.

3 Lord Jesus Christ,
you have come to us,
born as one of us,
Mary's Son—
led out to die on Calvary,
risen from death to set us free;
living Lord Jesus, help us see
you are Lord.

4 Lord Jesus Christ,
we would come to you,
live our lives for you,
Son of God;
all your commands we know are true,
your many gifts will make us new;
into our lives your power breaks through,
living Lord.

PATRICK APPLEFORD (1925–) altd.

374 *Intercessor* 11 10 11 10 C. H. H. PARRY (1848–1918)

1 O Christ, our Lord, we meet here as your people,
and pray that we may now accept your grace:
forgive us when we seek an earthly kingdom
in which we hope to find an honoured place.

2 Forgive us for our arrogant assumptions
that we alone have found Christ's holy way;
forgive us for the cowardly evasions
that modify your challenge to our day.

3 Forgive us for the mixture of our motives
when we are confident our love is pure;
forgive us for our unforgiving judgements
when of the Father's will we sound so sure.

4 Forgive us, Lord, for all our wilful blindness
to human suff'ring and to human need;
forgive us for our casual unkindness,
the hasty word and the begrudging deed.

5 And in forgiving grant us of your Spirit
the grace to lose our selves, and in the loss
to find redemption through a true devotion
that dares reflect the passion of your cross.

IAN ALEXANDER (1916–)*

375 *In my life, Lord*

BOB KILPATRICK (1952–)

1 In my life, Lord, be glorified, be glorified;
in my life, Lord, be glorified today.

2 In your Church, Lord, be glorified, be glorified;
in your Church, Lord, be glorified today.

3 In your world, Lord, be glorified, be glorified;
in your world, Lord, be glorified today.

BOB KILPATRICK (1952–) and compilers

376 *Richmond* CM

Melody by THOMAS HAWEIS (1734–1820) as adpt. by SAMUEL WEBBE the younger (1768–1843)

1 This is the day the Lord has made;
he calls the hours his own;
let heaven rejoice, let earth be glad,
and praise surround the throne.

2 Today he rose and left the dead,
and Satan's empire fell;
today the saints his triumphs spread,
and all his wonders tell.

3 Hosanna to the anointed King,
to David's holy Son!
Help us, O Lord; descend and bring
salvation from your throne.

4 Blest be the Lord: let us proclaim
his messages of grace;
who comes, in God his Father's name,
to save our sinful race.

5 Hosanna in the highest strains
the Church on earth can raise;
the highest heavens in which he reigns
shall give him nobler praise.

Psalm 118; Part 4 (based on vv. 24, 26) of para. by ISAAC WATTS (1674–1748)*

377 *The Lord's Day*

LES GARRETT (1944–)

1 This is the day,
    this is the day that the Lord has made,
        that the Lord has made;
  we will rejoice,
    we will rejoice and be glad in it,
        and be glad in it.
    This is the day that the Lord has made;
        we will rejoice and be glad in it.
  This is the day,
    this is the day that the Lord has made.

2 This is the day,
    this is the day when he rose again,
        when he rose again;
  we will rejoice,
    we will rejoice and be glad in it,
        and be glad in it.
    This is the day when he rose again;
        we will rejoice and be glad in it.
  This is the day,
    this is the day when he rose again.

3 This is the day,
    this is the day when the Spirit came,
        when the Spirit came;
  we will rejoice,
    we will rejoice and be glad in it,
        and be glad in it.
    This is the day when the Spirit came;
        we will rejoice and be glad in it.
  This is the day,
    this is the day when the Spirit came.

Psalm 118: 24 adpt. LES GARRETT (1944–)

378 *Morning Hymn* LM

F. H. BARTHÉLEMON (1741–1808)

1 Awake, my soul, and with the sun
thy daily stage of duty run;
shake off dull sloth, and joyful rise
to pay thy morning sacrifice.

2 By influence of the light divine
let thine own light to others shine;
reflect all heaven's propitious rays
in ardent love and cheerful praise.

3 Wake, and lift up thyself, my heart,
and with the angels bear thy part,
who all night long unwearied sing
high praise to the eternal King.

4 Lord, I my vows to thee renew;
disperse my sins as morning dew,
grant my first springs of thought and will,
and with thyself my spirit fill.

5 Direct, control, suggest this day
all I design, or do, or say;
that all my powers, with all their might,
in thy sole glory may unite.

6 Praise God, from whom all blessings flow.
praise him, all creatures here below,
praise him above, ye heavenly host,
praise Father, Son, and Holy Ghost.

THOMAS KEN (1637–1711)

379 *Carlisle* SM

CHARLES LOCKHART (1745–1815)

1 Awake and sing the song
of Moses and the Lamb;
wake every heart and every tongue
to praise the Saviour's name.

2 Sing of his dying love;
sing of his rising power;
sing how he intercedes above
for those whose sins he bore.

3 Sing, till we feel our hearts
ascending with our tongues;
sing, till the love of sin departs,
and grace inspires our songs.

4 Ye pilgrims on the road
to Zion's city, sing:
rejoice ye in the Lamb of God,
in Christ the eternal King.

5 Soon shall we hear him say,
ye blessèd children, come;
soon will he call us hence away,
and take his wanderers home.

6 There shall each raptured tongue
his endless praise proclaim,
and sing in sweeter notes the song
of Moses and the Lamb.

WILLIAM HAMMOND (1719–83)
altd. GEORGE WHITEFIELD, 1753
MARTIN MADAN, 1760
AUGUSTUS TOPLADY, 1776
W. J. HALL, 1836
and others

380 *Ratisbon* 77 77 77

Melody from WERNER'S *Choralbuch*, Leipzig, 1815

1 Christ, whose glory fills the skies,
Christ, the true, the only Light,
Sun of Righteousness, arise,
triumph o'er the shades of night;
Dayspring from on high, be near;
Daystar, in my heart appear.

2 Dark and cheerless is the morn
unaccompanied by thee;
joyless is the day's return,
till thy mercy's beams I see,
till they inward light impart,
glad my eyes, and warm my heart.

3 Visit then this soul of mine,
pierce the gloom of sin and grief;
fill me, radiancy divine,
scatter all my unbelief;
more and more thyself display,
shining to the perfect day.

CHARLES WESLEY (1707–88)

381 *Cross Deep* LM

BARRY ROSE (1934–)

1 Come, dearest Lord, descend and dwell
by faith and love in every breast;
then shall we know and taste and feel
the joys that cannot be expressed.

2 Come, fill our hearts with inward strength,
make our enlargèd souls possess
and learn the height and breadth and length
of thine unmeasurable grace.

3 Now to the God whose power can do
more than our thoughts or wishes know,
be everlasting honours done
by all the Church, through Christ his Son.

ISAAC WATTS (1674–1748)

382 *Nativity* CM

H. LAHEE (1826–1912)

1 Come, let us join our cheerful songs
with angels round the throne;
ten thousand thousand are their tongues,
but all their joys are one.

2 Worthy the Lamb that died, they cry,
to be exalted thus:
worthy the Lamb, our lips reply,
for he was slain for us.

3 Jesus is worthy to receive
honour and power divine;
and blessings more than we can give
be, Lord, for ever thine.

4 Let all the hosts of heaven combine
with air and earth and sea,
to lift in glorious songs divine
their endless praise to thee.

5 Let all creation join in one,
to bless the sacred name
of him that sits upon the throne,
and to adore the Lamb.

ISAAC WATTS (1674–1748)*

383 *St Mawes* 88 88 88 WALTER K. STANTON (1891–1978)

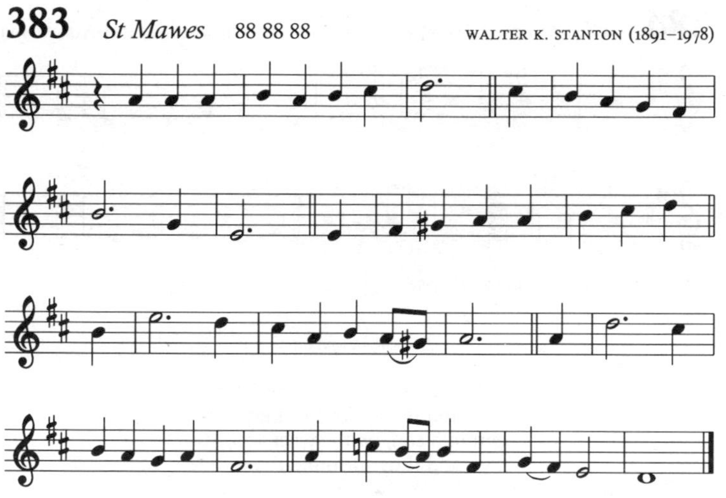

1 Come, let us with our Lord arise,
our Lord, who made both earth and skies;
who died to save the world he made,
and rose triumphant from the dead;
he rose, the Prince of life and peace,
and stamped the day for ever his.

2 This is the day the Lord has made,
that all may see his love displayed,
may feel his resurrection's power,
and rise again to fall no more,
in perfect righteousness renewed,
and filled with all the life of God.

3 Then let us render him his own,
with solemn prayer approach the throne,
with meekness hear the gospel word,
with thanks his dying love record;
our joyful hearts and voices raise,
and fill his courts with songs of praise.

CHARLES WESLEY (1707–88) altd.

384 *Windermere* SM

ARTHUR SOMERVELL (1863–1937)

Alternative tune: ST MICHAEL, no. 455.

Heavenly Joy on Earth

1 Come, we that love the Lord,
and let our joys be known;
join in a song with sweet accord,
and thus surround the throne.

2 Let those refuse to sing
that never knew our God;
but children of the heavenly King
may speak their joys abroad.

3 For we by grace have found
glory begun below;
celestial fruits on earthly ground
from faith and hope may grow.

4 The hill of Zion yields
a thousand sacred sweets,
before we reach the heavenly fields
or walk the golden streets.

5 There shall we see his face
and never, never sin;
there from the rivers of his grace
drink endless pleasures in.

6 Then let our songs abound,
and every tear be dry;
we're marching through Immanuel's ground
to fairer worlds on high.

ISAAC WATTS (1674–1748) altd.*

385 *Bow Brickhill* LM

SYDNEY H. NICHOLSON (1875–1947)

Alternative tune: EISENACH, no. 259.

1 Command thy blessing from above,
O God, on all assembled here;
behold us with a Father's love,
while we look up with filial fear.

2 Command thy blessing, Jesus, Lord;
may we thy true disciples be;
speak to each heart the mighty word,
say to the weakest, 'Follow me'.

3 Command thy blessing in this hour,
Spirit of truth, and fill this place
with humbling and exalting power,
with quickening and consuming grace.

4 O thou, our Maker, Saviour, Guide,
one true eternal God confessed,
may naught in life or death divide
the saints in thy communion blest.

5 With thee and these for ever bound,
may all who here in prayer unite,
with joyful songs thy throne surround,
rest in thy love and reign in light.

JAMES MONTGOMERY (1771–1854)*

386 *I will enter his gates*

Words and music by
LEONA VON BRETHORST, 1976

Capo 3(C)

E♭ (C) A♭ (F) E♭ (C)
I will en-ter his gates with thanks-giv-ing in my heart, I will

A♭ (F) Fm (Dm) B♭7 (G7)
en - ter his courts with praise, I will

E♭ (C) A♭ (F) E♭ (C) Cm (Am)
say this is the day that the Lord has___ made, I

A♭ (F) B♭7 (G7) E♭ (C)
will re - joice for he has made me glad.

A♭ (F) E♭ (C) Cm (Am)
He has made me glad, he has made me glad, I

A♭ (F) B♭7 (G7) E♭ (C) A♭ (F) E♭ (C)
will re - joice for he has made me glad.________

387 *Abridge* CM

ISAAC SMITH (1734–1805)

1 Great Shepherd of thy people, hear;
thy presence now display;
as thou hast given a place for prayer,
so give us hearts to pray.

2 Within these walls let holy peace,
and love and concord dwell;
here give the troubled conscience ease,
the wounded spirit heal.

3 May we in faith receive thy word,
in faith present our prayers;
and in the presence of our Lord
unburden all our cares.

4 The feeling heart, the seeing eye,
the humble mind bestow;
and shine upon us from on high,
that we in grace may grow.

JOHN NEWTON (1725–1807) altd.

388 *Parkside* 65 65 BERNARD S. MASSEY (1927–)

Alternative tune: CASWALL (BEMERTON), no. 451.

1 Jesus, stand among us
  in your risen power;
let this time of worship
  be a hallowed hour.

2 Breathe the Holy Spirit
  into every heart;
bid the fears and sorrows
  from each soul depart.

3 Thus with quickened footsteps
  we pursue our way,
watching for the dawning
  of eternal day.

WILLIAM PENNEFATHER (1816–73) altd.

389 *Cannock* LM

WALTER K. STANTON (1891–1978)

1 Jesus, thou joy of loving hearts,
the fount of life, the mind's true light,
from the best bliss that earth imparts
we turn to thee, our soul's delight.

2 Thy truth unchanged hath ever stood;
thou savest those that on thee call;
to them that seek thee thou art good;
to them that find thee, all in all.

3 We taste thee, O thou living bread,
and long to feast upon thee still;
we drink of thee, the fountain-head,
and thirst our souls from thee to fill.

4 Our restless spirits yearn for thee,
where'er our changeful lot is cast;
glad when thy gracious smile we see,
blest when our faith can hold thee fast.

5 O Jesus, ever with us stay,
make all our moments calm and bright;
chase the dark night of sin away,
shed o'er the world thy holy light.

Latin, 12th cent.
tr. RAY PALMER (1808–87)*

390 *Neander* 87 87 77 JOACHIM NEANDER (1650–80)

1 Open now thy gates of beauty,
 Zion, let me enter there,
where my soul in joyful duty
 waits for him who answers prayer:
O how blessed is this place,
filled with solace, light and grace!

2 Yes, my God, I come before thee,
 come thou also near to me;
where we find thee and adore thee,
 there a heaven on earth must be;
to my heart, O enter thou,
let it be thy temple now.

3 Thou my faith increase and quicken,
 let me keep thy gift divine;
howsoe'er temptations thicken,
 may thy word still o'er me shine,
as my pole-star through my life,
as my comfort in my strife.

4 Speak, O God, and I will hear thee,
 let thy will be done, indeed;
may I undisturbed draw near thee,
 while thou dost thy people feed:
here of life the fountain flows,
here is balm for all our woes.

BENJAMIN SCHMOLK (1672–1737)
tr. CATHERINE WINKWORTH (1827–78)

391 *Carlisle* SM

CHARLES LOCKHART (1745–1815)

1 Stand up and bless the Lord,
you people of his choice;
stand up and bless the Lord your God
with heart and soul and voice.

2 Though high above all praise,
above all blessing high,
who would not fear his holy name,
and laud and magnify?

3 O for the living flame
from his own altar brought,
to touch our lips, our minds inspire,
and wing to heaven our thought!

4 God is our strength and song,
and his salvation ours;
then be his love in Christ proclaimed
with all our ransomed powers.

5 Stand up and bless the Lord,
the Lord your God adore;
stand up and bless his glorious name
henceforth for evermore.

JAMES MONTGOMERY (1771–1854) altd.

392

Trisagion I A. GREGORY MURRAY (1905–92)

OR

Trisagion II A. GREGORY MURRAY (1905–92)

Greek liturgy, 4th-5th cent.
tr. Anon.

When the text is to be sung three times, use tunes in the order I, II, I.

393 *Kindle a flame*

Iona Community

394 *Eternal life*

Iona Community

from John 6: 68

395 *John One* 7 5 10 5

CARYL MICKLEM (1925–)

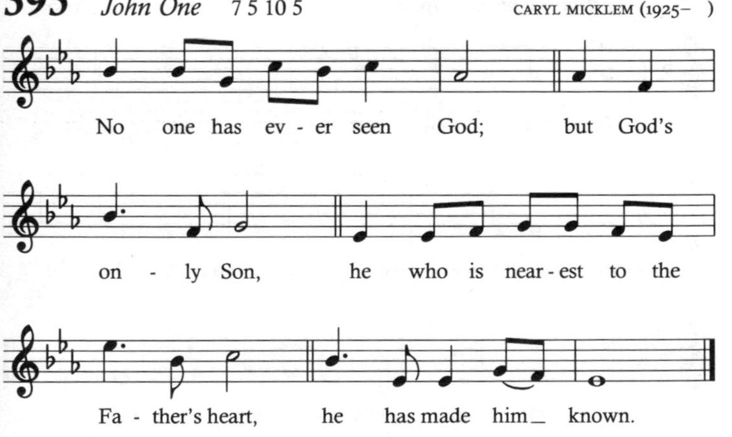

John 1: 18 (*New English Bible*)

396 *Adoramus te, Domine*

Taizé Community

397 *Edmondsham* 76 76

JOHN H. LORING (1906–)

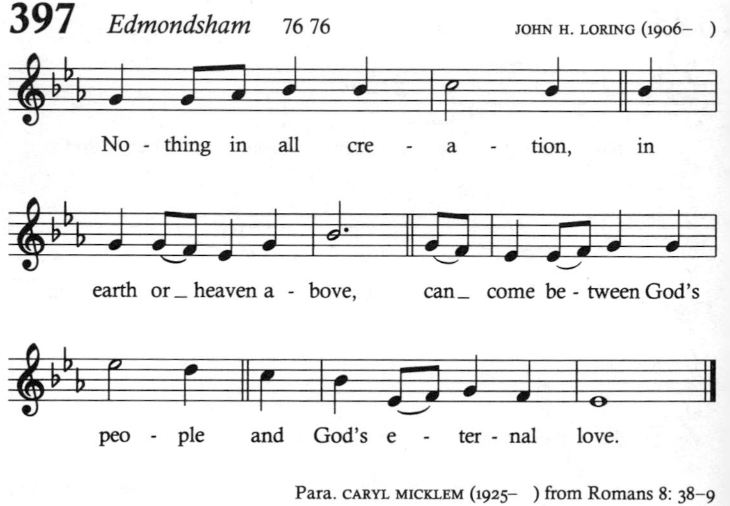

Para. CARYL MICKLEM (1925–) from Romans 8: 38–9

398 *Listen to me*

Taizé Community

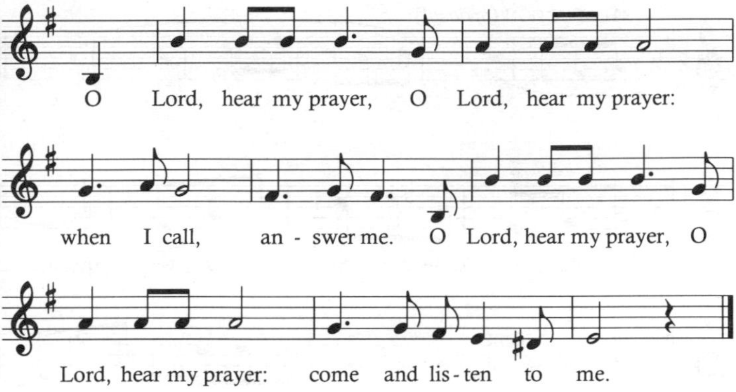

O Lord, hear my prayer, O Lord, hear my prayer:
when I call, an - swer me. O Lord, hear my prayer, O
Lord, hear my prayer: come and lis - ten to me.

399 *Stay with us*

Taizé Community

Stay with us, O Lord Je - sus Christ:
night will soon fall. Then stay with us, O
Lord Je - sus Christ: light in our dark - ness.

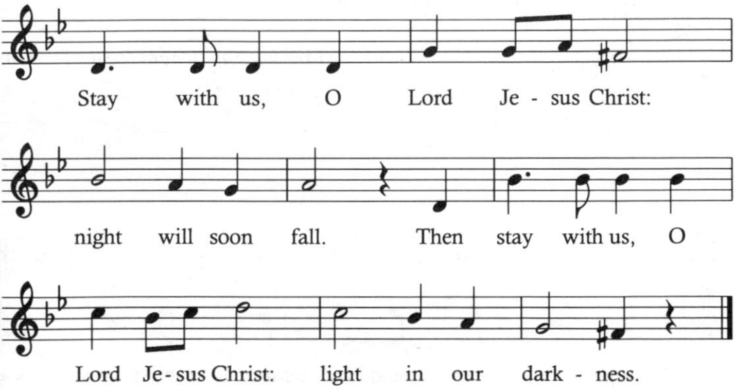

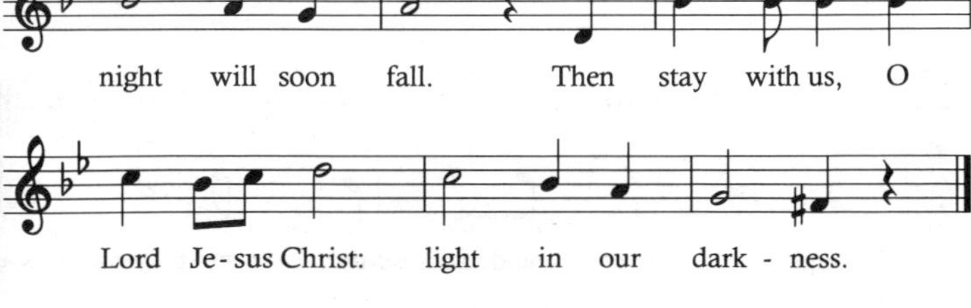

400 *Prayer Canticle*

ERIK ROUTLEY (1917–82)

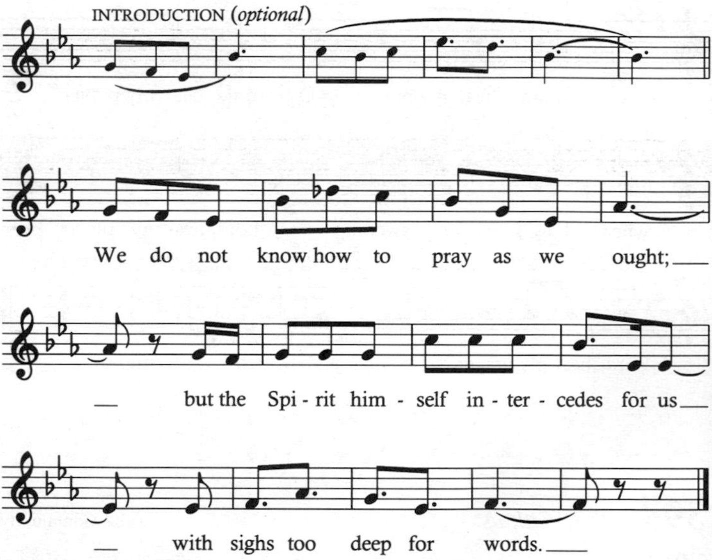
INTRODUCTION (*optional*)
We do not know how to pray as we ought; —
— but the Spi - rit him - self in - ter - cedes for us —
— with sighs too deep for words. —

Romans 8: 26 (*Revised Standard Version*)

401 *Through our lives*

Iona Community

Through our lives and — by our prayers,
your king - dom come.

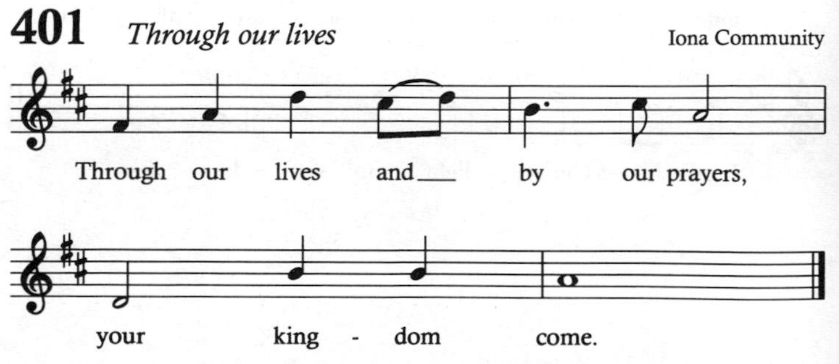

402 *Ubi caritas et amor*

Taizé Community

(Where there is tender care and love, God is present.)

403 *Laudate, omnes gentes* 76 76

Taizé Community

(Praise the Lord, all you peoples!)

404 *Stoner Hill* 10 10 10 10

WILLIAM H. HARRIS (1883–1973)

1 Lord of all good, our gifts we bring to thee,
use them thy holy purpose to fulfil:
tokens of love and pledges they shall be
that our whole life is offered to thy will.

2 We give our mind to understand thy ways,
hands, eyes, and voice to serve thy great design;
heart with the flame of thine own love ablaze,
till for thy glory all our powers combine.

3 Father, whose bounty all creation shows,
Christ, by whose willing sacrifice we live,
Spirit, from whom all life in fullness flows,
to thee with grateful hearts ourselves we give.

A. F. BAYLY (1901–84)

405 *Angel voices* 85 85 843

E. G. MONK (1819–1900)

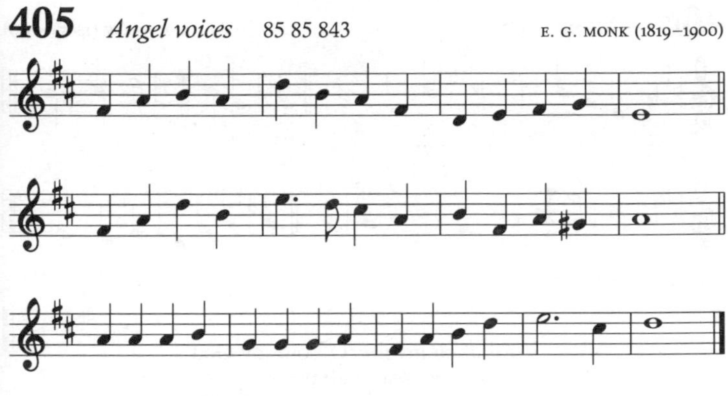

1 Angel voices ever singing
round thy throne of light,
angel harps for ever ringing
rest not day nor night;
thousands only live to bless thee,
and confess thee,
Lord of might.

2 Lord, we know that thou rejoicest
o'er each work of thine;
thou didst ears and hands and voices
for thy praise design;
craftsman's art and music's measure
for thy pleasure
all combine.

3 In thy house, great God, we offer
of thine own to thee,
and for thine acceptance proffer,
all unworthily,
hearts and minds and hands and voices,
in our choicest
psalmody.

4 Honour, glory, might and merit
thine shall ever be,
Father, Son, and Holy Spirit,
blessèd Trinity;
of the best that thou hast given
earth and heaven
render thee.

FRANCIS POTT (1832–1909) altd.

406 *Billing* CM

R. R. TERRY (1865–1938)

Alternative tune: ST FULBERT no. 418.

1 Fill thou my life, O Lord my God,
in every part with praise,
that my whole being may proclaim
thy being and thy ways.

2 Not for the lip of praise alone
nor ev'n the praising heart
I ask, but for a life made up
of praise in every part:

3 praise in the common things of life,
its goings out and in;
praise in each duty and each deed,
however small and mean.

4 Fill every part of me with praise;
let all my being speak
of thee and of thy love, O Lord,
poor though I be and weak.

5 So shalt thou, glorious Lord, from me
receive the glory due;
and so shall I begin on earth
the song for ever new.

6 So shall no part of day or night
from sacredness be free;
but all my life, in every step,
be fellowship with thee.

H. BONAR (1808–89) altd.

407 *North Coates* 65 65

T. R. MATTHEWS (1826–1910)

1 Jesus went to worship
in the synagogue;
with his friends and neighbours
sang his praise to God.

2 We, like Jesus, worship
in the Church today;
still, with friends and neighbours
sing our songs and pray.

3 When the service ended
Jesus took his praise
into streets and houses
spelling out God's ways.

4 People came to Jesus,
frightened, hurt, and sad;
helping them to worship,
Jesus made them glad.

5 Holy Spirit, help us
when this service ends,
still to follow Jesus,
still to be his friends.

6 When our neighbours meet us,
may they, with surprise,
catch a glimpse of Jesus
rising in our eyes.

ALAN GAUNT (1935–)*

408 *Westminster* CM

JAMES TURLE (1802–82)

1 My God, how wonderful thou art,
thy majesty how bright,
how beautiful thy mercy-seat
in depths of burning light!

2 How wonderful, how wonderful
the sight of thee must be,
thine endless wisdom, boundless power,
and awesome purity!

3 O how I fear thee, living God,
with deepest, tenderest fears,
and worship thee with trembling hope,
and penitential tears!

4 No earthly father loves like thee;
no mother half so mild
bears and forbears as thou hast done
with me, thy sinful child.

5 Yet I may love thee too, O Lord,
almighty as thou art,
for thou hast stooped to ask of me
the love of my poor heart.

6 O then this worse than worthless heart
in pity deign to take,
and make it love thee for thyself,
and for thy glory's sake.

7 Father of Jesus, love's reward,
what rapture will it be
to fall and worship at thy throne
and gaze and gaze on thee!

F. W. FABER (1814–63) altd.*

409 *Barford* CM

W. MOORE (1841–1930)

1 O God, in whom we live and move,
in whom we draw each breath,
God, filling all the height above,
and all the depths beneath:

2 our hands may build your hallowed shrine,
no bound your presence owns;
what highest heaven cannot confine,
the lowly heart enthrones.

3 You are about our path, and where
we seek to tread your ways;
all life is sacrament and prayer,
and every thought is praise.

4 And when we gather in your name,
to pray with one accord,
around, within us, still the same,
we find your presence, Lord.

5 In simple faith or solemn rite,
in head and heart and hand,
though you are hidden from our sight,
yet in our midst you stand.

6 Be with us, Lord; with us abide;
go with us where we go;
and, changeless in life's changing tide,
your presence we shall know.

G. W. BRIGGS (1875–1959)*

410 *Mit Freuden zart* 87 87 887

Later form of a melody in the Bohemian Brethren's *Kirchengeseng*, Berlin, 1566

1 Our Father God, thy name we praise,
to thee our hymns addressing,
and joyfully our voices raise
thy faithfulness confessing;
assembled by thy grace, O Lord,
we seek fresh guidance from thy Word;
now grant anew thy blessing.

2 Touch, Lord, the lips that speak for thee;
set words of truth before us,
that we may grow in constancy,
the light of wisdom o'er us.
Give us this day our daily bread;
may hungry souls again be fed;
may heavenly food restore us.

3 As with each other here we meet,
thy grace alone can feed us.
As here we gather at thy feet
we pray that thou wilt heed us.
The power is thine, O Lord divine,
the kingdom and the rule are thine.
May Jesus Christ still lead us!

from the Anabaptist *Ausbund*, 16th cent.
tr. E. A. PAYNE (1902–80)*

411 *Castleford* CM BENJAMIN CLIFFORD (1752–1811)

1 Now let us see thy beauty, Lord,
as we have seen before;
and by thy beauty quicken us
to love thee and adore.

2 How easy when with simple mind
thy loveliness we see,
to consecrate ourselves afresh
to duty and to thee!

3 Our every feverish mood is cooled,
and gone is every load,
when we can lose the love of self,
and find the love of God.

4 Lord, it is coming to ourselves
when thus we come to thee;
the bondage of thy loveliness
is perfect liberty.

5 So now we come to ask again
what thou hast often given,
the vision of that loveliness
which is the life of heaven.

BENJAMIN WAUGH (1839–1908) altd.*

412 *There's a quiet understanding*

E. R. (TEDD) SMITH (1927–)

Irregular

1 There's a quiet understanding
when we're gathered in the Spirit:
it's a promise that he gives us
when we gather in his name.
There's a love we feel in Jesus,
there's a manna that he feeds us:
it's a promise that he gives us
when we gather in his name.

2 And we know when we're together,
sharing love and understanding,
that our brothers and our sisters
feel the oneness that he brings.
Thank you, Jesus, thank you, Jesus,
for the way you love and feed us,
for the many ways you lead us,
thank you, thank you, Lord.

E. R. (TEDD) SMITH (1927–)*

413 *What a friend* 87 87 D

C. C. CONVERSE (1832–1918)

1 What a friend we have in Jesus,
all our sins and griefs to bear!
What a privilege to carry
everything to God in prayer!
O what peace we often forfeit,
O what needless pain we bear,
all because we do not carry
everything to God in prayer!

2 Have we trials and temptations,
is there trouble anywhere?
We should never be discouraged:
take it to the Lord in prayer.
Can we find a friend so faithful
who will all our sorrows share?
Jesus knows our every weakness:
take it to the Lord in prayer.

3 Are we weak and heavy-laden,
burdened with a load of care?
Jesus is our only refuge:
take it to the Lord in prayer.
Do your friends despise, forsake you?
Take it to the Lord in prayer;
in his arms he'll take and shield you,
you will find a solace there.

JOSEPH SCRIVEN (1819–86) altd.

414 *Engelberg* 10 10 10 with alleluia C. V. STANFORD (1852–1924)

1 When, in our music, God is glorified,
and adoration leaves no room for pride,
it is as though the whole creation cried:
Alleluia!

2 How often, making music, we have found
a new dimension in the world of sound,
as worship moved us to a more profound
Alleluia!

3 So has the Church, in liturgy and song,
in faith and love, through centuries of wrong,
borne witness to the truth in every tongue:
Alleluia!

4 And did not Jesus sing a psalm that night
when utmost evil strove against the Light?
Then let us sing, for whom he won the fight:
Alleluia!

5 Let every instrument be tuned for praise!
Let all rejoice who have a voice to raise!
and may God give us faith to sing always:
Alleluia!

F. PRATT GREEN (1903–)

STUART DAUERMANN (1944–)

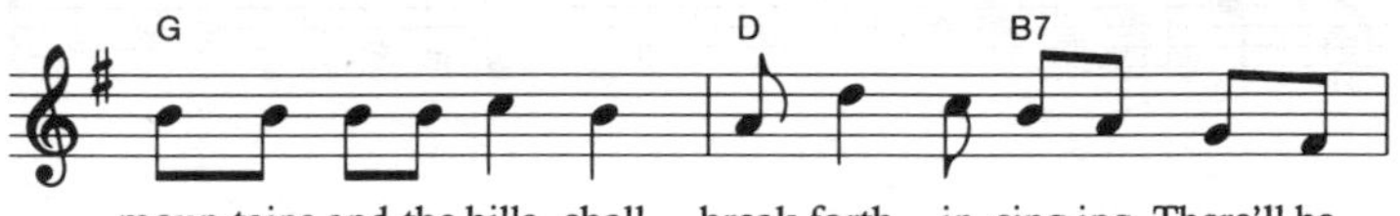

STUART DAUERMANN (1944–)*
based on Isaiah 55: 12

416 *Tallis's Canon* LM

THOMAS TALLIS (*c.*1505–85)
shortened by THOMAS RAVENSCROFT,
Psalmes, 1621

1 Glory to thee, my God, this night
for all the blessings of the light;
keep me, O keep me, King of kings,
beneath thine own almighty wings.

2 Forgive me, Lord, for thy dear Son,
the ill that I this day have done,
that with the world, myself, and thee,
I, ere I sleep, at peace may be.

3 Teach me to live, that I may dread
the grave as little as my bed;
teach me to die, that so I may
rise glorious at the judgement day.

4 O may my soul on thee repose,
and may sweet sleep mine eyelids close—
sleep that shall me more vigorous make
to serve my God when I awake.

5 When in the night I sleepless lie,
my mind with heavenly thoughts supply;
let no ill dreams disturb my rest,
no powers of darkness me molest.

6 Praise God, from whom all blessings flow;
praise him, all creatures here below;
praise him above, ye heavenly host;
praise Father, Son, and Holy Ghost.

THOMAS KEN (1637–1711) altd.

417 *Franconia* SM

W. H. HAVERGAL (1793–1870)
from a chorale in J. B. KÖNIG's
Harmonischer Liederschatz, 1738

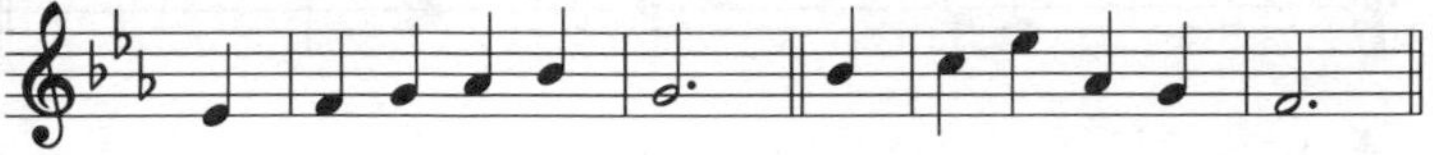

1 Lord Jesus, once a child,
Saviour of young and old,
receive *this little child* of ours (*these little ones*)
into your flock and fold.

2 You drank the cup of life,
its bitterness and bliss,
and loved us to the uttermost
for *such a child as this*. (*children such as these*.)

3 So help us, Lord, to trust
through this baptismal rite,
not in our own imperfect love,
but in your saving might.

4 Lord Jesus, for *her* sake, (*his/their*)
lend us your constant aid,
that *she*, when older, may rejoice (*he/they*)
we kept the vows we made.

F. PRATT GREEN (1903–)

418 *St Fulbert* CM

H. J. GAUNTLETT (1805–76)

Version I

1 We praise you, Lord, for Jesus Christ,
who died and rose again;
he lives to break the power of sin
and over death to reign.

2 We praise you that this child now shares
the freedom Christ can give,
has died to sin with Christ, and now
with Christ is raised to live.

3 We praise you, Lord, that now this child
is grafted to the vine,
is made a member of your house
and bears the cross as sign.

4 We praise you, Lord, for Jesus Christ,
he loves this child we bring:
he frees, forgives, and heals us all,
he lives and reigns as King.

JUDITH B. O'NEILL (1930–)

Version II

1 We praise you, Lord, for Jesus Christ,
who died and rose again;
he lives to break the power of sin
and over death to reign.

2 We praise you that these children share
the freedom Christ can give,
have died to sin with Christ, and now
with Christ are raised to live.

3 We praise you that these children, Lord,
are grafted to the vine,
are made full members of your house
and bear the cross as sign.

4 We praise you, Lord, for Jesus Christ,
he loves each child we bring:
he frees, forgives, and heals us all,
he lives and reigns as King.

JUDITH B. O'NEILL (1930–) altd.

419 *Liebster Immanuel* 11 10 11 10 (Dactylic)

Melody from *Himmels-Lust*, Jena, 1679

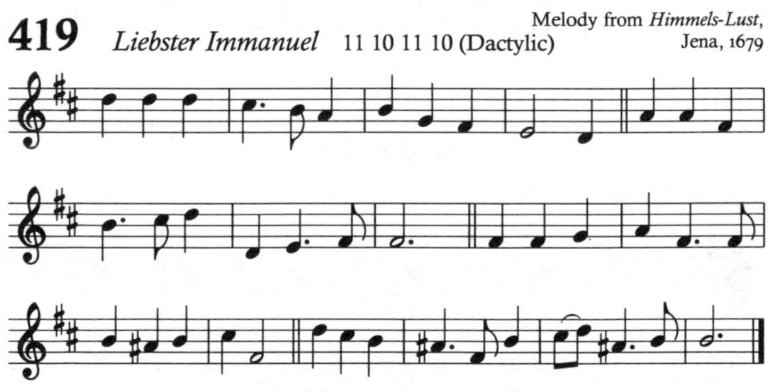

1 Word of the Father, the life of creation,
emptied of glory, among us you came;
born as a servant, assuming our weakness,
drank from the cup of our joy and our shame.

2 Each human child bears your image and likeness,
yet all are heirs to the sins of our earth;
once from death's flood you arose to redeem us,
water and Spirit now seal our rebirth.

3 Searching, you found us before we could name you,
loving, you suffered our pain and our loss;
strengthen this child through the faith of your people,
born in the glory which streams from the Cross.

COLIN THOMPSON (1945–)

420

FIRST TUNE

The Lord bless you arr. LOWELL MASON (1792–1872)

SECOND TUNE

Hadley Wood PAUL BATEMAN (1954–)

The Lord bless you and keep you:
the Lord make his face to shine upon you,
and be gracious unto you:
the Lord lift up his countenance upon you,
and give you peace.

from Numbers 6: 24–6

421 *Mit Freuden zart* 87 87 887

Later form of a melody in the Bohemian Brethren's *Kirchengeseng*, Berlin, 1566

1 All who believe and are baptized
shall see the Lord's salvation;
baptized into the death of Christ,
they are a new creation;
through Christ's redemption they shall stand
among the glorious heavenly band
of every tribe and nation.

2 With one accord, O God, we pray,
grant us your Holy Spirit,
and look on our infirmity
through Jesus' blood and merit;
O keep us in baptismal grace,
until at last we take our place
with all who life inherit.

THOMAS H. KINGO (1634–1703)
tr. G. A. T. RYGH (1860–1943) altd.*

422 *Crucifer* 10 10 with refrain SYDNEY H. NICHOLSON (1875–1947)

Lift high the Cross, the love of Christ proclaim
till all the world adore his sacred name!

1 Here we display God's foolishness, which came
to put the wisdom of this world to shame.
(1 Cor. 1: 18)

2 Our only boast is Jesus crucified;
we die with him and shall be glorified.
(Gal. 6: 14)

3 Bearing our human likeness as his own,
in death and suffering Christ took up his throne.
(Phil. 2: 8)

4 Sin's deadly bond which sealed our total loss
he set aside and nailed it to the Cross.
(Col. 2: 13)

5 All nameless powers that human life betray
are led as captives on his triumph day.
(Col. 2: 15)

6 May we, baptized according to his word,
take up his cup and drink it with our Lord.
(Mark 10: 38)

Refrain: GEORGE W. KITCHIN (1827–1912)
and M. R. NEWBOLT (1874–1956)
Verses: STEPHEN ORCHARD (1942–) and compilers

423 *Frère Jacques*

French traditional

A round in 4 parts

Wake up, sleeper! Wake up, sleeper!
Rise from the dead! Rise from the dead!
Christ will shine upon you. Christ will shine upon you.
You are light. You are light.

Ephesians 5: 14, 8
para. CHARLES ROBERTSON (1940–)

424 *Cross of Jesus* 87 87 (Trochaic)

JOHN STAINER (1840–1901)

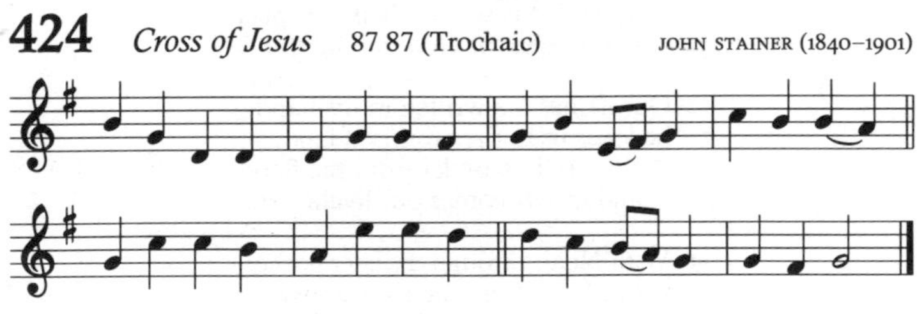

Water means Life

1 At the dawning of creation
when the world began to be,
God called forth the world's foundations
from the deep chaotic sea.

2 When the Lord delivered Israel
out of Egypt's bitter yoke,
then the parting of the waters
of the living water spoke.

3 Water from the rock of Moses,
water from the temple's side,
water from the heart of Jesus,
flow in this baptismal tide.

4 Thus united in this water
each to all, and each to Christ;
to his life of love he calls us
by his total sacrifice.

DAVID FOX (1956–)

425 *Herongate* LM

English traditional melody

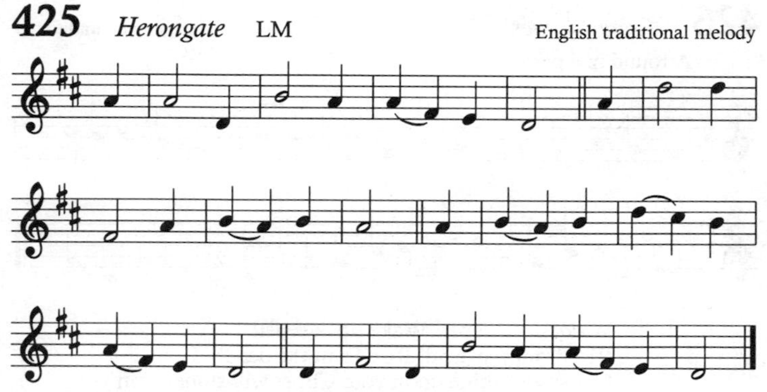

1 Now in the name of him, who sent
to preach by word and sacrament,
upon this new-born child we pray
the strength of God in doubtful day.

2 Our names are written in his hand;
he leads us to the promised land.
We rise in wonder from the flood
and love becomes our livelihood.

3 With Noah through disaster borne,
with Moses from the river drawn,
with Jonah from the sea released,
we celebrate this rising feast.

4 This water is a seal and sign
of costly love that makes us clean;
this love we see in Christ portrayed,
who rose triumphant from the dead.

5 We sing our thanks that old and young
so to the Church of Christ belong.
This is the covenant of grace;
we look salvation in the face.

FRED KAAN (1929–)

426 *Fredericktown* CHARLES R. ANDERS (1929–)

10 10 10 with alleluias

1 We know that Christ is raised and dies no more;
embraced by death, he broke its fearful hold;
and our despair he turned to blazing joy:

Alleluia! Alleluia! Alleluia!

2 We share by water in his saving death;
this union brings to being one new cell,
a living and organic part of Christ:

3 The Father's splendour clothes the Son with life;
the Spirit's fission shakes the Church of God;
baptized, we live with God the Three in One:

4 A new creation comes to life and grows
as Christ's new body takes on flesh and blood;
the universe restored and whole will sing:

JOHN B. GEYER (1932–) altd.*
based on Romans 6: 9

427 *Camano* 66 66 88

RICHARD PROULX (1937–)

Alternative tune: EASTVIEW, no. 432.

1 Dear Saviour, in your name,
in faith we gather here,
your word is still the same,
your presence ever near.
Now let the glory of your grace
be felt by all within this place.

2 We come before you, Lord,
to do your holy will;
may reverence for your Word
like gentle dew distil.
Yours to command; may we obey
and, joyful, run in all your way.

3 At this baptismal grave
your death and life we see,
we own your power to save
worked out on Calvary,
and ever near to bless with good
the soul that trusts your precious blood.

4 Let thoughts of earthly loss
or gain be all unknown;
this path so near your Cross
leads onward to the Crown.
Lord Jesus, guide us in your might,
till glory breaks as morning light.

JOSEPH ADAM (1841–1919)*

428 *Jackson (Byzantium)* CM

THOMAS JACKSON (1715–81)

1 I'm not ashamed to own my Lord,
or to defend his cause;
maintain the honour of his word,
the glory of his cross.

2 Jesus, my Lord—I know his name,
his name is all I trust;
nor will he put my soul to shame,
nor let my hope be lost.

3 Firm as his throne his promise stands,
and he can well secure
what I've committed to his hands,
till the decisive hour.

4 Then will he own my worthless name
before his Father's face;
and in the new Jerusalem
appoint my soul a place.

ISAAC WATTS (1674–1748)

429 *St George* SM

H. J. GAUNTLETT (1805–76)

1 Jesus our Lord and King,
to thee our praises rise;
to thee our bodies we present,
a living sacrifice.

2 Now justified by grace,
and made alive to God,
formed for thyself, to show thy praise,
we sound thy love abroad.

3 As dead indeed to sin,
from its dominion free,
henceforth, as not our own, but thine,
we follow only thee.

4 Baptized into thy death,
with thee again we rise,
to newness of a life of faith,
to new and endless joys.

5 Thy precious name we own,
and joyfully confess:
thou art our life, our hope, our crown,
our strength and righteousness.

Anon., 1858

430 *Norman* 87 87 (Trochaic) Melody from Doles's *Vierstimmiges Choralbuch*, Leipzig, 1785

1 Praise to God, almighty maker
of all things below, above;
for his might is in redemption
manifest as holy love.

2 Praise the Son who thus revealed him,
love incarnate shown to us,
living, suffering, dying, risen,
love through death victorious.

3 Here, redemption's wondrous story
we set forth in mystic rite:
see him die, the grave receive him,
see him rise, by God's great might.

4 Here, within the font we meet him;
here with him we buried lie;
here we plead his matchless merit;
here with him to sin we die.

5 Then, victorious through his passion,
from the grave with him we rise,
born again to do him service
in the strength his grace supplies.

6 Praise the Spirit, who is promised
here to be the gift divine,
making in our hearts his temple,
love, joy, peace, his holy sign.

7 Here, baptized, the Church we enter,
realm on earth of heaven above:
praise to Father, Son and Spirit,
sacred name of holy love.

WILLIAM ROBINSON (1888–1963)*

431 *Epiphany Hymn* 11 10 11 10 (Dactylic) J. F. THRUPP (1827–67)

1 Lord of the love that in Christ has reclaimed us
children of earth, to be heirs of your reign,
help us become what by grace you have named us,
take and transform what by sin we remain.

2 You sent your Son, in whose gift is our healing;
you gave your Church to bring sight to the blind:
help us accept what your love is revealing—
greatness in service, and losing to find.

3 Father of Jesus, your covenant-mercies
raised from death's darkness the self that was his;
raise us with him as your people, as voices
calling your world to become what it is.

CARYL MICKLEM (1925–)*

432 *Eastview* 66 66 88 J. VERNON LEE (1892–1959)

1 Now is eternal life,
if risen with Christ we stand,
in him to life re-born,
and held within his hand;
no more we fear death's ancient dread,
in Christ arisen from the dead.

2 The human mind so long
brooded o'er life's brief span;
was it, O God, for naught,
for naught that life began?
Thou art our hope, our vital breath;
shall hope undying end in death?

3 And God, the living God,
stooped down to share our state;
by death destroying death
Christ opened wide life's gate.
He lives, who died; he reigns on high;
who live in him shall never die.

4 Unfathomed love divine,
reign thou within my heart;
from thee nor depth nor height,
nor life nor death can part;
my life is hid in God with thee,
now and through all eternity.

5 Thee will I love and serve
now in time's passing day;
thy hand shall hold me fast
when time is done away,
in God's unknown eternal spheres
to serve him through eternal years.

G. W. BRIGGS (1875–1959)*

433 *Hereford* LM — S. S. WESLEY (1810–76)

1 O thou who camest from above,
the pure celestial fire to impart,
kindle a flame of sacred love
on the mean altar of my heart.

2 There let it for thy glory burn
with inextinguishable blaze;
and trembling to its source return,
in humble prayer and fervent praise.

3 Jesus, confirm my heart's desire
to work and speak and think for thee;
still let me guard the holy fire,
and still stir up thy gift in me:

4 ready for all thy perfect will,
my acts of faith and love repeat,
till death thine endless mercies seal,
and make my sacrifice complete.

CHARLES WESLEY (1707–88)

434 *St Ethelwald* SM W. H. MONK (1823–89)

1 Jesus invites his saints
to meet around his board;
here pardoned rebels sit and hold
communion with their Lord.

2 For food he gives his flesh,
he bids us drink his blood;
amazing favour! matchless grace
of our descending God!

3 This holy bread and wine
maintains our fainting breath,
by union with our living Lord,
and interest in his death.

4 Our heavenly Father calls
Christ and his members one;
we the young children of his love,
and he the first-born Son.

5 We are but several parts
of that same broken bread;
one body has its several limbs,
but Jesus is the Head.

6 Let all our powers be joined
his glorious name to raise;
pleasure and love fill every mind
and every voice be praise.

ISAAC WATTS (1674–1748) altd.*

435 *Ave virgo virginum*

76 76 D (Trochaic)

Melody from Horn's *Gesangbuch*, 1544 (rhythm slightly altered)

1 Christian people, raise your song,
chase away all grieving.
Sing your joy and be made strong
our Lord's life receiving.
Nature's gifts of wheat and vine
now are set before us:
as we offer bread and wine
Christ comes to restore us.

2 Come to welcome Christ today,
God's great revelation.
He has pioneered the way
of the new creation.
Greet him, Christ our risen King
gladly recognising,
as with joy we greet the spring
out of winter rising.

COLIN THOMPSON (1945–)

436 *Song 1* 10 10 10 10 10 10

ORLANDO GIBBONS (1583–1625)

He took

1 Dear Lord, to you again our gifts we bring,
this bread our toil, this wine our ecstasy,
poor and imperfect though they both must be;
yet you will take a heart-free offering.
Yours is the bounty, ours the unfettered will
to make or mar, to fashion good or ill.

He blessed

2 Yes, you will take and bless, and grace impart
to make again what once your goodness gave,
what we half crave, and half refuse to have,
a sturdier will, a more repentant heart.
You have on earth no hands, no hearts but ours;
bless them as yours, ourselves, our will, our powers.

He broke

3 Break bread, O Lord, break down our wayward wills,
break down our prized possessions, break them down;
let them be freely given as your own
to all who need our gifts, to heal their ills.
Break this, the bread we bring, that all may share
in your one living body, everywhere.

He gave

4 Our lips receive your wine, our hands your bread;
you give us back the selves we offered you,
won by the Cross, by Calvary made new,
a heart enriched, a life raised from the dead.
Grant us to take and guard your treasure well,
that we in you, and you in us may dwell.

H. C. A. GAUNT (1902–83)

437

First Tune

Worlebury 10 7 10 7 46 66 JOHN AINSLIE (1942–)

Second Tune

Jucunda laudatio 10 7 10 7 46 66 A. GREGORY MURRAY (1905–92)

1 Reap me the earth as a harvest to God;
gather and bring it again,
all that is his, to the Maker of all:
lift it and offer it high!

Bring bread, bring wine, give glory to the Lord.
Whose is the earth but God's?
Whose is the praise but his?

2 Go with your song and your music, with joy
go to the altar of God.
Carry your offerings, fruits of the earth,
work of your labouring hands:

3 Gladness and pity and passion and pain
—all that is mortal in us—
lay all before him, return him his gift—
God, to whom all shall go home:

LUKE CONNAUGHTON (1917–79)*

438 *Folksong* 98 98

English traditional melody
arr. JOHN WILSON (1905–92)

*This may be repeated before v. 4, or before v. 3 if the hymn has been so divided.

1 An upper room did our Lord prepare
for those he loved until the end;
and his disciples still gather there
to celebrate their Risen Friend.

2 A lasting gift Jesus gave his own—
to share his bread, his loving cup;
whatever burdens may bow us down,
he by his cross shall lift us up.

3 And after supper he washed their feet,
for service, too, is sacrament;
in him our joy shall be made complete—
sent out to serve, as he was sent.

4 No end there is! We depart in peace;
he loves beyond the uttermost;
in every room in our Father's house
he will be there, as Lord and Host.

F. PRATT GREEN (1903–)

439 *Platt's Lane* 56 64

EVELYN SHARPE (1884–1969)

1 As we break the bread
and taste the life of wine,
we bring to mind our Lord,
Man of all time.

2 Grain is sown to die;
it rises from the dead,
becomes through human toil
our common bread.

3 Pass from hand to hand
the living love of Christ!
Machines and people raise
bread for this feast.

4 Jesus binds in one
our daily life and work;
he is of humankind
symbol and mark.

5 Having shared the bread
that died to rise again,
we rise to serve the world,
scattered as grain.

FRED KAAN (1929–)*

440 *Raleigh* 66 66 88

EBENEZER PROUT (1835–1909)

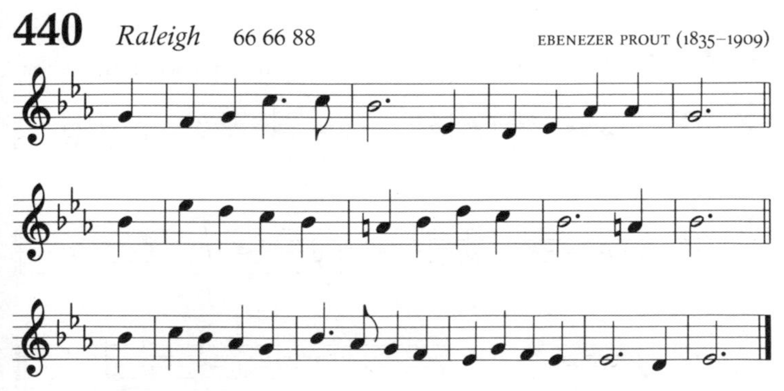

1 Author of life divine,
who hast a table spread,
furnished with mystic wine
and everlasting bread,
preserve the life thyself hast given,
and feed and train us up for heaven.

2 Our needy souls sustain
with fresh supplies of love,
till all thy life we gain,
and all thy fullness prove,
and, strengthened by thy perfect
grace,
behold without a veil thy face.

CHARLES WESLEY (1707–88)

441 *Belmont* CM

W. GARDINER'S *Sacred Melodies*, Vol. I, 1812
Melody probably by WILLIAM GARDINER (1769–1853)

1 Be known to us in breaking bread,
but do not then depart,
Saviour, abide with us, and spread
your table in our heart.

2 There sup with us in love divine;
your body and your blood,
that living bread, that heavenly wine,
be our immortal food.

JAMES MONTGOMERY (1771–1854) altd.

442 *Cassel* 77 77 77

German hymn melody, 17th cent.

1 Bread of heaven! on thee we feed,
for thy flesh is meat indeed;
ever may our souls be fed
with this true and living bread!
day by day with strength supplied,
through the life of him who died.

2 Vine of heaven! thy blood supplies
this blest cup of sacrifice;
'tis thy wounds our healing give;
to thy cross we look and live:
Jesus, may we ever be
rooted, grafted, built in thee.

JOSIAH CONDER (1789–1855) altd.

443 & 444

Les Commandemens de Dieu 98 98

Melody from *La Forme des Prières et Chants Ecclésiastiques*, Strasbourg, 1545

Alternative tune: RENDEZ À DIEU, no. 709.

443

1 Bread of the world, in mercy broken,
wine of the soul, in mercy shed,
by whom the words of life were spoken,
and in whose death our sins are dead:

2 look on the heart by sorrow broken,
look on the tears by sinners shed;
and be your feast to us the token
that by your grace our souls are fed.

REGINALD HEBER (1783–1826) altd.

444

1 Father, we give you thanks, who planted
your holy name within our hearts.
Knowledge and faith and life immortal
Jesus your Son to us imparts.

2 Lord, you have made all for your pleasure,
and given us food for all our days,
giving in Christ the bread eternal;
yours is the power, be yours the praise.

3 Watch o'er your Church, O Lord, in mercy,
save it from evil, guard it still,
and in your love unite, perfect it,
cleanse and conform it to your will.

4 As grain, once scattered on the hillsides,
was in the broken bread made one,
so may your world-wide Church be gathered
into your kingdom by your Son.

F. BLAND TUCKER (1895–1984) and others
based on the *Didache* (1st or 2nd cent.)

445 *Borough* 10 10 10 10 CYRIL V. TAYLOR (1907–91)

Alternative tune: STONER HILL, no. 404.

1 Come, risen Lord, and deign to be our guest;
nay, let us be thy guests; the feast is thine;
thyself at thine own board make manifest,
in thine own sacrament of bread and wine.

2 We meet, as in that upper room they met;
thou at the table, blessing, yet dost stand;
'This is my body': so thou givest yet;
faith still receives the cup as from thy hand.

3 One body we, one body who partake,
one Church united in communion blest;
one name we bear, one bread of life we break,
with all thy saints on earth and saints at rest,

4 one with each other, Lord, for one in thee,
who art one Saviour and one living Head;
then open thou our eyes, that we may see;
be known to us in breaking of the bread.

G. W. BRIGGS (1875–1959)

446 *Schmücke dich* 88 88 D (Trochaic) JOHANN CRÜGER (1598–1662)

1 Deck thyself, my soul, with gladness,
leave the gloomy haunts of sadness,
come into the daylight's splendour,
there with joy thy praises render
unto him whose grace unbounded
hath this wondrous banquet founded;
high o'er all the heavens he reigneth,
yet to dwell with thee he deigneth.

2 Sun, who all my life dost brighten;
Light, who dost my soul enlighten;
Joy, the best my heart e'er knoweth;
Fount, whence all my being floweth;
at thy feet I cry, my Maker,
let me be a fit partaker
of this blessed food from heaven,
for our good, thy glory, given.

3 Jesus, Bread of Life, I pray thee,
let me gladly here obey thee;
never to my hurt invited,
be thy love with love requited:
from this banquet let me measure,
Lord, how vast and deep its treasure;
through the gifts thou here dost give me,
as thy guest in heaven receive me.

JOHANN FRANCK (1618–77)
tr. CATHERINE WINKWORTH (1827–78)*

447

First Tune

Winchcombe CM LEONARD BLAKE (1907–89)

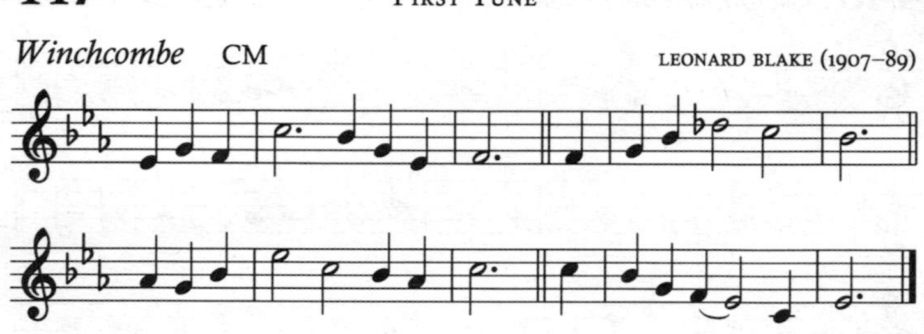

Second Tune

St Botolph CM GORDON SLATER (1896–1979)

1 I come with joy to meet my Lord,
   forgiven, loved, and free,
in awe and wonder to recall
   his life laid down for me.

2 I come with Christians far and near
   to find, as all are fed,
the new community of love
   in Christ's communion bread.

3 As Christ breaks bread and bids us share
   each proud division ends.
The love that made us, makes us one,
   and strangers now are friends.

4 And thus with joy we meet our Lord,
his presence, always near,
is in such friendship better known:
we see, and praise him here.

5 Together met, together bound,
we'll go our different ways,
and as his people in the world
we'll live and speak his praise.

BRIAN WREN (1936–)

448 *St Columba* 87 87 (Iambic) Ancient Irish hymn melody

1 Here, Lord, we take the broken bread
and drink the wine, believing
that by your life our souls are fed,
your parting gifts receiving.

2 As you have given, so we would give
ourselves for others' healing;
and as you lived, so we would live,
the Father's love revealing.

C. V. PILCHER (1879–1961) altd.*

449 *Eccles* 66 66

B. LUARD SELBY (1853–1918)

1 I hunger and I thirst;
Jesus, my manna be;
O living Water, burst
out of the rock for me!

2 O bruised and broken Bread,
my life-long needs supply:
as living souls are fed,
so feed me, or I die.

3 O true life-giving Vine,
let me your sweetness prove:
by your life strengthen mine,
refresh my soul with love.

4 Rough paths my feet have trod
since first their course began:
feed me, O Bread of God,
renew me, Son of Man.

5 For still the desert lies
my thirsting soul before:
O Living Water, rise
within me evermore!

J. S. B. MONSELL (1811–75) altd.*

450 *Gildas* SM

From a melody in M. WEISSE'S *Ein Neu Gesengbuchlen*, 1531

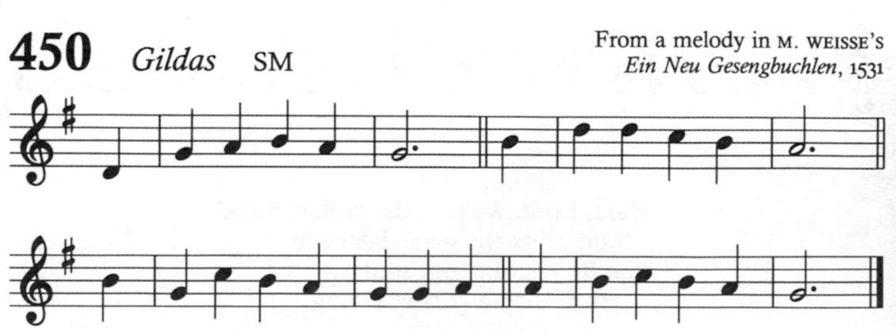

1 Jesus, we thus obey
thy last and kindest word;
here, in thine own appointed way,
we come to meet thee, Lord.

2 Our hearts we open wide
to make the Saviour room;
and lo! the Lamb, the Crucified,
the sinner's friend, is come!

3 His presence makes the feast;
and now our spirits feel
the glory not to be expressed,
the joy unspeakable.

4 Now let our souls be fed
with manna from above.
His banner over us is spread,
his everlasting love.

CHARLES WESLEY (1707–88) altd.*

451 *Caswall (Bemerton)* 65 65

FRIEDRICH FILITZ (1804–76)

1 Lamb of God, unblemished,
offered for our sin,
o'er our wayward spirits
gracious triumph win.

2 Love made you our brother,
love your anguish wrought;
love in you was sovereign,
love your lost ones sought.

3 By your holy passion,
and your endless love,
all that is unlike you
from our hearts remove.

4 By the cup of blessing
and the broken bread,
your renewing spirit
on us all be shed.

5 From each narrow purpose,
from all barren strife,
bring us to the fullness
of the heavenly life.

6 May each one partaking,
Saviour, be your guest
in the Father's kingdom,
there for ever blest.

H. ELVET LEWIS (1860–1953)*

452 *Let us break bread together*

Afro–American folk-song

10 10 with refrain

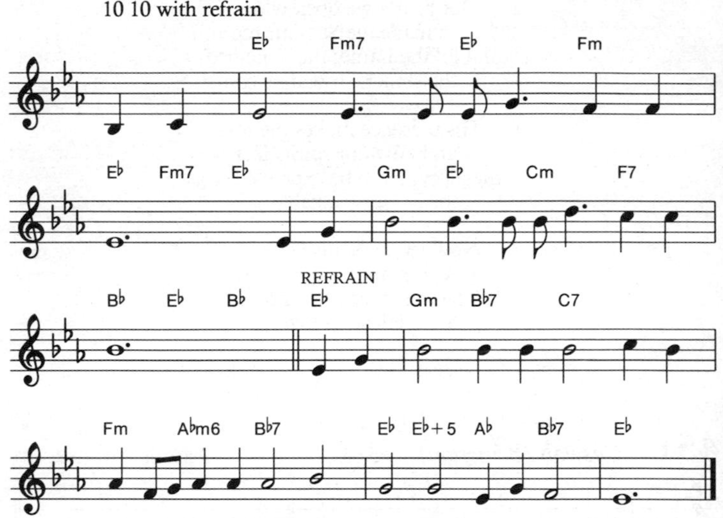

1 Let us break bread together in the Lord;
let us break bread together in the Lord:

when I fall on my knees,
with my face to the rising sun,
O Lord, have mercy on me.

2 Let us drink wine together in the Lord;
let us drink wine together in the Lord:

3 Let us praise God together in the Lord;
let us praise God together in the Lord:

based on an Afro–American Spiritual

Other verses or variations may be improvised; for example, when the hymn is sung during communion where a common loaf is shared: 'Let us break bread together, hand to hand . . .'.

453 *Linstead Market* 88 88 10 8

Jamaican folk-song
adpt. by DOREEN POTTER (1925–80)

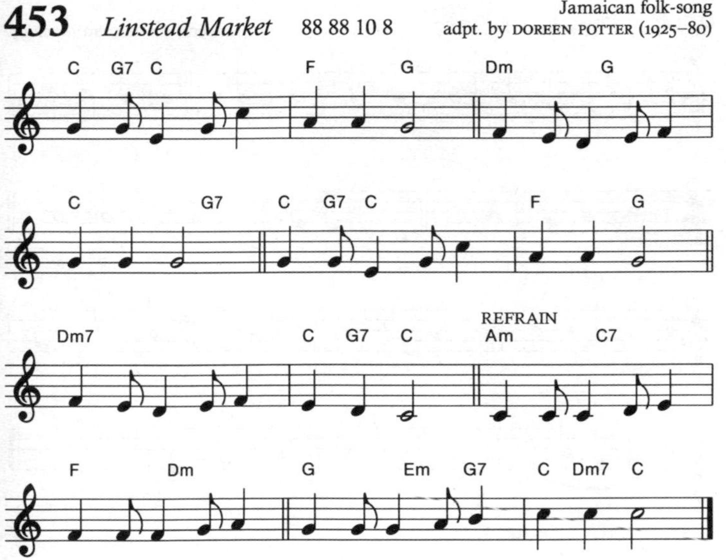

1 Let us talents and tongues employ,
reaching out with a shout of joy:
bread is broken, the wine is poured,
Christ is spoken and seen and heard.

Jesus lives again, earth can breathe again,
pass the Word around: loaves abound!

2 Christ is able to make us one,
at his table he set the tone,
teaching people to live to bless,
love in word and in deed express.

3 Jesus calls us in, sends us out
bearing fruit in a world of doubt,
gives us love to tell, bread to share:
God (Immanuel) everywhere!

FRED KAAN (1929–)*

454 *Picardy* 87 87 87

17th-cent. French carol melody

1 Let all mortal flesh keep silence
   and, with breathless awe, come near;
contemplate the Lord of heaven,
   present with his people here.
In the bread and wine, receive him:
   Christ the Lord, whom we revere.

2 Glorious king of endless ages,
   dwelling in God's holiness;
loving human nature dearly,
   grieving for our wickedness:
formed within the womb of Mary,
   born to bear our wretchedness.

3 Praised by all the hosts of heaven;
   praised by all created things;
every righteous soul, each prophet,
   martyr and apostle, sings
'Praise and glory in the highest,
   glory to the King of kings!'

4 Six-winged seraphim extol him,
   veil their faces, over-awed,
cherubim, all-seeing, praise him:
   'Holy, holy, holy Lord!
Alleluia! Alleluia!
   Christ, eternally adored!'

from the Liturgy of St James, *c.*4th cent
tr. ALAN GAUNT (1935–

455 *St Michael* SM

Composed or adpt. by
LOUIS BOURGEOIS in *Genevan Psalter*, 1551
further adpt. by WILLIAM CROTCH (1775–1847)

1 Lord of our highest love!
Let now thy peace be given;
fix all our thoughts on things above,
our hearts on thee in heaven.

2 Then, dearest Lord, draw near,
whilst we thy table spread:
and crown the feast with heavenly cheer,
thyself the living bread.

3 And when the loaf we break,
thine own rich blessing give,
may all with loving hearts partake,
and all new strength receive;

4 thankful that whilst we view
thy body bruised and torn,
life, health, and healing still accrue,
from stripes which thou hast borne.

5 Dear Lord, what memories crowd
around the sacred cup:
the upper room; Gethsemane;
thy foes; thy lifting up!

6 O scenes of suffering love,
enough our souls to win—
enough to melt our hearts, and prove
the antidote of sin.

G. Y. TICKLE (1819–88)

456 *Passion Chorale* 76 76 D

HANS LEO HASSLER (1562–1612)

1 O bread to pilgrims given,
  O food that angels eat,
O manna sent from heaven,
  for heaven-born natures meet!
Give us, for thee long pining,
  to eat till richly filled;
till, earth's delights resigning,
  our every wish is stilled.

2 O water, life-bestowing,
  forth from the Saviour's heart
a fountain purely flowing,
  a fount of love thou art:
O let us, freely tasting,
  our burning thirst assuage;
thy sweetness, never wasting,
  avails from age to age.

3 Jesus, this feast receiving,
  we thee unseen adore;
thy faithful word believing,
  we take, and doubt no more:
give us, thou true and loving,
  on earth to live in thee;
then, death the veil removing,
  thy glorious face to see.

RAY PALMER (1808–87) altd.
translated from *Mainz Gesangbuch*, 1661
formerly attrib. THOMAS AQUINAS (*c.*1227–74)

457 *Picardy* 87 87 87 17th-cent. French carol melody

Alternative tune: PANGE LINGUA, no. 228.

1 Now, my tongue, the mystery telling,
   of the glorious Body sing,
and the Blood, all price excelling,
   which the whole world's Lord and King,
in a Virgin's womb once dwelling,
   shed for this world's ransoming.

2 Born for us, and for us given,
   born to live like us below,
he, a man with us abiding,
   dwelt, the seeds of truth to sow;
and at last faced death undaunted,
   thus his greatest deed to show.

3 On the night of that last supper
   seated with his chosen band,
he, the paschal victim eating,
   first fulfils the law's command,
then, as food to his disciples,
   gives himself with his own hand.

4 Word made flesh! His word life-giving
gives his flesh our food to be,
bids us drink his blood, believing,
through his death, we life shall see:
blessèd they who thus receiving
are from death and sin set free.

5 Low in adoration bending,
now our hearts our God revere;
faith her aid to sight is lending,
though unseen the Lord is near;
ancient types and shadows ending,
Christ our Paschal Lamb is here.

6 Praise for ever, thanks and blessing,
thine, O gracious Father, be;
praise be thine, O Christ, who bringest
life and immortality;
praise be thine, thou quickening Spirit,
praise through all eternity.

THOMAS AQUINAS (*c.*1227–74)
tr. EDWARD CASWALL (1814–78) and others*

458 *St Thomas* SM

AARON WILLIAMS (1731–76)

1 The Son of God proclaim,
the Lord of time and space;
the God who bade the light break forth
now shines in Jesus' face.

2 He, God's creative Word,
the Church's Lord and Head,
here bids us gather as his friends
and share his wine and bread.

3 Behold his outstretched hands;
though all was in his power,
he took the towel and basin then,
and serves us in this hour.

4 The Lord of life and death
with wondering praise we sing;
we break the bread at his command,
and name him God and King.

5 We take this cup in hope;
for he, who gladly bore
the shameful cross, is risen again
and reigns for evermore.

BASIL E. BRIDGE (1927–)*

459 *Holborn* 10 10 10 10

ERIC H. THIMAN (1900–75)

Alternative tune: SURSUM CORDA, no. 731.

1 Thee we adore, O hidden Saviour, thee,
who in thy Supper with us deign'st to be;
both flesh and spirit in thy presence fail,
yet here thy presence we devoutly hail.

2 O blest memorial of our dying Lord,
who living bread to us doth here afford!
O may our souls for ever feed on thee,
and thou, O Christ, for ever precious be.

3 Fountain of goodness, Jesus, Lord and God,
cleanse us, unclean, in thy most cleansing flood;
increase our faith and love, that we may know
the hope and peace which from thy presence flow.

4 O Christ, whom now beneath a veil we see,
may what we thirst for soon our portion be,
to gaze on thee unveiled, and see thy face,
the vision of thy glory and thy grace.

THOMAS AQUINAS (*c.*1227–74)
tr. J. R. WOODFORD (1820–85)*

460 *Cross of Jesus* 87 87 (Trochaic) JOHN STAINER (1840–1901)

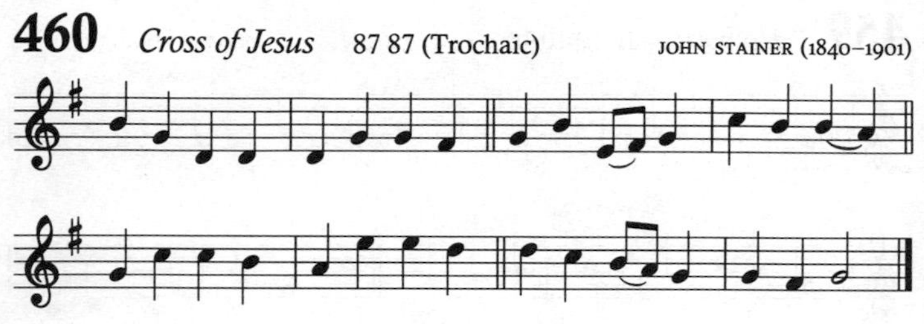

1 Thee we praise, high priest and victim,
of our hearts the shepherd-king;
living, dying, rising, saving;
now let alleluias ring.

2 Here, a dedicated priesthood,
we are met to worship thee;
all thy saints, on earth, in heaven,
humbly bend the adoring knee.

3 Here we see the mystery telling
of thy wondrous love for all;
here in prayer and sacred symbol
we thy boundless love recall.

4 See thy Body bruised and broken,
see thy Blood for us outpoured;
thou the Priest and thou the Victim,
holy, holy, holy Lord!

5 Now thou standest at thine altar
feeding us with food divine;
here thy flesh and blood thou givest,
making us most truly thine.

6 Lo! in adoration bending,
we receive what thou dost give;
join the angels' choir unending,
feed by faith on thee and live.

7 Praise to thee, eternal Saviour!
Praises from the earth ascend;
praises from the saints in heaven,
alleluias without end.

WILLIAM ROBINSON (1888–1963)*

461 *Ach Gott und Herr* 87 87 (Iambic)

Melody from *Andachts Zymbeln*, Freiburg, 1655
adpt. J. S. BACH (1685–1750)

1 Strengthen for service, Lord, the hands
that holy things have taken;
let ears that now have heard your songs
to clamour never waken.

2 Lord, may the tongues which 'Holy' sang
keep free from all deceiving;
the eyes which saw your love be bright,
your blessed hope perceiving.

3 May feet that tread your hallowed courts
from light be never banished;
may bodies by your Body fed
with your life be replenished.

Liturgy of Malabar
tr. C. W. HUMPHREYS (1840–1921)
and PERCY DEARMER (1867–1936) altd.*

462 *St Keverne* 14 14 14 15

C. S. LANG (1891–1971)

1 From glory to glory advancing, we praise thee, O Lord;
thy name with the Father and Spirit be ever adored,
from strength unto strength we go forward on Zion's highway,
to appear before God in the city of infinite day.

2 Thanksgiving and glory and worship and blessing and love,
one heart and one song have the saints upon earth and above.
O Lord, evermore to thy servants thy presence be nigh;
fit us by our service on earth for thy service on high.

Liturgy of St James
tr. C. W. HUMPHREYS (1840–1921) altd.*

463

FIRST TUNE

Warrington LM

RALPH HARRISON (1748–1810)

SECOND TUNE

Solothurn LM

Swiss traditional melody

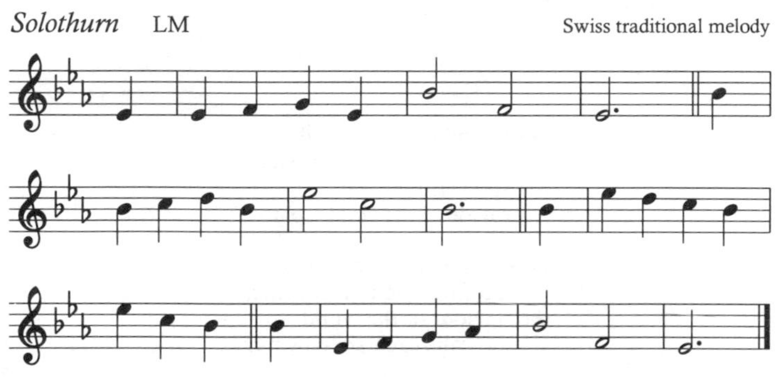

1 Now let us from this table rise
renewed in body, mind and soul;
with Christ we die and live again,
his selfless love has made us whole.

2 With minds alert, upheld by grace,
to spread the Word in speech and deed,
we follow in the steps of Christ,
at one with all in hope and need.

3 To fill each human house with love,
it is the sacrament of care;
the work that Christ began to do
we humbly pledge ourselves to share.

4 Then grant us courage, Father God,
to choose again the pilgrim way,
and help us to accept with joy
the challenge of tomorrow's day.

FRED KAAN (1929–)

464 *St Cecilia* 66 66 L. G. HAYNE (1836–83)

1 Glory and praise to God
who loves the human race;
his all-creating word
provides each child a place.

2 Glory and praise to Christ
who from the Father came,
the Saviour of the world,
who calls each child by name.

3 O Holy Spirit, come,
your gifts of grace instil,
all the good will of God
in *this new life* fulfil. (*these new lives*)

BRYN A. REES (1911–83)

465 *Sunset* 98 98 G. G. STOCKS (1877–1960)

1 With grateful hearts our faith professing,
we ask you, Lord, come to our aid:
that we, our children re-possessing,
may keep the vows that we have made.

2 We know that in your true providing
the young and old to Christ belong;
Lord, help us to be wise in guiding,
and make us in example strong.

3 Give to all parents love and patience,
each home with Christian graces fill,
protect all children in temptations,
and keep them safe in every ill.

4 Accept, O Lord, our dedication
to fill with love the growing mind,
that in this church and congregation
the young a living faith may find.

FRED KAAN (1929–)*

466 *Sussex Carol* 88 88 88

English traditional melody

1 As man and woman we were made,
 that love be found and life begun;
so praise the Lord who made us two,
 and praise the Lord when two are one:
praise for the love that comes to life
through child or parent, husband, wife.

2 Now Jesus lived and gave his love
 to make our life and loving new;
so celebrate with him today,
 and drink the joy he offers you
that makes the simple moment shine
and changes water into wine.

3 And Jesus died to live again;
 so praise the love that, come what may,
can bring the dawn and clear the skies,
 and waits to wipe all tears away;
and let us hope for what shall be,
believing where we cannot see.

4 Then spread the table, clear the hall,
   and celebrate till day is done;
let peace go deep between us all,
   and joy be shared by everyone:
laugh and make merry with your friends,
and praise the love that never ends!

BRIAN WREN (1936–)

467 *Herongate* LM

English traditional melody

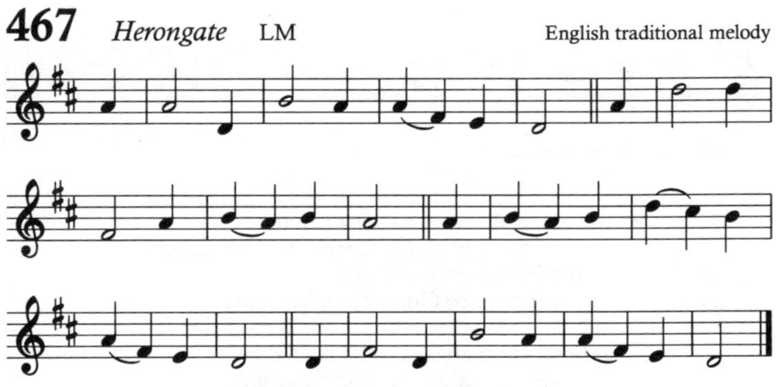

1 O God, your life-creating love
   this sacred trust to parents gave.
In Christ your power came from above
   your children here to claim and save.

2 Help us who now our pledges give
   the young to cherish, guard and guide,
to learn of Christ, and so to live
   that they may in your love abide.

3 Grant, Lord, as strength and wisdom grow,
   that every child your truth may learn.
Impart your light, that each may know
   your will, and life's true way discern.

4 Then home and child, kept in your peace,
   and guarded, Father, by your care,
will in the grace of Christ increase,
   and all your Kingdom's blessings share.

A. F. BAYLY (1901–84) altd.*

468 *Philadelphia* LM

Adpt. by SAMUEL WESLEY (1766–1837)
from 'Gregorian melody'

Alternative tune: MELCOMBE, no. 562.

1 Surprised by joy no song can tell,
no thought can compass, here we stand
to celebrate eternal Love,
to reach for God's almighty hand.

2 Beyond an angel's mind is this,
best gift, alone to mortals given;
the love of parent, lover, friend
brings straight to earth the bliss of heaven.

3 Faith, hope and love here come alive;
God's very being is made known
when, giving and forgiving all,
two are inseparably one.

4 For all this splendour, all this joy
is ours because a Father's care—
large, generous, patient, strong as death—
showed us in Christ what love can dare.

5 Your banner over us be love,
your grace refresh our travelling days,
your power sustain, your beauty cheer;
our words, our home, our lives be praise!

ERIK ROUTLEY (1917–82)

469 *As we are gathered*

JOHN DANIELS

Words anon., 1979*

470 Cambridge 66 65 65 (Irregular)
CHARLES WOOD (1866–1926)
ORGAN INTRODUCTION
VERSES
1. Christ, who knows all_ his sheep, will all_ in
2. I know my God_ is just,_ to him_ I
3. Lord Je - sus, take_ my spi - rit: I trust_ thy
safe - ty keep._ He will not lose_ his
whol - ly trust;_ all that I have,_ and
love_ and me - rit: take home this wan - dering
blood, nor in - ter - ces - sion: nor we the
am,_ all that I hope for: all's sure and
sheep, for thou_ hast sought it: this soul in
pur - chased good_ of his_ dear pas - sion.
seen_ to him,_ which I_ here grope for.
safe - ty keep,_ for thou_ hast bought it.
Org.

1 Christ, who knows all his sheep,
will all in safety keep.
He will not lose his blood,
nor intercession:
nor we the purchased good
of his dear passion.

2 I know my God is just,
to him I wholly trust;
all that I have, and am,
all that I hope for:
all's sure and seen to him,
which I here grope for.

3 Lord Jesus, take my spirit:
I trust thy love and merit:
take home this wandering sheep,
for thou hast sought it:
this soul in safety keep,
for thou hast bought it.

RICHARD BAXTER (1615–91)

471 *Komm, Herr, segne uns*

DIETER TRAUTWEIN (1928–)

11 11 5 66 5

1 Bless, and keep us, Lord, in your love united,
from your family never separated.
You make all things new
as we follow after;
whether tears or laughter,
we belong to you.

2 Blessing shrivels up when your children hoard it;
help us, Lord, to share, for we can afford it.
Blessing only grows
in the act of sharing,
in a life of caring,
love that heals and glows.

3 Fill your world with peace, such as you intended.
Teach us prize the earth, love, replenish, tend it.
Lord, uplift, fulfil
all who sow in sadness:
let them reap with gladness,
by your kingdom thrilled.

4 You renew our life, changing tears to laughter;
we belong to you, so we follow after.
Bless and keep us, Lord,
in your love united,
never separated
from your living Word.

DIETER TRAUTWEIN (1928–)
tr. FRED KAAN (1929–)

472 *St Matthew* DCM

Later form of a tune in *A Supplement to the New Version*, 1708
Probably by WILLIAM CROFT (1678–1727)

Alternative tune: DUNDEE, no. 129.

1 Come, let us join our friends above
  that have obtained the prize;
and on the eagle wings of love
  to joys celestial rise:
let all the saints terrestrial sing
  with those to glory gone;
for all the servants of our King,
  in earth and heaven, are one.

2 One family we dwell in him,
  one Church, above, beneath,
though now divided by the stream,
  the narrow stream of death:
one army of the living God,
  to his command we bow;
part of his host has crossed the flood,
  and part is crossing now.

3 Our spirits too shall quickly join,
  like theirs with glory crowned,
and shout to see our captain's sign,
  to hear his trumpet sound.
O that we now might grasp our guide!
  O that the word were given!
Come, Lord of hosts, the waves divide,
  and bring us safe to heaven.

CHARLES WESLEY (1707–88) altd.

473 *Ubi caritas* 13 12 12 12 12

A. GREGORY MURRAY (1905–92)

God is love, and where true love is, God himself is there.

1 Here in Christ we gather, love of Christ our calling.
Christ, our love, is with us, gladness be his greeting.
Let us love and serve him, God of all the ages.
Let us love sincerely, seeing Christ in others.
God is love, and where true love is, God himself is there.

2 When we Christians gather, members of his Body,
Christ, our Head, is with us, loving and beloved.
Here is sent the Spirit, one with Son and Father,
fire of love's indwelling, bond of peace among us.
God is love, and where true love is, God himself is there.

3 Grant us love's fulfilment, joy with all the blessed,
when we see your glory, risen Lord and Saviour.
Bathe us in your splendour, Light of all creation,
be our bliss for ever as we sing your praises.
God is love, and where true love is, God himself is there.

JAMES QUINN (1919–) altd.
adpt. from the Liturgy of Maundy Thursday

474 *Servant Song* 87 87 (Trochaic) RICHARD GILLARD (1953–)

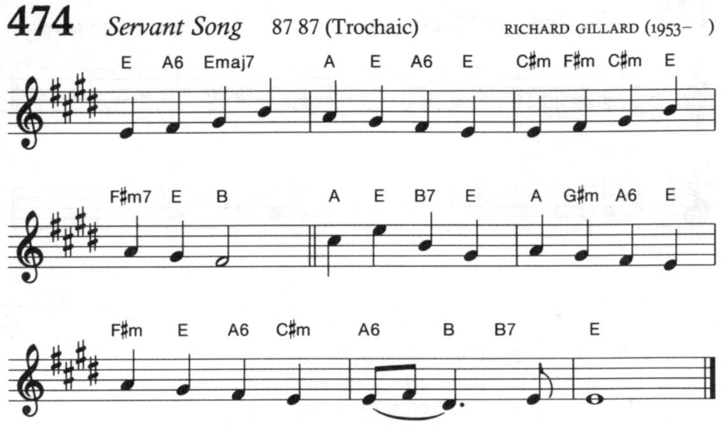

1 Brother, Sister, let me serve you,
let me be as Christ to you;
pray that I may have the grace to
let you be my servant too.

2 We are pilgrims on a journey,
and companions on the road;
we are here to help each other
walk the mile and bear the load.

3 I will hold the Christ-light for you
in the night-time of your fear;
I will hold my hand out to you,
speak the peace you long to hear.

4 I will weep when you are weeping;
when you laugh I'll laugh with you;
I will share your joy and sorrow
till we've seen this journey through.

5 When we sing to God in heaven
we shall find such harmony,
born of all we've known together
of Christ's love and agony.

6 Brother, Sister, let me serve you,
let me be as Christ to you;
pray that I may have the grace to
let you be my servant too.

RICHARD GILLARD (1953–) altd.

475 *Kingdom* 87 87 (Trochaic)

V. EARLE COPES (1921–)

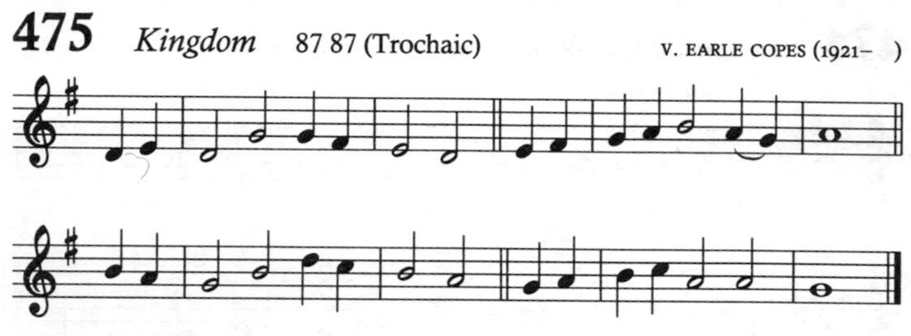

1 God, you meet us in our weakness
giving strength beyond our own,
by your Spirit, by your people,
showing we are not alone.

2 God, you meet us in our sorrows
with the comfort of your voice,
by your Spirit, by your people,
helping crying hearts rejoice.

3 God, you meet us in our neighbours,
when your strength and voice we need.
Yours the Spirit, we your people,
sharing love in word and deed!

GLEN BAKER (1932–)*

476 *Festus* LM

Adpt. from FREYLINGHAUSEN'S *Gesangbuch*, 1704

1 Jesus, where'er thy people meet,
there they behold thy mercy-seat:
where'er they seek thee, thou art found,
and every place is hallowed ground.

2 For thou, within no walls confined,
inhabitest the humble mind:
such ever bring thee where they come,
and going, take thee to their home.

3 Here may we prove the power of prayer,
to strengthen faith and sweeten care,
to teach our faint desires to rise,
and bring all heaven before our eyes.

4 Lord, we are few, but thou art near;
nor short thine arm, nor deaf thine ear;
O rend the heavens, come quickly down,
and make a thousand hearts thine own!

WILLIAM COWPER (1731–1800)

477 *Let there be love* 87 87 88 84

D. BILBROUGH

D. BILBROUGH, 1979*

478 *Lux aeterna* Irregular

PAUL BATEMAN (1954–)

Small notes are to fit the words of verses 4 and 5.

1 Many are the lightbeams from the one light.
   Our one light is Jesus.
Many are the lightbeams from the one light;
   we are one in Christ.

2 Many are the branches of the one tree.
   Our one tree is Jesus.
Many are the branches of the one tree;
   we are one in Christ.

3 Many are the gifts given, love is all one.
   Love's the gift of Jesus.
Many are the gifts given, love is all one;
   we are one in Christ.

4 Many ways to serve God, the Spirit is one;
   servant spirit of Jesus.
Many ways to serve God, the Spirit is one;
   we are one in Christ.

5 Many are the members, the body is one;
   members all of Jesus.
Many are the members, the body is one;
   we are one in Christ.

ANDERS FROSTENSON (1906–)
tr. DAVID LEWIS (1916–)

479 *Shalom chaverim*

Israeli traditional melody

Round

Traditional, para. compilers

For guitar use, play Dm chords throughout.
The letters indicate performance as a four-part round, the numbers as an eight-part round.

When the modern Hebrew version is sung, the word 'chaverim' (which means 'friends' or 'companions') should be pronounced with a soft 'ch' as in 'loch'. 'L'hitraot' means literally 'to see each other (again)'.

480 *Holly Lane* 76 777 6

PAMELA WARD (1946–)

1 The church is like a table,
  a table that is round.
It has no sides or corners,
no first or last, no honours;
here people are in one-ness
  and love together bound.

2 The church is like a table
  set in an open house;
no protocol for seating,
a symbol of inviting,
of sharing, drinking, eating;
  an end to 'them' and 'us'.

3 The church is like a table,
  a table for a feast
to celebrate the healing
of all excluded-feeling,
(while Christ is serving, kneeling,
  a towel round his waist).

4 The church is like a table,
  where every head is crowned.
As guests of God created,
all are to each related;
the whole world is awaited
  to make the circle round.

FRED KAAN (1929–)

481 *Illsley* LM

JOHN BISHOP (1665–1737)

The Resolution. Psalm 119: 96.
Written when I was silenced and cast out

1 They lack not friends who have thy love,
and may converse and walk with thee,
and with thy saints here and above,
with whom for ever I must be.

2 In the communion of thy saints
is wisdom, safety and delight;
and when my heart declines and faints,
they raise it by their heat and light.

3 As for my friends, they are not lost;
the several vessels of thy fleet,
though parted now, by tempests tossed,
shall safely in the haven meet.

4 Still we are centred all in thee,
members, though distant, of one Head;
in the same family are we,
by the same faith and spirit led.

5 Before thy throne we daily meet
as joint-petitioners to thee;
in spirit we each other greet,
and shall again each other see.

6 The heavenly hosts, world without end,
shall be my company above;
and thou, my best and surest friend,
who shall divide me from thy love?

RICHARD BAXTER (1615–91) altd.

482 *Yarnton* 89 85 BRIAN WREN (1936–)

1 We are not our own. Earth forms us,
human leaves on nature's growing vine,
fruit of many generations,
seeds of life divine.

2 We are not alone. Earth names us:
past and present, peoples near and far,
family and friends and strangers
show us who we are.

3 Through a human life God finds us;
dying, living, love is fully known,
and in bread and wine reminds us:
we are not our own.

4 Therefore let us make thanksgiving,
and with justice, willing and aware,
give to earth and all things living,
liturgies of care.

5 And if love's encounters lead us
on a way uncertain and unknown,
all the saints with prayer surround us:
we are not alone.

6 Let us be a house of welcome,
living stone upholding living stone,
gladly showing all our neighbours
we are not our own!

BRIAN WREN (1936–)

483

First Tune

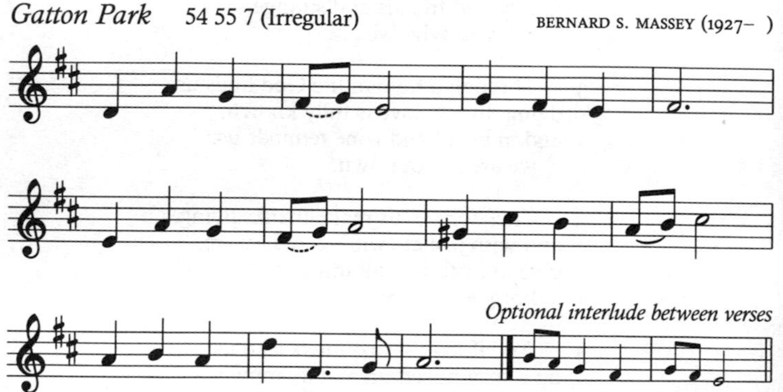

1 We are your people:
Lord, by your grace,
  you dare to make us
  Christ to our neighbours
of every nation and race.

2 How can we demonstrate
your love and care—
  speaking or listening?
  battling or serving?
help us to know when and where.

3 Called to portray you,
help us to live
  closer than neighbours,
  open to strangers,
able to clash and forgive.

4 Glad of tradition,
help us to see
  in all life's changing
  where you are leading,
where our best efforts should be.

5 Joined in community,
breaking your bread,
  may we discover
  gifts in each other,
willing to lead and be led.

6 Lord, as we minister
in different ways,
  may all we're doing
  show that you're living,
meeting your love with our praise.

BRIAN WREN (1936–   )

484 *Luther's Hymn* 87 87 887 *Geistliche Lieder*, 1535

1 We come unto our faithful God,
the Rock of our Salvation;
the eternal arms, that sure abode,
we make our habitation;
we seek thee as thy saints have sought;
we bring thee, Lord, the praise they brought,
in every generation.

2 The fire divine their steps that led
still goeth bright before us;
the heavenly shield around them spread
is still uplifted o'er us;
the grace those sinners that subdued,
the strength those weaklings that renewed,
doth vanquish, doth restore us.

3 Their joy unto their Lord we bring;
their song to us descendeth;
the Spirit who in them did sing
to us his music lendeth;
his song in them, in us, is one;
we raise it high, we send it on,—
the song that never endeth.

4 Ye saints to come, take up the strain,
the same sweet theme endeavour;
unbroken be the golden chain;
keep on the song for ever;
safe in the same dear dwelling-place,
rich with the same eternal grace,
bless the same boundless Giver.

T. H. GILL (1819–1906) altd.*

485 *Chilton Foliat* 10 10 10 10 G. C. MARTIN (1844–1916)

1 Almighty Father of all things that be,
our life, our work, we consecrate to thee,
whose heavens declare thy glory from above,
whose earth below is witness to thy love.

2 For well we know this weary, fallen earth
is yet thine own by right of its new birth,
since that great cross upreared on Calvary
redeemed it from its fault and shame to thee.

3 Thine still the changeful beauty of the hills,
the purple valleys flecked with silver rills,
the ocean glistening 'neath the golden rays;
they all are thine, and voiceless speak thy praise.

4 Thou dost the strength to worker's arm impart;
from thee the skilled musician's mystic art,
the grace of poet's pen or painter's hand,
to teach the loveliness of sea and land.

5 Then grant us, Lord, in all things thee to own,
to dwell within the shadow of thy throne,
to speak and work, to think, and live, and move,
reflecting thine own nature, which is love:

6 that so, by Christ redeemed from sin and shame,
and hallowed by thy Spirit's cleansing flame,
ourselves, our work, and all our powers may be
a sacrifice acceptable to thee.

ERNEST DUGMORE (1843–1925) altd.

486 *Intercessor* 11 10 11 10

C. H. H. PARRY (1848–1918)

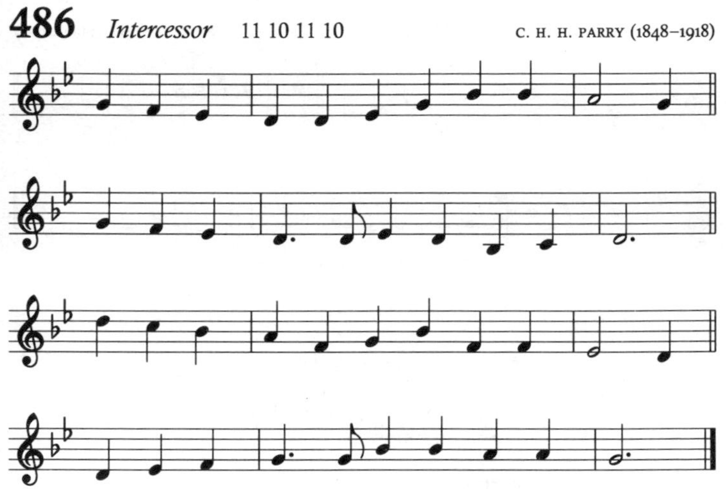

1 By gracious powers so wonderfully sheltered,
   and confidently waiting, come what may,
we know that God is with us night and morning,
   and never fails to greet us each new day.

2 Yet is this heart by its old foe tormented,
   still evil days bring burdens hard to bear;
O give our frightened souls the sure salvation
   for which, O Lord, you taught us to prepare.

3 And when this cup you give is filled to brimming
   with bitter suffering, hard to understand,
we take it thankfully and without trembling
   out of so good and so beloved a hand.

4 Yet when again in this same world you give us
   the joy we had, the brightness of your Sun,
we shall remember all the days we lived through,
   and our whole life shall then be yours alone.

DIETRICH BONHOEFFER (1906–45)
(written in prison, for the New Year 1945,
a few months before his execution)
tr. F. PRATT GREEN (1903–)

487 *Kilmarnock* CM

NEIL DOUGALL (1776–1862)

1 Awake, my soul, stretch every nerve,
and press with vigour on;
a heavenly race demands thy zeal,
and an immortal crown.

2 A cloud of witnesses around
holds thee in full survey:
forget the steps already trod
and onward urge thy way.

3 'Tis God's all-animating voice
that calls thee from on high;
'tis his own hand presents the prize
to thine aspiring eye:

4 that prize, with peerless glories bright,
which shall new lustre boast,
when victor's wreaths and monarchs' gems
shall blend in common dust.

5 Blest Saviour, introduced by thee
have I my race begun;
and, crowned with victory, at thy feet
I'll lay my honours down.

PHILIP DODDRIDGE (1702–51)*

488 *Samson* LM Adapted from G. F. HANDEL (1685–1759)

1 Awake, our souls; away, our fears;
let every trembling thought be gone;
awake, and run the heavenly race,
and put a cheerful courage on.

2 True, 'tis a strait and thorny road,
and mortal spirits tire and faint;
but they forget the mighty God
who feeds the strength of every saint—

3 thee, mighty God, whose matchless power
is ever new and ever young,
and firm endures, while endless years
their everlasting circles run!

4 From thee, the overflowing spring,
our souls shall drink a fresh supply,
while such as trust their native strength
shall faint away, and droop, and die.

5 Swift as an eagle cuts the air,
we'll mount aloft to thine abode;
on wings of love our souls shall fly,
nor tire amidst the heavenly road.

ISAAC WATTS (1674–1748)

489 *Slane* 10 10 10 10 (Dactylic) Irish traditional melody

1 Be thou my vision, O Lord of my heart,
naught be all else to me, save that thou art—
thou my best thought in the day and the night,
waking and sleeping, thy presence my light.

2 Be thou my wisdom, be thou my true word,
thou ever with me and I with thee, Lord;
thou my great Father, thy child let me be,
thou in me dwelling, and I one with thee.

3 Be thou my breastplate, my sword for the fight;
be thou my dignity, thou my delight,
thou my soul's shelter, and thou my strong tower;
raise thou me heav'nward, great Power of my power.

4 Riches I heed not, nor earth's empty praise,
thou mine inheritance, now and always;
thou and thou only, the first in my heart,
High King of heaven, my treasure thou art.

5 High King of heaven, thou heaven's bright sun,
grant me its joys after vict'ry is won;
heart of my own heart, whatever befall,
still be my vision, O Ruler of all.

Ancient Irish poem
tr. MARY E. BYRNE (1880–1931)
and ELEANOR H. HULL (1860–1935) altd.

490 *St Brelade* 66 88 6 CARYL MICKLEM (1925–)

1 Beyond the mist and doubt
    of this uncertain day,
I trust in your eternal name,
beyond all changes still the same,
    and in that name I pray.

2 Our restless intellect
    has all things in its shade,
but still to you my spirit clings,
serene beyond all shaken things,
    and I am not afraid.

3 Still in humility
    we know you by your grace,
for science's remotest probe
feels but the fringes of your robe:
    love looks upon your face.

DONALD WYNN HUGHES (1911–67) altd.

491 *Day by day* 56 667 3

D. AUSTIN (1932–)

F Gm C7 F Dm G7

Day by day, dear Lord, of thee three things I

C7 F D7 Gm Gm7

pray: to see thee more clear-ly, to love thee more

C C7 F B♭6 F C7 F

dear-ly, to fol-low thee more near-ly, day by day.

attrib. RICHARD OF CHICHESTER (*c.*1197–1253) altd.

492 *Repton* 8 6 88 6 (6)

C. H. H. PARRY (1848–1918)

1 Dear Lord and Father of mankind,
forgive our foolish ways!
Reclothe us in our rightful mind;
in purer lives thy service find,
in deeper reverence, praise.

2 In simple trust like theirs who heard
beside the Syrian sea
the gracious calling of the Lord,
let us, like them, without a word,
rise up and follow thee.

3 O Sabbath rest by Galilee!
O calm of hills above,
where Jesus knelt to share with thee
the silence of eternity
interpreted by love!

4 With that deep hush subduing all
our words and works that drown
the tender whisper of thy call,
as noiseless let thy blessing fall
as fell thy manna down.

5 Drop thy still dews of quietness,
till all our strivings cease;
take from our souls the strain and stress,
and let our ordered lives confess
the beauty of thy peace.

6 Breathe through the heats of our desire
thy coolness and thy balm;
let sense be dumb, let flesh retire;
speak through the earthquake, wind, and fire,
O still, small voice of calm!

J. G. WHITTIER (1807–92)

493 *Herongate* LM

English traditional melody

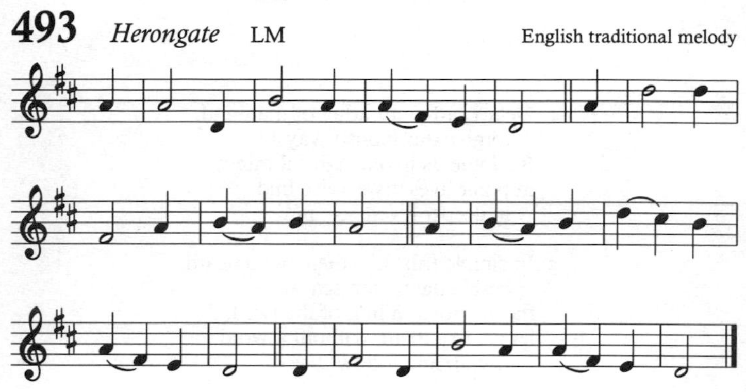

1 Dear Master, in whose life I see
all that I would, but fail to be,
let thy clear light for ever shine,
to shame and guide this life of mine.

2 Though what I dream and what I do
in my weak days are always two,
help me, oppressed by things undone,
O thou, whose deeds and dreams were one.

JOHN HUNTER (1848–1917)

494 *St Paul (Aberdeen)* CM

CHALMERS' *Collection*, Aberdeen, 1749

1 Father of peace, and God of love,
we own your power to save—
that power by which our Shepherd rose
victorious o'er the grave.

2 Him from the dead you brought again,
when, by his sacred blood,
confirmed and sealed for evermore
the eternal covenant stood.

3 O may your spirit seal our souls,
and mould them to your will,
that our weak hearts no more may stray,
but keep your precepts still;

4 that to perfection's sacred height
we nearer still may rise,
and all we think, and all we do,
be pleasing in your eyes.

Scottish Paraphrases, 1781, altd;
from Hebrews 13: 20–21
based on para. by PHILIP DODDRIDGE (1702–51)
(v. 1: DODDRIDGE; v. 4: prob. WILLIAM CAMERON (1751–1811))

495 *Sussex* 87 87 (Trochaic)

English traditional melody
adapt. R. VAUGHAN WILLIAMS (1872–1958)

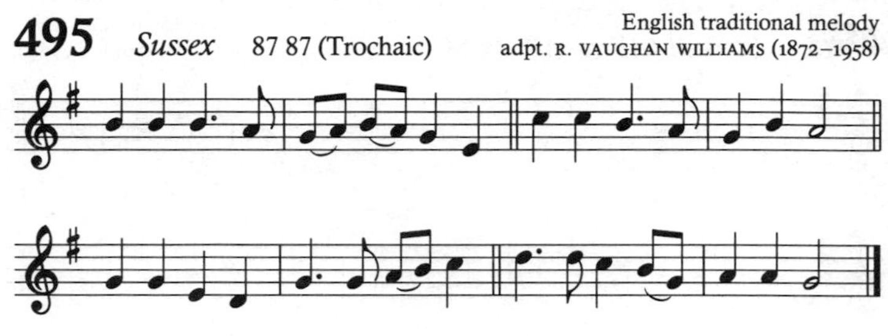

1 Father, hear the prayer we offer;
not for ease that prayer shall be,
but for strength that we may ever
live our lives courageously.

2 Not for ever in green pastures
do we ask our way to be;
but the steep and rugged pathway
may we tread rejoicingly.

3 Not for ever by still waters
would we idly rest and stay;
but would smite the living fountains
from the rocks along our way.

4 Be our strength in hours of weakness,
in our wanderings be our guide;
through endeavour, failure, danger,
Father, be thou at our side.

LOVE MARIA WILLIS (1824–1908) and others

496 *Duke Street* LM

Melody from BOYD's *Psalm & Hymn Tunes*, 1793
Later attrib. to JOHN HATTON (d. 1793)

1 Fight the good fight with all thy might;
Christ is thy strength, and Christ thy right;
lay hold on life, and it shall be
thy joy and crown eternally.

2 Run the straight race through God's good grace,
lift up thine eyes, and seek his face;
life with its way before us lies;
Christ is the path, and Christ the prize.

3 Cast care aside; and on thy guide
lean, and his mercy will provide;
lean, and the trusting soul shall prove
Christ is its life, and Christ its love.

4 Faint not nor fear, his arm is near;
he changeth not, and thou art dear;
only believe, and thou shalt see
that Christ is all in all to thee.

J. S. B. MONSELL (1811–75) altd.

497 *Gatescarth* 86 88 6

CARYL MICKLEM (1925–)

1 Give to me, Lord, a thankful heart
and a discerning mind:
give, as I play the Christian's part,
the strength to finish what I start
and act on what I find.

2 When, in the rush of days, my will
is habit-bound and slow
help me to keep in vision still
what love and power and peace can fill
a life that trusts in you.

3 By your divine and urgent claim
and by your human face
kindle our sinking hearts to flame
and as you teach the world your name
let it become your place.

4 Jesus, with all your Church I long
to see your kingdom come:
show me your way of righting wrong
and turning sorrow into song
until you bring me home.

CARYL MICKLEM (1925–)

498 *God be in my head*

H. WALFORD DAVIES (1869–1941)

God be in my head
  and in my understanding;
God be in my eyes
  and in my looking;
God be in my mouth
  and in my speaking;
God be in my heart
  and in my thinking;
God be at my end
  and at my departing.

from a *Book of Hours*, Sarum, 1514

499 *Carlisle* SM

CHARLES LOCKHART (1745–1815)

1 Have faith in God, my heart,
   trust and be unafraid;
God will fulfil in every part
   each promise he has made.

2 Have faith in God, my mind,
   although your light burns low;
God's mercy holds a wiser plan
   than you can fully know.

3 Have faith in God, my soul,
   his cross for ever stands;
and neither life nor death can pluck
   his children from his hands.

4 Lord Jesus, make me whole;
   grant me no resting-place,
until I rest, heart, mind and soul,
   the captive of your grace.

BRYN A. REES (1911–83) altd.

500 *Dunfermline* CM

Scottish Psalter, 1615

1 Jesus, united by thy grace
and each to each endeared,
with confidence we seek thy face,
and know our prayer is heard.

2 Help us to help each other, Lord,
each other's cross to bear,
let all their friendly aid afford
and feel each other's care.

3 Touched by the lodestone of thy love,
let all our hearts agree,
and ever toward each other move,
and ever move toward thee.

4 To thee, inseparably joined,
let all our spirits cleave;
O may we all the loving mind
that was in thee, receive.

5 This is the bond of perfectness,
thy spotless charity;
O let us, still we pray, possess
the mind that was in thee.

CHARLES WESLEY (1707–88) altd.

501 *Song 24* 10 10 10 10 ORLANDO GIBBONS (1583–1625)

Alternative tune: STONER HILL, no. 404.

1 I greet thee, who my sure Redeemer art,
my only trust and Saviour of my heart,
who pain didst undergo for my poor sake;
I pray thee from me anxious cares to take.

2 Thou art the King of mercy and of grace,
reigning omnipotent in every place:
so come, O King, and our whole being sway;
shine on us with the light of thy pure day.

3 Thou art the Life, by which alone we live,
and all our substance and our strength receive;
sustain us by thy faith and by thy power,
and give us strength in every trying hour.

4 Thou hast the true and perfect gentleness,
no harshness hast thou and no bitterness:
O grant to us the grace we find in thee,
that we may dwell in perfect unity.

5 Our hope is in no other save in thee;
our faith is built upon thy promise free;
Lord, give us peace, and make us calm and sure,
that in thy strength we evermore endure.

from *French Psalter*, Strasbourg, 1545
attrib. JOHN CALVIN (1509–64)
tr. ELIZABETH L. SMITH (1817–98), adpt. & altd.*

502 *Neumark* 98 98 88

GEORG NEUMARK (1621–81)

1 If thou but trust in God to guide thee,
   and hope in him through all thy ways,
he'll give thee strength, whate'er betide thee,
   and bear thee through the evil days;
who trusts in God's unchanging love
builds on the rock that naught can move.

2 Only be still, and wait his leisure
   in cheerful hope, with heart content
to take whate'er thy Father's pleasure,
   his all-discerning love, has sent;
nor doubt our inmost wants are known
to him who chose us for his own.

3 Sing, pray, and keep his ways unswerving;
   so do thine own part faithfully,
and trust his word,—though undeserving,
   thou yet shalt find it true for thee;
God never yet forsook at need
the soul that trusted him indeed.

GEORG NEUMARK (1621–81)
tr. CATHERINE WINKWORTH (1827–78) altd.*

503 *Bablock Hythe* DLM CARYL MICKLEM (1925–)

1 It is a thing most wonderful,
almost too wonderful to be,
that God's own Son should come from heaven
and die to save a child like me:
and yet I know that it is true;
he came to this poor world below,
and wept, and toiled, and mourned, and died,
only because he loved me so.

2 I sometimes think about the cross
and shut my eyes, and try to see
the cruel nails and crown of thorns,
and Jesus crucified for me:
but even could I see him die,
I could but see a little part
of that great love, which, like a fire,
is always burning in his heart.

3 It is most wonderful to know
his love for me so free and sure;
but still more wonderful to see
my love for him so faint and poor;
and yet I want to love thee, Lord;
O light the flame within my heart,
and I will love thee more and more,
until I see thee as thou art.

W. W. HOW (1823–97) altd.*

504 *Highwood* 11 10 11 10

R. R. TERRY (1865–1938)

1 Light of the world, from whom all truth proceeding
dawns on each heart that humbly seeks thy face,
lowly we wait on thee, and, thy hand leading,
follow thy guidance to thy holy place.

2 In thee, O God, all things had their beginning;
in thee, O Lord, all things shall find their end;
thou knowest all; and we our knowledge winning
by thee alone our widening bounds extend.

3 How marv'llous are the wonders thou hast taught us
and still dost teach us each succeeding day!
From darkness into light thy hand has brought us,
and points to fuller light along our way.

4 All knowledge is not ours to know; for round us
unmeasured heights are found and depths below;
thee would we know; thy love which sought and found us
gives all we need and all that we should know.

5 Though dark the path, thy lamp is brightly burning,
lighting our faltering footsteps through the night;
from thee we came, and unto thee returning,
Light of the world, in thee we find our light.

G. W. BRIGGS (1875–1959)*

505 *Llanllyfni* DSM

JOHN JONES (Talysarn), (1796–1857)
arr. DAVID JENKINS (1848–1915)

Alternative tune: ICH HALTE TREULICH STILL, no. 550.

Christian Freedom

1 Make me a captive, Lord,
and then I shall be free;
force me to render up my sword,
and I shall conqueror be.
I sink in life's alarms
when by myself I stand;
imprison me within thine arms,
and strong shall be my hand.

2 My heart is weak and poor
until it master find;
it has no spring of action sure—
it varies with the wind.
It cannot freely move,
till thou hast wrought its chain;
enslave it with thy matchless love,
and deathless it shall reign.

3 My power is faint and low
till I have learned to serve;
it wants the needed fire to glow,
it wants the breeze to nerve;
it cannot drive the world
until itself be driven;
its flag can only be unfurled
when thou shalt breathe from heaven.

4 My will is not my own
till thou hast made it thine;
if it would reach a monarch's throne
it must its crown resign;
it only stands unbent,
amid the clashing strife,
when on thy bosom it has leant
and found in thee its life.

GEORGE MATHESON (1842–1906)

506 *David's Harp* 88 88 88

ROBERT KING (*fl.*1676–1728)

1 Jesus, thy boundless love to me
no thought can reach, no tongue declare;
O knit my thankful heart to thee,
and reign without a rival there:
thine wholly, thine alone, I am;
Lord, with thy love my heart inflame.

2 Lord, grant that nothing in my soul
may dwell, but thy pure love alone:
O may thy love possess me whole,
my joy, my treasure, and my crown:
all coldness from my heart remove;
my every act, word, thought, be love.

3 Still let thy love point out my way,
what wondrous things thy love hath wrought;
still lead me lest I go astray;
direct my word, inspire my thought;
and if I fall, soon may I hear
thy voice, and know that love is near.

PAUL GERHARDT (1607–76)
tr. JOHN WESLEY (1703–91) altd.

507 *Aus der Tiefe (Heinlein)*

77 77

Melody from *Nürnbergisches Gesangbuch*, 1676–7, altd.
possibly by MARTIN HERBST (1654–81)

1 Never further than thy cross,
never higher than thy feet;
here earth's precious things seem dross,
here earth's bitter things grow sweet.

2 Gazing thus, our sin we see,
learn thy love while gazing thus—
sin, which laid the cross on thee,
love, which bore the cross for us.

3 Here we learn to serve and give,
and, rejoicing, self deny;
here we gather love to live,
here we gather faith to die.

4 Symbols of our liberty
and our service, here unite;
captives, by thy Cross set free,
soldiers of thy Cross, we fight.

5 Pressing onwards as we can,
still to this our hearts must tend,
where our earliest hopes began,
there our last aspirings end,—

6 till amid the hosts of heaven
we in thee redeemed, complete,
through thy Cross all sins forgiven,
cast our crowns before thy feet.

ELISABETH R. CHARLES (1828–96) altd.

508

FIRST TUNE

Caithness CM — Melody from *Scottish Psalter*, 1635

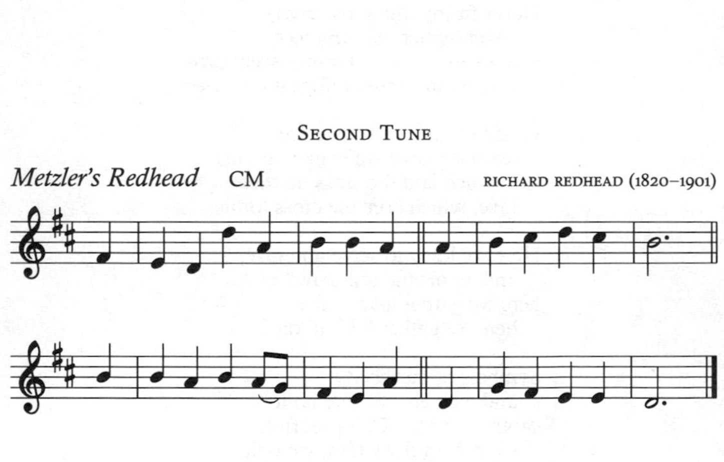

SECOND TUNE

Metzler's Redhead CM — RICHARD REDHEAD (1820–1901)

1 O Jesus Christ, grow thou in me
 and all things else recede;
my heart be daily nearer thee,
 from sin be daily freed.

2 Each day let thy supporting might
 my weakness still embrace;
my darkness vanish in thy light,
 thy life my death efface.

3 Let faith in thee and in thy might
 my every motive move,
be thou alone my soul's delight,
 my passion and my love.

4 Fill me with gladness from above,
 hold me by strength divine!
Lord, let the glow of thy great love
 through my whole being shine.

5 Make thoughts of self grow less and less,
 be thou my life and aim;
O make me daily, through thy grace,
 more worthy of thy name!

JOHANN C. LAVATER (1741–1801)
tr. attrib. ELIZABETH L. SMITH (1817–98)*

509 *Wolvercote* 76 76 D W. H. FERGUSON (1874–1950)

1 O Jesus, I have promised
to serve thee to the end;
be thou for ever near me,
my Master and my Friend;
I shall not fear the battle
if thou art by my side,
nor wander from the pathway
if thou wilt be my guide.

2 O let me feel thee near me;
the world is ever near,
I see the sights that dazzle,
the tempting sounds I hear;
my foes are ever near me,
around me and within;
but, Jesus, draw thou nearer,
and shield my soul from sin.

3 O let me hear thee speaking
in accents clear and still,
above the storms of passion,
the murmurs of self-will.
O speak to reassure me,
to hasten or control;
O speak, and make me listen,
thou guardian of my soul.

4 O Jesus, thou hast promised,
to all who follow thee,
that where thou art in glory
there shall thy servant be;
O guide me, call me, draw me,
uphold me to the end;
O give me grace to follow,
my Saviour and my Friend.

J. E. BODE (1816–74)*

510 *Taiwan* 9 9 10 6

C. M. KAO

1 O Lord, you are the life of the world,
O Lord, you are the life of the world,
come, live within me, come and enrich me
until I live like you.

2 O Lord, make me a lamp of new light,
O Lord, make me a lamp of new light,
so in the darkest and suffering places
I always shine for you.

3 O Lord, make me a spring of new life,
O Lord, make me a spring of new life,
so for the thirsty and crying people
I always flow like you.

C. M. KAO
tr. LILY KAO*

511 *St Margaret* 88 88 6

A. L. PEACE (1844–1912)

1 O Love that wilt not let me go,
I rest my weary soul in thee;
I give thee back the life I owe,
that in thine ocean depths its flow
may richer, fuller be.

2 O light that followest all my way,
I yield my flickering torch to thee;
my heart restores its borrowed ray,
that in thy sunshine's blaze its day
may brighter, fairer be.

3 O joy that seekest me through pain,
I cannot close my heart to thee;
I trace the rainbow through the rain,
and feel the promise is not vain,
that morn shall tearless be.

4 O Cross that liftest up my head,
I dare not ask to fly from thee;
I lay in dust life's glory dead,
and from the ground there blossoms red
life that shall endless be.

GEORGE MATHESON (1842–1906)

KAREN LAFFERTY (1948–)*
based on Matthew 6: 33, 7: 7 and Deuteronomy 8: 3

This hymn may be sung as a two-part canon, the second part entering when the first reaches the refrain.

513 *Third Mode Melody* DCM

THOMAS TALLIS (*c.*1505–85)

1 'Twixt gleams of joy and clouds of doubt
our feelings come and go;
our best estate is tossed about
in ceaseless ebb and flow.
No mood of feeling, form of thought,
is constant for a day;
but thou, O Lord, thou changest not:
the same thou art alway.

2 I grasp thy strength, make it mine own,
my heart with peace is blest;
I lose my hold, and then comes down
darkness, and cold unrest.
Let me no more my comfort draw
from my frail hold of thee,
in this alone rejoice with awe—
thy mighty grasp of me.

3 Out of that weak, unquiet drift
that comes but to depart,
to that pure heaven my spirit lift
where thou unchanging art.
Lay hold of me with thy strong grasp,
let thy almighty arm
in its embrace my weakness clasp,
and I shall fear no harm.

4 Thy purpose of eternal good
let me but surely know;
on this I'll lean—let changing mood
and feeling come or go—
glad when thy sunshine fills my soul,
not sad when clouds o'ercast,
since thou within thy sure control
of love dost hold me fast.

JOHN C. SHAIRP (1819–85)*

514 *St Stephen (Newington)* CM

WILLIAM JONES (1726–1800)

1 O for a heart to praise my God,
a heart from sin set free,
a heart that always feels thy blood
so freely shed for me;

2 a heart resigned, submissive, meek,
my great Redeemer's throne,
where only Christ is heard to speak,
where Jesus reigns alone;

3 a humble, lowly, contrite heart,
believing, true and clean;
which neither life nor death can part
from him that dwells within;

4 a heart in every thought renewed,
and filled with love divine;
perfect, and right, and pure, and good,
a copy, Lord, of thine!

5 Thy nature, gracious Lord, impart,
come quickly from above,
write thy new name upon my heart,
thy new, best name of love.

CHARLES WESLEY (1707–88) altd.

515 *Southwell* CM

H. S. IRONS (1834–1905)

1 We praise and bless thee, gracious Lord,
our Saviour kind and true,
for all the old things passed away,
for all thou hast made new.

2 The old security is gone
in which so long we lay;
the sleep of death thou hast dispelled,
the darkness rolled away.

3 New hopes, new purposes, desires
and joys, thy grace has given;
old ties are broken from the earth,
new ties attach to heaven.

4 But yet how much must be destroyed,
how much renewed must be,
before we fully stand complete
in likeness, Lord, to thee.

5 Thou, only thou, must carry on
the work thou hast begun;
of thine own strength thou must impart,
in thine own ways to run.

6 So shall we faultless stand at last
before thy Father's throne,
the blessedness for ever ours,
the glory all thine own.

KARL J. P. SPITTA (1801–59)
tr. JANE BORTHWICK (1813–97)*

516 *Philippian* 10 10 10 7

CARYL MICKLEM (1925–)

1 We praise you, Lord, for all that's true and pure—
clean lines, clear water, and an honest mind.
Grant us your truth, keep guard over our hearts,
fill all our thoughts with these things.

2 We praise you, Lord, for all that's excellent—
high mountain peaks, achievement dearly won.
Lift up our eyes, keep guard over our hearts,
fill all our thoughts with these things.

3 We praise you, Lord, for all of good report—
the spur to us of others' noble lives.
Show us your will, keep guard over our hearts,
fill all our thoughts with these things.

4 We praise you, Lord, the man of Nazareth—
you lived for others, now you live for all.
Jesus, draw near, keep guard over our hearts,
fill all our thoughts with these things.

CARYL MICKLEM (1925–)
based on Philippians 4: 6–8

517 *Bridegroom* 87 87 6

PETER CUTTS (1937–)

The first and second staves may each be sung by contrasted groups of voices, with the last line sung by all.

1 As the bride is to her chosen,
as the monarch to the realm,
as the keep unto the castle,
as the pilot to the helm,
so, Lord, art thou to me.

2 As the fountain in the garden,
as the candle in the dark,
as the treasure in the coffer,
as the manna in the ark,
so, Lord, art thou to me.

3 As the music at the banquet,
as the stamp unto the seal,
as the medicine to the fainting,
as the wine-cup at the meal,
so, Lord, art thou to me.

4 As the ruby in the setting,
as the honey in the comb,
as the light within the lantern,
as the parent in the home,
so, Lord, art thou to me.

5 As the sunshine in the heavens,
as the image in the glass,
as the fruit unto the fig-tree,
as the dew unto the grass,
so, Lord, art thou to me.

para. from JOHN TAULER (*c.*1300–61)
by EMMA BEVAN (1827–1909)*

518 *Father, I place into your hands*

JENNY HEWER

1 Father, I place into your hands
the things that I can't do.
Father, I place into your hands
the times that I've been through.
Father, I place into your hands
the way that I should go,
for I know I always can trust you.

2 Father, I place into your hands
my friends and family.
Father, I place into your hands
the things that trouble me.
Father, I place into your hands
the person I would be,
for I know I always can trust you.

3 Father, we love to see your face,
we love to hear your voice.
Father, we love to sing your praise,
and in your name rejoice.
Father, we love to walk with you
and in your presence rest,
for we know we always can trust you.

JENNY HEWER, 1975*

519 *Eisenach* LM

JOHANN SCHEIN (1586–1630)

1 For joys of service thee we praise,
whose favour crowneth all our days;
for humble tasks that bring delight,
when done, O Lord, as in thy sight.

2 Remove the selfishness that soils
our earthly gifts, our human toils;
and may we prove, in all we bring,
true sons and daughters of the King.

3 Accept our offerings, Lord most high,
our work, our purpose, sanctify;
and with our gifts may we have place
now in the kingdom of thy grace.

H. ELVET LEWIS (1860–1953)

520 *All Saints* 87 87 77

Later form of melody from *Geistreiches Gesangbuch*, Darmstadt, 1698

1 For ourselves no longer living,
   let us live for Christ alone;
of ourselves more strongly giving,
   go as far as he has gone:
one with God who chose to be
one with us to set us free.

2 If we are to live for others,
   share, as equals, human worth,
join the round of sisters, brothers,
   that encircles all the earth!
All the fullness earth affords,
is the people's, is the Lord's.

3 Fighting fear and exploitation
   is our daily common call;
finding selfhood, building nations,
   sharing what we have with all.
As the birds that soar in flight,
let us rise towards the light.

4 Let us rise and join the forces
   that combine to do God's will,
wisely using earth's resources,
   human energy and skill.
Let us now, by love released,
celebrate the future's feast!

FRED KAAN (1929–)*

521 *Angels' Song* LM

ORLANDO GIBBONS (1583–1625)

1 Forth in thy name, O Lord, I go,
my daily labour to pursue,
thee, only thee, resolved to know
in all I think or speak or do.

2 The task thy wisdom hath assigned
O let me cheerfully fulfil!
In all my works thy presence find,
and prove thy good and perfect will.

3 Thee may I set at my right hand,
whose eyes my inmost substance see,
and labour on at thy command,
and offer all my works to thee.

4 Give me to bear thine easy yoke,
and every moment watch and pray,
and still to things eternal look,
and hasten to thy glorious day;

5 for thee delightfully employ
whate'er thy bounteous grace hath given,
and run my course with even joy,
and closely walk with thee to heaven.

CHARLES WESLEY (1707–88) altd.

522 *Servant King* Irregular

GRAHAM KENDRICK (1950–)

1 From heaven you came, helpless babe,
entered our world, your glory veiled;
not to be served, but to serve,
and give your life that we might live.

This is our God, the Servant King,
he calls us now to follow him,
to bring our lives as a daily offering
of worship to the Servant King.

2 There in the garden of tears,
my heavy load he chose to bear;
his heart with sorrow was torn,
'Yet not my will but yours', he said.

3 Come see his hands and his feet,
 the scars that speak of sacrifice,
hands that flung stars into space
 to cruel nails surrendered.

4 So let us learn how to serve,
 and in our lives enthrone him;
each other's needs to prefer,
 for it is Christ we're serving.

GRAHAM KENDRICK (1950–)

523 *Sing Hosanna* 10 8 10 9 with refrain Traditional

1 Give me joy in my heart, keep me praising,
 give me joy in my heart, I pray;
give me joy in my heart, keep me praising,
 keep me praising till the break of day.

Sing hosanna! Sing hosanna!
Sing hosanna to the King of kings!
Sing hosanna! Sing hosanna!
Sing hosanna to the King!

2 Give me peace in my heart, keep me loving . . .

3 Give me love in my heart, keep me serving . . .

Traditional

524

FIRST TUNE

Song 24 10 10 10 10 ORLANDO GIBBONS (1583–1625)

SECOND TUNE

Winton 10 10 10 10 GEORGE DYSON (1883–1964)

1 Give me, O Christ, the strength that in thee lies,
that I may stand in every evil hour;
my poor heart faints unless to thee it flies,
resting its weakness in thy perfect power.

2 Give me to see the foes that I must fight,
powers of the darkness, throned where thou should'st reign,
read the directings of thy wrath aright,
lest, striking flesh and blood, I strike in vain.

3 Give me to wear the armour that can guard;
over my heart thy blood-bought righteousness,
faith for my shield, when fiery darts rain hard,
girded with truth, and shod with zeal to bless.

4 Give me to wield the weapon that is sure,
taking, through prayer, thy sword into my hand,
Word of thy wisdom, peaceable and pure,
so, Christ my Conqueror, I shall conqueror stand.

HENRY C. CARTER (1875–1954)*
based on Ephesians 6: 10–18

525 *Wych Cross* 88 88 88 ERIK ROUTLEY (1917–82)

1 He comes to us as one unknown
as, by the Galilean lake,
he came to those who knew him not:
he speaks the same words, 'Follow me',
and comes to set us to the tasks
he will fulfil in our own time.

2 As he commands and we obey,
he will reveal himself to us
in conflicts, toils and sufferings
encountered in his fellowship.
In our experience we shall learn,
as deepest mystery, who he is.

ALAN GAUNT (1935–)
adpt. from ALBERT SCHWEITZER (1875–1965)
The Quest of the Historical Jesus

526 *Samuel* 66 66 88 ARTHUR SULLIVAN (1842–1900)

1 Hushed was the evening hymn,
the temple-courts were dark,
the lamp was burning dim
before the sacred ark;
when suddenly a voice divine
rang through the silence of the shrine.

2 The old man meek and mild,
the priest of Israel, slept;
the little Levite child
watch in the temple kept;
and what from Eli's sense was sealed,
to Hannah's son the Lord revealed.

3 O give me Samuel's ear,
the open ear, O Lord,
alive and quick to hear
each whisper of thy word;
like him to answer to thy call,
and to obey thee first of all.

4 O give me Samuel's heart,
a lowly heart, that waits
when in thy house thou art,
or watches at thy gates;
by day and night a heart that still
moves at the breathing of thy will.

5 O give me Samuel's mind,
a sweet, unmurmuring faith,
obedient and resigned
to thee in life and death;
that I may read with childlike eyes
truths that are hidden from the wise.

J. D. BURNS (1823–64) altd.*

527 *Moab* 65 65 6665

JOHN ROBERTS (IEUAN GWYLLT) (1822–77)

Alternative tune: MONKS GATE, no. 557.

1 Jesus, our mighty Lord,
our strength in sadness,
the Father's conquering Word,
true source of gladness;
your Name we glorify,
O Jesus, throned on high;
you gave yourself to die
for our salvation.

2 Good Shepherd of your sheep,
your own defending,
in love your children keep
to life unending.
You are yourself the Way:
lead us then day by day
in your own steps, we pray,
O Lord most holy.

3 Glorious their life who sing,
with glad thanksgiving,
true hymns to Christ the King
in all their living:
all who confess his name,
come then with hearts aflame;
the God of peace acclaim
as Lord and Saviour.

CLEMENT OF ALEXANDRIA (*c.*170–?220)
tr. F. BLAND TUCKER (1895–1984)

528 *Quem pastores laudavere* 888 7

German carol melody,
14th cent.

1 Jesus, good above all other,
gentle child of gentle mother,
in a stable born our brother,
give us grace to persevere.

2 Jesus, cradled in a manger,
for us facing every danger,
living as a homeless stranger,
now become our King most dear.

3 Jesus, for your people dying,
risen Master, death defying,
Lord in heaven, your grace supplying,
keep us to your presence near.

4 Jesus, all our sorrows bearing,
you our thoughts and hopes are sharing,
while to us the truth declaring,
help us all that truth to hear.

5 Lord, in all our living guide us;
let no pride or hate divide us;
we'll go on with you beside us,
and with joy we'll persevere!

PERCY DEARMER (1867–1936) altd.*

529 *Nyland* 76 76 D Finnish melody

1 Light of the minds that know him:
may Christ be light to mine;
my sun in risen splendour,
my light of truth divine;
my guide in doubt and darkness,
my true and living way,
my clear light ever shining,
my dawn of heaven's day.

2 Life of the souls that love him:
may Christ be life indeed;
the living bread from heaven
on whom our spirits feed;
who died for love of sinners
to bear our guilty load,
and make of life's brief journey
a new Emmaus road.

3 Strength of the wills that serve him:
may Christ be strength to me,
who stilled the storm and tempest,
who calmed the tossing sea;
his Spirit's power to move me,
his will to master mine,
his cross to carry daily
and conquer in his sign.

4 May it be ours to know him
that we may truly love,
and loving, fully serve him
as serve the saints above;
till in that home of glory
with fadeless splendour bright,
we serve in perfect freedom
our Strength, our Life, our Light.

TIMOTHY DUDLEY-SMITH (1926–)*
based on a prayer of ST AUGUSTINE (354–430)

530 *Abbot's Leigh* 87 87 D

CYRIL V. TAYLOR (1907–91)

1 Living God, your joyful Spirit
  breaks the bounds of time and space,
rests in love upon your people,
  drawn together in this place.
Here we join in glad thanksgiving,
  here rejoice to pray and praise:
Lord of all our past traditions,
  Lord of all our future days.

2 As your bread may we be broken,
  scattered in community;
we who know your greatest blessings
  called to share Christ's ministry.
May we gently lead each other,
  share our hunger and our thirst;
learn that only through our weakness
  shall we know the strength of Christ.

3 Lord, when we grow tired of giving,
  feel frustration, hurt and strain,
by your Spirit's quiet compulsion,
  draw us back to you again.
Guide us through the bitter searching
  when our confidence is lost;
give us hope from desolation,
  arms outstretched upon a cross.

4 Living God, your power surrounds us,
  as we face the way Christ trod,
challenge us to fresh commitment
  to the purposes of God:
called to share a new creation,
  called to preach a living word,
promised all the joys of heaven,
  through the grace of Christ our Lord.

JILL JENKINS (1937–)*

531 *Slane* 10 11 11 12 Irish traditional melody

1 Lord of all hopefulness, Lord of all joy,
whose trust, ever child-like, no cares could destroy,
be there at our waking, and give us, we pray,
your bliss in our hearts, Lord, at the break of the day.

2 Lord of all eagerness, Lord of all faith,
whose strong hands were skilled at the plane and the lathe,
be there at our labours, and give us, we pray,
your strength in our hearts, Lord, at the noon of the day.

3 Lord of all kindliness, Lord of all grace,
your hands swift to welcome, your arms to embrace,
be there at our homing, and give us, we pray,
your love in our hearts, Lord, at the eve of the day.

4 Lord of all gentleness, Lord of all calm,
whose voice is contentment, whose presence is balm,
be there at our sleeping, and give us, we pray,
your peace in our hearts, Lord, at the end of the day.

'JAN STRUTHER' (1901–53)

532 *Snowshill* 10 11 11 11

WALTER K. STANTON (1891–1978)

1 Lord of creation, to you be all praise!
Most mighty your working, most wondrous your ways!
Your glory and greatness no mortal can tell,
and yet in the heart of the humble you dwell.

2 Lord of all power, I give you my will,
in joyful obedience your tasks to fulfil.
Your bondage is freedom, your service is song;
and, held in your keeping, my weakness is strong.

3 Lord of all wisdom, I give you my mind,
rich truth that surpasses my knowledge to find;
what eye has not seen and what ear has not heard
is taught by your Spirit and shines from your word.

4 Lord of all bounty, I give you my heart;
I praise and adore you for all you impart,
your love to inspire me, your counsel to guide,
your presence to shield me, whatever betide.

5 Lord of all being, I give you my all;
if e'er I disown you, I stumble and fall;
but, led in your service your word to obey,
I'll walk in your freedom to the end of the way.

JACK WINSLOW (1882–1974) altd.*

533 *Eastwood* 11 10 11 10 ERIC SHAVE (1901–)

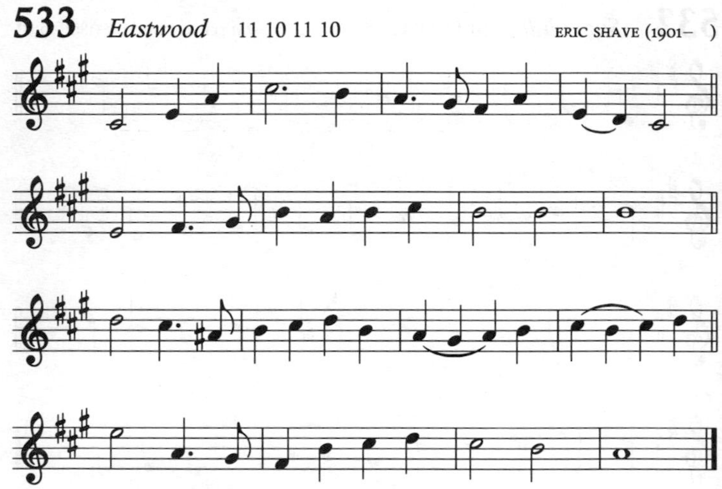

1 Lord of good life, the hosts of the undying
hail thee as conqueror on the heavenly field;
so we on earth, to their great song replying,
here to thy claim our earthly service yield.

2 Take thou our strength, for thou hast proved the stronger,
victor in wars our weakness never knew;
take thou our love, for thou hast loved the longer;
take thou our truth, for thou hast proved more true.

3 Take thou our courage, for thy trumpets call us
on where disciples shall new perils meet;
take thou our fears that weaken and enthral us,
tread them to dust beneath thy conquering feet.

4 Glory to God, who now to us has given
best of his gifts, the call to share his strife!
Glory to God, who bids us fight for heaven
here in the dust and joy of human life!

GEOFFREY HOYLAND (1889–1965)*

534 *Troy Court* LM

WALTER K. STANTON (1891–1978)

1 Lord, as I wake I turn to you,
yourself the first thought of my day;
my King, my God, whose help is sure,
yourself the help for which I pray.

2 There is no blessing, Lord, from you
for those who make their will their way,
no praise for those who will not praise,
no peace for those who will not pray.

3 Your loving gifts of grace to me,
those favours I could never earn,
call for my thanks in praise and prayer,
call me to love you in return.

4 Lord, make my life a life of love,
keep me from sin in all I do;
Lord, make your law my only law,
your will my will, for love of you.

BRIAN FOLEY (1919–)
based on Psalm 5

535 *Warrington* LM

RALPH HARRISON (1748–1810)

1 My gracious Lord, I own thy right
to every service I can pay;
and call it my supreme delight
to hear thy dictates and obey.

2 What is my being but for thee,
its sure support, its noblest end,
thy ever-smiling face to see
and serve the cause of such a friend?

3 I would not breathe for worldly joy,
or to increase my worldly good,
nor future days or powers employ
to spread a sounding name abroad;

4 but to my Saviour I would live,
to him who for my ransom died;
nor could untainted Eden give
such bliss as blossoms at his side.

5 His work my later years shall bless,
when youthful vigour is no more,
and my last hour of life confess
his love has animating power.

PHILIP DODDRIDGE (1702–51) altd.*

536 *Melcombe* LM SAMUEL WEBBE (1740–1816)

1 New every morning is the love
our wakening and uprising prove;
through sleep and darkness safely brought,
restored to life and power and thought.

2 New mercies each returning day,
hover around us while we pray;
new perils past, new sins forgiven,
new thoughts of God, new hopes of heaven.

3 If on our daily course our mind
be set to hallow all we find,
new treasures still, of countless price,
God will provide for sacrifice.

4 Old friends, old scenes, will lovelier be,
as more of heaven in each we see;
some softening gleam of love and prayer
shall dawn on every cross and care.

5 The trivial round, the common task
will furnish all we ought to ask.
Lord, help us, this and every day,
to live more nearly as we pray.

JOHN KEBLE (1792–1866) altd.*

537 *Winchester New* LM

Adpt. from a melody in *Musikalisches Hand-Buch*, Hamburg, 1690
arr. W. H. HAVERGAL (1793–1870)

1 O splendour of God's glory bright
who bringest forth the light from Light;
O Light, of light the fountain-spring;
O Day, our days illumining;

2 come, very Sun of truth and love,
come in thy radiance from above,
and shed the Holy Spirit's ray
on all we think or do today.

3 Teach us to work with all our might;
put Satan's fierce assaults to flight;
turn all to good that seems most ill;
help us our calling to fulfil.

4 Let joy be ours through all the day,
our thoughts as pure as morning ray,
our faith like noonday's glowing height,
our souls undimmed by shades of night.

5 O Christ, with each returning morn
thine image to our hearts is born;
O may we ever clearly see
our Saviour and our God in thee!

ST AMBROSE (340–97)
tr. JOHN CHANDLER (1806–76) and compilers of
Hymns Ancient & Modern, 1904 (altd. 1950)*

538 *Sandys* SM

English traditional carol from SANDYS' *Christmas Carols Ancient and Modern*, 1833

* v. 4

The Elixir

1 Teach me, my God and King,
in all things thee to see,
and what I do in anything
to do it as for thee.

2 A man that looks on glass
on it may stay his eye;
or if he pleaseth, through it pass,
and then the heaven espy.

3 All may of thee partake:
nothing can be so mean,
which, with this tincture, 'For thy sake',
will not grow bright and clean.

4 A servant with this clause
makes drudgery divine:
who sweeps a room, as for thy laws,
makes that and the action fine.

5 This is the famous stone
that turneth all to gold:
for that which God doth touch and own
cannot for less be told.

GEORGE HERBERT (1593–1633) altd.

539 *Angels' Song* LM

ORLANDO GIBBONS (1583–1625)

1 How blest are all the saints, our God,
who, having crossed the troubled sea,
have gained the harbour of your peace
and rest in your tranquillity.

2 Watch over us who voyage still,
with risk and danger yet to face;
remember all beset by storms
and hold them in your steadfast grace.

3 Our vessel's frail, the ocean wide,
but your love steers, and we aspire
to gain the peaceful shore at last,
the haven of our heart's desire.

4 Then we shall praise you endlessly,
great God to whom all praise is due,
for you have made us for yourself:
our hearts must find their rest in you.

ALAN GAUNT (1935–)
adpt. from ST AUGUSTINE (354–430)

540 *Llef* LM

G. H. JONES (1849–1919)

1 O Iesu mawr, rho d'anian bur
i eiddil gwan mewn anial dir;
i'w nerthu drwy'r holl rwystrau sy
ar ddyrys daith i'r Ganaan fry.

2 Pob gras sydd yn yr Eglwys fawr,
fry yn y nef neu ar y llawr,
caf feddu'r oll, eu meddu'n un
wrth feddu d'anian di dy hun.

3 Mi lyna'n dawel wrth dy draed,
mi ganaf am rinweddau'r gwaed;
mi garia'r groes, mi nofia'r don,
ond cael dy anian dan fy mron.

DAVID CHARLES (1762–1834)

1 Jesus, my Lord, grant your pure grace
to this poor wanderer on life's way;
strengthen my feeble steps, that I
may come to Canaan's shore one day.

2 Jesus, I trust that every grace,
treasured in heaven or here on earth,
will fill my heart when I have known
perfect delight in your new birth.

3 I will kneel faithful at your feet,
I'll witness to your saving blood;
with your new nature in my heart
I'll bear the cross and brave the flood.

tr. ENID A. EVANS (1926–) and
STEPHEN ORCHARD (1942–)*

541 *Cambridge* SM

Melody by R. HARRISON (1748–1810)

1 How blest are they, O Lord,
who stay themselves on thee;
who wait for thy salvation, Lord,
shall thy salvation see.

2 When we in darkness walk,
nor feel the heavenly flame,
then is the time to trust our God,
and call upon his name.

3 Soon shall our doubts and fears
subside at his control:
his loving-kindness shall break through
the midnight of the soul.

4 His grace will to the end
stronger and brighter shine,
nor present things, nor things to come,
shall quench the spark divine.

AUGUSTUS M. TOPLADY (1740–78) altd.

542 *Adoramus* 88 88 (Anapaestic)

PEGGY SPENCER PALMER (1900–87)

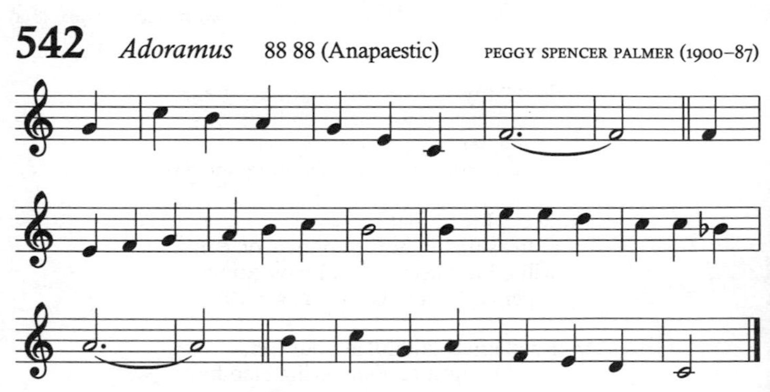

1 How good is the God we adore,
our faithful, unchangeable friend;
whose love is as great as his power,
and knows neither measure nor end.

2 'Tis Jesus, the first and the last,
whose Spirit shall guide us safe home;
we'll praise him for all that is past,
and trust him for all that's to come.

JOSEPH HART (1712–68) altd.

543 *Mannheim* 87 87 87

Melody adapted from a chorale by
FRIEDRICH FILITZ (1804–76)

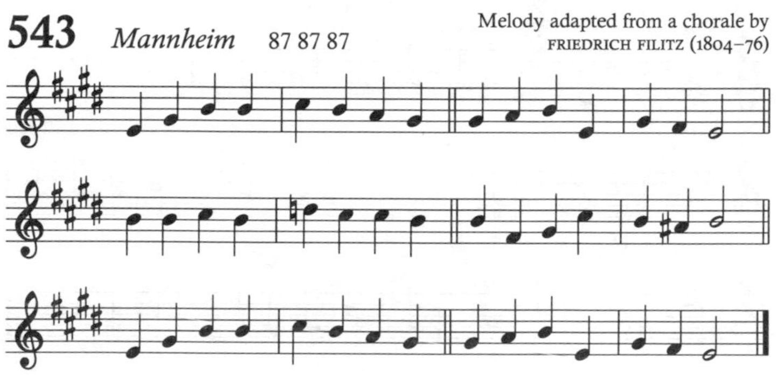

1 Lead us, heavenly Father, lead us
o'er the world's tempestuous sea;
guard us, guide us, keep us, feed us,
for we have no help but thee;
yet possessing every blessing
if our God our Father be.

2 Saviour, breathe forgiveness o'er us;
all our weakness thou dost know,
thou didst tread this earth before us,
thou didst feel its keenest woe;
lone and dreary, faint and weary,
through the desert thou didst go.

3 Spirit of our God, descending,
fill our hearts with heavenly joy,
love with every passion blending,
pleasure that can never cloy:
thus provided, pardoned, guided,
nothing can our peace destroy.

JAMES EDMESTON (1791–1867)

In verse 2 line 5 the word 'dreary' has its older meaning, 'sad', rather than the modern 'dismal' or 'gloomy'.

544

FIRST TUNE

Alberta 10 4 10 4 10 10 WILLIAM H. HARRIS (1883–1973)

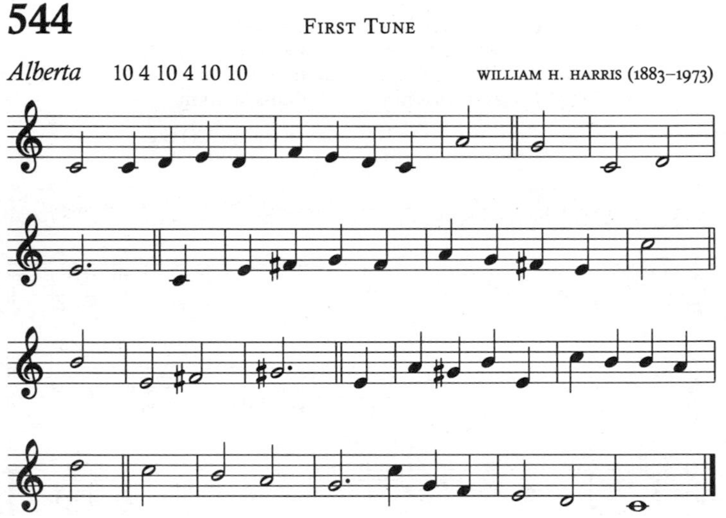

SECOND TUNE

Lux benigna 10 4 10 4 10 10 J. B. DYKES (1823–76)

1 Lead kindly light, amid the encircling gloom,
lead thou me on;
the night is dark, and I am far from home,
lead thou me on.
Keep thou my feet; I do not ask to see
the distant scene; one step enough for me.

2 I was not ever thus, nor prayed that thou
shouldst lead me on.
I loved to choose and see my path; but now
lead thou me on.
I loved the garish day and, spite of fears,
pride ruled my will: remember not past years.

3 So long thy power hath blest me, sure it still
will lead me on
o'er moor and fen, o'er crag and torrent, till
the night is gone,
and with the morn those angel faces smile,
which I have loved long since, and lost awhile.

J. H. NEWMAN (1801–90)

545 *Song 67* CM

Melody from PRYS's *Llyfr y Psalmau*, 1621, (rhythm altered)

The Covenant and Confidence of Faith

1 Lord, it belongs not to my care
whether I die or live;
to love and serve thee is my share,
and this thy grace must give.

2 If life be long, I will be glad
that I may long obey;
if short, yet why should I be sad
to soar to endless day?

3 Christ leads me through no darker rooms
than he went through before;
and who into God's kingdom comes
must enter by this door.

4 Come, Lord, when grace hath made me meet
thy blessèd face to see;
for if thy work on earth be sweet,
what will thy glory be?

5 My knowledge of that life is small;
the eye of faith is dim;
but 'tis enough that Christ knows all,
and I shall be with him.

RICHARD BAXTER (1615–91) altd.*

546 *Christchurch* 66 66 88

CHARLES STEGGALL (1826–1905)

1 March on, my soul, with strength,
march forward void of fear;
he who has led will lead
while year succeeds to year;
and as you travel on your way,
his hand shall hold you day by day.

2 March on, my soul, with strength;
in ease you dare not dwell;
high duty calls you forth;
then up, and serve him well!
Take up your cross, take up your sword,
and fight the battles of your Lord!

3 March on, my soul, with strength,
with strength, but not your own;
the conquest you will gain
through Christ your Lord alone;
his grace shall nerve your feeble arm,
his love preserve you safe from harm.

4 March on, my soul, with strength,
from strength to strength march on;
warfare shall end at length,
all foes be overthrown.
And then, my soul, if faithful now,
the crown of life awaits your brow.

WILLIAM WRIGHT (1859–1924) altd.*

547 *The People of God*

ESTELLE WHITE (1925–   )

PILGRIMAGE

1 'Moses, I know you're the man',
the Lord says.
'You're going to work out my plan',
the Lord says.
'Lead all the Israelites out of slavery,
and I shall make them a wandering race
called the people of God.'

So every day we're on our way,
for we're a travelling, wandering race;
we're the people of God.

2 'Don't get too set in your ways',
the Lord says.
'Each step is only a phase',
the Lord says.
'I'll go before you and I shall be a sign
to guide my travelling, wandering race;
you're the people of God.'

3 'No matter what you may do',
the Lord says,
'I shall be faithful and true,'
the Lord says.
'My love will strengthen you as you go along,
for you're my travelling, wandering race;
you're the people of God.'

4 'Look at the birds in the air,'
the Lord says.
'They fly unhampered by care',
the Lord says.
'You will move easier if you're travelling light,
for you're a wandering, vagabond race,
you're the people of God.'

5 'Foxes have places to go,'
the Lord says,
'but I've no home here below',
the Lord says.
'So if you want to be with me all your days,
keep up the moving and travelling on,
you're the people of God.'

ESTELLE WHITE (1925–)*

548 *Many Mansions* 55 54 D (Irregular) PETER CUTTS (1937–)

1 Nothing distress you,
nothing affright you,
everything passes,
God will abide.
Patient endeavour
accomplishes all things;
who God possesses
needs naught beside.

2 Lift your mind upward,
fair are his mansions,
nothing distress you,
cast fear away.
Follow Christ freely,
his love will light you,
nothing affright you,
in the dark way.

3 See the world's glory!
Fading its splendour,
everything passes,
all is denied.
Look ever homeward
to the eternal;
faithful in promise
God will abide.

4 Love in due measure
measureless Goodness;
patient endeavour,
run to Love's call!
Faith burning brightly
be your soul's shelter;
who hopes, believing,
accomplishes all.

5 Hell may assail you,
it cannot move you;
sorrows may grieve you,
faith may be tried.
Though you have nothing,
he is your treasure:
who God possesses
needs naught beside.

from 'Nada te turbe'
ST TERESA OF AVILA (1515–82)
tr. COLIN THOMPSON (1945–)

549 *Southcote* 9979 with refrain SYDNEY CARTER (1915–)

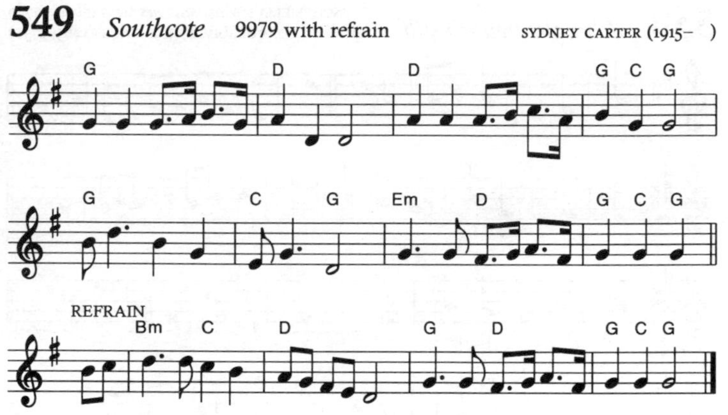

1 One more step along the world I go,
one more step along the world I go,
from the old things to the new
keep me travelling along with you:

And it's from the old I travel to the new;
keep me travelling along with you.

2 Round the corner of the world I turn,
more and more about the world I learn;
all the new things that I see
you'll be looking at along with me:

3 As I travel through the bad and good,
keep me travelling the way I should;
where I see no way to go
you'll be telling me the way, I know:

4 Give me courage when the world is rough,
keep me loving though the world is tough;
leap and sing in all I do,
keep me travelling along with you:

5 You are older than the world can be,
you are younger than the life in me;
ever old and ever new,
keep me travelling along with you:

SYDNEY CARTER (1915–)

550 *Ich halte treulich still* DSM

SCHEMELLI'S *Musikalisches Gesangbuch*, 1736
probably by J. S. BACH (1685–1750)

1 Put thou thy trust in God,
so safe shalt thou go on;
walk in his strength with faith and hope,
so shall thy work be done.
Give to the winds thy fears;
hope, and be undismayed;
God hears thy sighs and counts thy tears,
God shall lift up thy head.

2 Through waves, and clouds, and storms,
he gently clears thy way;
wait thou his time; so shall this night
soon end in joyous day.
Leave to his sovereign sway
to choose and to command;
so shalt thou wondering own, his way
how wise, how strong his hand.

3 Thou seest our weakness, Lord;
our hearts are known to thee:
O lift thou up the sinking hand,
confirm the feeble knee.
Let us, in life, in death,
thy steadfast truth declare,
and publish, with our latest breath,
thy love and guardian care.

PAUL GERHARDT (1607–76)
(freely) tr. JOHN WESLEY (1703–91) altd.

551 *Caithness* CM

Melody from *Scottish Psalter,* 1635

1 O for a closer walk with God,
  a calm and heavenly frame;
a light to shine upon the road
  that leads me to the Lamb.

2 Where is the blessedness I knew
  when first I saw the Lord?
Where is the soul-refreshing view
  of Jesus and his word?

3 What peaceful hours I once enjoyed,
  how sweet their memory still!
But they have left an aching void
  the world can never fill.

4 Return, O holy dove, return,
  sweet messenger of rest:
I hate the sins that made thee mourn
  and drove thee from my breast.

5 The dearest idol I have known,
  whate'er that idol be,
help me to tear it from thy throne
  and worship only thee.

6 So shall my walk be close with God,
  calm and serene my frame;
so purer light shall mark the road
  that leads me to the Lamb.

WILLIAM COWPER (1731–1800)

552 *Dominus regit me* 87 87 (Iambic) J. B. DYKES (1823–76)

Alternative tune: ST COLUMBA, no. 448.

1 The King of love my Shepherd is,
whose goodness faileth never;
I nothing lack if I am his
and he is mine for ever.

2 Where streams of living water flow
my ransomed soul he leadeth,
and where the verdant pastures grow
with food celestial feedeth.

3 Perverse and foolish oft I strayed,
but yet in love he sought me,
and on his shoulder gently laid,
and home, rejoicing, brought me.

4 In death's dark vale I fear no ill
with thee, dear Lord, beside me;
thy rod and staff my comfort still,
thy cross before to guide me.

5 Thou spread'st a table in my sight,
thy unction grace bestoweth;
and O what transport of delight
from thy pure chalice floweth!

6 And so through all the length of days
thy goodness faileth never;
Good Shepherd, may I sing thy praise
within thy house for ever.

H. W. BAKER (1821–77)

553 *Mountain Christians* 76 76 D attrib. JOHN MANNIN (1802–65)

1 To Abraham and Sarah
the call of God was clear:
'Go forth and I will show you
a country rich and fair.
You need not fear the journey,
for I have pledged my word
that you shall be my people
and I will be your God'.

2 From Abraham and Sarah
arose a pilgrim race,
dependent for their journey
on God's abundant grace;
and in their heart was written
by God this saving word:
that 'You shall be my people
and I will be your God'.

3 We of this generation
on whom God's hand is laid,
can journey to the future
secure and unafraid,
rejoicing in God's goodness
and trusting in this word:
that 'You shall be my people
and I will be your God'.

JUDITH FETTER, 1984

554 *St James* CM

R. COURTEVILLE (*c.*1676–1772)

1 Thou art the Way: to thee alone
from sin and death we flee;
and they who would the Father seek,
must seek him, Lord, by thee.

2 Thou art the Truth: thy word alone
true wisdom can impart;
thou only canst inform the mind,
and purify the heart.

3 Thou art the Life: the rending tomb
proclaims thy conquering arm;
and those who put their trust in thee
nor death nor hell shall harm.

4 Thou art the Way, the Truth, the Life:
grant us that Way to know,
that Truth to keep, that Life to win,
whose joys eternal flow.

G. W. DOANE (1799–1859) altd.

555 *Siyahamba*

South African traditional
arr. ANDERS NYBERG and compilers

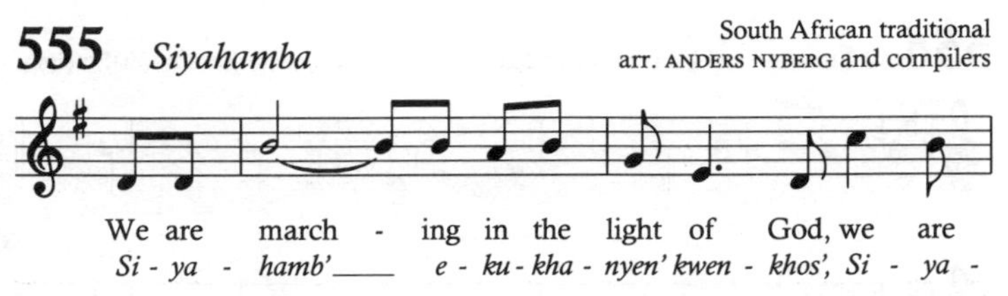

march-ing in the light of God. We are march-ing,
- hamb' e - ku-kha-nyen' kwen - khos'. Si - ya - ham - ba,

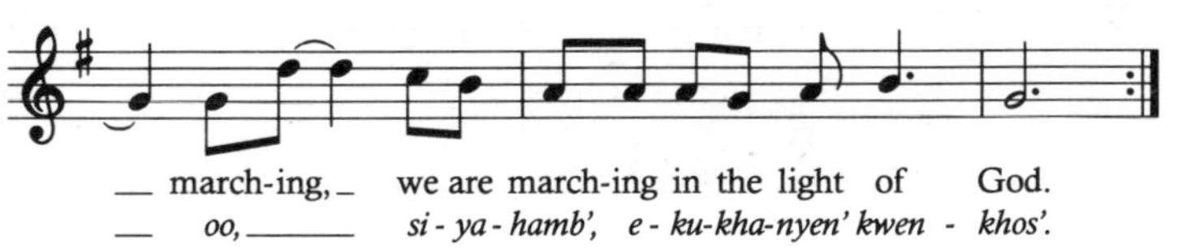

We are marching in the light of God.

Siyahamb' ekukhanyen' kwenkhos'.

South African traditional
tr. ANDERS NYBERG, 1984

556 *Stowey* 11 11 11 11 Irregular

English traditional melody

1 When a knight won his spurs in the stories of old,
he was gentle and brave, he was gallant and bold;
with a shield on his arm and a lance in his hand,
for God and for valour he rode through the land.

2 No charger have I, and no sword by my side,
yet still to adventure and battle I ride,
though back into storyland giants have fled,
and the knights are no more and the dragons are dead.

3 Let faith be my shield and let joy be my steed
'gainst the dragons of anger, the ogres of greed;
and let me set free, with the sword of my youth,
from the castle of darkness the power of the truth.

'JAN STRUTHER' (1901–53)

557 *Monks Gate* 65 65 6665

Adpt. from an English traditional melody
by R. VAUGHAN WILLIAMS (1872–1958)

1 Who would true valour see,
let him come hither;
one here will constant be,
come wind, come weather;
there's no discouragement
shall make him once relent
his first avowed intent
to be a pilgrim.

2 Who so beset him round
with dismal stories,
do but themselves confound;
his strength the more is.
No lion can him fright,
he'll with a giant fight,
but he will have a right
to be a pilgrim.

3 Hobgoblin nor foul fiend
can daunt his spirit;
he knows he at the end
shall life inherit.
Then fancies fly away,
he'll fear not what men say,
he'll labour night and day
to be a pilgrim.

JOHN BUNYAN (1628–88)

Bunyan's song from *The Pilgrim's Progress* is printed in its original form; but singers may prefer to alter the pronouns 'he' / 'him' / 'his' to suit the circumstances.

558 *Kelvingrove* 76 76 7776 Scottish traditional melody

1 Will you come and follow me,
if I but call your name?
Will you go where you don't know
and never be the same?
Will you let my love be shown,
will you let my name be known,
will you let my life be grown
in you and you in me?

2 Will you leave your self behind
if I but call your name?
Will you care for cruel and kind
and never be the same?
Will you risk the hostile stare
should your life attract or scare,
will you let me answer prayer
in you and you in me?

3 Will you love the 'you' you hide
if I but call your name?
Will you quell the fear inside
and never be the same?
Will you use the faith you've found
to reshape the world around
through my sight and touch and sound
in you and you in me?

4 Lord, your summons echoes true
when you but call my name.
Let me turn and follow you
and never be the same.
In your company I'll go
where your love and footsteps show.
Thus I'll move and live and grow
in you and you in me.

JOHN BELL (1949–) and
GRAHAM MAULE (1958–)

559 *Westminster Abbey* 87 87 87

Adpt. from an anthem by
HENRY PURCELL (1659–95)

1 Blessed city, heavenly Salem,
vision dear of peace and love,
who, of living stones upbuilded,
art the joy of heaven above:
we, with all thy holy people,
glorious to thy glory move.

2 Christ is made the sure foundation,
Christ the head and corner-stone,
chosen of the Lord and precious,
binding all the Church in one;
holy Zion's help for ever,
and her confidence alone.

3 All that dedicated city,
dearly loved of God on high,
in exultant jubilation
pours perpetual melody;
God, the One in Three, adoring
in glad hymns eternally.

4 To this temple where we call thee,
come, O Lord of Hosts, today;
with thy wonted loving-kindness
hear thy people as they pray;
and thy fullest benediction
shed within its walls for aye.

5 Here vouchsafe to all thy servants
what they ask of thee to gain,
what they gain from thee for ever
with the blessed to retain,
and hereafter in thy glory
evermore with thee to reign.

Latin, 7th cent.
tr. J. M. NEALE (1818–66) altd.*

560 *Abbot's Leigh* 87 87 D CYRIL V. TAYLOR (1907–91)

1 Glorious things of thee are spoken,
   Zion, city of our God;
he whose word cannot be broken
   formed thee for his own abode.
On the Rock of Ages founded,
   what can shake thy sure repose?
With salvation's walls surrounded,
   thou may'st smile at all thy foes.

2 See! The streams of living waters,
   springing from eternal love,
well supply thy sons and daughters,
   and all fear of want remove;
who can faint, while such a river
   ever flows, their thirst to assuage—
grace, which, like the Lord, the giver,
   never fails from age to age.

3 Saviour, if of Zion's city
   I, through grace, a member am,
let the world deride or pity,
   I will glory in thy name.
Fading is the worldling's pleasure,
   all his boasted pomp and show;
solid joys and lasting treasure
   none but Zion's children know.

JOHN NEWTON (1725–1807)

561 *Vienna* 77 77

J. H. KNECHT (1752–1817)

1 Christ, from whom all blessings flow,
perfecting the saints below,
hear us, who thy nature share,
who thy mystic body are.

2 Join us, in one spirit join,
let us still receive of thine;
still for more on thee we call,
thou who fillest all in all.

3 Closer knit to thee, our Head,
nourished, Lord, by thee, and fed,
let us daily growth receive,
more in Jesus Christ believe.

4 Never from thy service move,
needful to each other prove,
use the grace on each bestowed,
tempered by the art of God.

5 Love, like death, has all destroyed,
rendered all distinctions void;
names and sects and parties fall:
thou, O Christ, art all in all.

Cento from CHARLES WESLEY (1707–88) altd.

562 *Melcombe* LM

SAMUEL WEBBE (1740–1816)

1 Head of the Church, our risen Lord,
who by thy Spirit dost preside
o'er the whole body, by whose word
we all are ruled and sanctified:

2 our prayers and intercessions hear
for all thy family at large,
that all in their appointed sphere
their proper service may discharge.

3 So, through the grace derived from thee,
in whom all fullness dwells above,
may thy whole Church united be,
and edify itself in love.

JOSIAH CONDER (1789–1855) altd.
from *Gelasian Sacramentary*, 5th cent.

563 *Chichester* 668 668

JOHN BISHOP (1665–1737)

1 How pleased and blest was I
to hear the people cry,
Come, let us seek our God today!
Yes, with a cheerful zeal
we haste to Zion's hill,
and there our vows and honours pay.

2 Zion, thrice happy place
adorned with wondrous grace,
and walls of strength embrace thee round;
in thee our tribes appear,
to pray, and praise, and hear
the sacred gospel's joyful sound.

3 There David's greater Son
has fixed his royal throne,
he sits for grace and judgement there;
he bids the saint be glad,
he makes the sinner sad,
and humble souls rejoice with fear.

4 May peace attend thy gate,
and joy within thee wait
to bless the soul of every guest;
all those who seek thy peace
and wish for thine increase,
a thousand blessings on them rest.

5 My tongue repeats her vows,
Peace to this sacred house!
for there my friends and kindred dwell;
and since my glorious God
makes thee his blest abode,
my soul shall ever love thee well.

Psalm 122
para. ISAAC WATTS (1674–1748)*

564 *Vienna* 77 77

J. H. KNECHT (1752–1817)

1 Jesus, Lord, we look to thee,
let us in thy name agree;
show thyself the Prince of Peace,
bid our jarring conflicts cease.

2 By thy reconciling love
every stumbling-block remove;
each to each unite, endear;
come, and spread thy banner here.

3 Make us of one heart and mind,
courteous, merciful, and kind,
lowly, meek in thought and word,
altogether like our Lord.

4 Let us for each other care,
each the other's burden bear,
to thy Church the pattern give,
show how true believers live.

5 Free from anger and from pride,
let us thus in God abide;
all the depth of love express,
all the height of holiness.

CHARLES WESLEY (1707–88) altd.*

GRAHAM KENDRICK (1950–)

566 *Aurelia* 76 76 D S. S. WESLEY (1810–76)

Alternative tune: ST THEODULPH, no. 208.

1 The Church's one foundation
is Jesus Christ her Lord;
she is his new creation
by water and the word:
from heaven he came and sought her
to be his holy bride;
with his own blood he bought her,
and for her life he died.

2 Elect from every nation,
yet one o'er all the earth,
her charter of salvation
one Lord, one faith, one birth:
one holy name she blesses,
partakes one holy food,
and to one hope she presses
with every grace endued.

3 'Mid toil and tribulation,
and tumult of her war,
she waits the consummation
of peace for evermore;
till with the vision glorious
her longing eyes are blest,
and the great Church victorious
shall be the Church at rest.

4 Yet she on earth hath union
with God the Three in One,
and mystic sweet communion
with those whose rest is won:
O happy ones and holy!
Lord, give us grace that we,
like them, the meek and lowly,
on high may dwell with thee.

SAMUEL J. STONE (1839–1900)

567 *Thornbury* 76 76 D BASIL HARWOOD (1859–1949)

1 Thy hand, O God, has guided
thy flock, from age to age;
the wondrous tale is written,
full clear, on every page;
thy people owned thy goodness,
and we their deeds record;
and both of this bear witness:
one Church, one Faith, one Lord.

2 Thy heralds brought glad tidings
to greatest, as to least;
they summoned all to hasten
and share the great King's feast;
their gospel of redemption,
sin pardoned, earth restored,
was all in this enfolded:
one Church, one Faith, one Lord.

3 Thy mercy will not fail us,
nor leave thy work undone;
with thy right hand to help us,
the victory shall be won;
and then, by all creation,
thy name shall be adored,
and this shall be our anthem:
one Church, one Faith, one Lord.

E. H. PLUMPTRE (1821–91)*

568 *East Meads* 885 86 JOHN WILSON (1905–92)

1 Lord Christ, the Father's mighty Son,
whose work upon the cross was done
to give and receive,
make all our scattered churches one
that the world may believe.

2 To make us one your prayers were said.
To make us one you broke the bread
for all to receive.
Its pieces scatter us instead:
how can others believe?

3 Lord Christ, forgive us, make us new!
What our designs could never do
your love can achieve.
Our prayers, our work, we bring to you
that the world may believe.

4 We will not question or refuse
the way you work, the means you choose,
the pattern you weave,
but reconcile our warring views
that the world may believe.

BRIAN WREN (1936–)

569 *Tetherdown* 55 55 65 65

GERALD L. BARNES (1935–)

1 We pause to give thanks
and focus our thought
on how far our God
his people has brought.
We pause for affirming
our 'Yes' to his call,
pursuing his future:
life's fullness for all.

2 The future is here
as Christ sets us free;
we reach out in hope
for all that will be.
We go where he leads us,
to time's furthest ends,
to share in his mission
as partners and friends.

3 We rise and we risk
the course he has set,
to care for our world,
a world of 'not-yet';
at one in the Spirit,
we follow Christ's way
and put into practice
God's future today.

FRED KAAN (1929–)

570 *St Magnus* CM Probably by JEREMIAH CLARKE (*c*.1673–1707)

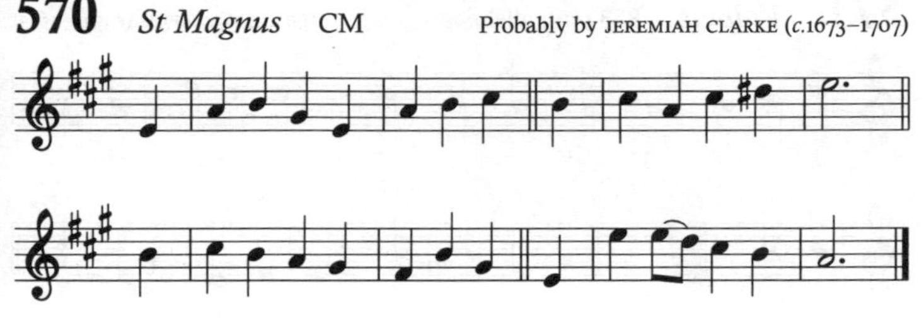

1 A glorious company we sing,
the Master and his friends,
he sent them forth to tell his love,
and all his love intends.

2 A faithful company we sing,
the steadfast martyr band;
for Christ and for his kingdom's cause
they boldly made their stand.

3 A loving company we sing,
whom Jesus sent to save
the sick, the hungry and the blind,
the outcast and the slave.

4 We join this glorious company
of Jesus and his friends,
to spread throughout this troubled world
his love that never ends.

A. F. BAYLY (1901–84) altd.*

571 *Vulpius* 888 with alleluias

MELCHIOR VULPIUS (*c.*1570–1615)

1 Christ is the King! O friends rejoice;
brothers and sisters, with one voice
tell all the earth he is your choice:

Alleluia! Alleluia! Alleluia!

2 O magnify the Lord, and raise
anthems of joy and holy praise
for Christ's brave saints of ancient days:

3 Christ through all ages is the same:
place the same hope in his great name,
with the same faith his word proclaim:

4 Let Love's unconquerable might
your scattered companies unite
in service to the Lord of light:

5 So shall God's will on earth be done,
new lamps be lit, new tasks begun,
and the whole Church at last be one:

G. K. A. BELL (1883–1958)*

572 *Light up the fire* Irregular

SUE MCCLELLAN, JOHN PAC, and KEITH RYCROFT

1 Colours of day dawn into the mind,
the day has begun, the night is behind.
Go down in the city, into the street,
and let's give the message to the people we meet:

So light up the fire and let the flame burn,
open the door, let Jesus return.
Take seeds of his Spirit, let the fruit grow,
tell the people of Jesus, let his love show.

2 Go through the park, on into the town;
the sun still shines on, it never goes down.
The light of the world is risen again;
the people of darkness are needing our friend.

3 Open your eyes, look into the sky;
the darkness has come, the Son came to die.
The evening draws on, the sun disappears,
but Jesus is living, his Spirit is here:

SUE MCCLELLAN, JOHN PAC, and KEITH RYCROFT, 1974*

573 *Benson* Irregular MILLICENT D. KINGHAM (b. 1866)

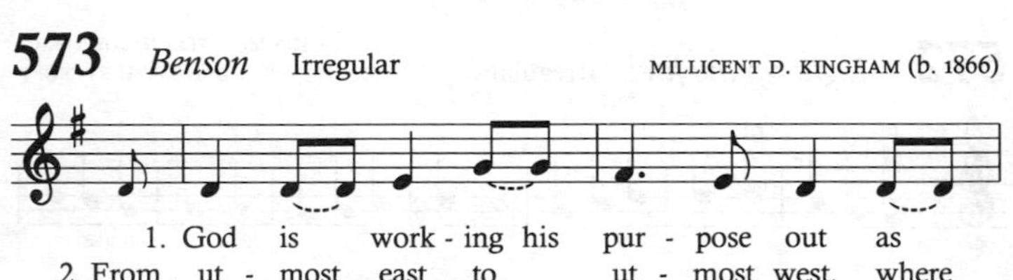

1. God is work - ing his pur - pose out as
2. From ut - most east to ut - most west, where
3. What can *we* do to work God's work, to
4. Let us go out in the strength of God, with the
5. All that *we* do can have no worth un -

year____ suc - ceeds__ to year;
hu - man feet have trod, by the
pros - per and in - crease________
ban - ner of Christ un - furled, that the
- less God bless - es the deed;

God is work - ing his pur - pose out, and the
voice of ma - ny____ mes - sen - gers goes
love and jus - tice through - out the world, the
light of the glo - ri - ous gos - pel of truth may
vain - ly we hope for the har - vest - tide till

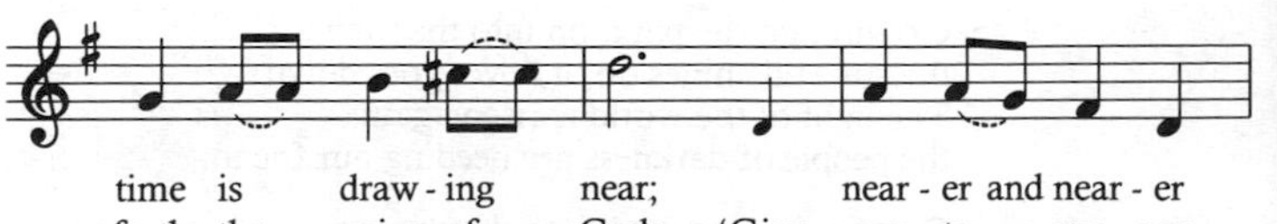

time is draw - ing near; near - er and near - er
forth the voice of God: 'Give ear to me, you
reign of the Prince of Peace? What can we do to
shine through-out the world: sin and sor - row
God a - wa - kens the seed; yet near - er and near - er

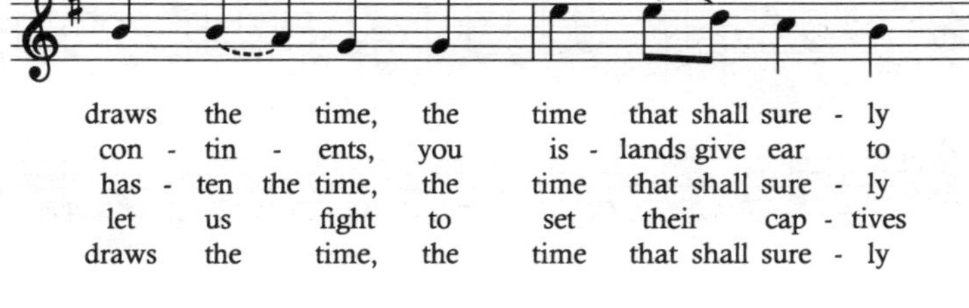

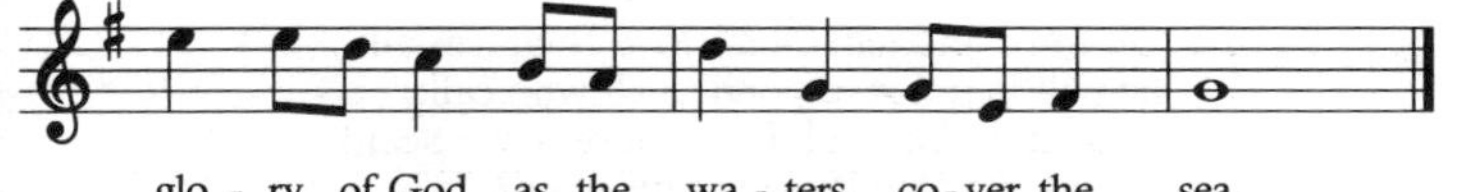

glo - ry of God as the wa - ters co - ver the sea.
glo - ry of God as the wa - ters co - ver the sea'.
glo - ry of God as the wa - ters co - ver the sea?
glo - ry of God as the wa - ters co - ver the sea.
glo - ry of God as the wa - ters co - ver the sea.

A. C. AINGER (1841–1919)*

574 *Yanworth* 10 10 10 10 JOHN BARNARD (1948–)

1 Go forth and tell! O Church of God, awake!
God's saving news to all the nations take:
proclaim Christ Jesus, Saviour, Lord and King,
that all the world his glorious praise may sing.

2 Go forth and tell! God's love embraces all;
he will in grace respond to all who call:
how shall they call if they have never heard
the gracious invitation of his word?

3 Go forth and tell! The doors are open wide:
share God's good gifts—let no one be denied;
live out your life as Christ your Lord shall choose,
your ransomed powers for his sole glory use.

4 Go forth and tell! O Church of God, arise!
Go in the strength which Christ your Lord supplies;
go till all nations his great name adore
and serve him, Lord and King for evermore.

JAMES E. SEDDON (1915–83)*

575 *Heathlands* 77 77 77 HENRY SMART (1813–79)

1 God of mercy, God of grace,
show the brightness of your face;
shine upon us, Saviour, shine,
fill your Church with light divine;
and your saving health extend
unto earth's remotest end.

2 Let the peoples praise you, Lord!
Be by all that live adored;
let the nations shout and sing
glory to their Saviour King;
at your feet their tribute pay
and your holy will obey.

3 Let the peoples praise you, Lord!
Earth shall all her fruits afford;
God to us his blessing give,
we to God devoted live:
all below, and all above,
one in joy and light and love.

H. F. LYTE (1793–1847) altd.*
based on Psalm 67

576 *Go tell everyone* Irregular HUBERT J. RICHARDS (1921–)

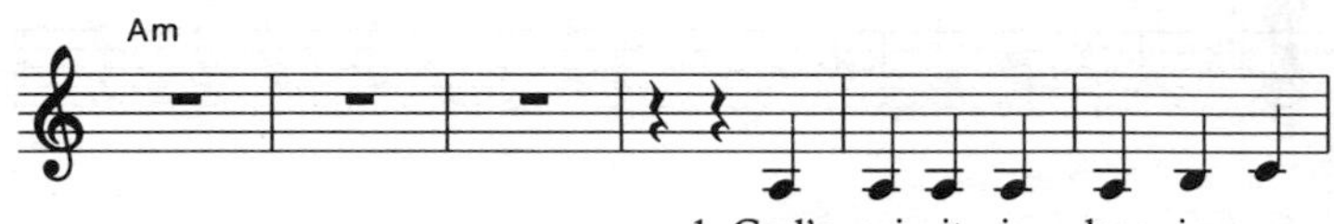

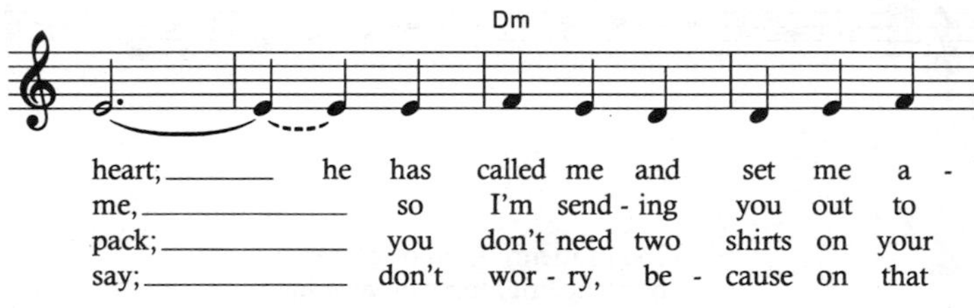

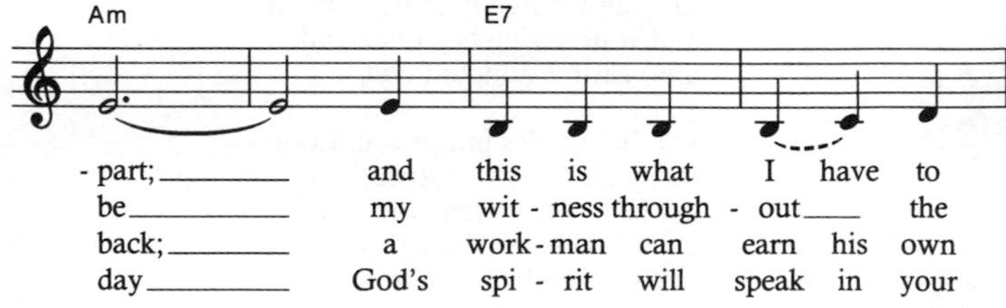

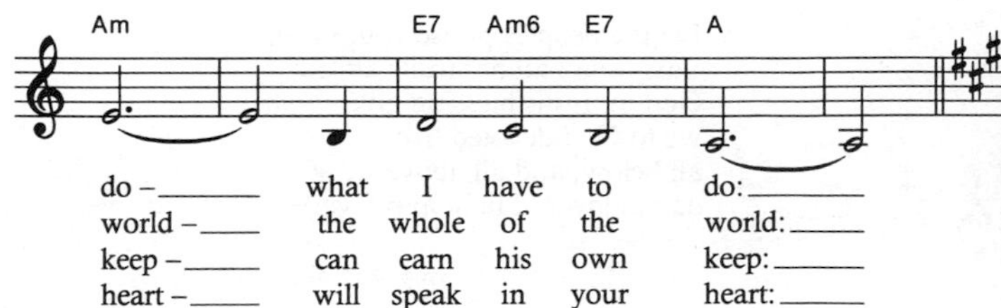

HUBERT J. RICHARDS (1921–)*
based on Luke 4: 18, in the version by
ALAN DALE (1902–79) (*New World*)
and on Matt. 10: 9,10,19,20

577 *Mainzer* LM

JOSEPH MAINZER (1801–51)

1 O Spirit of the living God,
in all thy plenitude of grace,
wherever human feet have trod,
descend on our rebellious race.

2 Give tongues of fire and hearts of love
to preach the reconciling word;
give power and unction from above,
whene'er the joyful sound is heard.

3 Be darkness, at thy coming, light;
confusion, order in thy path;
souls without strength inspire with might;
bid mercy triumph over wrath.

4 O Spirit of the Lord, prepare
all the round earth her God to meet;
breathe thou abroad like morning air,
till hearts of stone begin to beat.

5 Baptize the nations; far and nigh
the triumphs of the cross record;
the name of Jesus glorify,
till every kindred call him Lord.

6 God from eternity hath willed
all flesh shall his salvation see;
so be the Father's love fulfilled,
the Saviour's sufferings crowned through thee.

JAMES MONTGOMERY (1771–1854) altd.

578 *Rustington* 87 87 D

C. H. H. PARRY (1848–1918)

Alternative tune: CORINTH, no. 138.

1 Lord of light, whose name outshineth
all the stars and suns of space,
deign to make us thy co-workers
in the kingdom of thy grace.
Use us to fulfil thy purpose
in the gift of Christ thy Son:
Father, as in highest heaven,
so on earth thy will be done.

2 By the toil of patient workers
in some far outlying field;
by the courage where the radiance
of the cross is still revealed;
by the victories of meekness,
through reproach and suffering won:
Father, as in highest heaven,
so on earth thy will be done.

3 Grant that knowledge, still increasing,
at thy feet may lowly kneel;
with thy grace our triumphs hallow,
with thy charity our zeal.
Lift the nations from the shadows
to the gladness of the sun:
Father, as in highest heaven,
so on earth thy will be done.

4 By the prayers of faithful watchers,
never silent day or night;
by the cross of Jesus bringing
peace to all, and healing light;
by the love which passeth knowledge,
making all thy children one:
Father, as in highest heaven,
so on earth thy will be done.

H. ELVET LEWIS (1860–1953) altd.*

579 *Abbot's Leigh* 87 87 D

CYRIL V. TAYLOR (1907–91)

1 Lord, thy Church on earth is seeking
   thy renewal from above;
teach us all the art of speaking
   with the accent of thy love.
We would heed thy great commission:
   'Go now into every place—
preach, baptize, fulfil my mission,
   serve with love and share my grace'.

2 Freedom give to those in bondage,
   lift the burdens caused by sin.
Give new hope, new strength and courage,
   grant release from fears within.
Light for darkness; joy for sorrow;
   love for hatred; peace for strife:
these and countless blessings follow
   as the Spirit gives new life.

3 In the streets of every city
   where the bruised and lonely dwell,
let us show the Saviour's pity,
   let us of his mercy tell;
to all lands and peoples bringing
   all the richness of thy word,
till the world, thy praises singing,
   hails thee Christ, Redeemer, Lord.

HUGH SHERLOCK (1905–) altd.*

580 *Everton* 87 87 D

HENRY SMART (1813–79)

1 Lord, you give the great commission:
'Heal the sick and preach the word'.
Lest the Church neglect its mission
and the gospel go unheard,
help us witness to your purpose
with renewed integrity;
with the Spirit's gifts empower us
for the work of ministry.

2 Lord, you call us to your service:
'In my name baptize and teach'.
That the world may trust your promise,
life abundant meant for each,
give us all new fervour, draw us
closer in community;
with the Spirit's gifts empower us
for the work of ministry.

3 Lord, you make the common holy:
'This my body, this my blood'.
Let us all, for earth's true glory
daily lift life heavenward,
asking that the world around us
share your children's liberty;
with the Spirit's gifts empower us
for the work of ministry.

4 Lord, you show us love's true measure:
'Father, what they do, forgive'.
Yet we hoard as private treasure
all that you so freely give.
May your care and mercy lead us
to a just society;
with the Spirit's gifts empower us
for the work of ministry.

5 Lord, you bless with words assuring:
'I am with you to the end'.
Faith and hope and love restoring,
may we serve as you intend,
and, amid the cares that claim us,
hold in mind eternity;
with the Spirit's gifts empower us
for the work of ministry.

JEFFERY ROWTHORN (1934–)

581 *Northbrook* 11 10 11 10

R. S. THATCHER (1888–1957)

1 Sing, one and all, a song of celebration,
of love's renewal, and of hope restored,
as custom yields to ferment of creation,
and we, his Church, obey our living Lord.

2 Rejoice that still his Spirit is descending
with challenges that faith cannot refuse;
and ask no longer what is worth defending,
but how to make effective God's good news.

3 We need not now take refuge in tradition,
like those prepared to make a final stand,
but use it as a springboard of decision,
to follow him whose Kingdom is at hand.

4 Creative Spirit, let your word be spoken!
Your shock of truth invigorates the mind;
your miracles of grace shall be our token
that God in Christ is saving humankind.

F. PRATT GREEN (1903–)*

582 *Truro* LM

Melody from T. WILLIAMS'S *Psalmodia Evangelica*, 1789

1 Thanks be to God, whose Church on earth
has stood the tests of time and place,
and everywhere proclaims new birth
through Christ whose love reveals God's face.

2 Thanks be to God, whose Spirit sent
apostles out upon his way;
from east to west the message went;
on Greek and Roman dawned the day.

3 Thanks be to God, whose later voice
from west to east sent back the word
which, through the servants of his choice,
at last in every tongue was heard.

4 Thanks be to God who now would reach
his listeners in more global ways;
now each will send the news, and each
receive and answer it in praise.

5 Thanks be to God, in whom we share
today the mission of his Son;
may all his Church that time prepare
when, like the task, the world is one.

CARYL MICKLEM (1925–)

583 *The Bard of Armagh* 12 10 12 11 Irish traditional melody

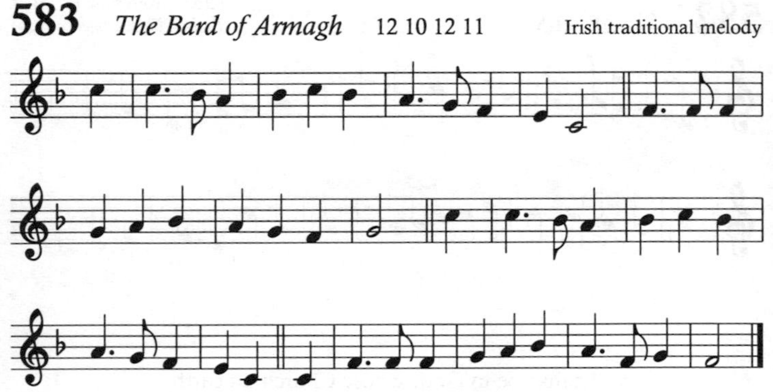

1 The Church is wherever God's people are praising,
singing their thanks for his goodness this day.
The Church is wherever disciples of Jesus
remember his story and walk in his way.

2 The Church is wherever God's people are helping,
caring for neighbours in sickness and need.
The Church is wherever God's people are sharing
the words of the Bible in gift and in deed.

CAROL R. IKELER (1920–)*

584 *St Clement* 98 98

C. C. SCHOLEFIELD (1839–1904)

1 The day thou gavest, Lord, is ended,
the darkness falls at thy behest;
to thee our morning hymns ascended,
thy praise shall sanctify our rest.

2 We thank thee that thy Church unsleeping,
while earth rolls onward into light,
through all the world her watch is keeping,
and rests not now by day or night.

3 As o'er each continent and island
the dawn leads on another day,
the voice of prayer is never silent,
nor dies the strain of praise away.

4 The sun that bids us rest is waking
our friends beneath the western sky,
and hour by hour fresh lips are making
thy wondrous doings heard on high.

5 So be it, Lord; thy throne shall never,
like earth's proud empires, pass away;
thy kingdom stands and grows for ever,
till all thy creatures own thy sway.

JOHN ELLERTON (1826–93) altd.

585 *Ein' feste Burg* 87 87 66 667

MARTIN LUTHER (1483–1546)

1 Our God stands like a fortress rock
with walls that will not fail us;
he helps us brace against the shock
of fears which now assail us.
The enemy of old
in wickedness is bold;
this seems his victory hour,
he fears no earthly power
and arms himself with cunning.

2 We win no battles through our might,
we fall at once, dejected;
the righteous one will lead our fight,
by God himself directed.
You ask, 'Who can this be?'
Christ Jesus, it is he,
eternal King and Lord,
God's true and living word,
no-one can stand against him.

3 And though the world seems full of ill,
with hungry devils prowling,
Christ's victöry is with us still,
we need not fear their howling.
The tyrants of this age
strut briefly on the stage:
their sentence has been passed.
We stand unharmed at last,
a word from God destroys them.

4 God's word and plan, which they pretend
is subject to their pleasure,
will bind their wills to serve God's end,
which we, who love him, treasure.
Then let them take our lives,
goods, children, husbands, wives,
and carry all away;
theirs is a short-lived day,
ours is the lasting kingdom.

MARTIN LUTHER (1483–1546)
tr. STEPHEN ORCHARD (1942–)*

586

FIRST TUNE

Meine Hoffnung 87 87 337

Later form of a melody by
JOACHIM NEANDER (1650–80)

SECOND TUNE

Michael 87 87 337

HERBERT HOWELLS (1892–1983)

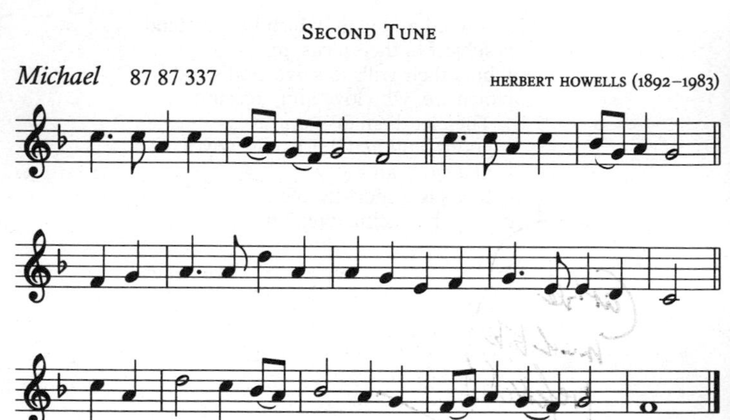

1 All my hope on God is founded;
he doth still my trust renew.
Me through change and chance he guideth,
only good and only true.
God unknown,
he alone
calls my heart to be his own.

2 Human pride and earthly glory,
sword and crown betray our trust;
what with care and toil is builded,
tower and temple, fall to dust.
But God's power
hour by hour
is my temple and my tower.

3 God's great goodness aye endureth,
deep his wisdom, passing thought;
splendour, light and life attend him,
beauty springeth out of naught.
Evermore
from his store
new-born worlds rise and adore.

4 Daily doth the almighty giver
bounteous gifts on us bestow;
his desire our soul delighteth
pleasure leads us where we go.
Love doth stand
at his hand;
joy doth wait on his command.

5 Still from earth to God eternal
sacrifice of praise be done,
high above all praises praising
for the gift of Christ his Son.
Christ doth call
one and all;
ye who follow shall not fall.

ROBERT BRIDGES (1844–1930) altd.*
based on JOACHIM NEANDER (1650–80)

587 *St Stephen (Newington)* CM WILLIAM JONES (1726–1800)

Alternative tune: ST ANDREW, no. 597.

1 Behold the amazing gift of love
the Father has bestowed,
that we, though sinners, should be called
the children of our God.

2 Concealed as yet this honour lies,
by this dark world unknown,
a world that knew not, when he came,
ev'n God's eternal Son.

3 High is the rank we now possess,
but higher we shall rise;
though what we shall hereafter be
is hid from mortal eyes.

4 But this we know, when he appears
we shall be like our Lord;
for we shall see him as he is
in glorious light adored.

1 John 3: 1, 2,
as in *Scottish Paraphrases*, 1781, altd.*

588 *Bishopthorpe* CM

Melody from *Select Portions of the Psalms*, c.1786

1 Blest be the everlasting God,
  the Father of our Lord,
be his abounding mercy praised,
  his majesty adored.

2 When from the dead he raised his Son
  to reign with him on high,
he gave our souls a lively hope
  that they should never die.

3 There's an inheritance divine
  reserved against that Day,
'tis uncorrupted, undefiled,
  and cannot fade away.

4 Saints by the power of God are kept
  till their salvation come;
we walk by faith as strangers here
  till Christ shall call us home.

ISAAC WATTS (1674–1748) altd.*
from 1 Peter 1 : 3–5

589 *Montgomery* 11 11 11 11

Melody from
*Magdalen Hospital Hymns, c.*1762

1 How firm a foundation, you saints of the Lord,
is laid for your faith in his excellent word;
what more can he say than to you he has said,
to all who for refuge to Jesus have fled?

2 'Fear not, I am with you, so be not dismayed;
for I am your God and will still give you aid:
I'll strengthen you, help you, and cause you to stand,
upheld by my righteous, omnipotent hand.

3 'When through the deep waters I call you to go,
the rivers of sorrow shall not overflow;
for I will be with you in trouble to bless,
and sanctify to you your deepest distress.

4 'When through fiery trials your pathway shall lie,
my grace all-sufficient shall be your supply;
the flame shall not hurt you, my only design
your dross to consume and your gold to refine.'

5 The soul that on Jesus has leaned for repose
he will not, he cannot, desert to its foes.
That soul, though all hell should endeavour to shake,
he never will leave, he will never forsake.

Author: 'K——.'
from JOHN RIPPON'S *Selection of Hymns*
from the best authors, 1787, altd.*

590 *Penlan* 76 76 D

DAVID JENKINS (1848–1915)

Alternative tune: LLANGLOFFAN, no. 604.

1 In heavenly love abiding,
no change my heart shall fear;
and safe is such confiding,
for nothing changes here:
the storm may roar without me,
my heart may low be laid,
but God is round about me,
and can I be dismayed?

2 Wherever he may guide me,
no want shall turn me back;
my Shepherd is beside me,
and nothing can I lack:
his wisdom ever waketh,
his sight is never dim;
he knows the way he taketh,
and I will walk with him.

3 Green pastures are before me,
which yet I have not seen;
bright skies will soon be o'er me,
where darkening clouds have been:
my hope I cannot measure,
my path to life is free;
my Saviour has my treasure,
and he will walk with me.

ANNA L. WARING (1823–1910)*

591 *Do not be afraid*

GERALD MARKLAND

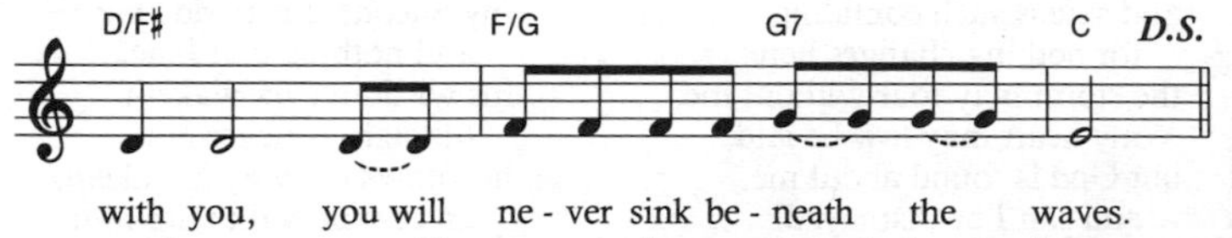

GERALD MARKLAND, 1978
from Isaiah 43: 1–4

592 *Nun danket all* CM *Praxis Pietatis Melica*, 1647

Unseen, not Unknown

1 Jesus, these eyes have never seen
that radiant form of thine;
the veil of sense hangs dark between
thy blessed face and mine.

2 I see thee not, I hear thee not,
yet art thou oft with me;
and earth hath ne'er so dear a spot
as where I meet with thee.

3 Yet, though I have not seen, and still
must rest in faith alone,
I love thee, dearest Lord, and will,
unseen, but not unknown.

4 When death these mortal eyes shall seal
and still this beating heart,
the rending veil shall thee reveal
all glorious as thou art.

RAY PALMER (1808–87)*

593 *Warwick* CM

SAMUEL STANLEY (1767–1822)

1 O Lord, I would delight in thee
and on thy care depend;
to thee in every trouble flee,
my best, my only friend.

2 When all created streams are dried
thy fullness is the same:
may I with this be satisfied,
and glory in thy name.

3 No good in creatures can be found
but may be found in thee;
I must have all things and abound,
while God is God to me.

4 He that has made my heaven secure
will here all good provide;
while Christ is rich can I be poor?
what can I want beside?

5 O Lord, I cast my care on thee;
I triumph and adore;
henceforth my great concern shall be
to love and please thee more.

JOHN RYLAND (1753–1825)

594 *Peace, perfect peace*

Words and music by KEVIN MAYHEW, 1977

595

FIRST TUNE

Clonmel 76 76 D

Irish traditional melody

SECOND TUNE

Craigmillar 76 76 D

ERIK ROUTLEY (1917–82)

Joy and Peace in Believing

1 Sometimes a light surprises
  the Christian while (s)he sings;
it is the Lord who rises
  with healing in his wings;
when comforts are declining,
  he grants the soul again
a season of clear shining
  to cheer it after rain.

2 In holy contemplation
  we sweetly then pursue
the theme of God's salvation,
  and find it ever new;
set free from present sorrow,
  we cheerfully can say:
let every unknown morrow
  bring with it what it may—

3 it can bring with it nothing
  but he will bear us through;
who gives the lilies clothing
  will clothe his people too;
beneath the spreading heavens
  no creature but is fed;
and he who feeds the ravens
  will give his children bread.

4 Though vine nor fig-tree neither
  expected fruit should bear;
though all the field should wither,
  nor flocks nor herds be there;
yet, God the same abiding,
  his praise shall tune my voice;
for, while in him confiding,
  I cannot but rejoice.

WILLIAM COWPER (1731–1800)*

596 *Crediton* CM

THOMAS CLARK (1775–1859)

1 Rejoice, believer, in the Lord
   who makes your cause his own:
the hope that's built upon his word
   can ne'er be overthrown.

2 Though many foes beset your road,
   and feeble is your arm,
your life is hid with Christ in God
   beyond the reach of harm.

3 Weak as you are, you shall not faint,
   or fainting, shall not die;
Jesus, the strength of every saint,
   will aid you from on high.

4 Though unperceived by mortal sense
   faith sees him always near,
a guide, a glory, a defence;
   then what have you to fear?

5 As surely as he overcame
   and triumphed once for you,
so surely you that love his name
   shall triumph in him too.

JOHN NEWTON (1725–1807) altd.

597 *St Andrew* CM

WILLIAM TANS'UR (*c.*1700–83)

1 The Saviour died, but rose again
triumphant from the grave;
and pleads our cause at God's right hand,
omnipotent to save.

2 Who then can e'er divide us more
from Jesus and his love,
or break the sacred chain that binds
the earth to heaven above?

3 Let troubles rise, and terrors frown,
and days of darkness fall;
through him all dangers we'll defy,
and more than conquer all.

4 Nor death nor life, nor earth nor hell,
nor time's destroying sway,
can e'er efface us from his heart,
or make his love decay.

5 Each future period love will bless,
as it has blessed the past;
he loved us from the first of time,
he loves us to the last.

from Romans 8: 34–39
Scottish Paraphrases, 1781 (no. 48, vv. 5–9)*

598 *Will your anchor hold?* Irregular W. J. KIRKPATRICK (1838–1921)

1 Will your anchor hold in the storms of life
when the clouds unfold their wings of strife?
When the strong tides lift, and the cables strain,
will your anchor drift, or firm remain?

We have an anchor that keeps the soul
steadfast and sure while the billows roll;
fastened to the Rock which cannot move,
grounded firm and deep in the Saviour's love!

2 Will your anchor hold in the straits of fear,
when the breakers roar and the reef is near?
While the surges rave, and the wild winds blow,
shall the angry waves your boat o'erflow?

3 Will your anchor hold in the floods of death,
when the waters cold chill your latest breath?
On the rising tide you can never fail;
while your anchor holds you will still prevail.

4 Will your eyes behold through the morning light
the city of gold and the harbour bright?
Will you anchor safe by the heavenly shore,
when life's storms are past for evermore?

PRISCILLA J. OWENS (1829–1907) altd.*

599 *Milton Abbas* 664 6664

ERIC H. THIMAN (1900–75)

1 Christ for the world! we sing,
the world to Christ we bring,
with loving zeal;
the poor, and them that mourn,
the faint and overborne,
sin-sick and sorrow worn,
for Christ to heal.

2 Christ for the world! we sing,
the world to Christ we bring,
with fervent prayer;
the wayward and the lost,
by restless passions tossed,
redeemed at countless cost
from dark despair.

3 Christ for the world! we sing,
the world to Christ we bring,
with one accord;
with us the work to share,
with us reproach to dare,
with us the cross to bear
for Christ our Lord.

4 Christ for the world! we sing,
the world to Christ we bring,
with joyful song;
the new-born souls, whose days,
reclaimed from error's ways,
inspired with hope and praise,
to Christ belong.

SAMUEL WOLCOTT (1813–86)*

600 *Christe sanctorum* 10 11 11 6

Melody from
Paris *Antiphoner*, 1681

1 Christ is the world's Light, he and none other;
born in our darkness, he became our Brother.
If we have seen him, we have seen the Father:
Glory to God on high.

2 Christ is the world's Peace, he and none other;
no one can serve him and despise a brother.
Who else unites us, one in God the Father?
Glory to God on high.

3 Christ is the world's Life, he and none other;
sold once for silver, murdered here, our Brother—
he, who redeems us, reigns with God the Father:
Glory to God on high.

4 Give God the glory, God and none other;
give God the glory, Spirit, Son and Father;
give God the glory, God in Man my brother:
Glory to God on high.

F. PRATT GREEN (1903–)*

601 *Rinkart* 67 67 66 66 J. S. BACH (1685–1750)

1 Christ is the world's true light,
its captain of salvation,
the daystar clear and bright
and joy of every nation;
new life, new hope awakes,
where'er we own his sway:
freedom her bondage breaks,
and night is turned to day.

2 In Christ all races meet,
their ancient feuds forgetting,
the whole round world complete,
from sunrise to its setting:
when Christ is throned as Lord,
all shall forsake their fear,
to ploughshare beat the sword,
to pruning-hook the spear.

3 One Lord, in one great name
unite us all who own thee;
cast out our pride and shame
that hinder to enthrone thee;
the world has waited long,
has travailed long in pain;
to heal its ancient wrong,
come, Prince of Peace, and reign.

G. W. BRIGGS (1875–1959) altd.*

602 *Lledrod* LM

Welsh hymn melody,
probably 18th-cent.

1 Forth in the peace of Christ we go;
 Christ to the world with joy we bring;
Christ in our minds, Christ on our lips,
 Christ in our hearts, the world's true King.

2 King of our hearts, Christ makes us kings;
 kingship with him his servants gain;
with Christ, the Servant-Lord of all,
 Christ's world we serve to share Christ's reign.

3 Priests of the world, Christ sends us forth,
 this world of time to consecrate,
our world of sin by grace to heal,
 Christ's world in Christ to recreate.

4 Prophets of Christ, we hear his Word:
 he claims our minds, to search his ways,
he claims our lips, to speak his truth,
 he claims our hearts, to sing his praise.

5 We are his Church, he makes us one:
 here is one hearth for all to find,
here is one flock, one Shepherd-King,
 here is one faith, one heart, one mind.

JAMES QUINN (1919–)

603 *Lord of the Years* 11 10 11 10

MICHAEL BAUGHEN (1930–)

1 Lord, for the years your love has kept and guided,
urged and inspired us, cheered us on our way,
sought us and saved us, pardoned and provided:
Lord of the years, we bring our thanks today.

2 Lord, for that Word, the Word of life which fires us,
speaks to our hearts and sets our souls ablaze,
teaches and trains, rebukes us and inspires us:
Lord of the Word, receive your people's praise.

3 Lord, for our land, in this our generation,
spirits oppressed by pleasure, wealth and care:
for young and old, for commonwealth and nation,
Lord of our land, be pleased to hear our prayer.

4 Lord, for our world, when we disown and doubt you,
loveless in strength, and comfortless in pain,
hungry and helpless, lost indeed without you:
Lord of the world, we pray that Christ may reign.

5 Lord, for ourselves; in living power remake us—
self on the cross and Christ upon the throne;
past put behind us, for the future take us,
Lord of our lives, to live for Christ alone.

TIMOTHY DUDLEY-SMITH (1926–) altd.

604 *Llangloffan* 76 86 D Welsh hymn melody

1 O crucified Redeemer,
whose life-blood we have spilt,
to you we raise our guilty hands,
and humbly own our guilt;
today we see your passion
spread open to our gaze;
the crowded street, the country road,
its Calvary displays.

2 We hear your cry of anguish,
we see your life outpoured,
where battlefields run red with blood,
our neighbours' blood, O Lord;
and in that other battle,
the fight for daily bread,
where might is right and self is king,
we see your thorn-crowned head.

3 The groaning of creation,
wrung out by pain and care,
the anguish of a million hearts
that break in dumb despair;
O crucified Redeemer,
these are your cries of pain;
O may they break our selfish hearts,
and love come in to reign.

TIMOTHY REES (1874–1939) altd.

605 *Bethany* 87 87 D HENRY SMART (1813–79)

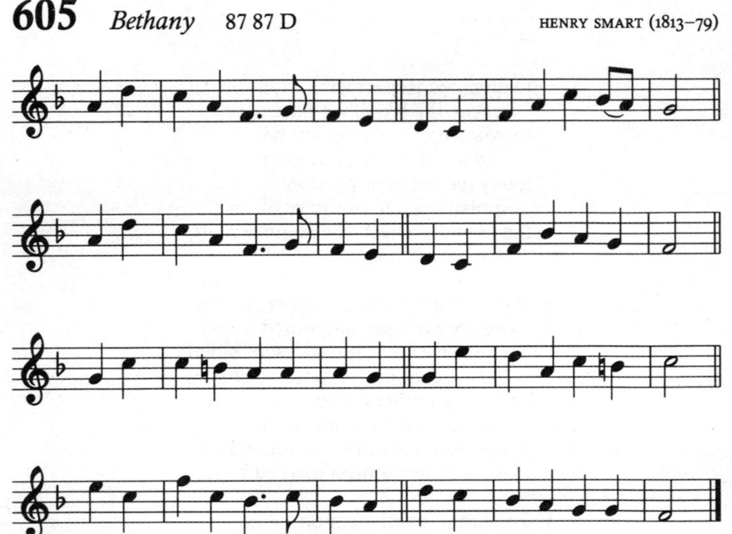

Alternative tune: EVERTON, no. 324.

1 Son of God, eternal Saviour,
source of life and truth and grace,
Son of Man, whose birth among us
hallows all our human race,
Christ our Head, who, throned in glory,
for your own will ever plead,
fill us with your love and pity,
heal our wrongs, and help our need.

2 As you, Lord, have lived for others,
so may we for others live;
freely have your gifts been granted,
freely may your servants give.
Yours the gold and yours the silver,
yours the wealth of sea and land,
we but stewards of your bounty,
held in trust as from your hand.

3 Come, O Christ, and reign above us,
King of love, and Prince of peace:
hush the storm of strife and passion,
bid its cruel discords cease:
by your patient years of toiling,
by your silent hours of pain,
quench our fevered thirst of pleasure,
shame our selfish greed of gain.

4 Son of God, eternal Saviour,
source of life and truth and grace,
Son of Man, whose birth among us
hallows all our human race,
in your love you prayed the Father
that your people should be one;
grant, O Christ, our hope's fruition,
here on earth your will be done.

S. C. LOWRY (1855–1932) altd.

606 *Fulda* LM GARDINER'S *Sacred Melodies*, 1815

1 Where cross the crowded ways of life,
where sound the cries of race and clan,
above the noise of selfish strife,
we hear your voice, O Son of Man.

2 In haunts of wretchedness and need,
on shadowed thresholds dark with fears,
from paths where hide the lures of greed,
we catch the vision of your tears.

3 From tender childhood's helplessness,
from human grief and burdened toil,
from famished souls, from sorrow's stress,
your heart has never known recoil.

4 The cup of water given for you
still holds the freshness of your grace;
yet long these multitudes to view
the strong compassion in your face.

5 O Master, from the mountainside
make haste to heal these hearts of pain;
among these restless throngs abide;
O tread the city's streets again,

6 till all the world shall learn your love,
and follow where your feet have trod;
till glorious from your heaven above,
shall come the city of our God.

F. M. NORTH (1850–1935) altd.

607 *Harrold* 66 66 88 BASIL E. BRIDGE (1927–)

1 This is the truth we hold,
source of the joy we share,
hope that can make us bold
trusting the name we bear;
that 'Christ has died' and 'Christ is risen,
in Christ shall all be made alive'.

2 This is the song of praise
echoing down the years,
true for the present days,
through all our doubts and fears;
for 'Christ has died' and 'Christ is risen,
in Christ shall all be made alive'.

3 Christ is the living Bread
Christ is the word to speak,
Christ is the way to tread,
Christ is the goal to seek;
for 'Christ has died' and 'Christ is risen,
in Christ shall all be made alive'.

4 One in the faith we share,
out in his name we go;
Jesus awaits us there,
longing that all should know
that 'Christ has died' and 'Christ is risen,
in Christ shall all be made alive'.

BASIL E. BRIDGE (1927–)*

608 *Sheltered Dale* 86 86 86 Melody by J. L. F. GLUECH, fl. 1814

At a Harvest Festival

(*The Resurrection of the world*
. . . the breath
of dawn that rustles through the trees
and that clear voice that saith:)

1 'Awake, awake to love and work!
The lark is in the sky,
the fields are wet with diamond dew,
the worlds awake to cry
their blessings on the Lord of Life,
as he goes meekly by.

2 Come, let thy voice be one with theirs,
shout with their shout of praise;
see how the giant sun soars up,
great lord of years and days;
so let the love of Jesus come,
and set thy soul ablaze:

3 to give, and give, and give again,
what God hath given thee;
to spend thy self nor count the cost:
to serve right gloriously
the God who gave all worlds that are,
and all that are to be.'

G. A. STUDDERT-KENNEDY (1883–1929)

609 *Abel* 76 76 D

REGINALD BARRETT-AYRES (1920–81)

1 'Am I my brother's keeper?'—
the muttered cry was drowned
by Abel's life-blood shouting
in silence from the ground.
For no man is an island
divided from the main,
the bell which tolled for Abel
tolled equally for Cain.

2 When Pilate called for water
and thought his hands were clean,
Christ counted less than order,
the man than the machine.
The crowd cried 'Crucify him!',
their malice wouldn't budge;
our rulers call for water,
and history's our judge.

3 As long as people hunger,
as long as people thirst,
and ignorance and illness
and warfare do their worst,
as long as there's injustice
in any of God's lands,
I am 'my brother's keeper';
I dare not wash my hands.

JOHN FERGUSON (1921–89)*

610 *Song 46* 10 10

ORLANDO GIBBONS (1583–1625)

1 Beloved, let us love: for love is of God;
in God alone has love its true abode.

2 Beloved, let us love: for they who love
are born of God, his children from above.

3 Beloved, let us love: for love is rest,
and they who have no love abide unblest.

4 Beloved, let us love: for love is light,
and those who have no love dwell in the night.

5 Beloved, let us love: for only thus
shall we behold that God who first loved us.

H. BONAR (1808–89) altd.*

611 *Ryburn* 88 88 88

NORMAN COCKER (1889–1953)

LOVE IN ACTION

1 Lord Christ, we praise your sacrifice,
your life in love so freely given.
For those who took your life away
you prayed, that they might be forgiven;
and there, in helplessness arrayed,
God's power was perfectly displayed.

2 Once helpless in your mother's arms,
dependent on her mercy then;
at last, by choice, in other hands
you were as helpless once again;
and, at their mercy, crucified,
you claimed your victory and died.

3 Though helpless and rejected then
you're now as risen Lord acclaimed;
for ever, by your sacrifice,
is God's eternal love proclaimed:
the love which, dying, brings to birth
new life and hope for all the earth.

4 So, living Lord, prepare us now
your willing helplessness to share;
to give ourselves in sacrifice
to overcome the world's despair;
in love to give our lives away
and claim your victory today.

ALAN GAUNT (1935–)

612 *Shipston* 87 87 (Trochaic) English traditional melody

1 God, whose farm is all creation,
take the gratitude we give;
take the finest of our harvest,
crops we grow that all may live.

2 Take our ploughing, seeding, reaping,
hopes and fears of sun and rain,
all our thinking, planning, waiting,
ripened in this fruit and grain.

3 All our labour, all our watching,
all our calendar of care,
in these crops of your creation,
take, O God: they are our prayer.

JOHN ARLOTT (1914–91) altd.

613 *Fulda* LM

GARDINER'S *Sacred Melodies*, 1815

1 Lord, speak to me, that I may speak
in living echoes of thy tone;
as thou hast sought, so let me seek
thy straying children, lost and lone.

2 O lead me, Lord, that I may lead
the wandering and the wavering feet;
O feed me, Lord, that I may feed
thy hungering ones with manna sweet.

3 O strengthen me, that while I stand
firm on the rock and strong in thee,
I may stretch out a loving hand
to wrestlers with the troubled sea.

4 O teach me, Lord, that I may teach
the precious things thou dost impart;
and wing my words that they may reach
the hidden depths of many a heart.

5 O use me, Lord, use even me,
just as thou wilt, and when, and where,
until thy blessed face I see,
thy rest, thy joy, thy glory share.

FRANCES RIDLEY HAVERGAL (1836–79)*

614 *Hermitage* 67 67

R. O. MORRIS (1886–1948)

1 Love came down at Christmas,
love all lovely, love divine;
love was born at Christmas,
star and angels gave the sign.

2 Worship we the Godhead,
love incarnate, love divine;
worship we our Jesus:
but wherewith for sacred sign?

3 Love shall be our token,
love be yours and love be mine,
love to God and all men,
love for plea and gift and sign.

CHRISTINA ROSSETTI (1830–94)

615 *Childhood* 888 6

'University of Wales'
A Students' Hymnal, 1923

1 O God of mercy, God of might,
in love and pity infinite,
teach us, as ever in thy sight,
to live our life to thee.

2 And thou, who cam'st on earth to die
that fallen ones might live thereby,
O hear us, for to thee we cry,
in hope, O Lord, to thee.

3 Teach us the lesson thou hast taught,
to feel for those thy blood hath bought;
that every word, and deed, and thought
may work a work for thee.

4 For all are neighbours, far and wide,
since thou, O Lord, for all hast died;
then teach us, whatsoe'er betide,
to love them all in thee.

5 In sickness, sorrow, want, or care,
whate'er it be, 'tis ours to share;
may we, where help is needed, there
give help as unto thee.

6 And may thy Holy Spirit move
all those who live, to live in love,
till thou shalt greet in heaven above
all those who give to thee.

GODFREY THRING (1823–1903)*

616 *Hispania* 10 10

Anon., 19th cent., adpt.

1 Peace with the Father, peace with Christ his Son,
peace with the Spirit, keep us ever one.

2 Love of the Father, love of Christ his Son,
love of the Spirit, make all Christians one.

3 Sin has divided those whom Christ made one;
Father, forgive us through your loving Son.

4 Send forth your Spirit, Father, from above
on us, your children, one with Christ in love.

5 Christians, forgive each other from your heart;
Christ be among us, nevermore to part.

JAMES QUINN (1919–)

617 *Old 120th* 66 66 66

Melody as in *Psalmes*, 1570

The Kingdom of God within

1 O thou not made with hands,
not throned above the skies,
nor walled with shining walls,
nor framed with stones of price,
more bright than gold or gem,
God's own Jerusalem!

2 Where'er the gentle heart
finds courage from above;
where'er the heart forsook
warms with the breath of love;
where faith bids fear depart,
City of God, thou art.

3 Thou art where'er the proud
in humbleness melts down;
where self itself yields up;
where martyrs win their crown;
where faithful souls possess
themselves in perfect peace.

4 Where in life's common ways
with cheerful feet we go;
where in his steps we tread
who trod the way of woe;
where he is in the heart,
City of God, thou art.

5 Not throned above the skies,
nor golden-walled afar,
but where Christ's two or three
in his name gathered are,
be in the midst of them,
God's own Jerusalem!

F. T. PALGRAVE (1824–97)

618 *Narenza* SM

Melody from
Catholicum Hymnologium Germanicum, 1584
adpt. W. H. HAVERGAL (1793–1870)

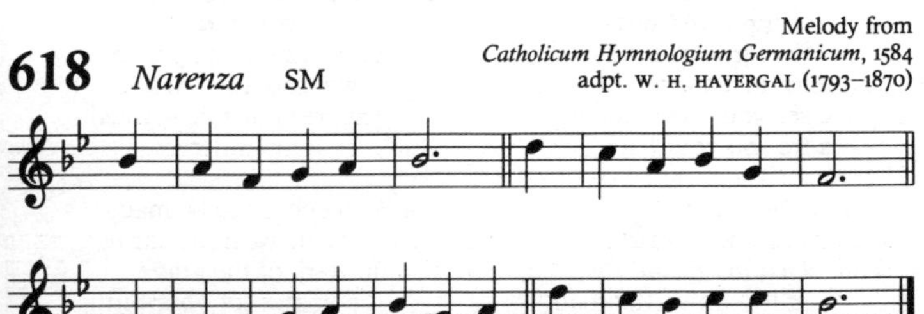

Alternative tune: WINDERMERE, no. 384.

1 We give thee but thine own,
whate'er the gift may be;
all that we have is thine alone,
a trust, O Lord, from thee.

2 May we thy bounties thus
as stewards true receive,
and gladly, as thou blessest us,
to thee our first-fruits give.

W. W. HOW (1823–1897)

619 *Paderborn* 55 55 65 65

German folk melody
adpt. in *Paderborn Gesangbuch*, 1765

1 We meet you, O Christ,
in many a guise;
your image we see
in simple and wise.
You live in a palace,
exist in a shack.
We see you, the gardener,
a tree on your back.

2 In millions alive,
away and abroad,
involved in our life
you live down the road.
Imprisoned in systems
you long to be free.
We see you, Lord Jesus,
still bearing your tree.

3 We hear you, O Man,
in agony cry.
For freedom you march,
in riots you die.
Your face in the papers
we read and we see.
The tree must be planted—
by human decree.

4 You choose to be made
at one with the earth;
the dark of the grave
prepares for your birth.
Your death is your rising,
creative your word:
the tree springs to life, and
our hope is restored.

FRED KAAN (1929–)

620 *Oriel* 87 87 87

From CASPAR ETT'S *Cantica Sacra*, 1840
adpt. W. H. MONK (1823–89)

1 For the healing of the nations,
   Lord, we pray with one accord;
for a just and equal sharing
   of the things that earth affords.
To a life of love in action
   help us rise and pledge our word.

2 Lead us, Father, into freedom;
   from despair your world release,
that, redeemed from war and hatred,
   all may come and go in peace.
Show us how through care and goodness
   fear will die and hope increase.

3 All that kills abundant living,
   let it from the earth be banned:
pride of status, race or schooling,
   dogmas that obscure your plan.
In our common quest for justice
   may we hallow life's brief span.

4 You, Creator-God, have written
   your great name on humankind;
for our growing in your likeness
   bring the life of Christ to mind;
that by our response and service
   earth its destiny may find.

FRED KAAN (1929–)

621 *Annue Christe* 12 12 12 12

French Church melody from *Paris Antiphoner*, 1681

1 Almighty Father, who for us thy Son didst give,
that all the nations through his precious death might live,
in mercy guard us, lest by sloth and selfish pride
we cause to stumble those for whom the Saviour died.

2 We are thy stewards; thine our talents, wisdom, skill;
our only glory that we may thy trust fulfil;
that we thy pleasure in our neighbour's good pursue,
if thou but workest in us both to will and do.

3 On just and unjust thou thy care dost freely shower;
make us thy children, free from greed and lust for power,
lest human justice, yoked with our unequal laws,
oppress the needy and neglect the humble cause.

4 Let not thy worship blind us to the claims of love;
but let thy manna lead us to the feast above,
to seek the country which by faith we now possess,
where Christ, our treasure, reigns in peace and righteousness.

GEORGE CAIRD (1917–84) altd.

622 *Vine and fig-tree*

Traditional

Beneath the shade of our vine and fig-tree
we'll live in peace and unafraid.
Beneath the shade of our vine and fig-tree
we'll live in peace and unafraid;

and into ploughshares turn our swords;
nations shall learn war no more;
and into ploughshares turn our swords;
nations shall learn war no more.

Beneath the shade of our vine and fig-tree
we'll live in peace and unafraid.
Beneath the shade of our vine and fig-tree
we'll live in peace and unafraid.

COLIN HODGETTS
based on Micah 4: 4*a* & 3*b*

623 *Song 1* 10 10 10 10 10 10 ORLANDO GIBBONS (1583–1625)

1 Eternal Ruler of the ceaseless round
   of circling planets singing on their way;
guide of the nations from the night profound
   into the glory of the perfect day;
rule in our hearts, that we may ever be
guided and strengthened and upheld by thee.

2 We are of thee, the children of thy love,
   the kindred of thy well-beloved Son;
descend, O Holy Spirit, like a dove
   into our hearts, that we may be as one:
as one with thee, to whom we ever tend;
as one with him, our brother and our friend.

3 We would be one in hatred of all wrong,
   one in our love of all things sweet and fair,
one with the joy that breaketh into song,
   one with the grief that trembleth into prayer,
one in the power that makes thy children free
to follow truth, and thus to follow thee.

4 O clothe us with thy heavenly armour, Lord,
   thy trusty shield, thy sword of love divine;
our inspiration be thy constant word;
   we ask no victories that are not thine:
give or withhold, let pain or pleasure be;
enough to know that we are serving thee.

J. W. CHADWICK (1840–1904)*

624 *Langham* 11 10 11 10 10 GEOFFREY SHAW (1879–1943)

1 Father Eternal, Ruler of Creation,
Spirit of life, by whom all things are made,
through the thick darkness covering every nation,
light to our blindness, come now to our aid!
Your kingdom come, O Lord, your will be done.

2 Rulers and peoples, still we stand divided,
and, sharing not our griefs, no joy can share;
by wars and tumults Love is mocked, derided,
his conquering cross no kingdom wills to bear:
Your kingdom come, O Lord, your will be done.

3 Envious of heart, blind-eyed, with tongues confounded,
nation by nation still goes unforgiven;
in wrath and fear, by jealousies surrounded,
building proud towers which shall not reach to heaven:
Your kingdom come, O Lord, your will be done.

4 Lust of possession causes desolations;
and meekness has no honour in the earth.
Led by no star, the rulers of the nations
still fail to bring us to the blissful birth:
Your kingdom come, O Lord, your will be done.

5 How shall we love you, holy, hidden Being,
unless we love the world which you have made?
O, give us surer love, for better seeing
your Word made flesh and in a manger laid:
Your kingdom come, O Lord, your will be done.

LAURENCE HOUSMAN (1865–1959) altd.*

625 *Rhuddlan* 87 87 87

Welsh traditional melody

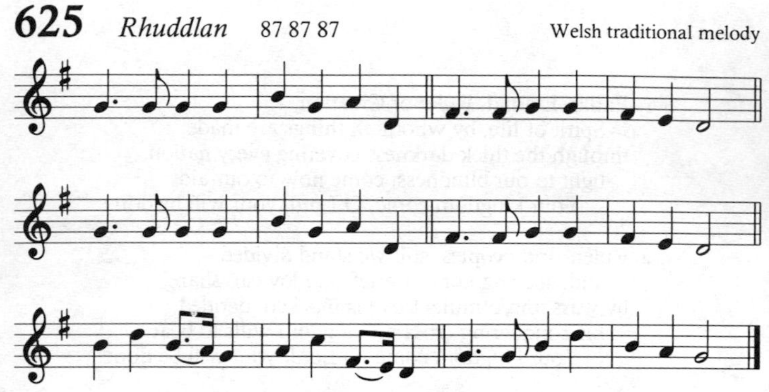

For Prisoners of Conscience

1 God of freedom, God of justice,
  God whose love is strong as death,
God who saw the dark of prison,
  God who knew the price of faith:
touch our world of sad oppression
  with your Spirit's healing breath.

2 Rid the earth of torture's terror,
  God whose hands were nailed to wood;
hear the cries of pain and protest,
  God who shed the tears and blood;
move in us the power of pity,
  restless for the common good.

3 Make in us a captive conscience
  quick to hear, to act, to plead;
make us truly sisters, brothers,
  of whatever race or creed:
teach us to be fully human,
  open to each other's need.

SHIRLEY ERENA MURRAY (1931–)*
Written in 1981 for *Amnesty International*

626 *Rhuddlan* 87 87 87

Welsh traditional melody

Alternative tune: ORIEL, no. 620.

1 Judge eternal, throned in splendour,
   Lord of lords and King of kings,
with thy living fire of judgement
   purge this land of bitter things;
over all its wide dominion
   spread the healing of thy wings.

2 Still the weary folk are pining
   for the hour that brings release;
and the city's crowded clangour
   cries aloud for sin to cease;
and the homesteads and the woodlands
   plead in silence for their peace.

3 Crown, O God, thine own endeavour;
   cleave our darkness with thy sword;
feed the faithless and the hungry
   with the richness of thy word;
cleanse the body of this nation
   through the glory of the Lord.

H. SCOTT HOLLAND (1847–1918) altd.*

627 *Callum* 65 74 64 74 PAUL BATEMAN (1954–)

SATISH KUMAR (1936–)
adpt. from the Hindu *Upanishads*, *c.*9th cent. BC

628 *New Jerusalem* 86 86 86 BERNARD S. MASSEY (1927–)

1 O holy City, seen by John,
where Christ, the Lamb, shall reign,
within whose four-square walls shall come
no night, nor need, nor pain,
and where the tears are wiped from eyes
that shall not weep again!

2 O shame to us who rest content
while lust and greed for gain
exploiting fear and misery
wring gold from human pain,
and bitter lips in blind despair
cry, 'Christ has died in vain!'

3 Give us, O God, the strength to build
the City that has stayed
too long a dream, whose laws of love,
for all the earth are made,
and where no sun need shine, since God's
pure light is now displayed.

4 Already we can see, by faith,
your City rising fair:
your presence with us challenges
all those who trust, to dare
to seize, in faith, the whole of life
and plant its glory there.

W. RUSSELL BOWIE (1882–1969)*
based on Revelation 21

629 Channel of Peace Irregular
SEBASTIAN TEMPLE (1928–)
D
1. Make me a chan-nel of your peace. Where
2. Make me a chan-nel of your peace. Where
3. Make me a chan-nel of your peace; for
Em A7
there is hat-red, let me bring your love; where
there's des-pair in life, let me bring hope; where
when we give we will our-selves re - ceive. It
Em
there is in - jur - y, your par-don, Lord; and
there is dark-ness, let me bring your light; and
is in par-don - ing that we are par - doned and in
Em7 A7 D Fine D7
where there's doubt, true faith in you:
where there's sad-ness, bring your joy: O
dy - ing that we gain e - ter-nal life.

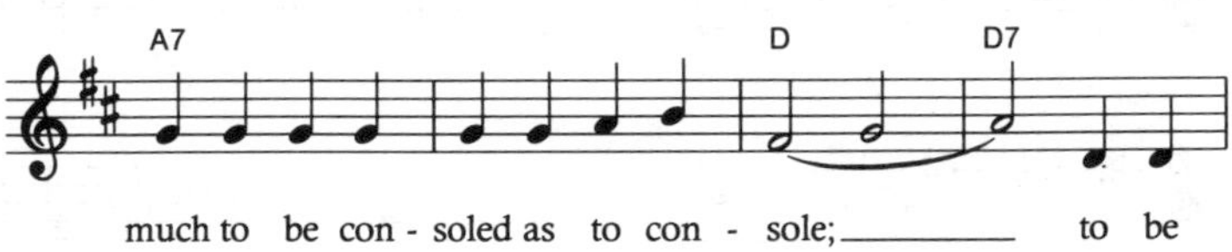

from a prayer sometimes attr. to ST FRANCIS (1182–1226)
arr. SEBASTIAN TEMPLE (1928–)*

630 *Farmborough* 88 88 88 ARTHUR S. WARRELL (1882–1939)

1 O Christ the Lord, O Christ the King,
who wide the gates of death didst fling,
whose place upon creation's throne
by Easter triumph was made known,
rule now on earth from realms above,
subdue the nations by thy love.

2 Lord, vindicate against our greed
the weak, whose tears thy justice plead,
thy pity, Lord, on those who lie
oppressed by war and tyranny;
show them the cross which thou didst bear,
give them the power which conquered there.

3 Let those whose pride usurps thy throne
acknowledge thou art Lord alone;
cause those whose lust racks humankind
thy wrath to know, thy mercy find;
make all this rebel world proclaim
the mighty power of thy blest name.

4 So shall creation's bondage cease,
its pangs of woe give birth to peace;
and all the earth, redeemed by thee,
shall know a glorious liberty:
O haste the time, make short the days,
till all our cries dissolve in praise!

R. T. BROOKS (1918–85) altd.*

631

FIRST TUNE

Sunderland SM HENRY SMART (1813–79)

SECOND TUNE

Hampton SM A. WILLIAMS'S *Psalmody* (*c.*1770)

1 O Lord our God, arise;
the cause of truth maintain,
and over all the peopled world
extend her blessed reign.

2 Thou Prince of Life, arise;
nor let thy glory cease;
far spread the conquests of thy grace
and bless the earth with peace.

3 Spirit of Power, arise;
expand thy quickening wing,
over a dark and ruined world
let light and order spring.

4 All on the earth, arise;
to God the Saviour sing;
from shore to shore, from earth to heaven,
let echoing anthems ring.

RALPH WARDLAW (1779–1853) altd.*

632 *Bellwoods* SM

JAMES HOPKIRK (1908–72)

Alternative tune: ST THOMAS, no. 458.

1 O Day of God, draw near
in beauty and in power,
come with your timeless judgement now
to match our present hour.

2 Bring to our troubled minds,
uncertain and afraid,
the quiet of a steadfast faith,
calm of a call obeyed.

3 Bring justice to our land,
that all may dwell secure,
and finely build for days to come
foundations that endure.

4 Bring to our world of strife
your sovereign word of peace,
that war may haunt the earth no more
and desolation cease.

5 O Day of God, draw near
as at creation's birth;
let there be light again, and set
your judgement in the earth.

R. B. Y. SCOTT (1899–1987) altd.*

633 *The Pollen of Peace* Irregular

Words and music by ROGER COURTNEY (1954–)

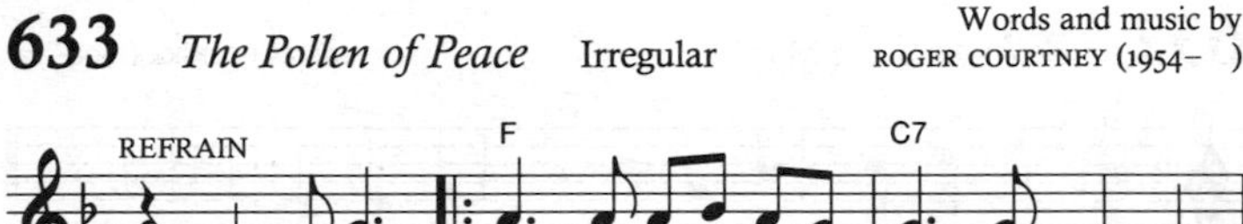

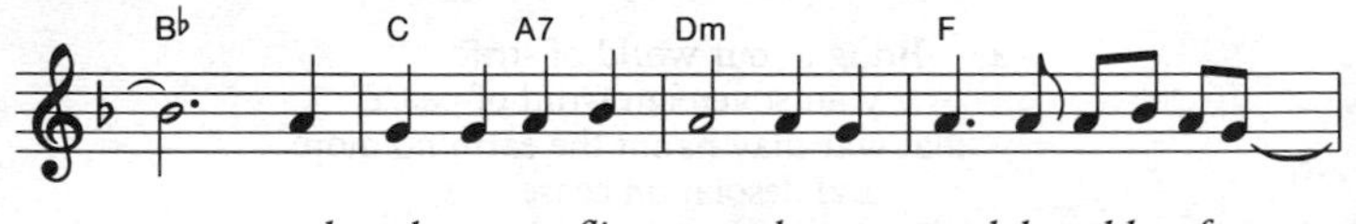

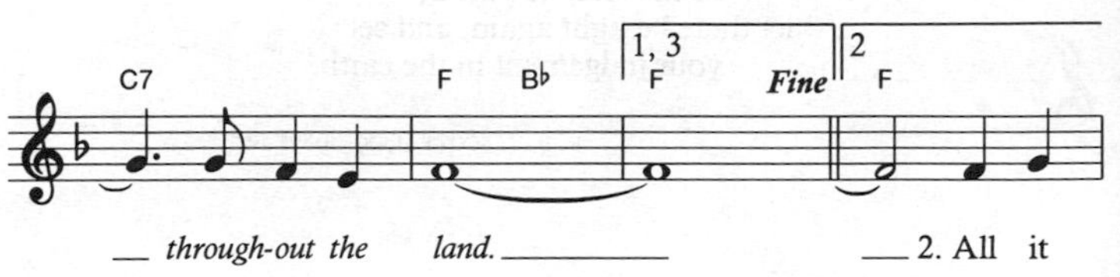

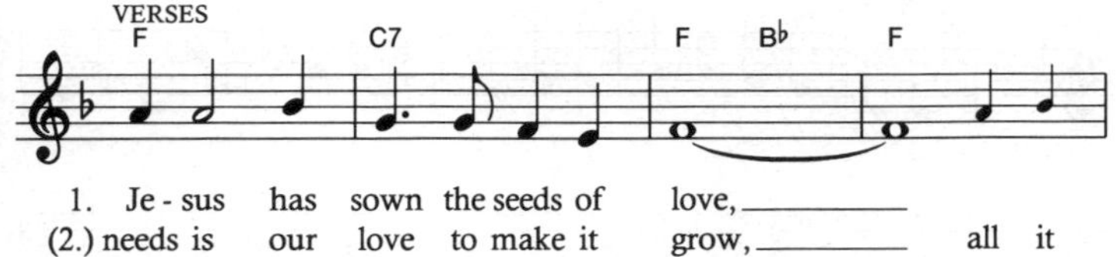
VERSES
F C7 F B♭ F
1. Je - sus has sown the seeds of love,
(2.) needs is our love to make it grow, all it

Am B♭ C7
Je - sus has launched the grey-winged dove. Let us
needs is our hope - ful-ness to show, and tell

F B♭ Gm C A7 Dm C7
make the flo - wer grow and let the peo - ple know that
those who choke with fear that the Prince of Peace is here: all it

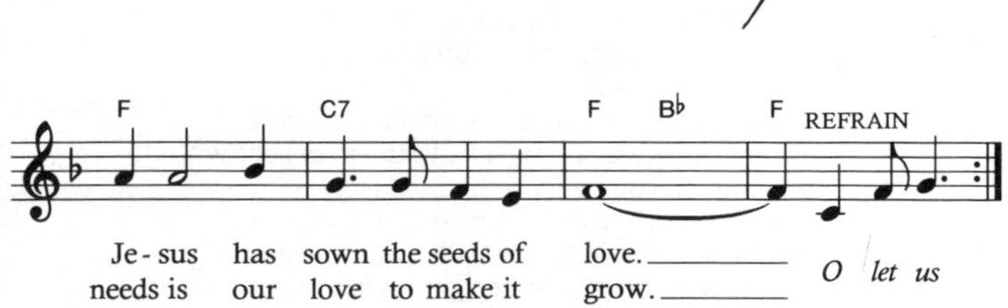
F C7 F B♭ F REFRAIN
Je - sus has sown the seeds of love.
needs is our love to make it grow.
O let us

634 *Song 1* 10 10 10 10 10 10

ORLANDO GIBBONS (1583–1625)

1 Pray for the Church afflicted and oppressed,
for all who suffer for the gospel's sake,
that Christ may show us how to serve them best
in that one kingdom Satan cannot shake.
But how much more than us they have to give
who by their dying show us how to live!

2 Pray for Christ's dissidents, who daily wait,
as Jesus waited in the olive grove,
the unjust trial, the pre-determined fate,
the world's contempt for reconciling love.
Shall all they won for us, at such a cost,
be by our negligence or weakness lost?

3 Pray that if times of testing should lay bare
what sort we are, who call ourselves his own,
we may be counted worthy then to wear,
with quiet fortitude, Christ's only crown:
the crown that in his saints he wears again—
the crown of thorns that signifies his reign.

F. PRATT GREEN (1903–)

635 *St Columba* 87 87 (Iambic) Ancient Irish hymn melody

1 Put peace into each other's hands
and like a treasure hold it,
protect it like a candle-flame,
with tenderness enfold it.

2 Put peace into each other's hands
with loving expectation;
be gentle in your words and ways,
in touch with God's creation.

3 Put peace into each other's hands
like bread we break for sharing;
look people warmly in the eye:
our life is meant for caring.

4 As at communion, shape your hands
into a waiting cradle;
the gift of Christ receive, revere,
united round the table.

5 Put Christ into each other's hands,
he is love's deepest measure;
in love make peace, give peace a chance,
and share it like a treasure.

FRED KAAN (1929–)

636 *Illsley* LM

JOHN BISHOP (1665–1737)

1 The Church of Christ, in every age
  beset by change but Spirit-led,
must claim and test its heritage
  and keep on rising from the dead.

2 Across the world, across the street,
  the victims of injustice cry
for shelter and for bread to eat,
  and never live until they die.

3 Then let the Servant Church arise,
  a caring Church, that longs to be
a partner in Christ's sacrifice,
  and clothed in Christ's humanity.

4 For he alone, whose blood was shed,
  can cure the fever in our blood,
and teach us how to share our bread
  and feed the starving multitude.

5 We have no mission but to serve,
  in full obedience to our Lord;
to care for all, without reserve,
  and spread his liberating Word.

F. PRATT GREEN (1903–)

637 *Air Falalalo* Irregular Scottish traditional melody

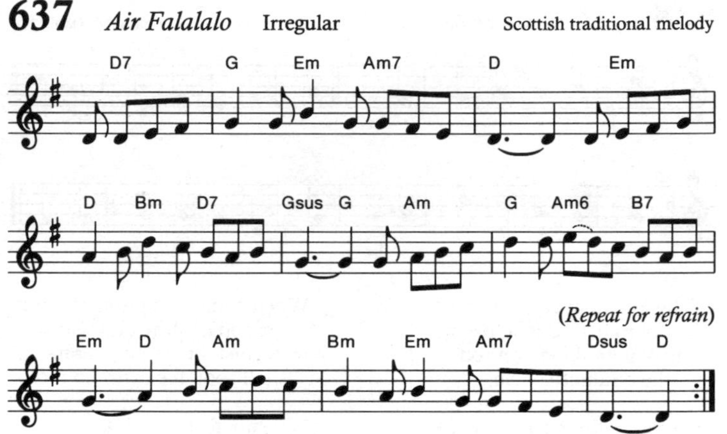

1 The Day of the Lord shall come, as prophets have told,
when Christ shall make all things new, no matter how old.
And some at the stars may gaze, and some at God's word,
in vain to predict the time, the Day of the Lord.

The desert shall spring to life, the hills shall rejoice;
the lame of the earth shall leap, the dumb shall find voice;
the lamb with the lion shall lie, and the last shall be first;
and nations for war no more shall study or thirst.

2 The Day of the Lord shall come—a thief in the night,
a curse to those in the wrong who think themselves right,
a pleasure for those in pain or with death at the door;
a true liberation for the prisoners and poor.

3 The Day of the Lord shall come and judgement be known,
as nations like sheep and goats come close to the throne.
Then Christ shall himself reveal, asking all to draw near
and see in his face all faces once ignored here.

4 The Day of the Lord shall come, but now is the time
to subvert earth's wisdom with Christ's folly sublime,
by loving the loveless, turning the tide and the cheek,
by walking beneath the cross in step with the weak.

JOHN BELL (1949–)
and GRAHAM MAULE (1958–)

638 *St Cecilia* 66 66

L. G. HAYNE (1836–83)

1 Thy kingdom come, O God;
thy rule, O Christ, begin;
break with thine iron rod
the tyrannies of sin.

2 Where is thy reign of peace
and purity and love?
When shall all hatred cease,
as in the realms above?

3 When comes the promised time,
the end of strife and war,
when lust, oppression, crime
shall spoil the earth no more?

4 We pray thee, Lord, arise,
and come in thy great might;
revive our longing eyes,
which languish for thy sight.

5 O'er lands both near and far
thick darkness broodeth yet;
arise, O Morning Star,
arise, and never set!

LEWIS HENSLEY (1824–1905) altd.*

639 *Gaudium et Spes* 10 3 12 6 4 8

BRIAN WREN (1936–)

1 This we can do for justice and for peace:
  we can pray,
and work to answer prayers that other people say.
This we can do in faith,
and see it through—
  for Jesus is alive today.

2 This we can do for justice and for peace:
  we can give
till everyone can take life in their hands, and live.
This we can do in love
and see it through—
  for Jesus is alive today.

3 This we can do for justice and for peace:
  we can see—
and help our neighbours see—what is, and what could be.
This we can do with truth
and see it through—
  for Jesus is alive today.

4 This we can do for justice and for peace:
  bring to light
whatever hurts and tramples down, or hides from sight.
This we can do with strength
and see it through—
  for Jesus is alive today.

5 This we can do for justice and for peace:
  we can hope
and, hoping, stride along our way while others grope.
This we can do till God
makes all things new—
  for Jesus is alive today.

BRIAN WREN (1936–)

640 *Ellers* 10 10 10 10 E. J. HOPKINS (1818–1901)

1 Saviour, again to thy dear name we raise
with one accord our parting hymn of praise;
guard thou the lips from sin, the hearts from shame,
that in thy house have called upon thy name.

2 Grant us thy peace, Lord, through the coming night;
turn thou for us its darkness into light;
from harm and danger keep thy servants free,
for dark and light are both alike to thee.

3 Grant us thy peace throughout our earthly life,
peace to thy Church from error and from strife;
peace to the world, the fruit of truth and love,
peace in each heart, thy Spirit from above.

4 Thy peace in sorrow, balm of every pain,
thy peace in death, the hope to rise again;
then, when thy voice shall bid our conflict cease,
call us, O Lord, to thine eternal peace.

JOHN ELLERTON (1826–93)*

641 *Herstmonceux* 4 666 68

EBENEZER PROUT (1835–1909)
adpt. ERIC H. THIMAN (1900–75)
and compilers

1 We pray for peace,
but not the easy peace
built on complacency
and not the truth of God;
we pray for real peace,
the peace God's love alone can seal.

2 We pray for peace,
but not the cruel peace
leaving God's poor bereft
and dying in distress;
we pray for real peace,
enriching all the human race.

3 We pray for peace,
and not the evil peace
defending unjust laws
and nursing prejudice,
but for the real peace
of justice, mercy, truth and love.

4 We pray for peace,
holy communion
with Christ our risen Lord
and every living thing;
God's will fulfilled on earth,
and all his creatures reconciled.

5 We pray for peace,
and, for the sake of peace,
look to the risen Christ,
who gives the grace we need
to serve the cause of peace
and make our own self-sacrifice.

6 God, give us peace;
if you withdraw your love
there is no peace for us,
nor any hope of it.
With you to lead us on,
through death or tumult, peace
will come.

ALAN GAUNT (1935–)*

642 *Uppsala* 10 10 11 11 PETER CUTTS (1937–)

1 We utter our cry: that peace may prevail!
that earth will survive and faith must not fail.
We pray with our life for the world in our care,
for people diminished by doubt and despair.

2 We cry from the fright of our daily scene
for strength to say 'No' to all that is mean:
designs bearing chaos, extinction of life,
all energy wasted on weapons of death.

3 We lift up our hearts for children unborn:
give wisdom, O God, that we may hand on,
replenished and tended, this good planet earth,
preserving the future and wonder of birth.

4 Creator of life, come, share out, we pray,
your Spirit on earth, revealing the Way
to leaders conferring round tables for peace;
that they may from bias and guile be released.

5 Come with us, Lord-Love, in protest and march,
and help us to fire with passion your Church,
to match all our statements and lofty resolve
with fervent commitment in action involved.

6 Whatever the ill or pressure we face,
Lord, hearten and heal, give insight and grace
to think and make peace with each heartbeat and breath,
choose Christ before Caesar and life before death!

FRED KAAN (1929–) 2009

643 *Go down, Moses* Irregular Afro–American Spiritual

1 When Israel was in Egypt's land,
Let my people go!
oppressed so hard they could not stand,
Let my people go!

Go down, Moses,
way down in Egypt's land;
tell old Pharaoh,
'Let my people go!'

2 No more shall they in bondage toil:
let them come out with Egypt's spoil.

3 The Lord told Moses what to do
to lead the children of Israel through.

4 O come along, Moses, you'll not get lost:
stretch out your rod, and come across.

5 When they reached the other shore
they sang a song of triumph o'er.

6 So let us all from bondage flee,
and Jesus, he will set us free.

Traditional (Afro–American Spiritual)*

644 *Angelus* LM

Founded on a melody in *Heilige Seelen-Lust*, 1657

1 At evening, when the sun was set,
the sick, O Lord, around you lay;
O in what various pains they met!
O with what joy they went away!

2 O Saviour Christ, our ills dispel:
for some are sick, and some are sad,
and some have never loved you well,
and some have lost the love they had;

3 and some are pressed with worldly care,
and some are tried with fear and doubt,
and some such grievous passions tear,
that only you can cast them out;

4 and none, O Lord, have perfect rest,
for none are wholly free from sin;
and those who long to serve you best
are conscious most of wrong within.

5 O Christ our Saviour, Son of Man;
you have been troubled, tempted, tried;
your kind but searching glance can scan
the very wounds that shame would hide.

6 Your touch has still its ancient power;
no word from you can fruitless fall;
hear in this solemn evening hour,
and in your mercy heal us all.

HENRY TWELLS (1823–1900)*

645 *Diva servatrix* 11 11 11 5

Melody from *Bayeux Antiphoner*, 1739

1 Father of mercy, God of consolation,
look on your people, gathered here to praise you,
pity our weakness, come in power to aid us,
source of all blessing.

2 Son of the Father, Lord of all creation,
come as our Saviour, Jesus, friend of sinners,
grant us forgiveness, lift our downcast spirit,
heal us and save us.

3 Joy-giving Spirit, be our light in darkness,
come to befriend us, help us bear our burdens,
give us true courage, breathe your peace around us,
stay with us always.

4 God in Three Persons, Father, Son and Spirit,
come to renew us, fill your Church with glory,
grant us your healing, pledge of resurrection,
foretaste of heaven.

JAMES QUINN (1919–)

646 *Acceptance* 76 76 D

BRENDA STEPHENSON (1947–)

1 Help us accept each other
as Christ accepted us;
teach us as sister, brother,
each person to embrace.
Be present, Lord, among us
and bring us to believe
we are *ourselves* accepted
and meant to love and live.

2 Teach us, O Lord, your lessons,
as in our daily life
we struggle to be human
and search for hope and faith.
Teach us to care for people,
for all—not just for some,
to love them as we find them
or as they may become.

3 Let your acceptance change us,
so that we may be moved
in living situations
to do the truth in love;
to practise your acceptance
until we know by heart
the table of forgiveness
and laughter's healing art.

4 Lord, for today's encounters
with all who are in need,
who hunger for acceptance,
for righteousness and bread,
we need new eyes for seeing,
new hands for holding on:
renew us with your Spirit;
Lord, free us, make us one!

FRED KAAN (1929–)

(Verse 3 line 7: for the 70 Times Table see Matthew 18: 21, 22)

647 *St Bernard* CM

Melody from *Tochter Sion*, Cologne, 1741, as adpt. in *Easy Hymn Tunes for Catholic Schools*, 1851

1 In Christ there is no East or West,
in him no South or North,
but one great fellowship of love
throughout the whole wide earth.

2 In him shall true hearts everywhere
their high communion find,
his service is the golden cord
close-binding humankind.

3 Join hands, then, all the human race,
whate'er your nation be;
all who my Father's image bear
are surely kin to me.

4 In Christ now meet both East and West,
in him meet South and North,
all Christlike souls are one in him,
throughout the whole wide earth.

'JOHN OXENHAM' (1852–1941) altd.*

648 *Chereponi* 7 7 9 with refrain TOM COLVIN (1925–)

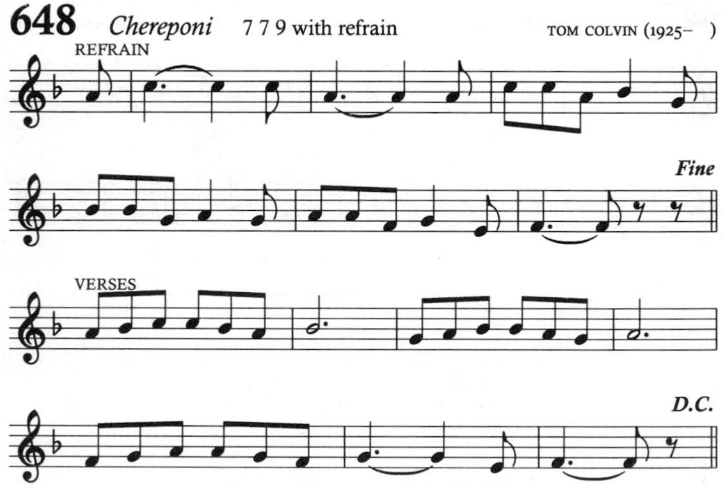

Jesu, Jesu,
fill us with your love,
show us how to serve
the neighbours we have from you.

1 Kneels at the feet of his friends,
silently washes their feet,
Master who acts as a slave to them:

2 Neighbours are rich, and are poor,
neighbours are black, and are white,
neighbours are near and are far away:

3 These are the ones we should serve,
these are the ones we should love.
All these are neighbours to us and you:

4 Kneel at the feet of our friends,
silently washing their feet,
this is the way we should live with you:

TOM COLVIN (1925–) altd.*

'Jesu' may be pronounced 'Yay-soo', as in many other languages.

649 *Let the world rejoice together*

Traditional Israeli folk-song

GEOFFREY GARDNER*

If sung through twice, get faster during the second time.

650 *Gonfalon Royal* LM

PERCY BUCK (1871–1947)

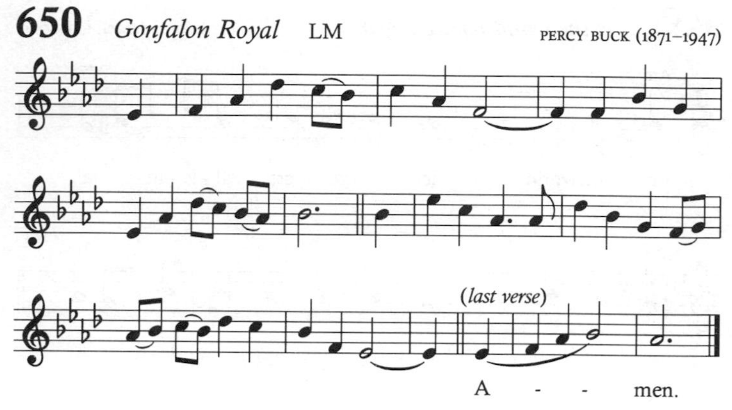

1 God with humanity made one
is seen in Christ, God's only Son:
in you, Lord Christ, the Son of Man,
we see God's reconciling plan.

2 To save a broken world you came,
and from chaotic depths reclaim
your whole creation, so we share
your reconciling work and care.

3 In you all humankind can see
the people God would have us be.
In you we find how God forgives,
through you, the Spirit in us lives.

4 Through us God calls the world again;
and constantly his love remains
with arms outstretched, to heal and bless
the refugees of emptiness.

5 Where race or creed or hate divide,
the Church, like God, must stand beside
and stretch out reconciling hands
to join, through suffering, every land.

6 Then give us strength, great Lord of life,
to work until all human strife
is reconciled, and all shall praise
your endless love, your glorious ways.
(Amen.)

DAVID FOX (1956–)

651 *Woodmansterne* 88 88 88

CARYL MICKLEM (1925–)

1 O God, by whose almighty plan
first order out of chaos stirred,
and life, responsive to your word
its fragile human form began;
grant us in light and love to grow,
your sovereign truth to seek and know.

2 O Christ, whose touch unveiled the blind,
whose presence warmed the lonely soul;
your love made broken sinners whole,
your faith cast devils from the mind.
Grant us your faith, your love, your care
to bring to sufferers everywhere.

3 O Holy Spirit, by whose grace
our skills abide, our wisdom grows,
in every healing work disclose
new paths to probe, new thoughts to trace.
Grant us your wisest way to go
in all we think, or speak, or do.

H. C. A. GAUNT (1902–83)*

652 *Drakes Broughton* 87 87 (Trochaic) EDWARD ELGAR (1857–1934)

1 God! When human bonds are broken
and we lack the love or skill
to restore the hope of healing,
give us grace and make us still.

2 Through that stillness, with your Spirit
come into our world of stress,
for the sake of Christ forgiving
all the failures we confess.

3 You in us are bruised and broken:
hear us as we seek release
from the pain of earlier living;
set us free and grant us peace.

4 Send us, God of new beginnings,
humbly hopeful into life.
Use us as a means of blessing:
make us stronger, give us faith.

5 Give us faith to be more faithful,
give us hope to be more true,
give us love to go on learning:
God! En-courage and renew!

FRED KAAN (1929–)

653 *Angelus* LM

Founded on a melody in *Heilige Seelenlust*, 1657

1 We cannot measure how you heal
or answer every sufferer's prayer,
yet we believe your grace responds
where faith and doubt unite to care.

2 The pain that will not go away,
the guilt that clings from things long past,
the fear of what the future holds
are present as if meant to last.

3 But present too is love which tends
the hurt we never hoped to find,
the private agonies inside,
the memories that haunt the mind.

4 Your hands, though bloodied on the cross,
survive to hold and heal and warn,
to carry all through death to life
and cradle children yet unborn.

5 So some have come who need your help,
and some have come to make amends:
your hands which shaped and saved the world
are present in the touch of friends.

6 Lord, let your Spirit meet us here
to mend the body, mind and soul,
to disentangle peace from pain
and make your broken people whole.

JOHN BELL (1949–)
and GRAHAM MAULE (1958–)

654 *Intercessor* 11 10 11 10

C. H. H. PARRY (1848–1918)

1 We turn to you, O God of every nation,
giver of good and origin of life;
your love is at the heart of all creation,
your hurt is people's pain in war and death.

2 We turn to you that we may be forgiven
for crucifying Christ on earth again.
We know that we have never wholly striven
to share with all the promise of your reign.

3 Free every heart from pride and self-reliance,
our ways of thought inspire with simple grace;
break down among us barriers of defiance,
speak to the soul of all the human race.

4 On all who work on earth for right relations
we pray the light of love from hour to hour.
Grant wisdom to the leaders of the nations,
the gift of carefulness to those in power.

5 Teach us, good Lord, to serve the need of others,
help us to give and not to count the cost.
Unite us all to live as sisters, brothers,
defeat our Babel with your Pentecost!

FRED KAAN (1929–)*

655 *Winchcombe* CM LEONARD BLAKE (1907–89)

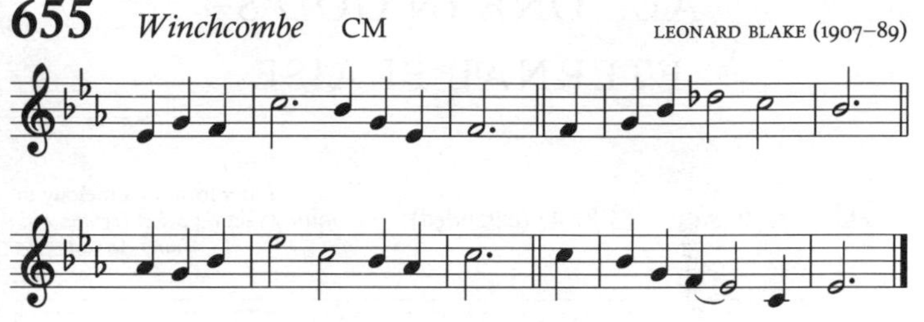

1 When Christ was lifted from the earth
his arms stretched out above
through every culture, every birth,
to draw an answering love.

2 Still east and west his love extends
and always, near or far,
he calls and claims us as his friends
and loves us as we are.

3 Where generation, class or race
divides us to our shame,
he sees not labels but a face,
a person and a name.

4 Thus freely loved, though fully known,
may I in Christ be free
to welcome and accept his own
as Christ accepted me.

BRIAN WREN (1936–)
from John 12: 32, 33 and Romans 15: 7

ALL ONE IN GOD'S ETERNAL PRAISE

656 *Helmsley* 87 87 47 (extended)

Later form of a melody in JOHN WESLEY'S *Select Hymns with Tunes Annext*, 1765

1 Lo! He comes with clouds descending,
once for favoured sinners slain;
thousand thousand saints attending
swell the triumph of his train:
Alleluia! (*3 times*)
God appears on earth to reign.

2 Every eye shall now behold him
robed in awesome majesty;
we, who set at naught and sold him,
crucified him on the tree:
Lord, have mercy, (*3 times*)
let us all thine Advent see.

3 Those dear tokens of his passion
still his dazzling body bears,
cause of endless exultation
to his ransomed worshippers:
Sing hosanna! (*3 times*)
see the risen Lord appears!

4 Yea, Amen, let all adore thee,
high on thine eternal throne:
Saviour, take the power and glory,
claim the kingdom for thine own;
O come quickly, (*3 times*)
Alleluia! Come, Lord, come!

CHARLES WESLEY (1707–88)
and JOHN CENNICK (1718–55)
altd. MARTIN MADAN (1726–90)*

657 *Gopsal* 66 66 88 G. F. HANDEL (1685–1759)

1 Rejoice, the Lord is King;
  your Lord and King adore;
mortals, give thanks and sing,
  and triumph evermore:

  Lift up your heart, lift up your voice:
  rejoice, again I say, rejoice!

2 Jesus the Saviour reigns,
  the God of truth and love;
when he had purged our stains
  he took his seat above:

3 His kingdom cannot fail;
  he rules o'er earth and heaven;
the keys of death and hell
  are to our Jesus given:

4 He sits at God's right hand
  till all his foes submit,
and bow to his command,
  and fall beneath his feet:

5 Rejoice in glorious hope;
  Jesus the judge shall come,
and take his servants up
  to their eternal home:

  We soon shall hear the archangel's voice,
  the trump of God shall sound, rejoice!

CHARLES WESLEY (1707–88)

658 *Sine nomine*

R. VAUGHAN WILLIAMS (1872–1958)

10 10 10 with alleluias

(*vv. 1, 5*)

1 For all the saints who from their labours rest,
who thee by faith before the world confessed,
thy name, Lord Jesus, be for ever blessed:

Alleluia! Alleluia!

2 Thou wast their Rock, their Fortress and their Might,
thou, Lord, their Captain in the well-fought fight,
in deepest darkness thou their one true light:

3 O may thy servants, faithful, true, and bold,
fight as the saints who nobly fought of old,
and win with them the victors' crown of gold:

4 O blest communion, fellowship divine!
We feebly struggle, they in glory shine;
Yet all are one in thee, for all are thine:

5 From earth's wide bounds, from ocean's farthest coast,
through gates of pearl streams in the countless host,
and sings to Father, Son and Holy Ghost:

W. W. HOW (1823–97)*

659 *Regnator orbis* 11 11 11 11 (Dactylic)

Adpt. from a melody in *Paris Antiphoner*, 1681

1 What of those sabbaths? what glory! what grandeur!
kept by the saints in celestial splendour:
rest for the weary, reward of endurance;
God, all in all, their delight and assurance!

2 There in Jerusalem, past comprehending,
peace is perfected and joy never ending;
there where fulfilment precedes aspiration,
always exceeding the heart's expectation.

3 What of the monarch there, what of the treasure,
what of the peace, of the rest and the pleasure?
How can they tell us the rapturous story:
those who encounter ineffable glory!

4 Meanwhile, we wait for the great celebration,
making our way to our true destination:
coming from Babylon, exile and sadness,
home to Jerusalem, city of gladness.

5 There all distress will be done with for ever;
there we will sing songs of Zion, and never
never cease praising; our songs ever soaring,
praising you, Lord, and for ever adoring.

6 Sabbath on sabbath, in endless succession;
sabbaths unending, delight past expression;
joy unrestrained, and eternity ringing:
we, with the angels, eternally singing!

7 Give God the glory and glad adoration,
from whom and *through* whom and *in* whom, creation
comes into being, with us to inherit
joy in the Father, the Son and the Spirit.

PETER ABELARD (1079–1142)
tr. ALAN GAUNT (1935–)

660 *Highwood* 11 10 11 10 R. R. TERRY (1865–1938)

1 Hark what a sound, and too divine for hearing,
stirs on the earth and trembles in the air!
Is it the thunder of the Lord's appearing?
Is it the music of his people's prayer?

2 Surely he cometh, and a thousand voices
shout to the saints, and to the deaf are dumb;
surely he cometh, and the earth rejoices,
glad in his coming who hath sworn: I come!

3 This hath he done, and shall we not adore him?
This shall he do, and can we still despair?
Come, let us quickly fling ourselves before him,
cast at his feet the burden of our care.

4 Through life and death, through sorrow and through sinning,
he shall suffice me, for he hath sufficed:
Christ is the end, for Christ was the beginning,
Christ the beginning, for the end is Christ.

F. W. H. MYERS (1843–1901) altd.

661 *Coe Fen* DCM

KEN NAYLOR (1931–91)

Alternative tune: SOLL'S SEIN, no. 311.

1 How shall I sing that majesty
which angels do admire?
Let dust in dust and silence lie;
sing, sing, ye heavenly choir.
Thousands of thousands stand around
thy throne, O God most high;
ten thousand times ten thousand sound
thy praise; but who am I?

2 Thy brightness unto them appears,
while I thy footsteps trace;
a sound of God comes to my ears;
but they behold thy face:
I shall, I fear, be dark and cold,
with all my fire and light;
yet when thou dost accept their gold,
Lord, treasure up my mite.

3 Enlighten with faith's light my heart,
inflame it with love's fire,
then shall I sing and take my part
with that celestial choir.
They sing, because thou art their Sun;
Lord, send a beam on me;
for where heaven is but once begun,
there alleluias be.

4 How great a being, Lord, is thine,
which doth all beings keep!
Thy knowledge is the only line
to sound so vast a deep:
thou art a sea without a shore,
a sun without a sphere;
thy time is now and evermore,
thy place is everywhere.

JOHN MASON (1646–94)*

662 *Ewing* 76 76 D

ALEXANDER EWING (1830–95)

1 Arise, arise, good Christian,
 let right to wrong succeed;
let penitential sorrow
 to heavenly gladness lead,
to light that has no evening,
 that knows no moon or sun,
the light so new and golden,
 the light that is but one.

2 Brief life is here our portion,
 brief sorrow, short-lived care;
the life that knows no ending,
 the tearless life, is there.
And he whom now we trust in
 shall then be seen and known,
and they who know and see him
 shall have him for their own.

3 There God our King and Portion,
in fullness of his grace,
we then shall see for ever,
and worship face to face.
Then all the halls of Zion
shall ever stand complete,
and in the land of beauty
all things of beauty meet.

4 Jerusalem the golden,
with milk and honey blest,
beneath thy contemplation
sink heart and voice oppressed.
I know not, O I know not
what radiant light is there,
what glory and communion,
what bliss beyond compare.

5 There is the throne of David,
and there, from sin released,
the song of them that triumph,
the shout of them that feast;
the Cross is all their splendour,
the Crucified their praise:
his laud and benediction
thy ransomed people raise.

BERNARD OF CLUNY (12th cent.)
tr. J. M. NEALE (1818–66) altd.*

663

FIRST TUNE

R. H. PRICHARD (1811–87)

Hyfrydol 87 87 D

SECOND TUNE

Love Divine 87 87 (Trochaic) JOHN STAINER (1840–1901)

Alternative tune: BLAENWERN, no. 95.

1 Love divine, all loves excelling,
joy of heaven, to earth come down,
fix in us thy humble dwelling,
all thy faithful mercies crown.
Jesus, thou art all compassion,
pure, unbounded love thou art;
visit us with thy salvation,
enter every trembling heart.

2 Come, almighty to deliver,
let us all thy life receive;
suddenly return, and never,
never more thy temples leave.
Thee we would be always blessing,
serve thee as thy hosts above,
pray, and praise thee without ceasing,
glory in thy perfect love.

3 Finish then thy new creation,
pure and spotless let us be;
let us see thy great salvation,
perfectly restored in thee;
changed from glory into glory,
till in heaven we take our place,
till we cast our crowns before thee,
lost in wonder, love and praise.

CHARLES WESLEY (1707–88)

664 *San Rocco* CM

DEREK WILLIAMS (1945–)

Alternative tune: JACKSON (BYZANTIUM) no. 722.

1 Give me the wings of faith to rise
within the veil, and see
the saints above, how great their joys,
how bright their glories be.

2 Once they were mourning here below,
their faces wet with tears;
they wrestled hard, as we do now,
with sins and doubts and fears.

3 I ask them whence their victory came;
they, with united breath,
ascribe their conquest to the Lamb,
their triumph to his death.

4 They marked the footsteps that he trod;
his zeal inspired their breast;
and, following their incarnate God,
possess the promised rest.

5 Our glorious leader claims our praise
for his own pattern given;
while the long cloud of witnesses
show the same path to heaven.

ISAAC WATTS (1674–1748)*

665 *Laus Deo* 87 87 (Trochaic)

Composed or adapted by
RICHARD REDHEAD (1820–1901)

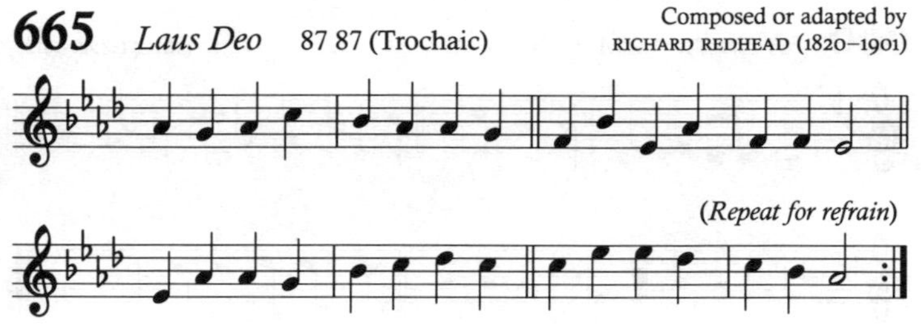

1 Round the Lord in glory seated,
  cherubim and seraphim
filled his temple, and repeated
  each to each the alternate hymn:

'Lord, thy glory fills the heaven;
  earth is with its fullness stored;
unto thee be glory given,
  holy, holy, holy Lord.'

2 Heaven is still with glory ringing,
  earth takes up the angels' cry,
'Holy, holy, holy', singing,
  'Lord of hosts, the Lord most high':

3 With his seraph train before him,
  with his holy Church below,
thus unite we to adore him,
  bid we thus our anthem flow:

RICHARD MANT (1776–1848) altd.
based on Isaiah 6: 1–3

666 *Nativity* CM

H. LAHEE (1826–1912)

The Church Militant learning the Church Triumphant's Song

1 Sing we the song of those who stand
around the eternal throne,
of every kindred, clime and land,
a multitude unknown.

2 Life's poor distinctions vanish here;
today the young, the old,
our Saviour and his flock appear,
one Shepherd and one fold.

3 Toil, trial, suffering still await
on earth the pilgrim-throng;
yet learn we in our lowly state
the Church Triumphant's song.

4 Worthy the Lamb for sinners slain,
cry the redeemed above,
blessing and honour to obtain,
and everlasting love.

5 Worthy the Lamb, on earth we sing,
who died our souls to save;
henceforth, O death, where is your sting,
your victory, O grave?

6 Then, Alleluia! power and praise
to God in Christ be given!
May all who now this anthem raise
renew the song in heaven.

JAMES MONTGOMERY (1771–1854)*

667 *Northampton* 77 77 C. J. KING (1859–1934)

1 Songs of praise the angels sang,
heaven with alleluias rang,
when creation was begun,
when God spoke and it was done.

2 Songs of praise awoke the morn
when the Prince of Peace was born;
songs of praise arose when he
captive led captivity.

3 Heaven and earth must pass away,
songs of praise shall crown that day;
God will make new heavens, new earth,
songs of praise shall hail their birth.

4 And shall we alone be dumb
till that glorious kingdom come?
No! The Church delights to raise
psalms and hymns and songs of praise.

5 Saints below, with heart and voice,
still in songs of praise rejoice,
learning here, by faith and love,
songs of praise to sing above.

6 Borne upon their dying breath,
songs of praise shall conquer death;
then, amidst eternal joy,
songs of praise their powers employ.

JAMES MONTGOMERY (1771–1854) altd.*

668 *Mendip* CM

English traditional melody

1 There is a land of pure delight,
where saints immortal reign;
infinite day excludes the night,
and pleasures banish pain.

2 There everlasting spring abides,
and never-withering flowers;
death, like a narrow sea, divides
this heavenly land from ours.

3 Sweet fields beyond the swelling flood
stand dressed in living green;
so to the Jews old Canaan stood,
while Jordan rolled between.

4 But timorous mortals start and shrink
to cross this narrow sea,
and linger shivering on the brink
and fear to launch away.

5 O could we make our doubts remove,
those gloomy doubts that rise,
and see the Canaan that we love
with unbeclouded eyes;

6 could we but climb where Moses stood,
and view the landscape o'er,
not Jordan's stream, nor death's cold flood,
should fright us from the shore.

ISAAC WATTS (1674–1748)

PSALMS AND CANTICLES

INTRODUCTION TO THE PSALMS AND CANTICLES

The musical settings of the **Psalms** which follow are of four types, one in metre and three in prose.

1. Metrical (e.g. Psalm 1, and including some texts commonly used as hymns). These are set to regular hymn-tunes. A Doxology in Common Metre will be found at no. 25 if required.

2. Those pointed for Anglican Chant (e.g. Psalm 18). These should be sung as nearly as possible in the rhythms and stress patterns of ordinary speech, and the pointing is designed to facilitate this. The bar-lines and note-values in the music are there only to show how to match music to words and the duration of notes is wholly subservient to the text. A raised point (·) shows how to divide a group of syllables between two notes of music. Bold type is to be disregarded when singing: it shows how the lines may be apportioned for responsive reading. A concluding Doxology (Gloria) will be found, pointed for Anglican Chant, inside the back cover of the book, if required.

3. Those pointed for Psalm Tones (e.g. Psalm 65). These have fewer note-changes to the line than Anglican Chant. The mark | in each line of words indicates the place at which the Tone's reciting note is left for the remaining three notes of each phrase. The final stressed syllable of each line should coincide with the last of these notes, and any remaining syllables should be lightly sung on the same note. Otherwise everything said above about Anglican Chant applies here also. Where an Antiphon is provided, this is sung in strict musical time. Usually the Antiphon may begin and end the Psalm; where specific instructions apply, they will be found on the page. The concluding Antiphon takes the place of a Doxology. Once again the bold type is for spoken reading only, and when spoken these Psalms may be used with or without the Antiphon (said by the congregation) at beginning and end.

4. Those pointed in the way associated with the names of Joseph Gelineau and Gregory Murray (e.g. Psalm 8). Like those set to Psalm Tones, these have Antiphons; unlike those others, though, these Psalms are sung in bars of equal duration. The syllables shown in bold type are lengthened as may be necessary to fill the bar. When these texts are read responsively, it is suggested that the leader reads the verses and the congregation responds with the Antiphon(s) as indicated. No Doxology is given for these Psalms.

The **Canticles** fall mainly into the same four types as the Psalms. All may be spoken; and for some no musical setting is given. Where a pattern for responsive reading is not indicated by bold type, the Antiphon(s) should be used as a congregational response.

NOTE ON THE PERFORMANCE OF ANGLICAN CHANT

Music can quite wonderfully irradiate words, not least in Psalms or other poetic prose sung to what we call (without sectarian significance) 'Anglican Chant'. In this we enjoy melody and four-part harmony, savour fine prose rolling off our tongues in the natural rhythms of good speech, and have all the range of emphasis and vivid expression which elocutionary English affords, untrammelled by a metrical beat.

It follows that the musical notation of Anglican Chant gives only the pitch of notes, but no indication whatever of their length or rhythm. The length of a note is strictly the time it would take to speak the syllable or syllables allotted to it. When a note has only one short syllable, such as 'in', 'of', 'the', or one of the many found in multi-syllabic words, it is a case of 'touch and go' even where there are several in succession, e.g. ' . . . | words of | my dis-|tress' (Psalm 22). Avoid any deadening tendency to sing these short syllables too slowly and heavily. The last syllable of a line should neither be prolonged nor zealously cut off. With rehearsal, this will all become as natural as in speech. The organist will need nimble fingers, and should memorize the chant and mentally sing the words.

The pointing seeks to match the various syllabic accents with the various musical stresses (there are some, even though there is no regular beat), and generally to help the free flow of both words and music. Better the golden rule 'Sing as you would speak' than an elaborate system of markings; so our markings are minimal, but will indicate clearly enough which syllables are to be sung to which notes, and sometimes which syllables have to be spread over two notes. The second note of a 'spread' syllable should be tucked in quickly and lightly ('slurred'); if the next bar also has a spread syllable, it is usually musically effective to shorten both notes of that bar.

Above all, do not let chanting be dull: with fluent articulation there must be a vivid expression of meaning and mood, whether it be tenderness or triumph, prayer or praise. Herein lies our true worship.

William White

669 PSALM 1

Sri Lampang 10 8 10 8 Thai traditional melody

1 Happy are they who walk in God's wise way;
happy who shun the sinful choice;
happy who find their pleasure in God's law,
happy who heed God's righteous voice.

2 Theirs is the life where duty and delight
nourish each other blissfully;
as when beside a broad and generous stream
proudly stands ever green the tree.

3 Fretful and anxious are the sinners' days,
barren and lonely is their path;
like wind on dust the judgement of the Lord
scatters their pride in sudden wrath.

4 Lord, in your mercy spare me, keep me still;
let me not choose the sinner's way.
Promise and law you equally have given:
let them be my delight today.

Psalm 1
para. ERIK ROUTLEY (1917–82)

670 PSALM 8

ANTIPHON (*before verse 1 and after verse 4*) A. GREGORY MURRAY (1905–92)

(♩ = 𝅝 of Psalm)

How great is your name, O Lord, our God, _ through all the earth!

PSALM

JOSEPH GELINEAU (1920–)

1. Your **ma**jesty is **praised** above the **hea**vens;
2. When I see the **hea**vens, the **work** of your **hands**,
3. Yet you have **made** us little **less** than **gods**,
4. **all** of them, **sheep** and **cat**tle,

(1.) on the **lips** of **chil**dren and of **babes**
(2.) the **moon** and the **stars** which you ar-**ranged**,
(3.) and **crowned** us with **glo**ry and **ho**nour;
(4.) yes, **e**ven the **sa**vage **beasts**,

(1.) you have found **praise** to **foil** your **en**emy,
(2.) what are **we** that you should **keep** us in **mind**,
(3.) gave us **power** over the **works** of your **hand**,
(4.) **birds** of the **air** and **fish**

(1.) to **si**lence the **foe** and the **re**bel.
(2.) men and **wo**men that you **care** for **us**?
(3.) put **all** things **un**der our **feet**,
(4.) that **make** their **way** through the **wa**ters.

671 PSALM 13

New Thirteenth Irregular JOHN BELL (1949–)

1 How long, O Lord,
 will you quite forget me?
How long, O Lord,
 will you turn your face from me?
How long, O Lord,
 must I suffer in my soul?
How long, how long,
 O Lord?

2 How long, O Lord,
 must this grief possess my heart?
How long, O Lord,
 must I languish night and day?
How long, O Lord,
 shall my enemy oppress?
How long, how long,
 O Lord?

3 Look now, look now,
 and answer me, my God;
give light, give light,
 lest I sleep the sleep of death,
lest my enemies
 rejoice at my downfall;
look now, look now,
 O Lord.

Psalm 13: 1–4
para. JOHN BELL (1949–)
and GRAHAM MAULE (1958–)

672 PSALM 18

T. A. WALMISLEY (1814–56)

1 I love you O | Lord my | strength,
O Lord my | stronghold, · my | crag and · my | haven.
My God, my rock in whom I | put my | trust,
my shield, the horn of my salvation and my refuge; |
you are | worthy · of | praise.

2 I will | call up·on the | Lord,
and so shall I be | saved __ | from my | enemies.
The breakers of | death rolled | over me,
and the torrents of ob-|livi·on | made · me a-|fraid.

3 The cords of | hell en-|tangled me,
and the | snares of | death were | set for me.
I called upon the | Lord in · my dis-|tress,
and | cried · out to | God for | help.

4 He heard my voice from his | heavenly | dwelling;
my cry of | anguish | came to · his | ears.
He reached down from on | high and | grasped me;
he | drew me | out of · great | waters.

5 He delivered me from my strong enemies, and from |
those who | hated me;
for | they __ | were too | mighty for me.
They confronted me in the | day of · my dis-|aster,
but the | Lord was | my sup-|port.

2nd half
He brought me out into an | open | place;
he | rescued me · be-|cause · he de-|lighted in me.

Psalm 18: 1–6, 16–19

673 PSALM 19

THOMAS NORRIS (1741–90)

1 The heavens declare the | glory · of | God,
  and the | firma·ment | shows his | handiwork.
One day tells its | tale · to an-|other,
  and one night imparts | knowledge | to an-|other.

2 Although they have no | words or | language,
  and their | voices | are not | heard,
their sound has gone out into | all __ | lands,
  and their | message · to the | ends · of the | world.

3 In the deep has he set a pa-|vilion · for the | sun;
  it comes forth like a | bridegroom | out of · his | chamber;
it rejoices like a champion to | run its | course.
  It goes from the | utter·most | edge of · the | heavens

2nd half
and runs to the | end of it · a-|gain;
  nothing is | hidden · from its | burning | heat.

JOHN CAMIDGE (THE YOUNGER) (1790–1859)

*Second chant**

4 The law of the Lord is perfect and re-|vives the | soul;
the testimony of the Lord is | sure · and gives | wisdom · to the | innocent.
The statutes of the Lord are just and re-|joice the | heart;
the commandment of the Lord is | clear · and gives | light · to the | eyes.

5 The fear of the Lord is clean and en-|dures for | ever;
the judgements of the Lord are true and | righteous | alto-|gether.
More to be desired are they than gold, more than | much fine | gold,
sweeter far than honey, than | honey | in the | comb.

6 By them also is your | servant · en-|lightened,
and in keeping them | there is | great re-|ward.
How can we tell how | often · we of-|fend?
Cleanse me | from my | secret | faults.

7 Above all, keep your servant from pre-|sumptu·ous | sins;
let them | not · get do-|minion | over me;
then I shall be | whole and | sound,
and | innocent · of a | great of-|fence.

2nd half

Let the words of my mouth and the meditation | of my | heart be acceptable in your sight,
O Lord, my | strength and | my re-|deemer.

Psalm 19

*If desired, this Psalm may be sung without a change of chant, or may begin at v. 4.

674 PSALM 19

Allein Gott 87 87 887

Geistliche Lieder, Leipzig, 1539
adpt. from an Easter Gloria, 1524

1 God's perfect law revives the soul,
his word makes wise the simple;
God's clear commands rejoice the heart,
his light the eye enlightens;
God's fear is pure, his judgements just,
more to be sought than pure fine gold,
sweeter by far than honey.

2 Lord, who can tell the secret faults
that have dominion over me?
Hold back your servant from self-will
and break its power to bind me.
May all I think and all I say
be now acceptable to you,
my Rock and my Redeemer.

Psalm 19: 7–14
Metrical version by I. R. PITT-WATSON (1923–)

675 PSALM 20

JAMES TURLE (1802–82)

OR

G. A. MACFARREN (1813–87)

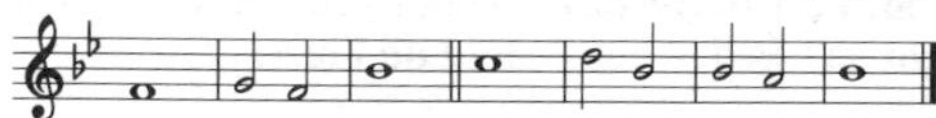

1 May the Lord answer you in the | day of | trouble,
the name of the | God of | Jacob · de-|fend you;
send you help from his | holy | place,
and | strengthen · you | out of | Zion;

2 remember all your offerings and ac-|cept your · burnt | sacrifice;
grant you your heart's desire and | prosper | all your | plans.
We will shout for joy at your victory, and triumph in the | name of · our | God;
may the Lord | grant all | your re-|quests.

3 Now I | know · that the | Lord
gives | victory · to | his a-|nointed;
he will answer him out of his | holy | heaven,
with the victorious | strength of | his right | hand.

2nd half
Some put their trust in chariots and | some in | horses,
but we will call upon the | name · of the | Lord our | God.

Psalm 20: 1–7

676 PSALM 22

JOSEPH BARNBY (1838–96)

1 My God, my God, why have | you for-| saken me,
and are so far from my cry and from the | words of | my dis-| tress?
O my God, I cry in the daytime but you | do not | answer;
by night as | well, · but I | find no | rest.

2 Yet | you are · the | Holy One,
enthroned upon the | prai —| ses of | Israel.
Our ancestors put their | trust in | you;
they | trusted · and | you de-| livered them.

3 They cried out to you and | were de-| livered;
they trusted in you and | were not | put to | shame.
But as for me, I am a | worm · and a | nobody,
scorned by | all · and des-| pised · by the | people.

4 All who see me | laugh me · to | scorn;
they curl their lips and | wag their | heads __ | saying,
'He trusted in the Lord; | let him · de-| liver him;
let him | rescue · him | if · he de-| lights in him.'

5 **Yet you are he who took me | out of · the | womb,**
and kept me | safe up·on my | mother's | breast.
I have been entrusted to you ever since | I was | born;
you were my God when I was | still in · my | mother's | womb.

6 **Be not far from me, for | trouble · is | near,**
and | there is | none to | help.
I am poured out like water; all my bones are | out of | joint;
my heart within my | breast is | melting | wax.

7 My mouth is dried out | like a | pot-sherd;
my tongue sticks to the roof of my mouth;
and you have | laid me · in the | dust of · the | grave.
Packs of dogs close me in, and gangs of evil-doers | circle · a-| round me;
they pierce my hands and my | feet; I can | count · all my | bones.

8 **They | stare and | gloat over me;**
they divide my garments among them;
they cast | lots __ | for my | clothing.
Be not far a-|way O | Lord;
you are my | strength __, | hasten · to | help me.

9 **Save me | from the | sword,**
my | life · from the | power · of the | dog.
Save me from the | lion's | mouth,
my wretched body from the | horns of | wild __ | bulls.

THOMAS NORRIS (1741–90)

10 **I will declare your | name to · my | people;**
in the midst of the congre-|gation | I will | praise you.
Praise the Lord | you that | fear him;
stand in awe of him O offspring of Israel;
all you of | Jacob's | line give | glory.

11 For he does not despise nor abhor the | poor in · their | poverty;
neither does he hide his face from them;
but when they | cry to | him he | hears them.
My praise is of him in the | great as-|sembly;
I will perform my vows in the | presence · of | those who | worship him.

12 The poor shall eat and be satisfied,
and those who seek the | Lord shall | praise him:
'May your | heart __ | live for | ever!'
All the ends of the earth shall remember and | turn · to the | Lord,
and all the families of the | nations · shall | bow be-|fore him.

13 For kingship be-|longs · to the | Lord;
he | rules __ | over · the | nations.
To him alone all who sleep in the earth bow | down in | worship;
all who go down to the | dust __ | fall be-|fore him.

14 My soul shall live for him; my de-|scendants · shall | serve him;
they shall be | known · as the | Lord's for | ever.
They shall come and make known to a people | yet un-|born
the saving | deeds that | he has | done.

Psalm 22: 1–11, 14–31

677 PSALM 23

University CM

Melody from JOHN RANDALL'S *Psalm and Hymn Tunes*, 1794
Probably by CHARLES COLLIGNON (1725–85)

1 The God of love my Shepherd is,
and he that doth me feed;
while he is mine and I am his,
what can I want or need?

2 He leads me to the tender grass,
where I both feed and rest;
then to the streams that gently pass:
in both I have the best.

3 Or if I stray, he doth convert,
and bring my mind in frame,
and all this not for my desert,
but for his holy name.

4 Yea, in death's shady black abode
well may I walk, not fear;
for thou art with me, and thy rod
to guide, thy staff to bear.

5 Surely thy sweet and wondrous love
shall measure all my days;
and, as it never shall remove,
so neither shall my praise.

Psalm 23
para. GEORGE HERBERT (1593–1633)

678 PSALM 23

JOSEPH GELINEAU (1920–)

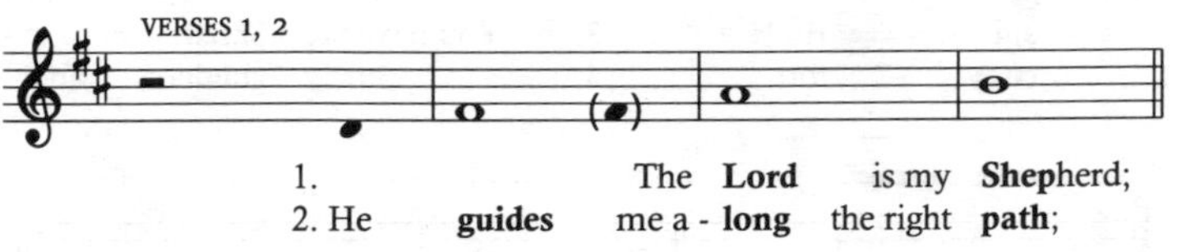

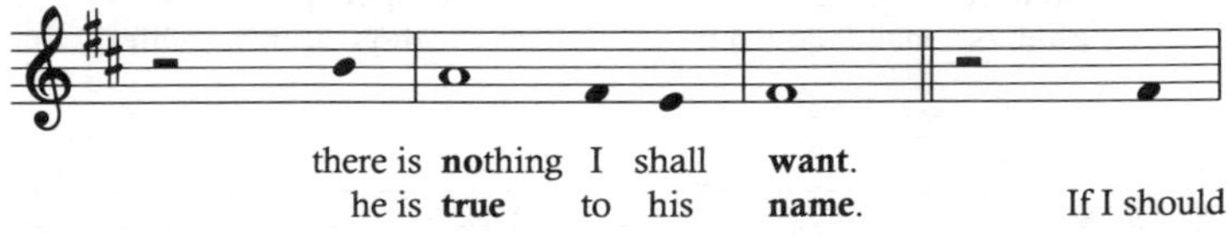

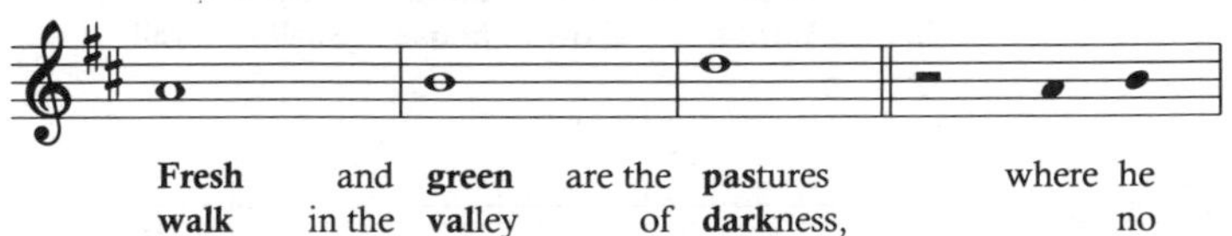

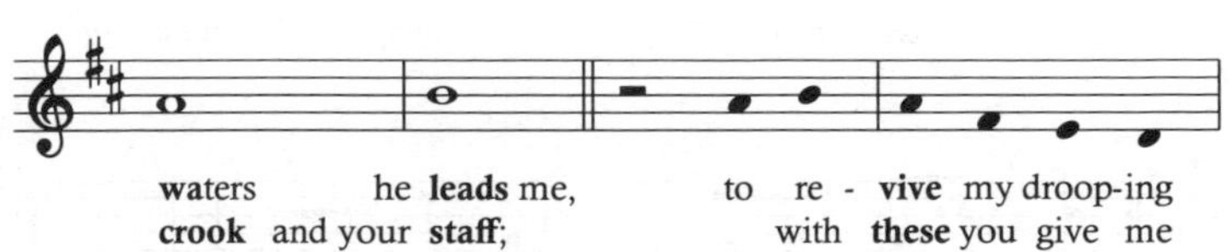

The Antiphon (p. 746) may be used after verses 1 and 4.

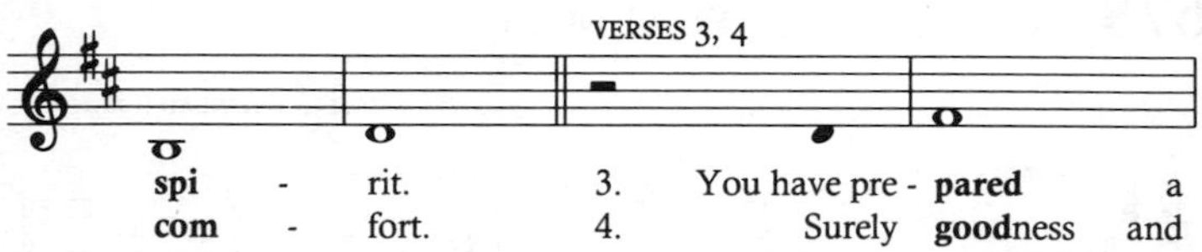
VERSES 3, 4
spi - rit. 3. You have pre - **pared** a
com - fort. 4. Surely **good**ness and

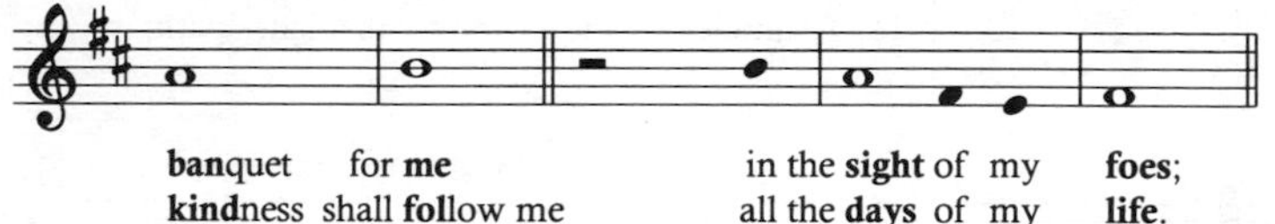
banquet for **me** in the **sight** of my **foes**;
kindness shall **fol**low me all the **days** of my **life**.

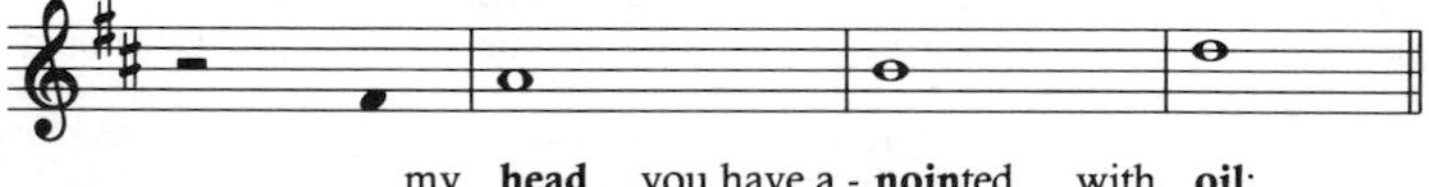
my **head** you have a - **noin**ted with **oil**;
In the **Lord's** own **house** shall I **dwell**

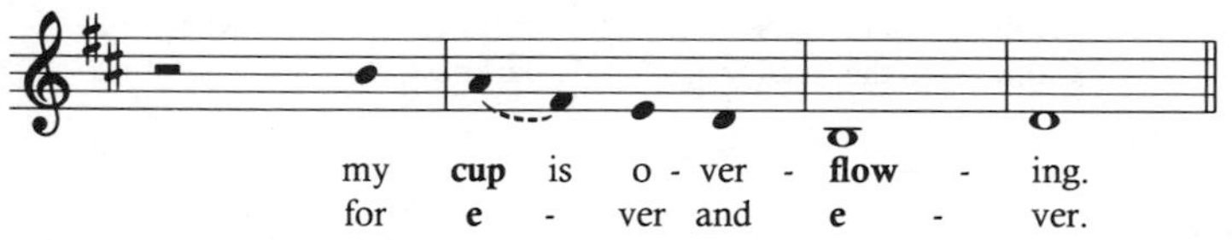
my **cup** is o - ver - **flow** - ing.
for **e** - ver and **e** - ver.

ANTIPHON (♩ = 𝅝 of Psalm)
A. GREGORY MURRAY (1905–92)
The Lord_ is my Shep-herd, no-thing shall I want: he

leads me by safe___ paths, no-thing shall I fear.

679 PSALM 23

Crimond CM

Melody ascribed to JESSIE IRVINE (1836–87)
but more probably by DAVID GRANT (1833–93)

Alternative tune: WILTSHIRE no. 685.

1 The Lord's my Shepherd, I'll not want:
he makes me down to lie
in pastures green; he leadeth me
the quiet waters by.

2 My soul he doth restore again,
and me to walk doth make
within the paths of righteousness,
ev'n for his own name's sake.

3 Yea, though I walk through death's dark vale,
yet will I fear no ill;
for thou art with me, and thy rod
and staff me comfort still.

4 My table thou hast furnishèd
in presence of my foes;
my head thou dost with oil anoint,
and my cup overflows.

5 Goodness and mercy all my life
shall surely follow me;
and in God's house for evermore
my dwelling-place shall be.

Psalm 23
Metrical version by WILLIAM WHITTINGHAM (1524–79) altd.

680 PSALM 24

Tones by JOSEPH GELINEAU (1920–)

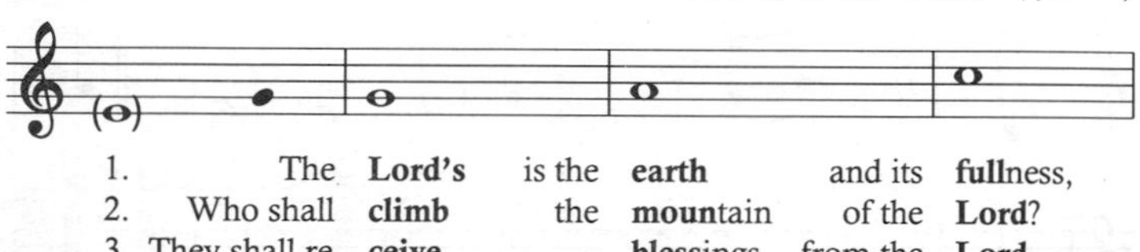

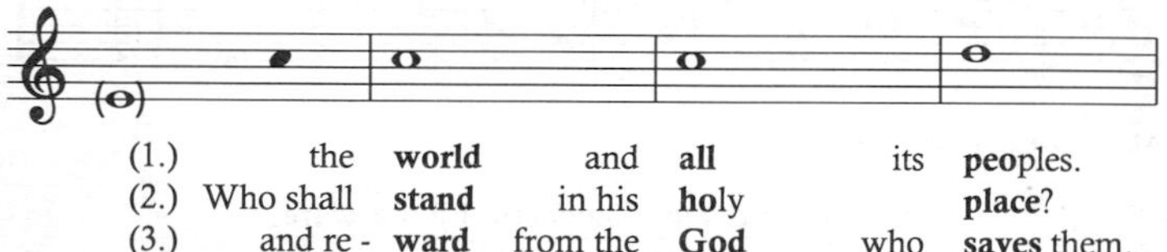

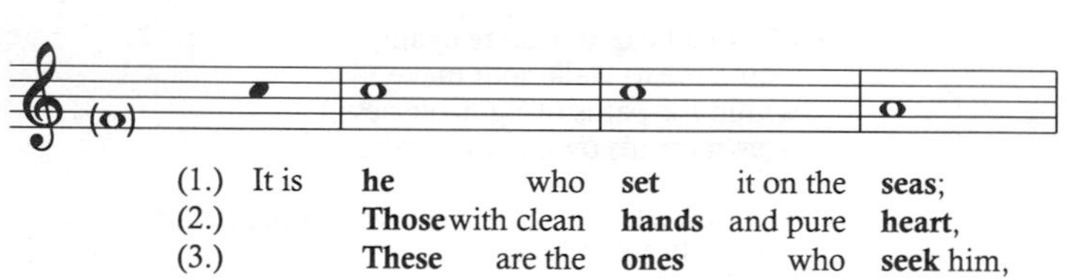

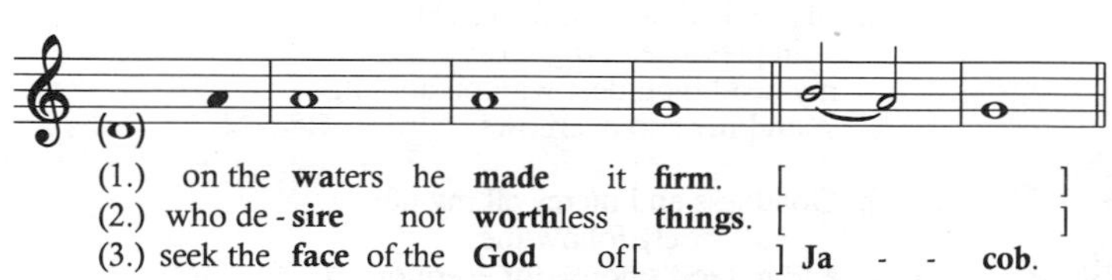

It is suggested that Antiphon I be sung at the beginning and after each of verses 1–3, and Antiphon II after verses 4–7.

ANTIPHON I

A. GREGORY MURRAY (1905–92)

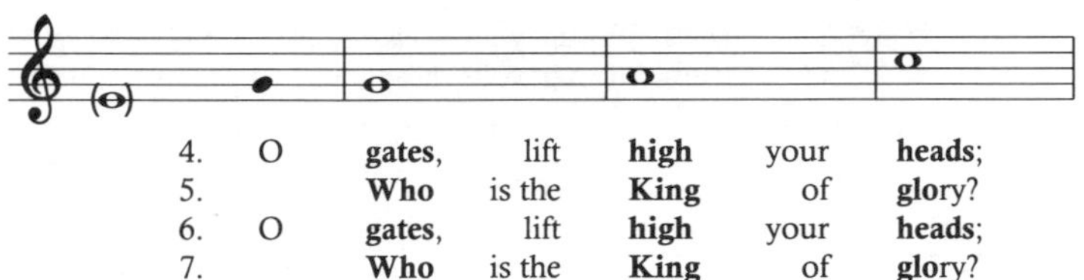

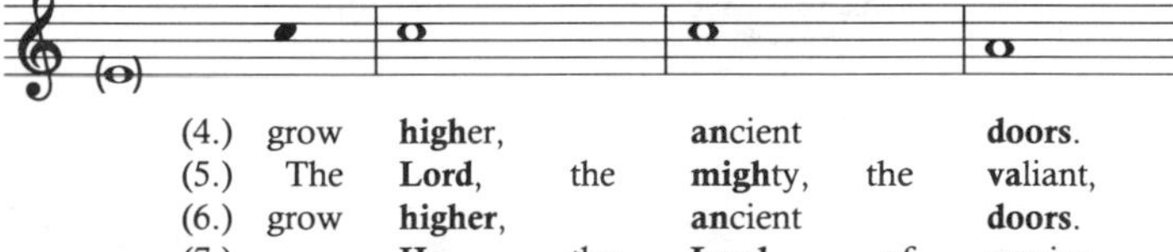

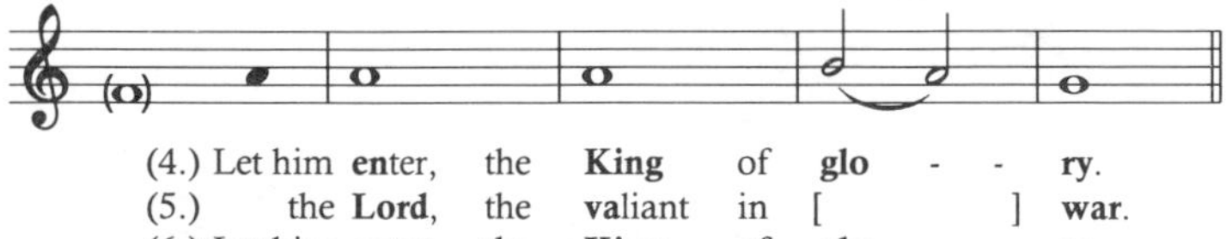

ANTIPHON II

JOSEPH GELINEAU (1920–)

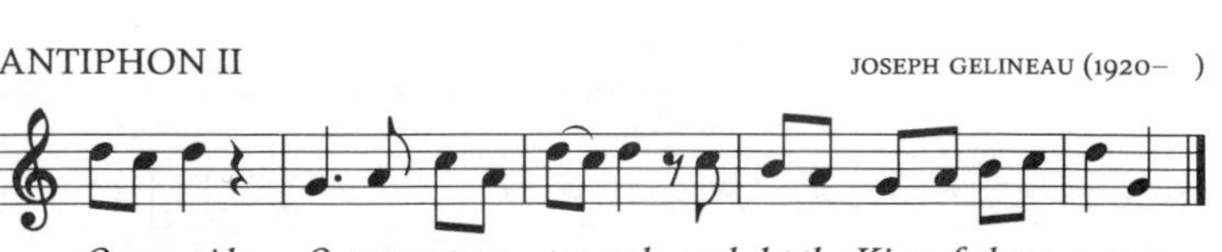

681 PSALM 24

St George's, Edinburgh ANDREW MITCHELL THOMSON (1778–1831)
DCM irreg. with coda

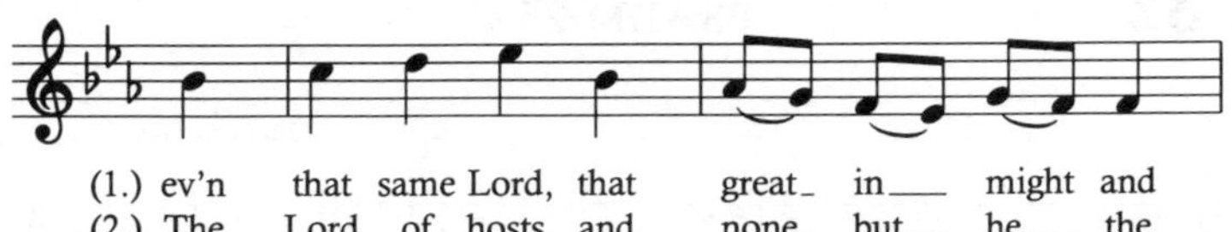

strong in bat - tle is, ev'n that same Lord, that
King of glo - ry is. The Lord of hosts, and

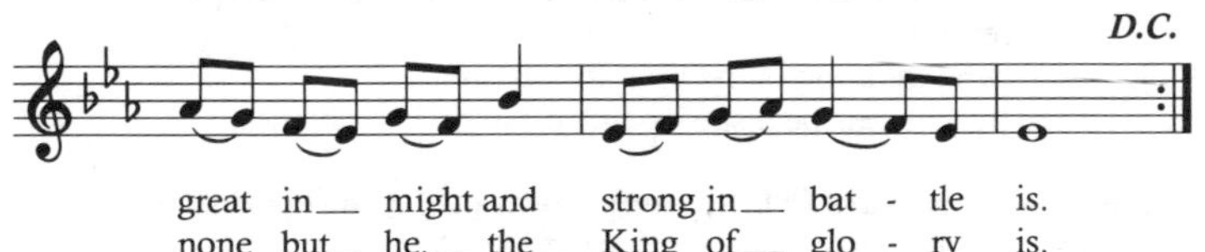

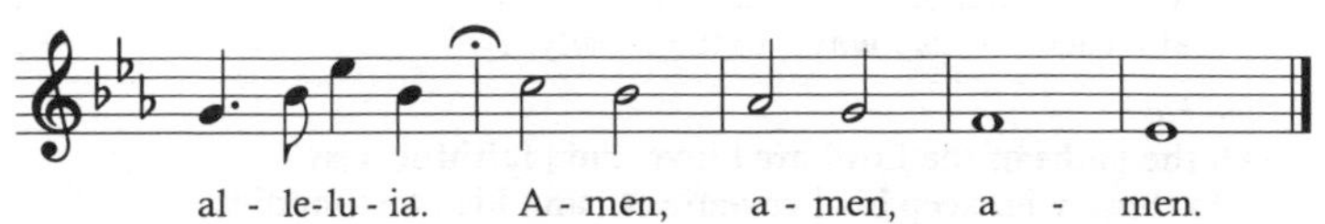

Psalm 24: 7–10
Scottish Metrical Psalter, 1650

682 PSALM 25

E. EDWARDS (1830–1907)

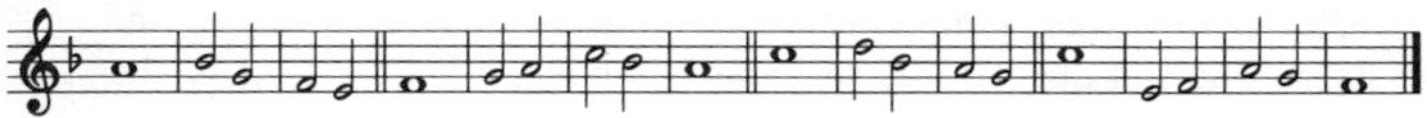

OR

SAMUEL WESLEY (1766–1837)

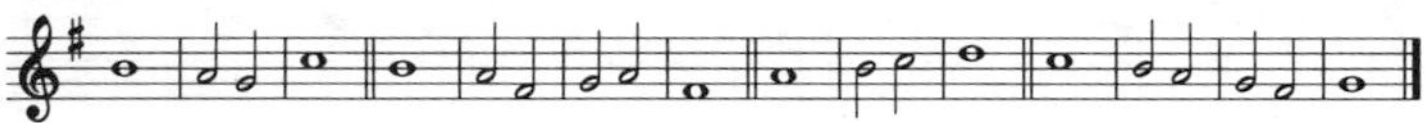

1 To you O Lord I lift up my soul; **my God, I put my | trust in | you;**
let me not be humiliated, nor let my | enem·ies | triumph | over me.
Let none who look to you be | put to | shame;
let the treacherous be disap-|pointed | in their | schemes.

2 **Show me your ways O Lord, and | teach me · your | paths.**
Lead me | in your | truth and | teach me,
for you are the | God of · my sal-|vation;
in you have I | trusted | all the · day | long.

3 **Remember O Lord your com-|passion · and | love,**
for | they are · from | ever-|lasting.
Remember not the sins of my youth and | my trans-|gressions;
remember me according to your love,
and for the | sake of · your | goodness · O | Lord.

4 Gracious and | upright · is the | Lord;
therefore he teaches | sinners | in his | way.
He guides the humble in | doing | right,
and | teaches · his | way · to the | lowly.

2nd half
All the paths of the Lord are | love and | faithful·ness
to those who keep his | coven·ant | and his | testimonies.

Psalm 25: 1–10

683 PSALM 27

Festus LM Adpt. from FREYLINGHAUSEN'S *Gesangbuch*, 1704

1 The Lord Jehovah is my light,
  my saving strength; whom shall I fear,
who shall my trusting soul affright
  when he, my Lord, my Life, is near?

2 One thing have I desired of God,
  and that I seek with heart sincere:
that I may dwell in his abode,
  and serve him still with holy fear;

3 that I the beauty of the Lord
  may see, and in his courts enquire;
roam through the treasures of his Word
  till all my thoughts to him aspire.

4 For then in trouble, I shall be
  o'ershadowed with his sheltering love;
his secret tent shall cover me,
  and an unfailing refuge prove.

5 Upon a rock he sets my feet,
  he lifts my head above my foes;
he makes me for his service meet,
  and gives me in his strength repose.

6 Then in his courts with fervent songs
  the sacrifice of joy I'll bring;
my life, redeemed, to him belongs,
  and of his love I'll ever sing.

Psalm 27: 1, 4–7
para. G. Y. TICKLE (1819–88)

684 PSALM 27

Christus der ist mein Leben 76 76 MELCHIOR VULPIUS (*c.*1570–1615)

1 God is my strong salvation;
what foe have I to fear?
In darkness and temptation
my light, my help is near.

2 Though hosts encamp around me,
firm to the fight I stand;
what terror can confound me,
with God at my right hand?

3 Place on the Lord reliance,
my soul with courage wait;
his truth is your assurance
when faint and desolate.

4 His might your heart shall strengthen,
his love your joy increase;
mercy your days shall lengthen,
the Lord will give you peace.

JAMES MONTGOMERY (1771–1854)*
based mainly on Psalm 27: 1–3, 14

685 PSALM 34

Wiltshire CM

GEORGE T. SMART (1776–1867)

1 Through all the changing scenes of life,
in trouble and in joy,
the praises of my God shall still
my heart and tongue employ.

2 Of his deliverance I will boast,
till all that are distressed
from mine example comfort take,
and soothe their griefs to rest.

3 O magnify the Lord with me,
with me exalt his name;
when in distress to him I called,
he to my rescue came.

4 The hosts of God encamp around
the dwellings of the just;
deliverance he affords to all
who on his succour trust.

5 O make but trial of his love;
experience will decide
how blest are they, and only they,
who in his truth confide.

6 Fear him, ye saints, and you will then
have nothing else to fear;
make you his service your delight,
your wants shall be his care.

Psalm 34: 1–4, 7–9
para. N. TATE (1652–1715) and
N. BRADY (1659–1726) *New Version*, 1696; altd.

686 PSALM 34

PART I

JOHN GOSS (1800–80)

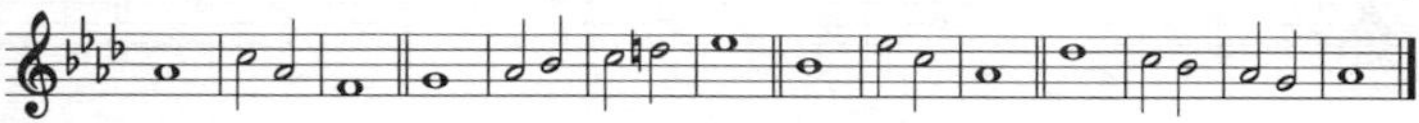

1 I will bless the | Lord at | all times;
his praise shall | ever · be | in my | mouth.
I will | glory · in the | Lord;
let the | humble | hear · and re-|joice.

2 Proclaim with me the | greatness · of the | Lord;
let us ex-|alt his | name to-|gether.
I sought the | Lord · and he | answered me,
and delivered me | out of | all my | terror.

3 **Look upon him | and be | radiant,**
and let not your | faces | be a-|shamed.
I called in my affliction and the | Lord __ | heard me,
and | saved me · from | all my | troubles.

4 **The angel of the Lord encompasses | those who | fear him,**
and | he __ | will de-|liver them.
Taste and see that the | Lord is | good;
happy are | they who | trust in | him.

5 Fear the Lord, | you that · are his | saints,
for those who | fear him | lack __ | nothing.
The young lions lack, and | suffer | hunger,
but those who seek the | Lord lack | nothing · that is | good.

(*continued*)

PART II

J. BOOTH (1852–1929)

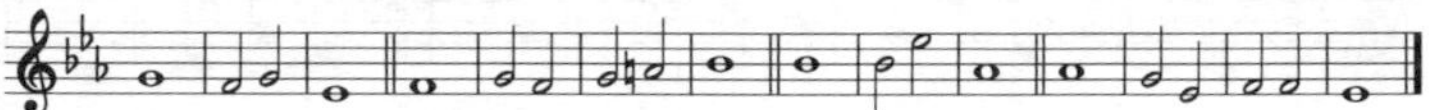

6 Come children and | listen · to | me:
I will | teach you · the | fear of · the | Lord.
Who a-|mong you · loves | life
and desires long | life · to en-|joy pros-|perity?

7 Keep your tongue from | evil-|speaking,
and your | lips from | lying | words.
Turn from evil | and do | good;
seek | peace ___ | and pur-|sue it.

8 **The eyes of the Lord are up-|on the | righteous,**
and his ears are | open | to their | cry.
The face of the Lord is against | those · who do | evil,
to root out the re-|membrance · of them | from the | earth.

9 **The righteous cry, and the | Lord ___ | hears them,**
and de-|livers them · from | all their | troubles.
The Lord is near to the | broken-|hearted,
and will save | those whose | spirits · are | crushed.

Psalm 34: 1–18

687 PSALM 36

London New CM

Melody from the *Scottish Psalter*, 1635,
as given in JOHN PLAYFORD'S *Psalms*, 1671

1 Thy mercy, Lord, is in the heavens;
thy truth doth reach the clouds;
thy justice is like mountains great;
thy judgements deep as floods.

2 Lord, thou preservest all that lives;
how precious is thy grace!
Therefore in shadow of thy wings
people their trust shall place.

3 They with the fullness of thy house
shall be well satisfied;
from rivers of thy pleasures thou
wilt drink to them provide;

4 because of life the fountain pure
remains alone with thee,
and in that purest light of thine
we clearly light shall see.

Psalm 36: 5–9
Scottish Metrical Psalter, 1650*

688 PSALM 40

Adpt. ROBERT SIMPSON (1790–1832)
Ballerma CM from a melody by F. H. BARTHÉLEMON (1741–1808)

1 I waited for the Lord my God,
  and patiently did bear;
at length to me he did incline
  my voice and cry to hear.

2 He took me from a fearful pit,
  and from the miry clay,
and on a rock he set my feet,
  establishing my way.

3 He put a new song in my mouth,
  our God to magnify;
many shall see it, and shall fear,
  and on the Lord rely.

4 O blessed is the one whose trust
  upon the Lord relies;
respecting not the proud, nor such
  as turn aside to lies.

Psalm 40: 1–4
Scottish Metrical Psalter, 1650*

689 PSALM 42

Martyrdom CM

HUGH WILSON (1766–1824)
adpt. R. A. SMITH (1780–1829)

1 As pants the hart for cooling streams
when heated in the chase,
so longs my soul, O God, for thee,
and thy refreshing grace.

2 For thee, my God, the living God,
my thirsty soul doth pine;
O when shall I behold thy face,
thou Majesty divine?

3 God of my strength, how long shall I,
like one forgotten, mourn—
forlorn, forsaken, and exposed
to my oppressor's scorn?

4 Why restless, why cast down, my soul?
Hope still, and thou shalt sing
the praise of him who is thy God,
thy health's eternal spring.

Psalm 42: 1, 2, 9, 11
para. N. TATE (1652–1715)
and N. BRADY (1659–1726) altd.

690

PSALM 43

First Tune

Martyrs CM — Melody from *Scottish Psalter*, 1615 (1635 rhythm)

Second Tune

Cheshire CM — Melody from ESTE's *Psalmes*, 1592 (rhythm slightly altd.)

1 O send thy light forth and thy truth;
let them be guides to me,
and bring me to thy holy hill,
ev'n where thy dwellings be.

2 Then will I to God's altar go,
to God my chiefest joy:
yea, God, my God, thy name to praise,
my harp I will employ.

3 Why art thou then cast down, my soul?
What should discourage thee?
And why with vexing thoughts art thou
disquieted in me?

4 Still trust in God; for him to praise
good cause I yet shall have:
he is my everlasting health,
my God that doth me save.

Psalm 43: 3–5
Scottish Metrical Psalter, 1650*

691 PSALM 46

Stroudwater CM W. ANCHORS' *Psalmody*, *c.*1721

1 God is our refuge and our strength,
in straits a present aid;
therefore, although the earth remove,
we will not be afraid:

2 though hills amidst the seas be cast;
though waters roaring make,
and troubled be; yea though the hills
by swelling seas do shake.

3 A river is, whose streams make glad
the city of our God,
the holy place, wherein the Lord
most high hath his abode.

4 God in the midst of her doth dwell;
nothing shall her remove:
God unto her an helper will,
and that right early, prove.

Psalm 46: 1–5
Scottish Metrical Psalter, 1650

692 PSALM 46

Adpt. from MARTIN LUTHER (1483–1546)

1 God is our | refuge · and | strength,
a very | present | help in | trouble.
Therefore we will not fear though the | earth be | moved,
and though the mountains be | toppled · into the |
depths of · the | sea;

2 though its waters | rage and | foam,
and though the mountains | tremble | at its | tumult.
Unison **The Lord of | hosts is | with us;**
the God of | Jacob | is our | stronghold.

3 There is a river whose streams make glad the | city · of | God,
the holy habi-|tation · of the | Most __ | High.
God is in the midst of her; she shall | not be · over-|thrown;
God shall | help her · at the | break of | day.

4 The nations make much ado, and the | kingdoms · are | shaken;
God has spoken, and the | earth shall | melt a-|way.
Unison **The Lord of | hosts is | with us;**
the God of | Jacob | is our | stronghold.

5 Come now and look upon the | works · of the | Lord,
what awesome | things · he has | done on | earth.
It is he who makes war to cease in | all the | world;
he breaks the bow, and shatters the spear,
and | burns the | shields with | fire.

6 'Be still then, and know that | I am | God.
I will be exalted among the nations;
I will be ex-|alted | in the | earth.'
Unison **The Lord of | hosts is | with us;**
the God of | Jacob | is our | stronghold.

Psalm 46

693 PSALM 47

JOSEPH GELINEAU (1920–)

1. All **peo**ples, **clap** your **hands**,
2. He sub - **dues** **peo**ples **un**der us
3. God goes **up** with **shouts** of **joy**:
4. God is **king** of **all** the **earth**.
5. The **lead**ers of the **peo**ple are as - **sem**bled

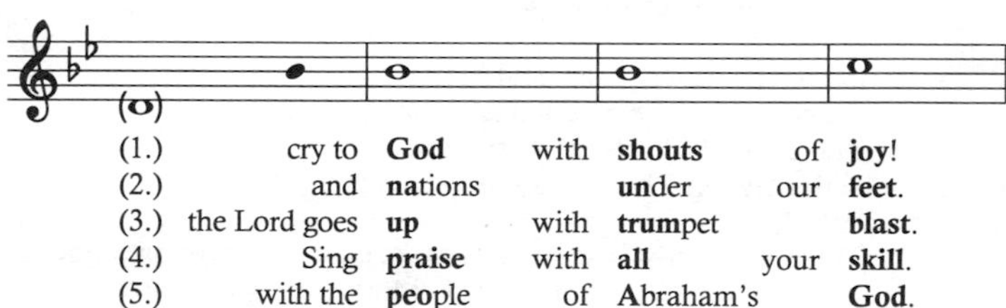

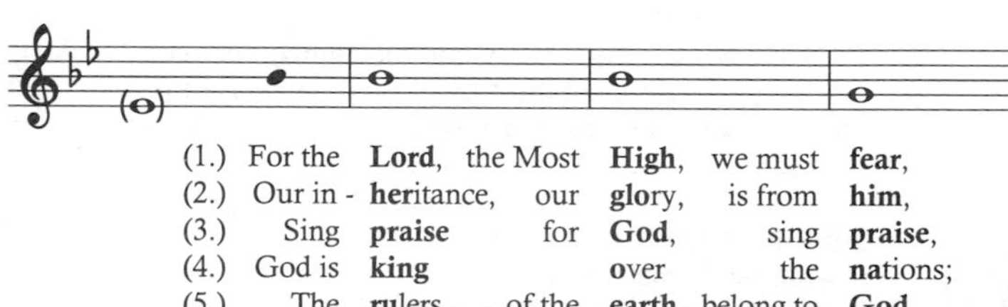

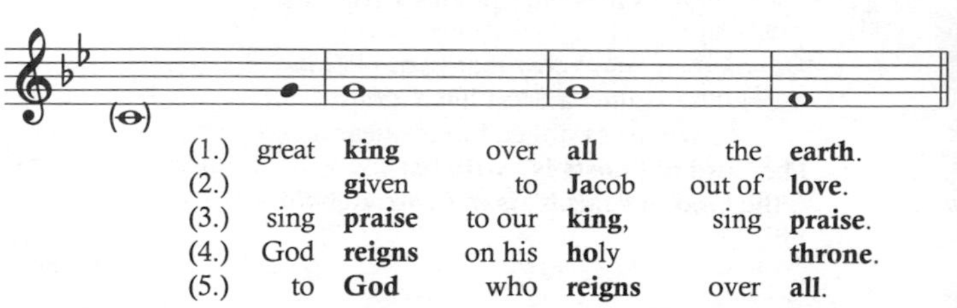

ANTIPHON (♩ = 𝅝 of Psalm) A. GREGORY MURRAY (1905–92)

The Antiphon may be used at the beginning, at the end, and after any or all other verses.

694

PSALM 51

PART I

L. FLINTOFT (1678–1727)

1 Have mercy on me O God, according to your | loving-|kindness;
in your great compassion | blot out | my of-|fences.
Wash me through and | through · from my | wickedness,
and | cleanse me | from my | sin.

2 For I | know · my trans-|gressions,
and my | sin is | ever · be-|fore me.
Against you | only · have I | sinned,
and done what is | evil | in your | sight.

3 And so you are justified | when you | speak,
and | upright | in your | judgement.
Indeed I have been | wicked · from my | birth,
a sinner | from my | mother's | womb.

4 For behold, you look for | truth · deep with-|in me,
and will make me under-|stand __ | wisdom | secretly.
Purge me from my sin, and | I shall · be | pure;
wash me, and | I shall · be | clean in-|deed.

(*continued overleaf*)

PSALM 51
(*continued*)

PART II

E. J. HOPKINS (1818–1901)

5 Make me hear of | joy and | gladness,
that the body you have | broken | may re-|joice.
Hide your | face from · my | sins,
and | blot out | all · my in-|iquities.

6 Create in me a clean | heart O | God,
and re-|new a · right | spirit · with-|in me.
Cast me not a-|way from · your | presence,
and take not your | holy | Spirit | from me.

7 Give me the joy of your | saving | help again,
and sus-|tain me · with your | bounti·ful | Spirit.
I shall teach your | ways · to the | wicked,
and | sinners | shall re-|turn to you.

8 **Deliver me from death O God, and my tongue shall | sing of · your | righteousness,**
O | God of | my sal-|vation.
Open my | lips O | Lord,
and my | mouth · shall pro-|claim your | praise.

9 Had you desired it I would have | offered | sacrifice,
but you | take · no de-|light in · burnt | offerings.
The sacrifice of God is a | troubled | spirit;
a broken and contrite heart O | God, · you will | not des-|pise.

Psalm 51: 1–17

If desired, the first chant may be used throughout the Psalm.

695 PSALM 51

Song 24 10 10 10 10 ORLANDO GIBBONS (1583–1625)

1 O God be gracious to me in your love,
and in your mercy pardon my misdeeds;
wash me from guilt and cleanse me from my sin,
for well I know the evil I have done.

2 Against you, Lord, you only have I sinned,
and what to you is hateful I have done;
I own your righteousness in charging me,
I know you justified should you condemn.

3 Take hyssop, sprinkle me and make me clean,
wash me and make me whiter than the snow;
fill me with gladness and rejoicing, Lord,
and let my broken frame know joy once more.

4 O turn your face, dear God, from my misdeeds,
and blot out all the sins that sully me;
create in me a clean and contrite heart,
renew my soul in faithfulness and love.

5 Drive me not from your presence, gracious Lord,
nor keep your Holy Spirit far from me;
restore my soul with your salvation's joy,
and with a willing spirit strengthen me.

Psalm 51: 1–4, 7–12
para. I. R. PITT-WATSON (1923–)

696 PSALM 62

GEORGE THALBEN-BALL (1896–1987)

OR

G. C. MARTIN (1844–1916)

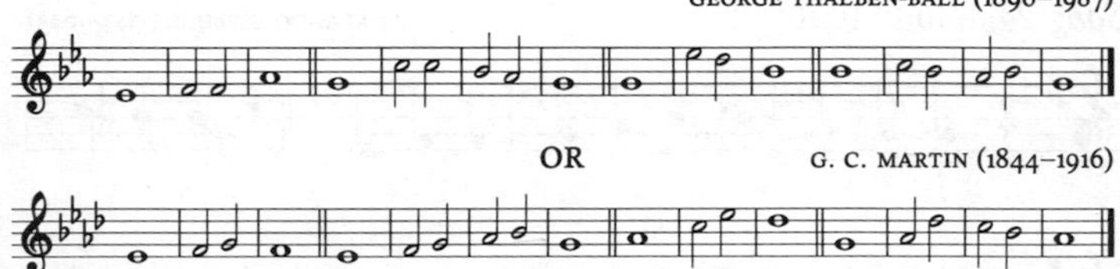

1 For God alone my soul in | silence | waits;
from | him comes | my sal-|vation.
He alone is my | rock and · my sal-|vation,
my stronghold, so that I | shall not · be | greatly | shaken.

2 How long will you assail me to crush me, | all of · you to-|gether,
as if you were a leaning | fence, a | toppling | wall?
They seek only to bring me down from my | place of | honour;
lies | are their | chief de-|light.

2nd half
They | bless with · their | lips,
but | in their | hearts they | curse.

3 For God alone my soul in | silence | waits;
truly, my | hope __ | is in | him.
He alone is my | rock and · my sal-|vation,
my stronghold, so that | I shall | not be | shaken.

4 In God is my | safety · and my | honour;
God is my strong | rock __ | and my | refuge.
Put your trust in him | always · O | people,
pour out your hearts be-|fore him, · for | God is · our | refuge.

5 Those of high degree are but a | fleeting | breath,
even those of | low e·state | cannot · be | trusted.
Set both on a | scale to-|gether
they are | lighter | than a | breath.

6 Put no | trust in · ex-|tortion;
in robbery | take no | empty | pride;
though | wealth in-|crease,
set | not your | heart up-|on it.

7 God has spoken once, | twice · have I | heard it,
that | power · be-|longs to | God.
Steadfast love is | yours O | Lord,
for you repay all ac-|cording | to their | deeds.

Psalm 62

697 PSALM 63

Wainwright LM RICHARD WAINWRIGHT (1758–1825)

1 O God, thou art my God alone,
early to thee my soul shall cry,
a pilgrim in a land unknown,
a thirsty land whose springs are dry.

2 O could I be as I have been
when, praying in the holy place,
thy power and glory I have seen,
and marked the footsteps of thy grace!

3 Yet through this rough and thorny maze
I follow hard on thee, my God;
thine hand unseen upholds my ways;
I safely tread where thou hast trod.

4 Thee, in the watches of the night,
when I remember on my bed,
thy presence makes the darkness light;
thy guardian wings are round my head.

5 Better than life itself thy love,
dearer than all beside to me;
for whom have I in heaven above,
or what on earth, compared with thee?

6 Praise, with my heart, my mind, my voice,
for all thy mercy I will give;
my soul shall still in God rejoice;
my tongue shall bless thee while I live.

JAMES MONTGOMERY (1771–1854) altd.*
based on Psalm 63: 1–8 (*AV*)

698 PSALM 65

ANTIPHON (*at beginning and end*) BRENDA STEPHENSON (1947–)

TONE

1 You are to be praised, O | God, in Zion;
to you shall vows be performed | in Jerusalem.
To you that hear prayer shall | all flesh come,
because of | their transgressions.
Our sins are stron-|ger than we are,
but you will | blot them out.

2 Happy are they | whom you choose
and draw to your | courts to dwell there!
they will be satisfied by the beauty | of your house,
by the holiness | of your temple.
Awesome things will you show us in your righteousness,
O God of | our salvation,
O hope of all the ends of the earth
and of the seas that are | far away.

3 You make fast the mountains | by your power;
they are girded a-|bout with might.
You still the roaring | of the seas,
the roaring of their waves, and the clamour | of the peoples.
Those who dwell at the ends of the earth will tremble at your |
marvellous signs;
you make the dawn and the dusk to | sing for joy.

4 You visit the earth and water | it abundantly;
you make it very plenteous; the river of God is | full of water.
You pre-|pare the grain,
for so you provide | for the earth.
You drench the furrows and smooth | out the ridges;
with heavy rain you soften the ground and | bless its increase.

5 **You crown the year | with your goodness,**
and your paths over-|flow with plenty.
May the fields of the wilderness be | rich for grazing,
and the hills be | clothed with joy.
May the meadows cover themselves with flocks,
and the valleys cloak them-|selves with grain;
let them shout for | joy and sing.

Psalm 65

699 PSALM 67

JOSEPH GELINEAU (1920–)

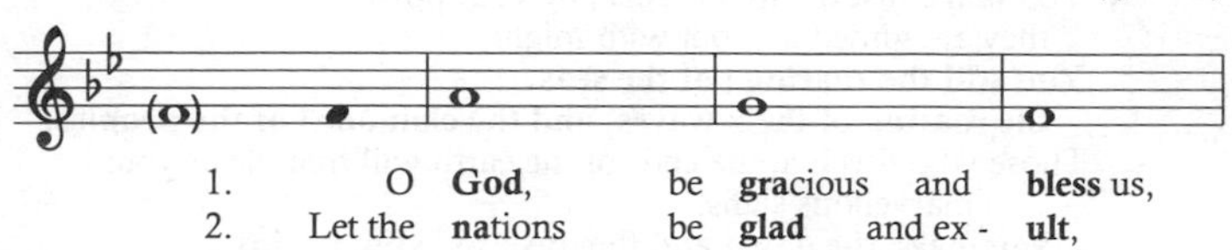

1. O **God**, be **gra**cious and **bless** us,
2. Let the **na**tions be **glad** and ex - **ult**,
3. The **earth** has **yield**ed its **fruit**,

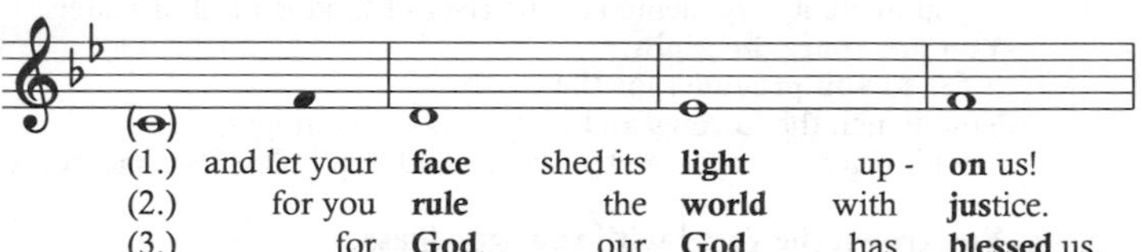

(1.) and let your **face** shed its **light** up - **on** us!
(2.) for you **rule** the **world** with **jus**tice.
(3.) for **God**, our **God**, has **bless**ed us.

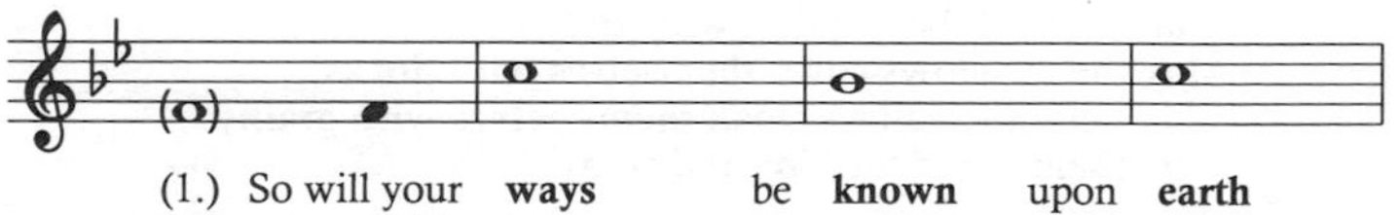

(1.) So will your **ways** be **known** upon **earth**
(2.) With **fair**ness you **rule** the **peo**ples,
(3.) May **God** still **give** us his **bless**ing

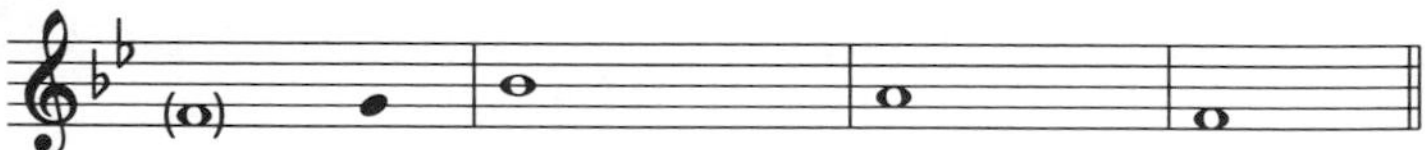

(1.) and all **na**tions learn your **sa**ving **help**.
(2.) you **guide** the **na**tions on **earth**.
(3.) till the **ends** of the **earth** re - **vere** him.

ANTIPHON (*after each verse; also at the beginning if desired*)
(♩ = 𝅝 of Psalm) PETER PEACOCK

Let the peo-ples praise you, O God, _ let all the peo-ples praise you!

700 PSALM 72

WILLIAM BOYCE (1711–79)

OR

G. C. MARTIN (1844–1916)

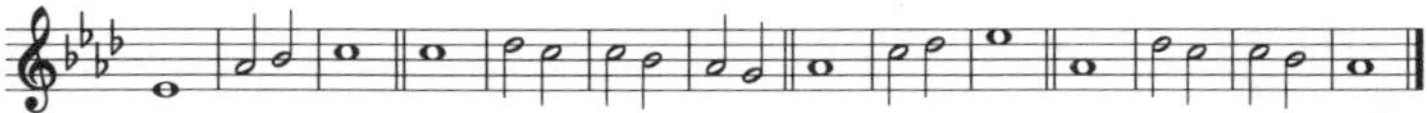

1 Give the king your | justice · O | God,
and your | righteousness · to the | king's __ | son;
that he may rule your | people | righteously
and the | poor __ | with __ | justice;

2 that the mountains may bring pros-|perity · to the | people,
and the | little | hills bring | righteous·ness.
He shall defend the needy a-|mong the | people;
he shall rescue the | poor and | crush the · op-|pressor.

3 He shall live as long as the sun and | moon en-|dure,
from one gener-|ation | to an-|other.
He shall come down like rain upon the | mown __ | field,
like | showers · that | water · the | earth.

4 In his time shall the | righteous | flourish;
there shall be abundance of peace till the | moon shall | be no | more.
The kings of Tarshish and of the | isles · shall pay | tribute,
and the kings of Arabia and | Saba | offer | gifts.

5 **All kings shall bow | down be-|fore him,**
and all the | nations | do him | service.
For he shall deliver the poor who cries | out · in dis-|tress,
and the op-|pressed who | has no | helper.

(*continued overleaf*)

PSALM 72
(continued)

WILLIAM BOYCE (1711–79)

OR

G. C. MARTIN (1844–1916)

6 He shall have pity on the | lowly · and | poor;
he shall pre- | serve the | lives · of the | needy.
He shall redeem their lives from op- | pression · and | violence,
and dear shall their | blood be | in his | sight.

7 Long | may he | live!
and may there be | given to · him | gold · from A- | rabia;
may prayer be | made for · him | always,
and may they | bless him | all the · day | long.

8 May there be abundance of | grain · on the | earth,
growing thick | even | on the | hilltops;
may its fruit | flourish · like | Lebanon,
and its grain like | grass up- | on the | earth.

9 May his name re- | main for | ever
and be established as | long as · the | sun en- | dures;
may all the nations | bless them·selves in | him
and | call __ | him __ | blessèd.

10 Blessed be the Lord God, the | God of | Israel,
who a- | lone does | wondrous | deeds!
And blessed be his glorious | name for | ever!
and may all the earth be filled with his | glory. A- | men. A- | men.

Psalm 72: 1–7, 10–19

701 PSALM 80

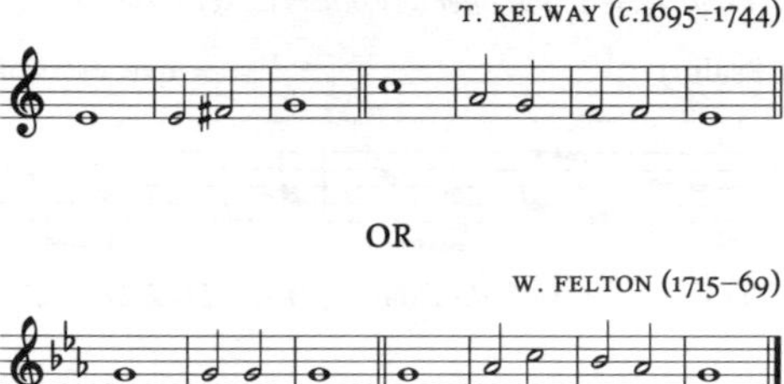

1 Hear O Shepherd of Israel, leading | Joseph · like a | flock;
shine forth, you that are en-|throned up-|on the | cherubim.

2 In the presence of Ephraim, Benjamin | and Man-|asseh,
stir up your | strength and | come to | help us.

3 **Restore us, O | God of | hosts;**
show the light of your countenance, | and we | shall be | saved.

4 O Lord | God of | hosts;
how long will you be angered des-|pite the | prayers of · your | people?

5 You have fed them with the | bread of | tears;
you have given them | bowls of | tears to | drink.

6 **You have made us the de-|rision · of our | neighbours,**
and our | ene·mies | laugh us · to | scorn.

7 **Restore us, O | God of | hosts;**
show the light of your countenance, | and we | shall be | saved.

Psalm 80: 1–7

702 PSALM 84

ANTIPHON I (*before verse 1, and after any others except verse 7*)

(♩ = 𝅝 of Psalm) A. GREGORY MURRAY (1905–92)

How love-ly is your dwell-ing place, Lord, God of hosts.

JOSEPH GELINEAU (1920–)

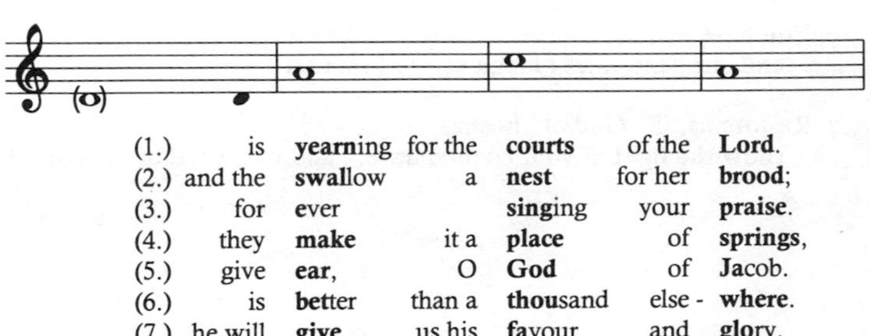

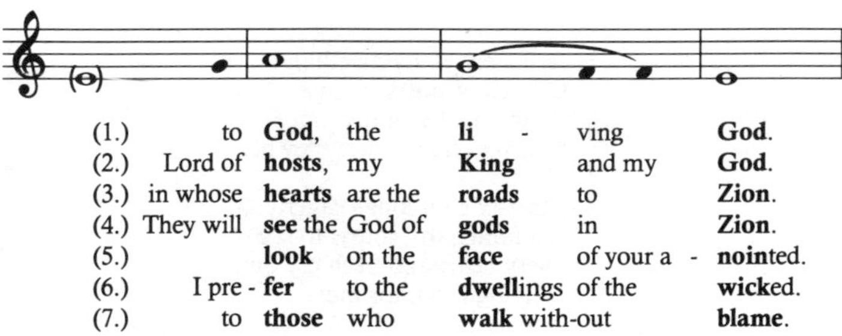

ANTIPHON II (*after verse 7, and any others; may be used alternately with Antiphon I*)

703 PSALM 84

Harington (Retirement) CM HENRY HARINGTON (1727–1816)

1 How lovely is thy dwelling-place,
O Lord of hosts, to me!
The tabernacles of thy grace
how pleasant, Lord, they be!

2 My thirsty soul longs eagerly,
yea faints, thy courts to see,
my very heart and flesh cry out,
O living God, for thee.

3 Bless'd are they in thy house that dwell,
they ever give thee praise.
Bless'd is the one whose strength thou art,
in whose heart are thy ways.

4 For God the Lord's a sun and shield:
he'll grace and glory give;
and will withhold no good from them
that uprightly do live.

5 O thou that art the Lord of hosts,
that one is truly blest,
who by assurèd confidence
on thee alone doth rest.

Psalm 84: 1, 2, 4, 5, 11, 12
Scottish Metrical Psalter, 1650*

704 PSALM 85

Canterbury 77 77

Simplified from *Song 13*
ORLANDO GIBBONS (1583–1625)

1 Lord, thine heart in love hath yearned
  and restored thy fallen land,
Israel's favour is restored,
  thou hast freed thy captive band.

2 Thou hast borne thy people's sin,
  covered all their deeds of ill;
all thy wrath is gathered in,
  and thy burning anger still.

3 Wilt thou not in mercy turn?
  Turn, and be our life again,
that thy people's heart may burn
  with the gladness of thy reign.

4 Show us now thy tender love;
  thy salvation, Lord, impart;
I the voice divine would prove,
  listening in my silent heart.

5 Faithfulness and truth shall meet,
  peace and righteousness embrace;
God bestow his goodness sweet,
  justice go before his face.

Psalm 85: 1–3, 6–8*a*, 10–13
from the metrical version of
JOHN KEBLE (1792–1866)*

705

PSALM 90

St Anne CM

Probably by WILLIAM CROFT (1678–1727)

1 Our God, our help in ages past,
our hope for years to come,
our shelter from the stormy blast,
and our eternal home:

2 under the shadow of thy throne
thy saints have dwelt secure;
sufficient is thine arm alone,
and our defence is sure.

3 Before the hills in order stood,
or earth received her frame;
from everlasting thou art God,
to endless years the same.

4 A thousand ages in thy sight
are like an evening gone;
short as the watch that ends the night
before the rising sun.

5 Time, like an ever-rolling stream,
bears all our years away;
they fly forgotten, as a dream
dies at the opening day.

6 Our God, our help in ages past,
our hope for years to come,
be thou our guard while troubles last,
and our eternal home.

ISAAC WATTS (1674–1748) altd.
based on Psalm 90: 1–6

706

PSALM 91

WILLIAM KNYVETT (1779–1856) from HANDEL

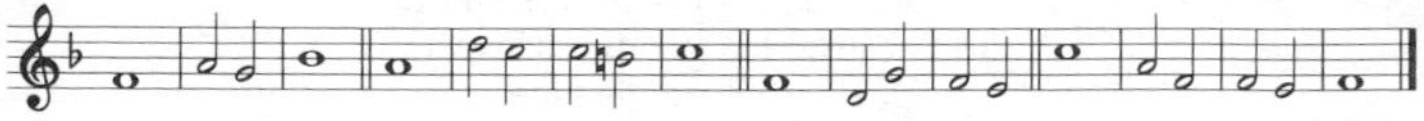

OR

J. P. HARDING (1850–1911)

1 They who dwell in the shelter of the | Most __ | High
abide under the | shadow | of the · al-|mighty.
I will say to the Lord, 'You are my | refuge · and my | stronghold,
my God, in | whom I | put my | trust'.

2 He shall deliver you from the | snare of · the | hunter
and | from the | deadly | pestilence.
He shall cover you with his pinions,
and you shall find refuge | under · his | wings;
his faithfulness shall | be a | shield and | buckler.

3 You shall not be afraid of any | terror · by | night,
nor of the | arrow · that | flies by | day;
of the plague that | stalks · in the | darkness,
nor of the | sickness · that lays | waste at | mid-day.

4 A thousand shall fall at your side,
and | ten thousand · at your | right hand,
but it | shall not | come near | you.
Your eyes have | only · to be-|hold
to see the re-|ward __ | of the | wicked.

5 Because you have made the | Lord your | refuge,
and the Most | High your | habi-|tation,
there shall no | evil · be-|fall you,
neither shall any | plague come | near your | dwelling.

6 For he shall give his | angels | charge over · you,
to | keep you · in | all your | ways.
They shall bear you | in their | hands,
lest you dash your | foot a-|gainst a | stone.

7 You shall tread upon the | lion and | adder;
you shall trample the young lion and the | serpent | under · your | feet.
Because you are bound to me in love, | therefore · will I de-|liver · you;
I will protect you, be-|cause you | know my | name.

8 You shall call upon me, and | I will | answer · you;
I am with you in trouble; I will | rescue · you and | bring you · to | honour.
With long life | will I | satisfy · you,
and | show you | my sal-|vation.

Psalm 91

707

PSALM 95

J. WILSON'S *A Selection of Psalm Tunes*
Edinburgh, 1825

Dublin (Howard) CM

1 O come, and let us to the Lord
in songs our voices raise,
with joyful noise let us the Rock
of our salvation praise.

2 Let us before his presence come
with praise and thankful voice;
let us sing psalms to him with grace,
and make a joyful noise.

3 The Lord's a great God, and great King
above all gods he is;
depths of the earth are in his hand,
the strength of hills is his.

4 To him the spacious sea belongs,
for he the same did make;
the dry land also from his hands
its form at first did take.

5 O come and let us worship him,
let us bow down withal,
and on our knees before the Lord
our Maker let us fall.

Psalm 95: 1–6
Irish Metrical Psalter, 1880

708 PSALM 96

ANTIPHON (*at beginning and end*) BRENDA STEPHENSON (1947–)

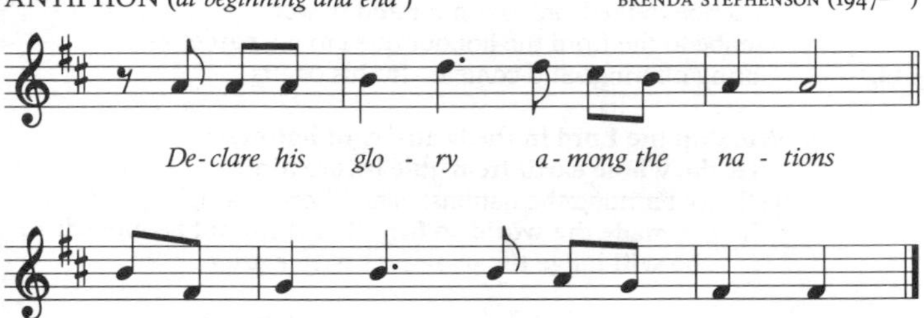

TONE A. GREGORY MURRAY (1905–92)

1 Sing to the Lord | a new song;
sing to the Lord, | all the earth.
Sing to the Lord and | bless his name;
proclaim the good news of his salvation from | day to day.

2 Declare his glory a-|mong the nations
and his wonders a-|mong all peoples.
For great is the Lord and greatly | to be praised;
he is more to be feared | than all gods.

3 As for the gods of the nations, they | are but idols;
but it is the Lord who | made the heavens.
O the majesty and magnificence | of his presence!
O the power and the splendour | of his sanctuary!

(*continued overleaf*)

4 Ascribe to the Lord, you families | of the peoples,
ascribe to the Lord ho-|nour and power.
Ascribe to the Lord the honour due | to his name;
bring offerings and come in-|to his courts.

5 **Worship the Lord in the beau-|ty of holiness;**
let the whole earth trem-|ble before him.
Tell it out among the nations: 'The | Lord is king!
he has made the world so firm that it cannot be moved;
he will judge the peo-|ples with equity'.

6 Let the heavens rejoice, and let the | earth be glad;
let the sea thunder and all | that is in it;
let the | field be joyful
and all that | is therein.

7 Then shall all the trees of the wood shout for joy
before the Lord | when he comes,
when he comes to | judge the earth.
He will judge the | world with righteousness
and the peoples | with his truth.

Psalm 96

709

PSALM 98

Rendez à Dieu 98 98 D

Melody from *La Forme des Prières et Chants Ecclésiastiques*, Strasbourg, 1545 (2nd line as in *Genevan Psalter*, 1551)

1 New songs of celebration render
to him who has great wonders done.
Awed by his love, his foes surrender
and fall before the mighty one.
He has made known his great salvation
which all his friends with joy confess:
He has revealed to every nation
his everlasting righteousness.

2 Joyfully, heartily resounding,
let every instrument and voice
peal out the praise of grace abounding,
calling the whole world to rejoice.
Trumpets and organs, set in motion
such sounds as make the heavens ring;
all things that live in earth and ocean,
make music for your mighty king.

3 Rivers and seas and torrents roaring,
honour the Lord with wild acclaim;
mountains and stones look up adoring
and find a voice to praise his name.
Righteous, commanding, ever glorious,
praises be his that never cease;
just is our God, whose truth victorious
establishes the world in peace.

Psalm 98: 1, 2, 4–9
para. ERIK ROUTLEY (1917–82)*

710 PSALM 98

J. DAVY (1763–1824)

1 Sing to the | Lord a · new | song,
for | he has · done | marvel·lous | things.
With his right hand and his | holy | arm
has he | won · for him-|self the | victory.

2 The Lord has made | known his | victory;
his righteousness has he openly | shown · in the |
sight of · the | nations.
He remembers his mercy and faithfulness to the |
house of | Israel,
and all the ends of the earth have seen the |
victo·ry | of our | God.

3 Shout with joy to the Lord | all you | lands;
lift up your | voice, re-|joice and | sing.
Sing to the | Lord · with the | harp,
with the | harp · and the | voice of | song.

4 With trumpets and the | sound · of the | horn
shout with | joy be·fore the | King, the | Lord.
Let the sea make a noise and | all · that is | in it,
the | lands and | those who | dwell therein.

5 Let the rivers clap their hands,
and let the hills ring | out with | joy,
before the Lord when he | comes to | judge the | earth.
In righteousness shall he | judge the | world
and the | peo —|ples with | equity.

Psalm 98

711 PSALM 100

ANTIPHON (*at beginning and end*) BRENDA STEPHENSON (1947–)

TONE

1 Be joyful in the Lord, | all you lands;
serve the | Lord with gladness
and come before his presence | with a song.

2 **Know this: the Lord him-|self is God;**
he himself has made us, and | we are his;
we are his people and the sheep | of his pasture.

3 Enter his gates | with thanksgiving;
go into his | courts with praise;
give thanks to him and call up-|on his name.

4 **For the | Lord is good;**
his mercy is | everlasting;
and his faithfulness endures from | age to age.

Psalm 100

712 PSALM 100

Old Hundredth LM

Later form of melody
in the *Genevan Psalter*, 1551

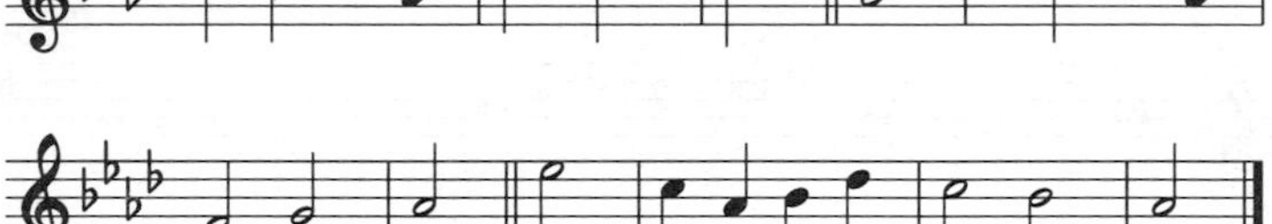

1 All people that on earth do dwell,
sing to the Lord with cheerful voice;
him serve with mirth, his praise forth tell;
come ye before him and rejoice.

2 The Lord, ye know, is God indeed;
without our aid he did us make;
we are his folk, he doth us feed;
and for his sheep he doth us take.

3 O enter then his gates with praise,
approach with joy his courts unto;
praise, laud and bless his name always,
for it is seemly so to do.

4 For why: the Lord our God is good,
his mercy is for ever sure;
his truth at all times firmly stood,
and shall from age to age endure.

Psalm 100
metrical version by
WILLIAM KETHE (publ. 1560–61) altd.

713

PSALM 100

Psalm 100 FRED DUNN

Psalm 100: 1, 2, 4*a*, 5*a*
versified by FRED DUNN, 1977

714 PSALM 103

H. WALFORD DAVIES (1869–1941)

1 Bless the Lord | O my | soul,
   and all that is within me | bless his | holy | name.
Bless the Lord | O my | soul,
   and for-|get not | all his | benefits.

2 He forgives | all your | sins,
   and | heals all | your in-|firmities;
he redeems your | life · from the | grave,
   and crowns you with | mercy · and | loving-|kindness.

3 He satisfies you with | good __ | things,
   and your | youth · is re-|newed · like an | eagle's.
The Lord executes | righteousness · and | judgement
   for | all who | are op-|pressed.

4 He made his ways | known to | Moses,
   and his | works · to the | children · of | Israel.
The Lord is full of com-|passion · and | mercy,
   slow to | anger · and of | great __ | kindness.

5 **He will not | always · ac-|cuse us,**
   nor will he | keep his | anger · for | ever.
He has not dealt with us ac-|cording · to our | sins,
   nor rewarded us ac-|cording | to our | wickedness.

6 For as the heavens are | high a·bove the | earth,
   so is his mercy | great up·on | those who | fear him.
As far as the | east is · from the | west,
   so far has he re-|moved our | sins __ | from us.

(*continued*)

H. WALFORD DAVIES (1869–1941)

7 As a father | cares · for his | children,
so does the | Lord · care for | those who | fear him.

8 **For he himself knows whereof | we are | made;**
he re-| members · that | we are · but | dust.

9 Our days are | like the | grass;
we | flourish · like a | flower · of the | field;

10 **when the wind goes over it, | it is | gone,**
and its | place shall | know it · no | more.

First chant 11 But the merciful goodness of the Lord endures for ever on | those who | fear him,
and his | righteousness · on | children's | children;
on those who | keep his | coven·ant,
and re-| member · his com-| mandments · and | do them.

12 The Lord has set his | throne in | heaven,
and his kingship | has do-| minion · over | all.
Bless the Lord you angels of his,
you mighty ones who | do his | bidding,
and | hearken · to the | voice of · his | word.

13 Bless the Lord all | you his | hosts,
you ministers of | his who | do his | will,
Bless the Lord all you works of his,
in all | places of · his do-| minion;
bless the | Lord __ | O my | soul.

Psalm 103

715 PSALM 103

Tiverton CM

JACOB (?) GRIGG (*c*.1790)
in JOHN RIPPON'S *Selection of Psalm and Hymn Tunes*, 1796

1 O thou my soul, bless God the Lord;
and all that in me is
be stirrèd up, his holy name
to magnify and bless.

2 Bless, O my soul, the Lord thy God,
and not forgetful be
of all his gracious benefits
he hath bestowed on thee;

3 all thine iniquities who doth
most graciously forgive;
who thy diseases all and pains
doth heal, and thee relieve;

4 who doth redeem thy life, that thou
to death may'st not go down;
who thee with loving-kindness doth
and tender mercies crown;

5 who with abundance of good things
doth satisfy thy mouth;
so that, ev'n as the eagle's age,
renewèd is thy youth.

6 O bless the Lord, all ye his works,
wherewith the world is stored
in his dominions everywhere,
my soul, bless thou the Lord.

Psalm 103: 1–5, 22
Scottish Metrical Psalter, 1650

716 PSALM 103

Dundrennan SM CARYL MICKLEM (1925–)

1 My soul, repeat his praise,
whose mercies are so great,
whose anger is so slow to rise,
so ready to abate.

2 High as the heavens are raised
above the ground we tread,
so far the riches of his grace
our highest thoughts exceed.

3 His power subdues our sins;
and his forgiving love,
far as the east is from the west,
doth all our guilt remove.

4 The pity of the Lord
to those that fear his name,
is such as tender parents feel;
he knows our feeble frame.

5 Our days are as the grass,
or like the morning flower;
if one sharp blast sweep o'er the field,
it withers in an hour.

6 But thy compassions, Lord,
to endless years endure,
and children's children ever find
thy words of promise sure.

Psalm 103: 8, 11–17
para. ISAAC WATTS (1674–1748)

717 PSALM 106

Dunfermline CM

Scottish Psalter, 1615

1 Give praise and thanks unto the Lord,
for bountiful is he;
his tender mercy doth endure
unto eternity.

2 Who can express God's mighty works,
or show forth all his praise?
Blessèd are they that judgement keep,
and justly do always.

3 Remember me, Lord, with that love
which thou to thine dost bear;
with thy salvation, O my God,
to visit me draw near,

4 that I thy chosen's good may see,
and in their joy rejoice,
and may with thine inheritance
exult with cheerful voice.

Psalm 106: 1–5
Scottish Metrical Psalter, 1650*

718 PSALM 107

E. HIGGINS (d. 1769)

1 Give thanks to the Lord for | he is | good,
and his | mercy · en-|dures for | ever.
Let all those whom the Lord has re-|deemed pro-|claim
that he re-|deemed them · from the | hand · of the | foe.

2nd half
He gathered them | out of · the | lands;
from the east and from the west,
from the | north and | from the | south.

WILLIAM WHITE (1908–)

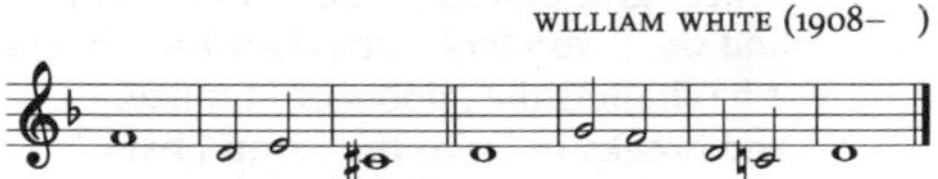

Second chant 2 Some wandered in | desert | wastes;
they found no way to a | city · where | they might |
dwell.

3 **They were | hungry · and | thirsty;**
their | spirits | languished · with-|in them.

First chant 4 Then they cried to the | Lord · in their | trouble,
and he de-|livered them · from | their dis-|tress.
He put their feet on a | straight __ | path,
to go to a | city · where | they might | dwell.

5 Let them give thanks to the | Lord · for his | mercy
and the | wonders · he | does for · his | children.
For he | satisfies · the | thirsty,
and fills the | hungry · with | good __ | things.

(*continued overleaf*)

PSALM 107
(*continued*)

Second chant 6 Some sat in darkness | and deep | gloom,
bound | fast in | misery · and | iron;

7 **because they rebelled against the | words of | God**
and despised the | counsel · of the | Most __ | High.

8 So he humbled their | spirits with · hard | labour;
they stumbled, and | there was | none to | help.

First chant 9 **Then they cried to the | Lord · in their | trouble,**
and he de-|livered them · from | their dis-|tress.
He led them out of darkness and | deep __ | gloom,
and | broke their | bonds a-|sunder.

10 Let them give thanks to the | Lord · for his | mercy
and the | wonders · he | does for · his | children.
For he shatters the | doors of | bronze,
and breaks in | two the | iron | bars.

Second chant 11 Some were fools and took to re-|bel·lious | ways;
they were af-|flicted · be-|cause of · their | sins.

12 **They abhorred all | manner · of | food,**
and drew | near to | death's __ | door.

First chant 13 Then they cried to the | Lord · in their | trouble,
and he de-|livered them · from | their dis-|tress.
He sent forth his | word and | healed them,
and | saved them | from the | grave.

14 Let them give thanks to the | Lord · for his | mercy
and the | wonders · he | does · for his | children.
Let them offer a | sacrifice · of | thanksgiving,
and tell of his | acts with | shouts of | joy.

PSALM 107
(*continued*)

Second chant 15 Some went down to the | sea in | ships,
and plied their | trade in | deep __ | waters;

16 **they beheld the | works · of the | Lord**
and his | wonders | in the | deep.

17 Then he spoke, and a stormy | wind a-| rose,
which tossed | high the | waves · of the | sea.

18 **They mounted up to the heavens and fell |**
back to · the | depths;
their hearts | melted · be-| cause of · their | peril.

19 They reeled and | staggered · like | drunkards,
and were | at their | wits' __ | end.

First chant 20 **Then they cried to the | Lord · in their | trouble,**
and he de-| livered them · from | their dis-| tress.
He stilled the | storm · to a | whisper
and | quieted · the | waves · of the | sea.

2nd half
Then were they glad be-| cause of · the | calm,
and he brought them to the | harbour | they were |
bound for.

21 Let them give thanks to the | Lord for · his | mercy
and the | wonders · he | does for · his | children.
Let them exalt him in the congre-| gation of · the | people,
and | praise him · in the | council · of the | elders.

Psalm 107: 1–32

719 PSALM 111

adpt. JOSEPH CORFE (1740–1820)
from HENRY LAWES (1596–1662)

OR

ROBERT COOKE (1768–1814)

1 Alleluia! I will give thanks to the Lord with my | whole __ | heart,
in the assembly of the | upright, · in the | congre-|gation.
Great are the | deeds · of the | Lord!
They are | studied · by | all · who de-|light in them.

2 His work is full of | majesty · and | splendour,
and his | righteousness · en-|dures for | ever.
He makes his marvellous | works to · be re-|membered;
the Lord is | gracious · and | full of · com-|passion.

3 He gives food to | those who | fear him;
he is ever | mindful | of his | covenant.
He has shown his people the | power of · his | works
in | giving them · the | lands · of the | nations.

4 The works of his hands are | faithfulness · and | justice;
all | his com-|mandments · are | sure.
They stand fast for | ever · and | ever,
because they are | done in | truth and | equity.

5 He sent redemption to his people;
he commanded his | covenant · for | ever;
holy and | awesome | is his | name.
The fear of the Lord is the be-|ginning · of | wisdom;
those who keep his commandments have a good
understanding; his | praise en-|dures for | ever.

Psalm 111

720 PSALM 113

Laudate Pueri HEINZ WERNER ZIMMERMAN (1930–)

1 Praise the Lord!
Praise, you servants of the Lord,
praise the name of the Lord!
Blessèd be the name of the Lord!
Blessèd be the name of the Lord
from this time forth and for evermore!
Praise the Lord! Praise the Lord!

2 Praise the Lord!
Thanks and praises sing to God,
day by day to the Lord!
High above the nations is God.
High above the nations is God,
his glory high over earth and sky.
Praise the Lord! Praise the Lord!

3 Praise the Lord!
Praise and glory give to God!
Who is like unto him?
Raising up the poor from the dust,
raising up the poor from the dust,
he makes them dwell in his
heart and home.
Praise the Lord! Praise the Lord!

4 Praise the Lord!
Praise, you servants of the Lord,
praise the love of the Lord!
Giving to the homeless a home,
giving to the homeless a home,
he fills their hearts with new hope and joy.
Praise the Lord! Praise the Lord!

Psalm 113: 1–5, 7
para. MARJORIE JILLSON (1931–)

721 PSALM 116

H. WALFORD DAVIES (1869–1941)

1 I | love the | Lord,
because he has heard the | voice of · my | suppli-|cation,
because he has in-|clined his | ear to · me
when-|ever · I | called up-|on him.

2 The cords of | death en-|tangled · me;
the grip of the grave took hold of me; I | came to |
grief and | sorrow.
Then I called upon the | name of · the | Lord:
'O Lord I | pray you, | save my | life.'

3 **Gracious is the | Lord and | righteous;**
our | God is | full of · com-|passion.
The Lord watches | over · the | inno·cent;
I was | brought · very | low, and he | helped me.

2nd half
Turn again to your | rest · O my | soul,
for the | Lord has | treated · you | well.

4 For you have rescued my | life from | death,
my eyes from | tears · and my | feet from | stumbling.
I will walk in the | presence of · the | Lord
in the | land __ | of the | living.

Psalm 116: 1–9

722 PSALM 116

Jackson (Byzantium) CM THOMAS JACKSON (1715–81)

1 I'll of salvation take the cup,
and on the Lord's name call:
I'll pay my vows now to the Lord
before his people all.

2 Thank-offerings I to thee will give,
and on the Lord's name call.
I'll pay my vows now to the Lord
before his people all.

3 Within the courts of God's own house,
within the midst of thee,
O city of Jersualem,
praise to the Lord give ye.

Psalm 116: 13, 14, 17–19
Scottish Metrical Psalter, 1650*

723

PSALM 117

Lasst uns erfreuen
88 44 88 with alleluias

Melody from
Geistliche Kirchengesäng, Cologne, 1623
arr. R. VAUGHAN WILLIAMS (1872–1958)

1 From all that dwell below the skies
let the Creator's praise arise.
Alleluia! Alleluia!
Let the Redeemer's name be sung
through every land, by every tongue.
Alleluia! Alleluia!
Alleluia! Alleluia!
Alleluia!

2 Eternal are thy mercies, Lord:
eternal truth attends thy word.
Alleluia! Alleluia!
Thy praise shall sound from shore to shore,
till suns shall rise and set no more.
Alleluia! Alleluia!
Alleluia! Alleluia!
Alleluia!

ISAAC WATTS (1674–1748)
based on Psalm 117

724 PSALM 118

J. L. HOPKINS (1819–73)

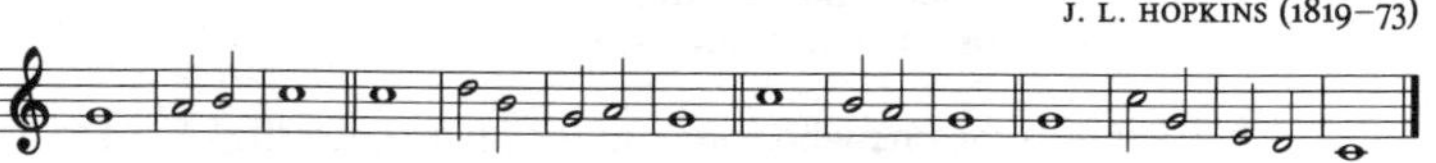

1 The Lord is my | strength and · my | song,
and he has be-|come __ | my sal-|vation.
There is a sound of exul-|tation and | victory
in the | tents __ | of the | righteous:

2 'The right hand of the Lord has triumphed!
The right hand of the | Lord · is ex-|alted!
The right | hand · of the | Lord has | triumphed!'
I shall not | die but | live,
and de-|clare the | works · of the | Lord.

3 The Lord has | punished · me | sorely,
but he did not | hand me | over · to | death.
Open for me the | gates of | righteousness;
I will enter them; I will offer | thanks __ |to the | Lord.

(*continued overleaf*)

PSALM 118
(*continued*)

J. L. HOPKINS (1819–73)

4 'This is the | gate · of the | Lord;
those who are | right·eous | may __ | enter.'
I will give thanks to you, | for you | answered me,
and have be-| come __ | my sal-| vation.

5 The same stone which the | builders · re-| jected
has be-| come the | chief __ | cornerstone.
This is the | Lord's __ | doing,
and it is | marvel·lous | in our | eyes.

6 On this day the | Lord has | acted;
we will re-| joice __ | and be | glad in it.
Hosanna, | Lord, ho-| sanna!
Lord | send us | now suc-| cess.

7 Blessèd is the one who comes in the | name of · the | Lord;
we | bless you · from the | house of · the | Lord.
God is the Lord; he has | shined up-| on us;
form a procession with branches up to the | horns __ |
of the | altar.

8 **'You are my God, and | I will | thank you;**
you are my | God, and | I will · ex-| alt you.'
Give thanks to the Lord, for | he is | good;
his | mercy · en-| dures for | ever.

Psalm 118: 14–29

725 PSALM 121

ANTIPHON (*at beginning and end*) BRENDA STEPHENSON (1947–)

TONE A. GREGORY MURRAY (1905–92)

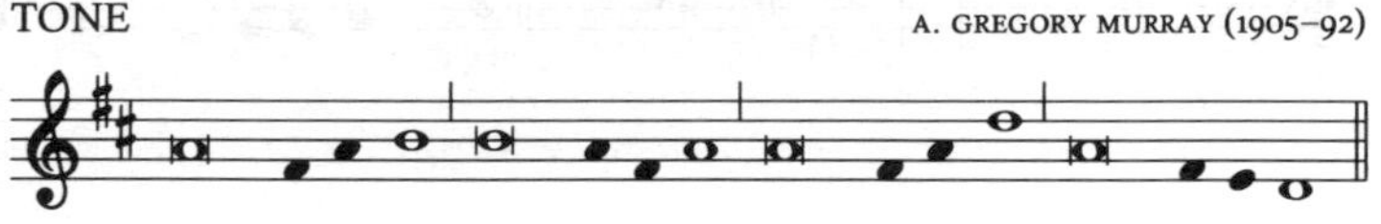

1 I lift up my eyes | to the hills;
from where is my | help to come?
My help comes | from the Lord,
the maker of | heaven and earth.

2 He will not let your | foot be moved
and he who watches over you will not | fall asleep;
behold, he who keeps watch | over Israel
shall neither slum-|ber nor sleep;

3 the Lord himself | watches over you;
the Lord is your shade at | your right hand,
so that the sun shall not strike | you by day,
nor the | moon by night.

4 The Lord shall preserve you | from all evil;
it is he who shall | keep you safe.
The Lord shall watch over your going out and your | coming in,
from this time forth for | evermore.

Psalm 121

726 PSALM 121

Dundee (French) CM *Scottish Psalter*, 1615

1 I to the hills will lift mine eyes;
from whence doth come mine aid?
My safety cometh from the Lord,
who heaven and earth hath made.

2 Thy foot he'll not let slide, nor will
he slumber that thee keeps.
Behold, he that keeps Israel,
he slumbers not, nor sleeps.

3 The Lord thee keeps; the Lord thy shade
on thy right hand doth stay.
The moon by night thee shall not smite,
nor yet the sun by day.

4 The Lord shall keep thy soul; he shall
preserve thee from all ill;
henceforth thy going out and in
God keep for ever will.

Psalm 121
Scottish Metrical Psalter, 1650

727 PSALMS 122 and 133

York CM *Scottish Psalter*, 1615

1 I joy'd when to the house of God,
go up, they said to me.
Jerusalem, within thy gates
our feet shall standing be.

2 Pray that Jerusalem may have
peace and felicity.
Let them that love thee and thy peace
have still prosperity.

3 Behold how good a thing it is,
and it becomes us well,
as those whom peace and kinship bind,
in unity to dwell.

4 Therefore I wish that peace may still
within thy walls remain,
and ever may thy palaces
prosperity retain.

5 Now, for my friends' and kindred's sakes,
peace be in thee, I'll say.
And for the house of God our Lord,
I'll seek thy good alway.

Psalm 122: 1, 2, 6–9 and Psalm 133: 1
Scottish Metrical Psalter, 1650, altd.*

728 PSALM 130

JAMES TURLE (1802–82)

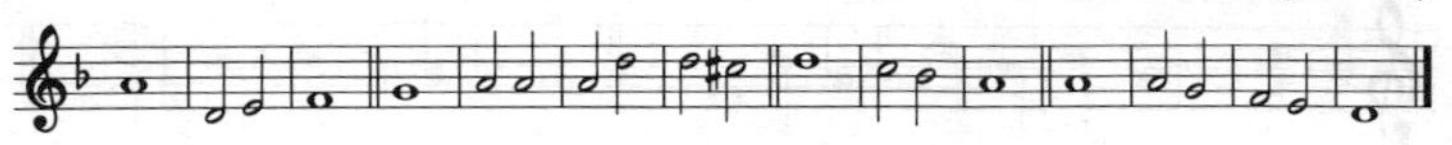

OR

WILLIAM CROFT (1678–1727)

1 Out of the depths have I | called to · you O | Lord;
Lord | hear __ | my __ | voice;

2 **let your ears con-| sider | well**
the | voice of · my | suppli-| cation.

3 If you Lord were to note what is | done a-| miss,
O | Lord __ | who could | stand?

4 **For there is for-| giveness · with | you;**
there-| fore you | shall be | feared.

5 I wait for the Lord; my | soul __ | waits for him;
in his | word __ | is my | hope.

6 **My soul waits for the Lord more than they that |**
watch · for the | morning;
yes, more than | they that | watch · for the | morning.

7 O Israel, | wait · for the | Lord,
for with the | Lord __ | there is | mercy.

8 **With him there is | plenteous · re-| demption,**
and he shall redeem | Israel · from | all their | sins.

Psalm 130

729 PSALM 131

ANTIPHON (*at beginning and end*) BRENDA STEPHENSON (1947–)

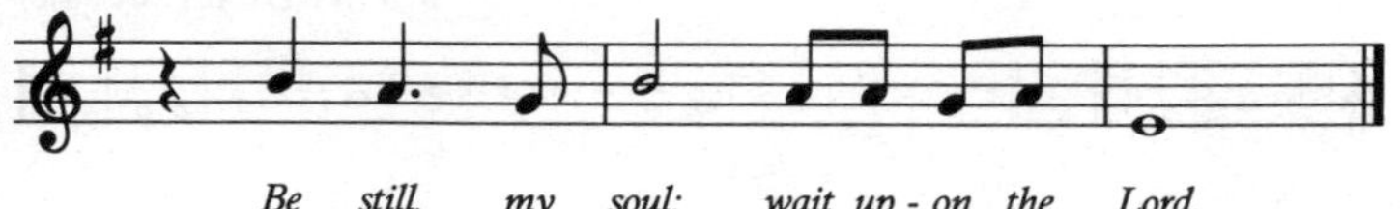

TONE A. GREGORY MURRAY (1905–92)

1 O Lord, I | am not proud;
  I have no | haughty looks.
I do not occupy myself | with great matters,
  or with things that are too | hard for me.

2 But I | still my soul
  and | make it quiet,
like a child upon its | mother's breast;
  my soul is quiet-|ed within me.

3 O | Israel,
  wait up-|on the Lord,
from | this time forth
  for | evermore.

Psalm 131

730 PSALM 139

W. H. HAVERGAL (1793–1870)

OR

G. C. MARTIN (1844–1916)

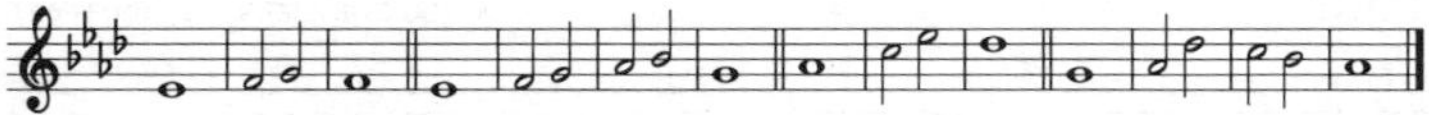

1 Lord, you have searched me | out and | known me;
you know my sitting down and my rising up;
you dis-|cern my | thoughts · from a-|far.
You trace my | journeys · and my | resting-places,
and are ac-|quainted · with | all my | ways.

2 Indeed there is not a | word on · my | lips,
but you O Lord | know it | alto-|gether.
You press upon me be-|hind · and be-|fore,
and | lay your | hand up-|on me.

2nd half
Such knowledge is too | wonder·ful | for me;
it is so | high that · I | cannot · at-|tain to it.

3 Where can I | go then · from your | spirit?
where can I | flee — | from your | presence?
If I climb up to | heaven, · you are | there;
if I make the grave my | bed, · you are | there — | also.

4 If I take the | wings of · the | morning,
and dwell in the | utter·most | parts of · the | sea,
even there your | hand will | lead me,
and your | right hand | hold me | fast.

5 **If I say 'Surely the | darkness · will | cover me,**
and the light a-| round me | turn to | night',
darkness is not dark to you; the night is as |
bright as · the | day;
darkness and light to | you are | both a-| like.

6 For you yourself created my | inmost | parts;
you knit me to-| gether · in my | mother's | womb.
I will thank you because I am | marvellous·ly | made;
your works are wonderful, | and I | know it | well.

7 **My body was not hidden from you while I was being |**
made in | secret
and | woven · in the | depths of · the | earth.
Your eyes beheld my limbs, yet un-| finished · in the | womb;
all of them were | written | in your | book;

2nd half
they were | fashioned · day by | day,
when as | yet __ | there was | none of them.

8 How deep I find your | thoughts O | God!
How | great __ | is the | sum of them!
If I were to count them, they would be more in |
number · than the| sand;
to count them all, my life span would | need to |
be like | yours.

9 Search me out O God, and | know my | heart;
try me and | know my | restless | thoughts.
Look well whether there be any | wicked·ness | in me,
and lead me in the | way · that is | ever-| lasting.

Psalm 139: 1–18, 23–4

731 PSALM 139

Sursum corda 10 10 10 10 ALFRED M. SMITH (1879–1971)

1 You are before me, Lord, you are behind,
and over me you have spread out your hand;
such knowledge is too wonderful for me,
too high to grasp, too great to understand.

2 Then where, Lord, from your Spirit shall I go,
and where, Lord, from your presence shall I fly?
If I ascend to heaven you are there,
and still are with me though in hell I lie;

3 and if I take my flight into the dawn,
or if I dwell on ocean's farthest shore,
your mighty hand will rest upon me still,
and your right hand will guard me evermore.

4 If I should say 'Darkness will cover me,
and I shall hide within the vale of night',
surely the darkness is not dark to you,
the night is as the day, the darkness light.

5 Search me, O God, search me and know my heart;
try me, O God, my mind and spirit try;
keep me from any path that gives you pain,
and lead me in the everlasting way.

Psalm 139: 5–12, 23, 24
metrical version by
I. R. PITT-WATSON (1923–)*

732

PSALM 145

Duke Street LM

Melody from BOYD'S *Psalm & Hymn Tunes*, 1793
Later attrib. JOHN HATTON (d. 1793)

1 O Lord, thou art my God and King;
thee will I magnify and praise;
thee will I bless, and gladly sing
unto thy holy name always.

2 Each day I rise I will thee bless,
and praise thy name time without end.
Much to be praised and great God is;
his greatness none can comprehend.

3 Age unto age thy works shall praise,
declare the marvels done by thee:
and I will tell thy glorious ways,
the honour of thy majesty.

4 Thy wondrous works I will record;
by nations shall the might be told
of all thy dreadful acts, O Lord,
and I thy greatness will unfold.

5 They utter shall abundantly
the memory of thy goodness great,
and shall sing praises cheerfully,
whilst they thy righteousness relate.

Psalm 145: 1–7
Scottish Metrical Psalter, 1650*

733

PSALM 145

FIRST VERSION

E. J. HOPKINS (1818–1901)

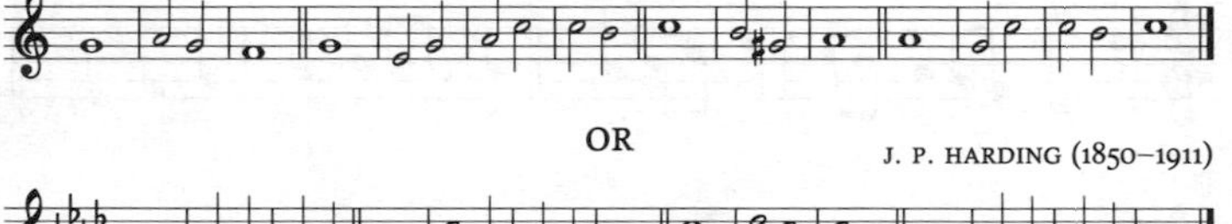

OR

J. P. HARDING (1850–1911)

1 The Lord is gracious and | full of · com-|passion,
slow to ¦ anger · and of | great __ | kindness.
The Lord is | loving · to | every·one,
and his compassion is | over | all his | works.

2 All your works | praise you · O | Lord,
and your | faithful | servants | bless you.
They make known the | glory · of your | kingdom,
and | speak __ | of your | power;

3 that the peoples may | know of · your | power
and the glorious | splendour | of your | kingdom.
Your kingdom is an ever-|lasting | kingdom;
your dominion en-|dures through-|out all | ages.

4 The Lord is faithful in | all his | words,
and | merciful · in | all his | deeds.
The Lord upholds | those who | fall;
he lifts up | those · who are | bowed __ | down.

5 The eyes of all wait up-|on you · O | Lord,
and you | give them · their | food in · due | season.
You open | wide your | hand,
and satisfy the needs of | every | living | creature.

6 The Lord is righteous in | all his | ways,
and | loving · in | all his | works.
The Lord is near to those who | call up-|on him,
to all who | call up-|on him | faithfully.

7 He fulfils the desire of | those who | fear him;
he | hears their | cry and | helps them.
My mouth shall speak the | praise · of the | Lord;
let all flesh bless his holy | name for | ever · and | ever.

Psalm 145: 8–19, 21

733

PSALM 145
Second Version

ANTIPHON (*at beginning and end*) BRENDA STEPHENSON (1947–)

TONE IAN FORRESTER (1956–)

1 The Lord is gracious and full | of compassion,
slow to anger and | of great kindness.
The Lord is loving to | everyone,
and his compassion is over | all his works.

2 All your works praise | you, O Lord,
and your faithful | servants bless you.
They make known the glory | of your kingdom,
and speak | of your power;

3 that the peoples may know | of your power
and the glorious splendour | of your kingdom.
Your kingdom is an ever-|lasting kingdom;
your dominion endures through-|out all ages.

4 The Lord is faithful in | all his words,
and merciful in | all his deeds.
The Lord upholds | those who fall;
he lifts up those who | are bowed down.

5 The eyes of all wait upon | you, O Lord,
and you give them their food | in due season.
You open | wide your hand,
and satisfy the needs of every | living creature.

6 The Lord is righteous in | all his ways,
and loving in | all his works.
The Lord is near to those who | call upon him,
to all who call up-|on him faithfully.

7 He fulfils the desire of | those who fear him;
he hears their | cry and helps them.
My mouth shall speak the praise | of the Lord;
let all flesh bless his holy name for e-|ver and ever.

Psalm 145: 8–19, 21

734 PSALM 146

Lucerne (Dresden) 888 D JOHANN SCHMIDLIN (1722–72)

1 I'll praise my maker while I've breath,
and when my voice is lost in death,
praise shall employ my nobler powers:
my days of praise shall ne'er be past,
while life and thought and being last,
or immortality endures.

2 Happy the one whose hopes rely
on Israel's God! He made the sky,
and earth and sea, with all their train:
his truth for ever stands secure;
he saves the oppressed; he feeds the poor,
and none shall find his promise vain.

3 The Lord pours eyesight on the blind:
the Lord supports the fainting mind;
he sends the labouring conscience peace;
he helps the stranger in distress,
the widow and the fatherless,
and grants the prisoner sweet release.

4 I'll praise him while he lends me breath;
and when my voice is lost in death,
praise shall employ my nobler powers:
my days of praise shall ne'er be past,
while life and thought and being last,
or immortality endures.

Psalm 146: 1, 2, 5–9
para. ISAAC WATTS (1674–1748) altd.

735 PSALM 150

C. V. STANFORD (1852–1924)

1. O praise God in his ho-li-ness: praise him in the fir-ma-ment

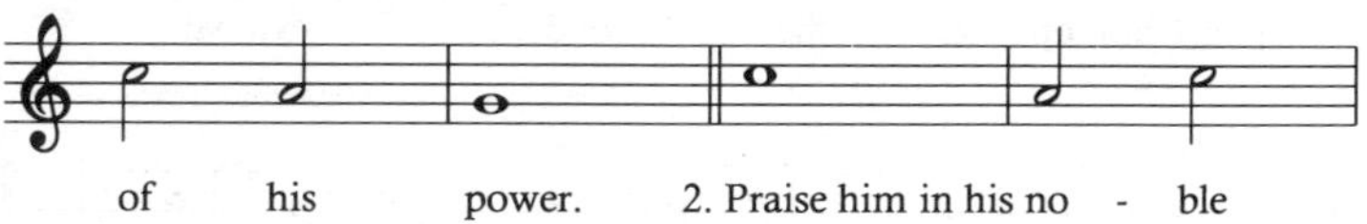

of his power. 2. Praise him in his no - ble

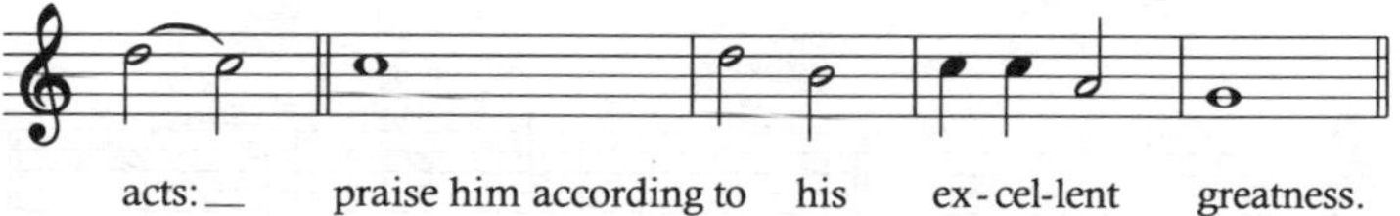

acts: praise him according to his ex-cel-lent greatness.

3. Praise him in the sound of the trum-pet: praise him up-on the

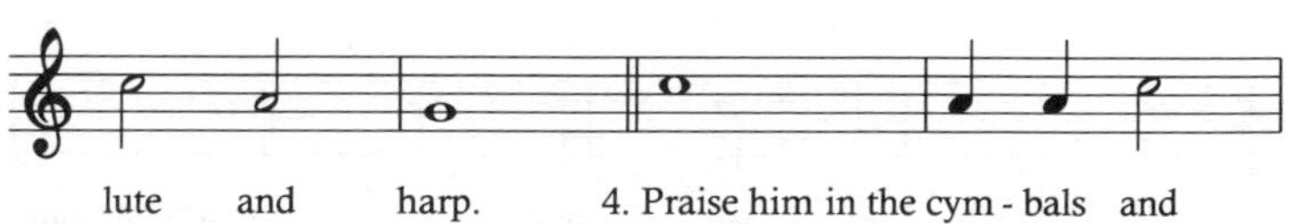

lute and harp. 4. Praise him in the cym-bals and

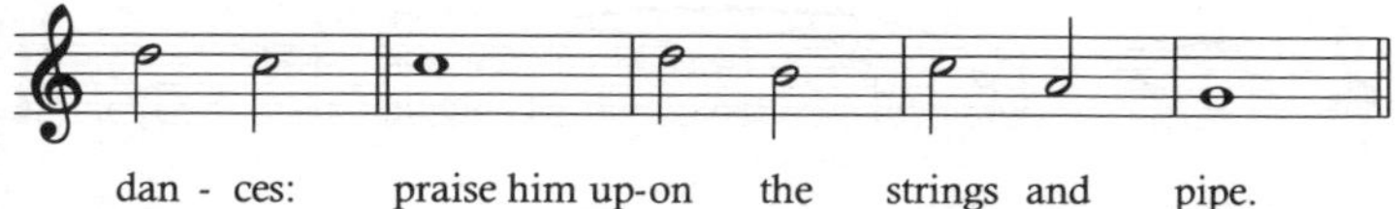

dan-ces: praise him up-on the strings and pipe.

(*continued*)

Book of Common Prayer

736 VENITE

J. NARES (1715–83)

OR

W. FELTON (1715–69)

OR

G. A. MACFARREN (1813–87)

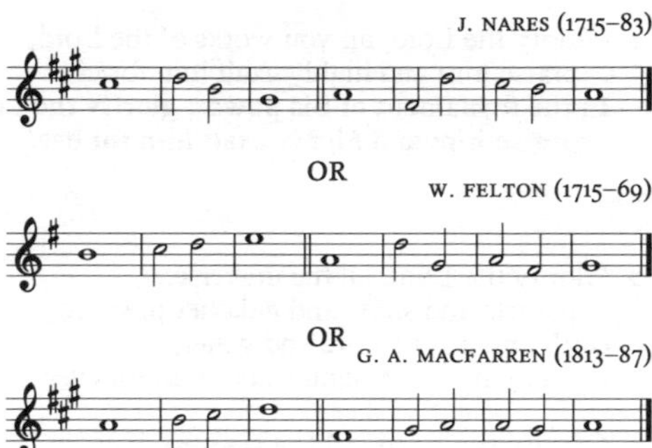

1 O come let us | sing · to the | Lord;
let us shout in triumph to the | rock of | our sal-|vation.

2 Let us come before his | face with | thanksgiving,
and cry | out to · him | joyfully · in | psalms.

3 For the Lord is a | great ___ | God;
and a | great ___ | king a·bove | all gods.

4 In his hands are the | depths · of the | earth;
and the peaks of the | mountains · are | his ___ | also.

5 The sea is | his · and he | made it;
his hands | moulded | dry ___ | land.

6 Come let us worship and | bow ___ | down,
and | kneel be·fore the | Lord our | maker.

7 For he him-|self is · our | God;
**we are the people of his | pasture · and the |
sheep of · his | hand.**

8 If only you would hear his | voice to-|day;
for he | comes to | judge the | earth.

9 **He shall judge the | world with | righteousness,
and the | peoples | with his | truth.**

from Psalms 95 and 96

737 A SONG OF CREATION

1 Glorify the Lord, all you works of the Lord,
praise him and highly exalt him for ever.
In the firmament of his power, glorify the Lord,
praise him and highly exalt him for ever.

2 Glorify the Lord, all the universe,
planets and stars, and galaxies in space,
earth and air, and fire and water,
praise him and highly exalt him for ever.

3 **Glorify the Lord, all the seasons,**
winds and sunshine, mists and snow,
thunder and lightning, day and night,
praise him and highly exalt him for ever.

4 Glorify the Lord, all the world,
mountains and plains, rivers and oceans,
plant-life and fish, birds and animals,
praise him and highly exalt him for ever.

5 **Glorify the Lord, all humankind,**
children and parents, women and men,
powerless and powerful, living and dying,
praise him and highly exalt him for ever.

6 Glorify the Lord, all the people of God,
servants and sinners, humble and holy,
painters and poets, makers of music,
praise him and highly exalt him for ever.

7 **Glorify the Lord, all his Church,**
apostles and martyrs, teachers and ministers,
one holy priesthood of all believers,
praise him and highly exalt him for ever.

based on the 'Song of the Three' (Apocrypha)
(cf. Daniel 3: 57–90, in the *Jerusalem Bible*)

738

BENEDICTUS

(The Song of Zechariah)

E. CUTLER (1831–1916)

OR

JOSEPH BARNBY (1838–96)

1 Blessed be the Lord, the | God of | Israel,
who has come to his | people · and | set them | free.
The Lord has raised up for us a | mighty | Saviour,
born of the | house of · his | servant | David.

2 Through the holy prophets God | promised · of | old
to save us from our enemies, from the | hands of |
all who | hate us,
to show | mercy · to our | forebears,
and to re-|member his | holy | covenant.

3 This was the oath God swore to our | father | Abraham:
to set us | free from · the | hands of · our | enemies,
free to worship him with-|out __ | fear,
holy and righteous before him, | all the | days of · our | life.

4 And you child shall be called the prophet of the | Most __ | High,
for you will go before the | Lord · to pre-|pare his | way,
to give his people | knowledge · of sal-|vation
by the for-|giveness | of their | sins.

5 In the tender com-|passion of · our | God
the dawn from on | high shall | break up-|on us,
to shine on those who dwell in darkness and the |
shadow · of | death,
and to guide our | feet · into the | way of | peace.

Luke 1: 68–79

739 MAGNIFICAT

(The Song of Mary)

THOMAS ATTWOOD (1765–1838)

OR

GEORGE THALBEN-BALL (1896–1987)

OR

H. WALFORD DAVIES (1869–1941)

1 My soul proclaims the | greatness · of the | Lord.
My spirit re-|joices · in | God my | Saviour,
who has looked with favour on his | lowly | servant.
From this day all gene-|rations · will | call me | blessèd.

2 The Almighty has | done great | things for me,
and | holy | is his | name.
God has mercy on | those who | fear him,
from gene-|ration · to | gene-|ration.

3 The Lord has shown | strength · with his | arm,
and scattered the | proud in | their con-|ceit,
casting down the | mighty · from their | thrones,
and | lifting | up the | lowly.

2nd half
God has filled the hungry with | good __ | things,
and sent the | rich a-|way __ | empty.

4 He has come to the aid of his | servant | Israel,
to re-|member · the | promise · of | mercy;
the promise | made to · our | forebears,
to | Abraham and · his | children · for | ever.

Luke 1: 46–55

740 MAGNIFICAT

(The Song of Mary)

Woodlands 10 10 10 10 WALTER GREATOREX (1877–1949)

Alternative tune: WINTON, no. 524(*ii*).

1 Tell out, my soul, the greatness of the Lord!
Unnumbered blessings, give my spirit voice;
tender to me the promise of his word;
in God my Saviour shall my heart rejoice.

2 Tell out, my soul, the greatness of his name!
Make known his might, the deeds his arm has done;
his mercy sure, from age to age the same;
his holy name—the Lord, the Mighty One.

3 Tell out, my soul, the greatness of his might!
Powers and dominions lay their glory by;
proud hearts and stubborn wills are put to flight,
the hungry fed, the humble lifted high.

4 Tell out, my soul, the glories of his word!
Firm is his promise, and his mercy sure.
Tell out, my soul, the greatness of the Lord
to children's children and for evermore!

TIMOTHY DUDLEY-SMITH (1926–), based on
Luke 1: 46–55 in the *New English Bible*

741 A SONG OF THE INCARNATION

A. GREGORY MURRAY (1905–92)

1 The grace of God has dawned u-| pon the world
with heal-| ing for all.
The people who | walked in darkness
have seen | a great light:

2 **light has | dawned upon us,**
dwellers in a land as | dark as death.
For a boy has been | born for us,
a son gi-| ven to us.

3 God | is love;
and his love was disclosed to | us in this,
that he sent his | only Son
into the world to | bring us life.

4 **We know how generous our Lord Jesus | Christ has been:**
he was rich, yet for our sake he | became poor,
so that | through his poverty
we might | become rich.

5 God has spoken to us | in the Son
whom he has made heir to the whole | universe.
The Word became flesh; he came to | dwell among us,
and we saw his glory, such glory as befits the Father's only Son,
full of | grace and truth.

Titus 2: 11; Isaiah 9: 2, 6*a*;
1 John 4: 9; 2 Cor. 8: 9;
Hebrews 1: 2; John 1: 14

742 NUNC DIMITTIS

(The Song of Simeon)

FIRST VERSION

C. GIBBONS (1615–76)

OR

Tonus Parisianus I

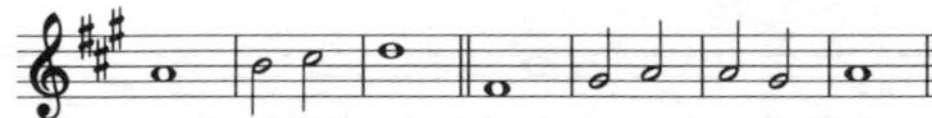

OR

G. A. MACFARREN (1813–87)

1 Now, Lord, you let your servant | go in | peace:
your | word has | been ful-|filled.

2 My own eyes have | seen the · sal-|vation
which you have prepared in the | sight of | every | people:

3 a light to re-|veal you · to the | nations,
and the | glory of · your | people | Israel.

Luke 2: 29–32

742 NUNC DIMITTIS

SECOND VERSION

ANTIPHON (*at beginning and end*) BRENDA STEPHENSON (1947–)

TONE

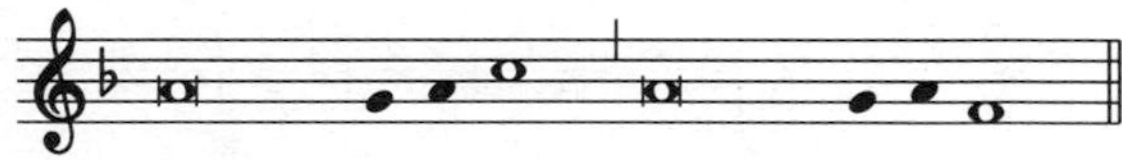

1 Now, Lord, you let your servant | go in peace:
your word has | been fulfilled.

2 My own eyes have seen | the salvation
which you have prepared in the sight of | every people:

3 a light to reveal you | to the nations,
and the glory of your | people Israel.

Luke 2: 29–32

743 THE BEATITUDES

WILLIAM LLEWELLYN (1925–)

INTRODUCTION

NB Each bar, whether $\frac{2}{4}$ or $\frac{3}{4}$, is to have the same duration.

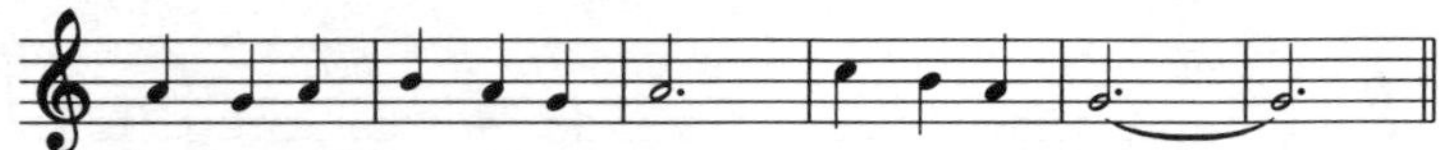

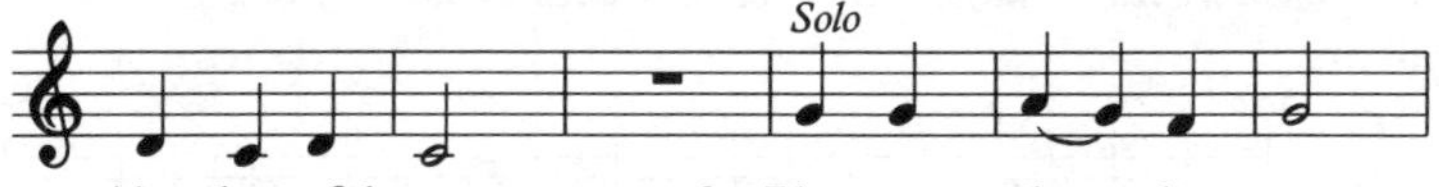

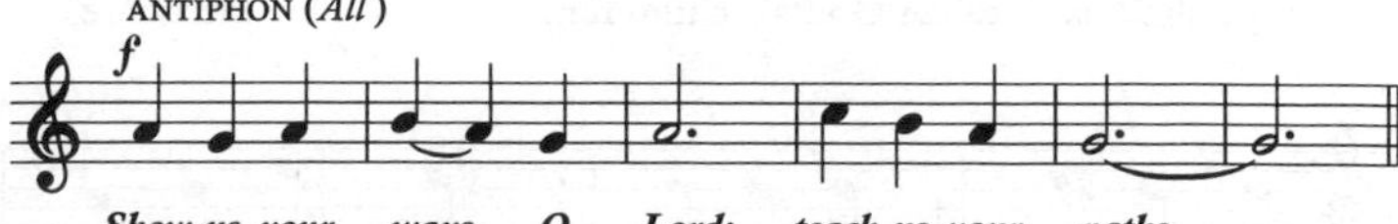

(continued)

Solo
4. Blest are they that hun-ger and thirst af - ter right-eous-ness:
All
for they shall___ be filled.
Solo
5. Blest are___ the mer-ci-ful:
All
for they shall ob - tain mer-cy.
ANTIPHON (All)
f
Show us your ways, O Lord: teach us your paths.____
Solo
6. Blest are the pure_ in heart:
All
for they shall see God.
Solo
7. Blest are___ the peace-ma-kers:
All
for they shall be called God's child-ren.
Solo
8. Blest are they which are per - se - cu - ted for right-eous-ness'

Show us your ways, O Lord: teach us your paths.

1 Blest are the poor in spirit:
for theirs is the kingdom of heaven.

2 Blest are they that mourn:
for they shall be comforted.

3 Blest are the meek:
for they shall inherit the earth.

Show us your ways, O Lord: teach us your paths.

4 Blest are they that hunger and thirst after righteousness:
for they shall be filled.

5 Blest are the merciful:
for they shall obtain mercy.

Show us your ways, O Lord: teach us your paths.

6 Blest are the pure in heart:
for they shall see God.

7 Blest are the peacemakers:
for they shall be called God's children.

8 Blest are they which are persecuted for righteousness' sake:
the kingdom of heaven is theirs.

Show us your ways, O Lord: teach us your paths.

Psalm 25: 4 and Matthew 5: 3–10

744 THE GREAT COMMANDMENTS

Hear, O Israel:
The Lord our God, the Lord is one.
Love the Lord your God
with all your heart,
with all your soul,
with all your mind,
and with all your strength.

This is the first and the great commandment.

The second is like it:
Love your neighbour as yourself.

There is no commandment greater than these.

Mark 12: 29–31 and Matthew 22: 38, 39

745 *New Commandment*

Source unknown

'A new commandment I give unto you,
 that you love one another as I have loved you;
 that you love one another as I have loved you.
By this shall all know you are my disciples:
 if you have love one for another;
by this shall all know you are my disciples:
 if you have love one for another.'

John 13: 34, 35

746 *Dieu, nous avons vu*

12 12 with refrain

JEAN LANGLAIS (1907–91)

God, your glory we have seen in your Son,
full of truth, full of heavenly grace;
in Christ make us live, his love shine on our face,
and the nations will see in us the triumph you have won.

1 In the fields of this world his good news he has sown,
and sends us out to reap till the harvest is done:

2 In his love like a fire that consumes he passed by;
the flame has touched our lips; let us shout 'Here am I!':

3 He was broken for us, God-forsaken his cry,
and still the bread he breaks; to ourselves we must die:

4 He has trampled the grapes of new life on his cross;
now drink the cup and live; he has filled it for us:

5 He has founded a kingdom that none shall destroy;
the corner-stone is laid: go to work, build with joy!

DIDIER RIMAUD (1922–)
refrain tr. R. E. C. JOHNSON (1913–) altd.
verses tr. BRIAN WREN (1936–)

A solo singer or small group may sing first the refrain and then each verse, the congregation responding with the refrain in each case.

747 SALVATOR MUNDI

A. GREGORY MURRAY (1905–92)

1 Saviour of the world, Lord Jesus, | Son of God,
come in power and help us, we | humbly pray.
You have freed us by your cross and | precious blood;
save us and help us, we | humbly pray.

2 You saved your disciples when they had | almost drowned;
hear us and save us, we | humbly pray.
In your great mercy loose us | from our sins;
forgive us and help us, we | humbly pray.

3 Make yourself known as our Saviour and might-|y Deliverer;
save us that we may praise you, we | humbly pray.
Draw near, as you have promised, from the throne | of your glory;
look upon us and hear our cry, we | humbly pray.

4 Come again and dwell with us, Lord | Jesus Christ;
stay with us for ever, we | humbly pray.
When you appear in power | and great glory,
make us one with you in your glor-|ious kingdom.

Thanks be to God. **Alleluia! Amen!**

Anon., attrib. HENRY ALLON (1818–92)*
based on a Latin prayer

The last line should be used only when the Canticle is spoken.

748 A SONG OF RESURRECTION

(The Easter Anthems)

W. CROTCH (1775–1847)

OR

R. GOODSON (1655–1718)

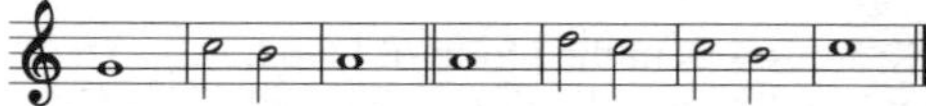

1 Christ our Passover has been | sacri·ficed | for us,
so let us | cele-|brate the | feast,

2 **not with the old leaven of cor-|ruption · and | wickedness,**
but with the unleavened | bread of · sin-|cerity · and | truth.

3 Christ, once raised from the dead, | dies no | more:
death has | no more · do-|minion | over him.

4 **In dying he died to sin, | once for | all;**
in | living · he | lives to | God.

5 See yourselves therefore as | dead to | sin,
and alive to God in | Jesus | Christ our | Lord.

6 **Christ has been | raised · from the | dead,**
the | firstfruits · of | those who | sleep.

7 For as by | man came | death,
by man has come also the resur-|rection | of the | dead.

8 **For as in | Adam · all | die,**
even so in Christ shall | all be | made a-|live.

1 Corinthians 5: 7, 8 and 15: 20–2; Romans 6: 9–11

749 A SONG OF CHRIST'S GLORY

G. C. MARTIN (1844–1916)

1 Christ Jesus was in the | form of | God,
but he | did not | cling · to e-|quality with · God.
He emptied himself, taking the | form of · a | servant,
and bore the | human | likeness · as his | own.

2 Being found in human | form he | humbled himself,
and became obedient unto | death, even | death · on a | cross.
Therefore God has | highly · ex-|alted him,
and be-|stowed on · him the | name a·bove | every name;

3 that at the name of Jesus every | knee should | bow,
in heaven and on | earth and | in the | depths,
and every tongue confess that Jesus | Christ is | Lord,
to the | glory · of | God the | Father.

Philippians 2: 6–11

750 *Fredericktown*

CHARLES R. ANDERS (1929–)

10 10 10 with alleluias

Alternative tune: SINE NOMINE, no. 658.

1 All praise to thee, for thou, O King divine,
didst yield the glory that of right was thine,
that in our darkened hearts thy grace might shine:

Alleluia! Alleluia! Alleluia!

2 Thou cam'st to us in lowliness of thought:
by thee the outcast and the poor were sought;
and by thy death was God's salvation wrought:

3 Let this mind be in us which was in thee,
who wast a servant that we might be free,
obedient unto death on Calvary:

4 Wherefore, by God's eternal purpose, thou
art high exalted o'er all creatures now,
and given the Name to which all knees shall bow:

5 Let every tongue confess with one accord,
in heaven and earth, that Jesus Christ is Lord,
and God the Father be by all adored:

F. BLAND TUCKER (1895–1984)*
based on Philippians 2: 5–11

751 *Veni Creator Spiritus* LM with doxology Mechlin melody

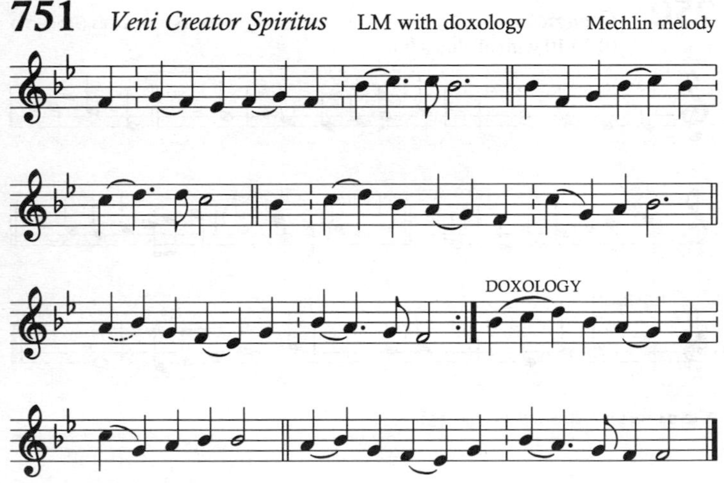

1 Come, Holy Ghost, our souls inspire,
and lighten with celestial fire;
thou the anointing Spirit art,
who dost thy sevenfold gifts impart.

2 Thy blessèd unction from above
is comfort, life, and fire of love;
enable with perpetual light
the dullness of our blinded sight.

3 Anoint and cheer our soilèd face
with the abundance of thy grace:
keep far our foes, give peace at home:
where thou art guide no ill can come.

4 Teach us to know the Father, Son,
and thee, of both, to be but One;
that through the ages all along
this may be our endless song:

Praise to thy eternal merit,
Father, Son, and Holy Spirit.

Latin, 9th cent.
tr. JOHN COSIN (1594–1672)

This alternative version of verse 1 may be used if preferred:

Come, Holy Spirit, souls inspire
and lighten with celestial fire;
thou the anointing Spirit art,
who dost thy sevenfold gifts impart.

752 A SONG OF THE FIRST-BORN

IAN FORRESTER (1956–)

1 Christ is the image of the | unseen God,
the first-born of | all creation;
for in him all | things were made,
in heaven | and on earth.

2 Through | him and for him
all | things were made;
he exists | before all things,
and holds | them in unity.

3 The Church | is his body,
and he | is its head;
he is | the beginning,
the first-born | from the dead.

4 **God made | all his fullness**
to | dwell in him,
to recon-|cile through him
all creation | to himself,

5 every-|thing on earth
and every-|thing in heaven,
when | he made peace
by his death | on the cross.

from Colossians 1: 15–20

753 A SONG OF LOVE

1 Beloved, let us love one another,
for love is from God.
Everyone who loves is born of God and knows God:
the unloving do not know God; for God is love.

2 In this was the love of God made known among us:
that God sent his only Son into the world that we might live through him.
For God loved the world so much that he gave his only Son,
that all who have faith in him may not die but have eternal life.

3 If God thus loved us we ought also to love one another.
We love because he first loved us.
If we love one another, God himself dwells in us;
his love is perfected in us.

4 There is no fear in love;
perfect love casts out fear.
Love bears everything, believes everything,
hopes everything, endures everything.

5 For I am persuaded that neither death nor life,
nor things present, nor things to come,
nor anything else in all creation
will be able to separate us from the love of God in Christ Jesus our Lord.

1 John 4: 7–9; John 3: 16; 1 John 4: 11, 19, 12*b*, 18;
1 Corinthians 13: 7; Romans 8: 38, 39

This Canticle is spoken, but the Antiphon printed below may suitably be sung after each verse and at the beginning.

Taizé Community

(Where there is tender care and love, God is present.)

754 A SONG OF PRAISE FOR ALL THE SAINTS

BUNTY NEWPORT (1927–)

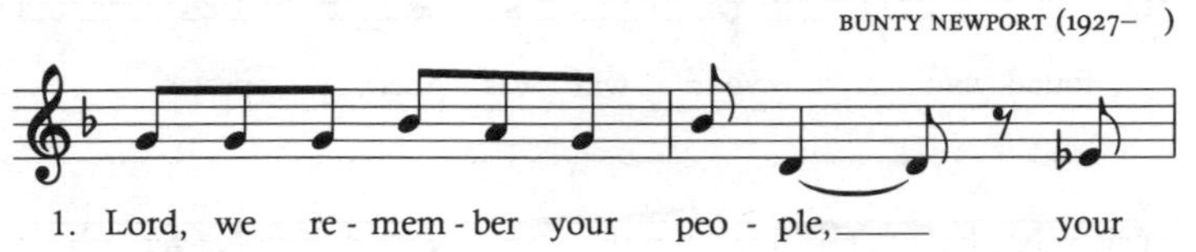

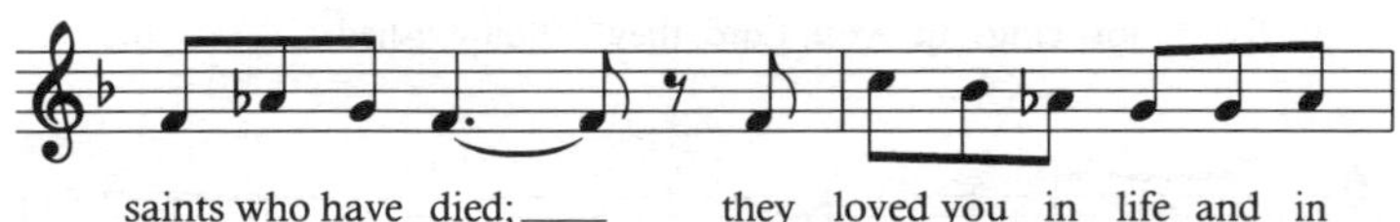

ANTIPHON (*after each verse*) ***Fine***

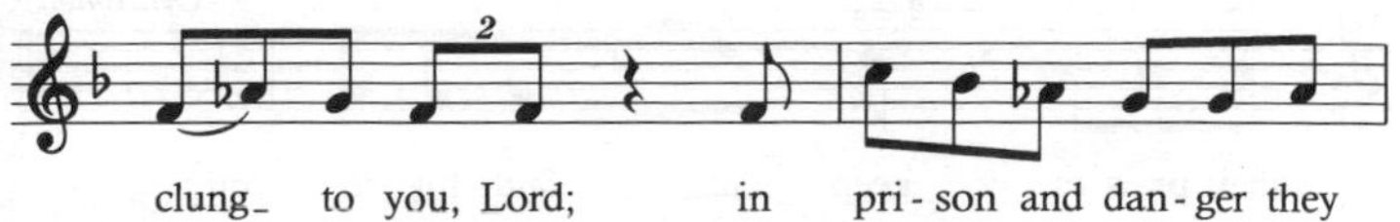

JUDITH B. O'NEILL (1930–)

755 TE DEUM

Mainzer LM JOSEPH MAINZER (1801–51)

1 We praise, we worship thee, O God,
thy sovereign power we sound abroad:
all nations bow before thy throne,
and thee the eternal Father own.

2 Loud alleluias to thy name
angels and seraphim proclaim:
the heavens and all the powers on high
with rapture constantly do cry,

3 'O holy, holy, holy Lord!
Thou God of hosts, by all adored;
earth and the heavens are full of thee,
thy light, thy power, thy majesty.'

4 Apostles join the glorious throng
and swell the loud immortal song;
prophets enraptured hear the sound
and spread the alleluia round.

5 Victorious martyrs join their praise
and shout the omnipotence of grace,
while all thy Church through all the earth
acknowledge and extol thy worth.

6 Glory to thee, O God most high!
Father, we praise thy majesty,
the Son, the Spirit, we adore:
one Godhead, blest for evermore.

'Te Deum laudamus' (Latin, 4th cent.), part 1;
tr. Anon., in Philip Gell's *Collection*, 1815, altd.

756 TE DEUM

1 We praise | you O | God,
we ac-|claim __ | you as | Lord;
all cre-|ation | worships you,
the | Father | ever-|lasting.

2 To you all angels, all the | powers of | heaven,
the cherubim and seraphim, | sing in | endless | praise:
Holy, holy, holy Lord, God of | power and | might,
heaven and | earth are | full of · your | glory.

3 The glorious company of a-|postles | praise you;
the noble | fellowship · of | prophets | praise you;
the white-robed army of | martyrs | praise you;
throughout the world the | holy | Church ac-|claims you

4 **Father, of | majesty · un-|bounded,**
your | true and | only | Son,
worthy of | all __ | praise,
the Holy Spirit, | advo-|cate and | guide.

5 You Christ are the | king of | glory,
the e-|ternal | Son of · the | Father.
When you took our flesh to | set us | free
you humbly | chose the | Virgin's | womb.

6 You overcame the | sting of | death,
and opened the kingdom of | heaven to | all be-|lievers.
You are seated at God's right | hand in | glory.
We believe that you will | come to | be our | judge.

7 Come then Lord, and | help your | people,
bought with the | price of | your own | blood,
and bring us | with your | saints
to | glory | ever-|lasting.

SET A — E. J. HOPKINS (1818–1901)

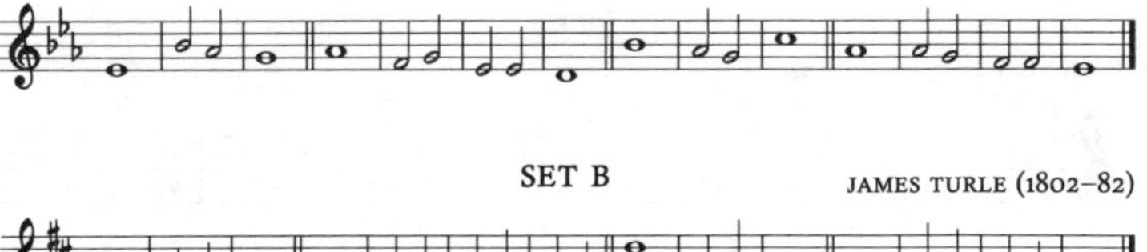

SET B — JAMES TURLE (1802–82)

8 Save your people Lord, and | bless · your in-|heritance.
Govern and up-|hold them | now and | always.
Day by | day we | bless you.
We | praise your | name for | ever.

9 Keep us today Lord from | all __ | sin.
Have | mercy on · us, | Lord, have | mercy.
Lord show us your | love and | mercy,
for we have | put our | trust in | you.

2nd half
In you Lord | is our | hope:
let us | never · be | put to | shame.

This Canticle may end at verse 7.

757 TE DEUM

ANTIPHON I (𝅝 = 𝅝 of verses)

ERIK ROUTLEY (1917–82)

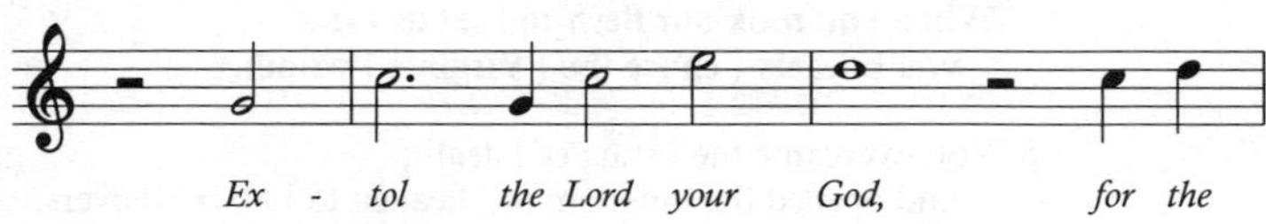

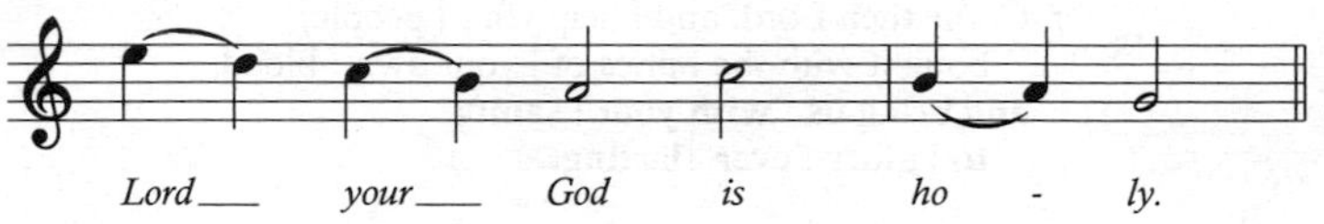

VERSES 1–5

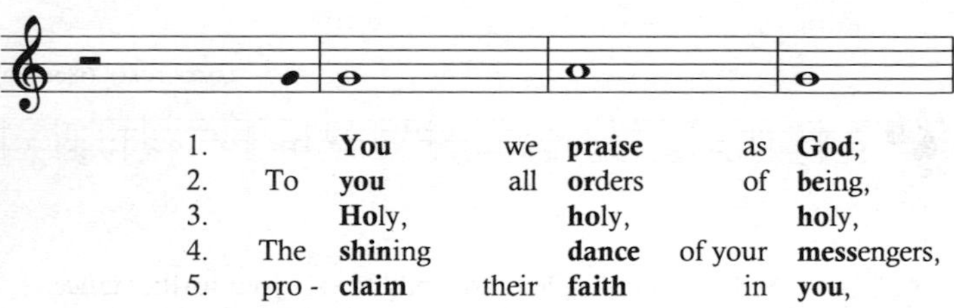

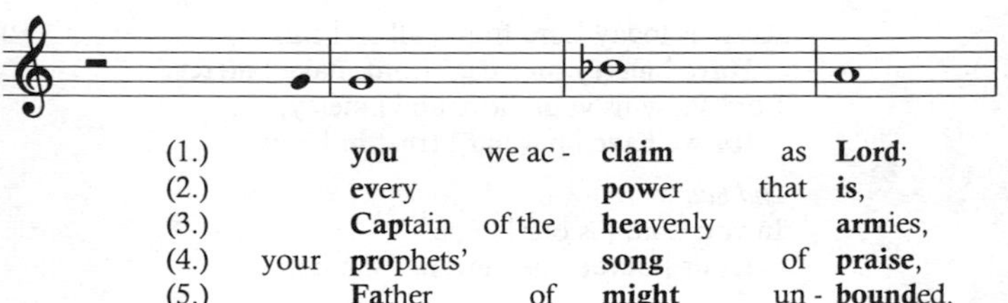

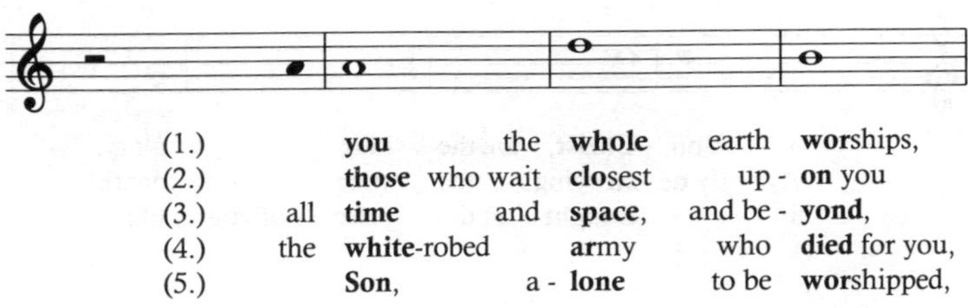

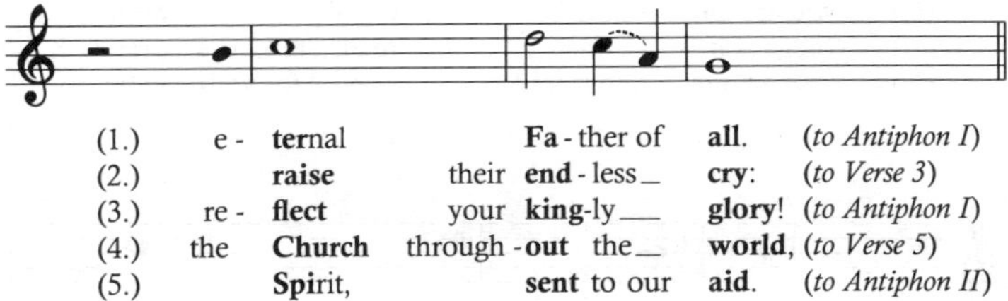

ANTIPHON II (o = o of verses)

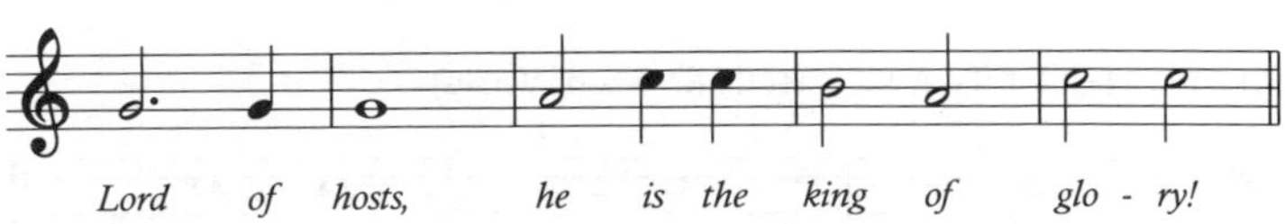

(Verses 6–8 overleaf)

VERSES 6–8

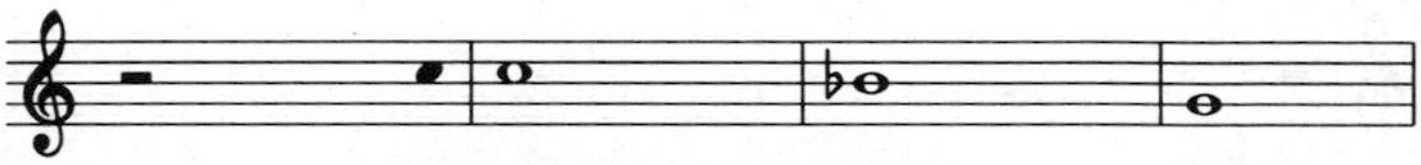

6. You, **Christ**, are the **king** of **glory**,
7. By de - **stroying** the **sting** of **death**
8. **Bought** at the **price** of your **life**

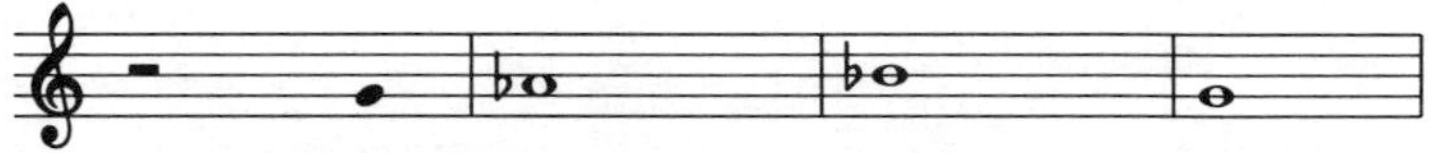

(6.) you are the **Father's** e - **ternal** **Son**.
(7.) you gave be - **lievers** a **road** to God's **presence**,
(8.) we your **household** **pray** for your **help**:

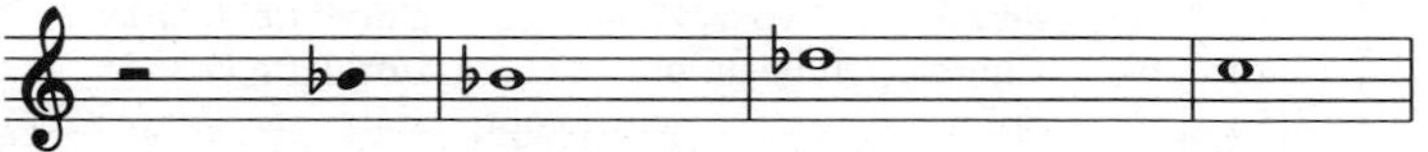

(6.) When to **save** the **world** you became **man**,
(7.) where you **sit** en - **throned** in **light**;
(8.) **give** us the **fullness** of **life**

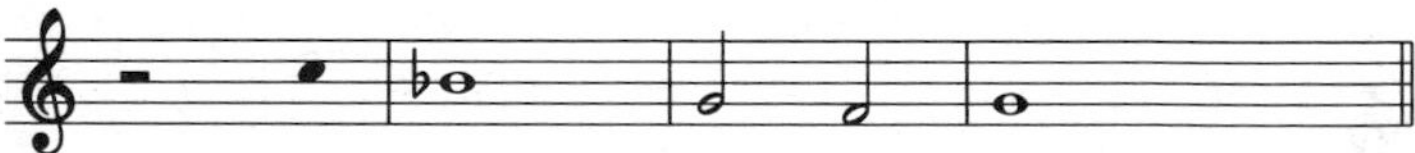

(6.) you did not **shrink** from a **hu** - man **birth.** (*to Antiphon II*)
(7.) we a - **wait** your **com**ing as **Judge**. (*to Verse 8*)
(8.) for **ever** with **all** who are **yours**. (*to Antiphon II*)

AFTER THE LAST ANTIPHON (𝅗𝅥 = 𝅝 of Verses)

Latin, *c.*400, tr. ALAN LUFF (1928–)

758 GREAT AND WONDERFUL

1 Great and wonderful are your deeds, Lord God Almighty!
Just and true are your ways, King of the ages!
Who shall not revere and praise your name, O Lord?
For you alone are holy.
All nations shall come and worship you,
for your judgements have been revealed.

2 You are worthy, our Lord and God, to receive
salvation and glory, honour and power,
for you created all things,
and by your will they were created and have their being;
and your judgements are true and just!

3 You are worthy, Lamb that was slain,
for by your blood you have redeemed for God
from every family and language and people and nation
a Kingdom of priests to serve our God on earth.

To him who sits on the throne, and to the Lamb,
be blessing and honour and glory and might
for ever and ever. Amen!

1) Revelation 15: 3*b*, 4
2) Revelation 4: 11; 16: 7*b*
3) Revelation 5: 9, 10, 13*b*

CONFESSIONS OF FAITH

759 THE APOSTLES' CREED

I believe in God, the Father almighty,
creator of heaven and earth.

I believe in Jesus Christ, God's only Son, our Lord,
who was conceived by the Holy Spirit,
born of the Virgin Mary,
suffered under Pontius Pilate,
was crucified, died, and was buried;
he descended to the dead.
On the third day he rose again;
he ascended into heaven,
he is seated at the right hand of the Father,
and he will come to judge the living and the dead.

I believe in the Holy Spirit,
the holy catholic Church,
the communion of saints,
the forgiveness of sins,
the resurrection of the body,
and the life everlasting. Amen.

760 THE NICENE CREED

We believe in one God,
the Father, the Almighty,
maker of heaven and earth,
of all that is, seen and unseen.

We believe in one Lord, Jesus Christ,
the only Son of God,
eternally begotten of the Father,
God from God, Light from Light,
true God from true God,
begotten, not made,
of one Being with the Father;
through him all things were made.

For us and for our salvation
he came down from heaven,
was incarnate of the Holy Spirit and the Virgin Mary
and became truly human.
For our sake he was crucified under Pontius Pilate;
he suffered death and was buried.
On the third day he rose again
in accordance with the Scriptures;
he ascended into heaven
and is seated at the right hand of the Father.
He will come again in glory to judge the living and the dead,
and his kingdom will have no end.

We believe in the Holy Spirit, the Lord, the giver of life,
who proceeds from the Father (and the Son),
who with the Father and the Son is worshipped and glorified,
who has spoken through the prophets.
We believe in one holy catholic and apostolic Church.
We acknowledge one baptism for the forgiveness of sins.
We look for the resurrection of the dead,
and the life of the world to come. Amen.

761 THE NATURE, FAITH AND ORDER OF THE UNITED REFORMED CHURCH

(*Version II, as approved by the General Assembly,* 1990)

With the whole Christian Church
the United Reformed Church believes in one God,
Father, Son and Holy Spirit.
The living God, the only God,
ever to be praised.
The life of faith to which we are called
is the Spirit's gift,
continually received
through the Word, the Sacraments
and our Christian life together.

(*continued overleaf*)

We acknowledge the gift
and answer the call,
giving thanks for the means of grace.

The highest authority
for what we believe and do
is God's Word in the Bible,
alive for his people today
through the help of the Spirit.

We respond to this Word,
whose servants we are
with all God's people
through the years.

We accept with thanksgiving to God
the witness to the catholic faith
in the Apostles' and Nicene Creeds.
We acknowledge the declarations
made in our own tradition
by Congregationalists, Presbyterians
and Churches of Christ
in which they stated the faith
and sought to make its implications clear.

Faith alive and active:
gift of an eternal source,
renewed for every generation.

We conduct our life together
according to the Basis of Union
in which we give expression to our faith
in forms which we believe contain
the essential elements of the Church's life,
both catholic and reformed;
but we affirm our right and readiness,
if the need arises,
to change the Basis of Union
and to make new statements of faith
in ever new obedience to the Living Christ.

Our crucified and risen Lord,
who leads us in our faith
and brings it to perfection.

Held together in the Body of Christ
through the freedom of the Spirit,
we rejoice in the diversity of the Spirit's gifts
and uphold the rights of personal conviction.
For the sake of faith and fellowship
it shall be for the church to decide
when differences of conviction
hurt our unity and peace.

We commit ourselves
to speak the truth in love
and grow together
in the peace of Christ.

We believe that
Christ gives his Church a government
distinct from the government of the state.
In the things that affect obedience to God
the Church is not subordinate to the state,
but must serve the Lord Jesus Christ,
its only Ruler and Head.
Civil authorities are called
to serve God's will of justice and peace for all humankind,
and to respect the rights of conscience and belief.

While we ourselves
are servants in the world
as citizens of God's eternal kingdom.

We affirm our intention
to go on praying and working,
with all our fellow Christians,
for the visible unity of the Church
in the way Christ chooses,
so that people and nations
may be led to love and serve God
and praise him more and more for ever.

Source, Guide, and Goal
of all that is:
to God be eternal glory.

Amen.

762 *National Anthem* 664 6664

Origin uncertain
(popularized in 1745)

God save our gracious Queen,
long live our noble Queen,
  God save the Queen!
Send her victorious,
happy and glorious,
long to reign over us;
  God save the Queen!

Anon., *c.*1745, altd.

COPYRIGHT ACKNOWLEDGEMENTS

The United Reformed Church and Oxford University Press are grateful to those who have given permission for copyright material to be included. Every effort has been made to trace copyright owners, and apologies are extended to anyone whose rights have inadvertently not been acknowledged. Any omissions or inaccuracies of copyright detail will be corrected in subsequent printings if valid claims have been received by the publisher.

The texts of the following canticles (and the pointing of the prose psalms and canticles) are by the compilers: *A Song of Creation* (737); *Salvator Mundi* (747); *A Song of Love* (753); and *Great and Wonderful* (758). The text of the *Order of Service* (1–20) and the *Confessions of Faith* (759–61) is from the 1989 *Service Book* of the URC, who hold the copyright. Adaptations of non-copyright texts made by the compilers are also property of the URC. Application for the use of material controlled by the URC and by OUP should be made in the first instance to the Hymn Copyright Manager, OUP, 7 Hatherley Street, London SW1P 2QT. Congregations may without prior application reproduce for one-time worship services any item bearing a URC copyright notice provided that the copyright acknowledgement is included on all copies. Permission to use all other items (whether in temporary or permanent form) should be sought from the respective owners. A list of the main copyright owners appears on page 1120 of the Full Music Edition; for any information not included there, please write to OUP (as above), enclosing a reply-paid envelope.

An acknowledgement has been placed next to a hymn where the copyright owner has requested this as a condition of granting permission. However, such on-page matter has been kept to a minimum, and users should refer to the complete list of copyright information which follows.

Texts from the following sources are acknowledged:

The Alternative Service Book, 1980: 748, 749 (from *An Anglican Prayer Book* 1989 [The Church of the Province of Southern Africa] with amendments)

The Book of Alternative Services, © 1985 The General Synod of the Anglican Church of Canada: 752 (*A Song of the First-Born*)

The Daily Office Revised, ed. Ronald C. D. Jasper (SPCK): 736 (*The Venite*)

The Grail Psalms: An Inclusive Language Version (Wm. Collins): 670, 678, 680, 693, 699, 702; by permission of A. P. Watt Ltd. on behalf of The Grail, England

Psalms from *The Book of Common Prayer of the American Episcopal Church*, 1979 (with minor adaptations): 672, 673, 675, 676, 682, 686, 692, 694, 696, 698, 700, 701, 706, 708, 710, 711, 714, 718, 719, 721, 724, 725, 728, 729, 730, 733.

The English translations of the *Benedictus* (738), *Magnificat* (739), *Nunc Dimittis* (742), and *Te Deum* (756) were prepared by the International Consultation on English Texts in 1975 and revised in 1988 by the English Language Liturgical Consultation.

5 Music: (*a*) and (*c*) © Les Presses de Taizé, published by Wm. Collins Ltd.
(*b*) © P. Bateman.

6 Music: © P. Bateman.

7 Music: © Les Presses de Taizé, published by Wm. Collins Ltd.

9 Music: (*a*) © Iona Community,

Wild Goose Publications, Pearce Institute, Govan, Glasgow G51 3UT. (*b*) and (*c*) © Les Presses de Taizé, published by Wm. Collins Ltd.

13 Music: Oxford University Press.

14 Music: (*a*) © Iona Community/Wild Goose Publications. (*b*) © P. Bateman.

15–17 Music: © P. Bateman.

20 Music: (*a*) Oxford University Press. (*c*)–(*f*) Executors of E. Thiman.

28 Words and Music: © Christian Conference of Asia.

29 Copyright © 1972 Maranatha! Music USA. Administered by CopyCare Ltd., 8 Marshfoot Lane, Hailsham, Sussex, BN27 2RA.

30 Copyright © 1976, 1981 Maranatha! Music USA. Administered by CopyCare Ltd.

33 Words: Stainer & Bell Ltd. Music: Oxford University Press from the *Revised Church Hymnary*, 1927.

35 Words: Stainer & Bell Ltd. Music: © G. L. Barnes.

41 Music: Oxford University Press from the *Revised Church Hymnary*, 1927.

42 Words: Stainer & Bell Ltd. Music: © F. Jackson.

44 Words: © Oxford University Press. Music: © D. Williams.

45 Words: © David Higham Associates.

46 Words and Music: Stainer & Bell Ltd.

48 Words: © Oxford University Press.

52 Words: Oxford University Press.

53 Music: United Reformed Church.

56 Words: Copyright © 1979 Hymn Society of America, Texas Christian University, Fort Worth, TX 76129, USA. Music: © P. Bateman.

57 Music: (*i*) © G. Hawkins.

60 Words: Stainer & Bell Ltd. Music: Copyright © 1977 Hope Publishing Company, Carol Stream, Illinois 60188, USA. All rights reserved.

64 Words: © T. Dudley-Smith. Music: © M. Baughen/Jubilate Hymns Ltd.

65 Words and Music: The Chansitor Press (for Wheaton Publishers) from *The Nursery Song & Picture Book*.

70 Words: © P. G. Jarvis.

75 Words: v.2 © H. M. Thwaites.

79 Words: © J. Quinn, by permission of Geoffrey Chapman (a division of Cassell plc). Music: Oxford University Press.

80 Words: © E. Cosnett. Music: © The Executors of John Dykes Bower.

82 Words: The Methodist Publishing House. Music: The Executors of W. K. Stanton.

83 Music: (*i*) © Carl Fischer Inc., New York. All rights reserved; international copyright secured. (*ii*) United Reformed Church.

84 Words: Oxford University Press.

85 Words and Music: Stainer & Bell Ltd.

86 Words: Copyright © 1967 Hope Publishing Company. All rights reserved.

87 Words: Stainer & Bell Ltd. Music: Oxford University Press.

88 Words: Stainer & Bell Ltd.

89 Words: Stainer & Bell Ltd. Music: (*i*) Copyright © 1971 Faber Music Ltd. from the *New Catholic Hymnal*. (*ii*) © P. Bateman.

90 Words and Music: Copyright © 1965 Josef Weinberger Ltd.

91 Words and Music: © The Caribbean Conference of Churches.

96 Copyright © 1923, renewal 1951, Hope Publishing Company. All rights reserved.

97 Music: (*ii*) © M. Archer.

99 Words: © J. W. Shore. Music: © P. L. Wright.

101 Words: © C. P. Thompson.

105 Words: © Christian Conference of Asia.
107 Words: © Iona Community/Wild Goose Publications.
108 Words: Stainer & Bell Ltd. (tr.). Music: © L. A. Lundberg.
110 Words and Music: © C. Micklem.
111 Words: © 1977 Hope Publishing Company. Music: © C. Micklem.
112 Words: © Oxford University Press. Music: (*i*) © C. Micklem; (*ii*) Oxford University Press.
114 Music: (*i*) Copyright © 1976 Hinshaw Music Inc.; (*ii*) The Public Trustee, for the Executors of Basil Harwood.
117 © 1953 Stuart K. Hine. Administered worldwide (excluding USA & Continental America) by Thankyou Music, Lottbridge Drove, Eastbourne, East Sussex, BN23 6NT.
122 Words: © D. Fox.
123 Words and Music: Stainer & Bell Ltd.
131 Words: McCrimmon Publishing Co. Ltd. Music: Oxford University Press.
136 Music: Oxford University Press.
141 Copyright © 1986 Thankyou Music.
142 Words: Tr. © Blandford Press (a division of Cassell plc).
145 Music: Oxford University Press from the *English Hymnal*.
148 Words: Oxford University Press from the *Oxford Book of Carols*.
151 Words and Music: © M. Perry/Jubilate Hymns.
152 Words: Stainer & Bell Ltd. Music: © R. Jacquet.
156 Words: United Reformed Church.
165 Words: Oxford University Press from the *Oxford Book of Carols*; v.2 © W. T. Pennar Davies.
166 Copyright © 1972 High-Fye Music Ltd, 8/9 Frith Street, London W1V 5TZ; all rights reserved.
173 Words: Oxford University Press from the *English Hymnal*.
174 Music: The Dohnavur Fellowship.
175 Words: Copyright © 1978 Lutheran Book of Worship, Augsburg Fortress, USA.
177 Words and Music: United Reformed Church.
178 Words: © Iona Community/ Wild Goose Publications.
180 Words and Music: © Iona Community/Wild Goose Publications.
183 Music: (*i*) Oxford University Press.
185 Music: Broomhill Church of Scotland, Glasgow.
186 Music: Oxford University Press.
188 Words and Music: Stainer & Bell Ltd.
189 Words: Stainer & Bell Ltd.
194 Words: v.3 © D. McIlhagga. Music: © The Church of St Charles Borromeo, Skillman, New Jersey, USA.
195 Words and Music: Stainer & Bell Ltd.
196 Words: Copyright © Josef Weinberger Ltd. Music: Oxford University Press.
197 Words: Stainer & Bell Ltd.
199 Words: © Methodist Church Division of Education and Youth.
200 Words: Mrs M. Rees. Music: (*i*) © G. L. Barnes; (*ii*) © P. Bateman.
201 Music: Oxford University Press from the *English Hymnal*.
202 Words: Oxford University Press.
204 Words: Canterbury Press from the *New English Hymnal*.
207 Music: © The John Ireland Trust, 35 St Mary's Mansions, London W2 1SQ.
210 Words: Stainer & Bell Ltd.
212 Words: © Church Pension Fund, USA.
213 Words: Stainer & Bell Ltd. Music: United Reformed Church.
214 Words: © F. E. V. Pilcher. Music: © L. Bartlett.
216 Words: Stainer & Bell Ltd.
219 Music: ©; owner untraced.
221 Words: Stainer & Bell Ltd.
222 Words: A. R. Mowbray Ltd. (a division of Cassell plc). Music: OUP.

225 Words and Music: Oxford University Press.
226 Words: Oxford University Press from the *English Hymnal*.
228 Words: Stainer & Bell Ltd.
229 Music: Hymns Ancient & Modern Ltd.
230 Words: Stainer & Bell Ltd.
231 Music: ©; owner untraced.
234 Copyright © 1973 The Word of God, PO Box 8617, Ann Arbor, MI 48107, USA.
237 Words: Stainer & Bell Ltd. Music: Oxford University Press.
238 Words: Hymns Ancient & Modern Ltd.
239 Music: (*i*) Oxford University Press.
240 Words: ©; owner untraced. Music: (*ii*) Oxford University Press from *Enlarged Songs of Praise*.
241 Copyright © 1983 Thankyou Music.
243 Words: Oxford University Press from the *Oxford Book of Carols*.
245 Words: Oxford University Press from *Enlarged Songs of Praise*.
247 Words: (*ii*) Stainer & Bell Ltd.
249 Words and Music: © C. Micklem.
251 Words: Oxford University Press.
260 Words: Oxford University Press.
263 Words: Stainer & Bell Ltd. Music: © P. Bateman.
267 Music: The Executors of John Dykes Bower.
268 Copyright © 1979 Springtide/Word Music (a division of Word [UK] Ltd.). Administered by CopyCare Ltd.
270 Words: © T. H. Evans.
271 Copyright © 1978 Springtide/Word Music (a division of Word [UK] Ltd.). Administered by CopyCare Ltd.
272 Music: (*ii*) Novello & Co. Ltd.
273 Words: Oxford University Press.
275 Words: © C. P. Thompson. Music: Oxford University Press.
276 Copyright © 1959, renewed 1987, Manna Music Inc. Administered by Thankyou Music.
279 Copyright © 1974, 1975 Celebration. Administered in Europe by Thankyou Music.
282 Words: Tr. © E. A. Evans and S. C. Orchard.
287 Words: Stainer & Bell Ltd.
288 Music: © The Church Pension Fund, USA.
294 Music: Oxford University Press from the *English Hymnal*.
296 Music: United Reformed Church.
298 Words: Copyright © 1971 Faber Music Ltd. from the *New Catholic Hymnal*.
300 Words: Copyright © Hymn Society of America, Texas Christian University, Fort Worth, TX 76129, USA. All rights reserved. Music: ©; owner untraced.
302 Music: ©; owner untraced.
303 Music: Broomhill Church of Scotland, Glasgow.
304 Words: © T. Dudley-Smith. Music: © G. Hawkins.
305 Music: Oxford University Press.
306 Words: United Reformed Church.
307 Words: © C. Micklem. Music: © 1958 Pilgrim Press, USA.
308 © 1935, 1963 Sparrow Corporation, PO Box 5010, 101 Winners Circle, Brentwood, TN 37024, USA.
309 Words: © M. Baughen/Jubilate Hymns.
311 Words: Oxford University Press from *Enlarged Songs of Praise*.
314 Music: (*i*) United Reformed Church; (*ii*) © P. Bateman.
315 Music: ©; owner untraced.
318 Words: © Mrs V. Caird.
319 Words: Copyright © 1954 renewed 1982 by Hope Publishing Company.
322 Words (adpt. from *Enlarged Songs of Praise* and *English Hymnal*): Oxford University Press. Music: Oxford University Press from the *English Hymnal*.
323 Music: Oxford University Press.
325 Words: United Reformed Church. Music: Oxford University Press.
326 Words: © 1982 Hymn Society of America, Texas Christian University, Fort Worth, TX 76129, USA.

COPYRIGHT ACKNOWLEDGEMENTS

327 Words: © B. E. Bridge.
328 Music: Hymns Ancient & Modern Ltd.
329 Words and Music: Oxford University Press.
334 Words: The Society of the Sacred Mission.
337 Words: © C. G. Hambly.
338 Words: Stainer & Bell Ltd.
339 Words and Music: Oxford University Press.
340 Words: Oxford University Press. Music: © P. Bateman.
341 Words: © C. P. Thompson.
342 Words: This translation (Stainer & Bell Ltd.) from Dietrich Bonhoeffer: *Letters and Papers from Prison* is made by permission of SCM Press. Music: United Reformed Church.
343 Words: Oxford University Press from *Planting Trees and Sowing Seeds*. Music: Copyright © 1967 Concordia Publishing House.
344 Words: © E. F. Downs.
346 Music: Oxford University Press from the *English Hymnal*.
347 Music: © The Iona Community/Wild Goose Publications.
349 Music: Oxford University Press from the *English Hymnal*.
350 Words: Oxford University Press from *Enlarged Songs of Praise*. Music: © R. Connolly.
352 Music: ©; owner untraced.
353 Music: Oxford University Press from the *English Hymnal*.
354 Words: Stainer & Bell Ltd. Music: The Governors of Repton School.
360 Music: The Representatives of the late Gwenlyn Evans.
361 Words: Oxford University Press. Music: Hymns Ancient & Modern Ltd.
362 Music: Oxford University Press.
366 Music: Oxford University Press.
367 Words: © C. Simmonds.
368 Music: © B. S. Massey.
373 Copyright © 1960 Josef Weinberger Ltd.
374 Words: © I. P. Alexander.
375 Copyright © 1978 Bob Kilpatrick Music, PO Box 2383, Fair Oaks, CA 95628, USA. All rights reserved; international copyright secured.
377 Copyright © 1967, 1980 Scripture in Song, administered by Thankyou Music.
381 Music: © B. Rose.
383 Music: Oxford University Press from the *BBC Hymn Book*.
385 Music: Hymns Ancient & Modern Ltd.
386 Copyright © 1976 Maranatha! Music USA. Administered by CopyCare Ltd.
388 Music: © B. S. Massey.
389 Music: Oxford University Press.
392 Music: © A. G. Murray.
393 © Iona Community/Wild Goose Publications.
394 © Iona Community/Wild Goose Publications.
395 Words: (*New English Bible*) © Oxford and Cambridge University Presses. Music: © C. Micklem.
396 © Les Presses de Taizé; published by Wm. Collins Ltd.
397 Words: par. © C. Micklem. Music: © J. Loring.
398 © Les Presses de Taizé; published by Wm. Collins Ltd.
399 © Les Presses de Taizé; published by Wm. Collins Ltd.
400 Music: Stainer & Bell Ltd.
401 © Iona Community/Wild Goose Publications.
402 © Les Presses de Taizé; published by Wm. Collins Ltd.
403 © Les Presses de Taizé; published by Wm. Collins Ltd.
404 Words and Music: Oxford University Press.
407 Words: Stainer & Bell Ltd.
409 Words: Oxford University Press from *Enlarged Songs of Praise*.
410 Words: Tr. ©; owner untraced.
412 Copyright © 1973 Hope Publishing Company; all rights reserved.
414 Words: Stainer & Bell Ltd.
415 Copyright © 1975 Lillenas

Publishing Company/Thankyou Music.
417 Words: Stainer & Bell Ltd.
418 Words: © J. B. O'Neill.
419 Words: © C. P. Thompson.
420 Music: (*ii*) © P. Bateman.
421 Words: Tr. ©; owner untraced.
422 Words and Music: Hymns Ancient & Modern Ltd.
423 Words: (par.) © C. Robertson.
424 Words: © D. Fox.
425 Words: Stainer & Bell Ltd. Music: Oxford University Press from the *English Hymnal.*
426 Words: © J. Geyer. Music: Copyright © 1978 *Lutheran Book of Worship*, Augsburg Fortress, USA.
427 Music: Copyright © 1980 GIA Publications, 7404 S. Mason Avenue, Chicago, Illinois 60638, USA; all rights reserved.
430 Words: © The Executors of William Robinson.
431 Words: © C. Micklem.
432 Words: Oxford University Press. Music: United Reformed Church.
435 Words: © C. P. Thompson.
436 Words: Oxford University Press. Music: Harmony from the *English Hymnal.*
437 Words: McCrimmon Publishing Co. Ltd. Music: (*i*) Geoffrey Chapman (a division of Cassell plc); (*ii*) © A. G. Murray.
438 Words: Stainer & Bell Ltd. Music: Oxford University Press.
439 Words: Stainer & Bell Ltd. Music: Oxford University Press from *Enlarged Songs of Praise.*
444 Words: © The Church Pension Fund, USA.
445 Words and Music: Oxford University Press.
447 Words: Oxford University Press. Music: (*i*) Lady Dunbar of Hempriggs: (*ii*) Oxford University Press.
448 Words: © F. E. V. Pilcher.
451 Words: The Executors of H. E. Lewis.
453 Words: Stainer & Bell Ltd.
454 Words: Stainer & Bell Ltd.
458 Words: © B. E. Bridge.
459 Music: United Reformed Church.
460 Words: United Reformed Church.
462 Music: Novello & Co. Ltd.
463 Words: Stainer & Bell Ltd.
464 Words: © Mrs M. Rees.
465 Words: © Stainer & Bell Ltd. Music: The Governors of Repton School.
466 Words: Oxford University Press. Music: Harmony Stainer & Bell Ltd.
467 Words: © Oxford University Press. Music: Oxford University Press from the *English Hymnal.*
468 Words: Oxford University Press.
469 Copyright © 1979 Springtide (a division of Word [UK] Ltd.). Administered by CopyCare Ltd.
471 Words and Music: © D. Trautwein; tr. Stainer & Bell Ltd.
473 Words: © J. Quinn, by permission of Geoffrey Chapman (a division of Cassell plc). Music: © A. G. Murray.
474 Copyright © Scripture in Song, administered in Europe by Thankyou Music.
475 Words: © G. Baker. Music: © 1959 Abingdon Press.
477 Copyright © 1979 Dave Bilbrough Songs, administered by Thankyou Music.
478 Words: © A. Frostenson; tr. World Council of Churches, Geneva. Music: © P. Bateman.
480 Words and Music: Stainer & Bell Ltd.
482 Words and Melody: Oxford University Press. Music: Arrangement © 1989 Hope Publishing Co.; all rights reserved.
483 Words: Oxford University Press. Music: (*i*) © C. Micklem; (*ii*) © B. S. Massey.
486 Words: Dietrich Bonhoeffer; official tr. is in *Letters and Papers from Prison*, Enlarged Edition, SCM Press 1971. This versification by F. Pratt Green (Stainer & Bell Ltd.) is made by permission of SCM Press.
490 Words: © Methodist Publishing House. Music: © C. Micklem.

491 Music: © D. Austin.
493 Music: Oxford University Press from the *English Hymnal*.
495 Music: Oxford University Press from the *English Hymnal*.
497 Words and Music: © C. Micklem.
498 Music: Oxford University Press for the Trustees of the Walford Davies Estate.
499 Words: © Mrs M. Rees.
503 Music: © C. Micklem.
504 Words: Oxford University Press from *Prayers and Hymns for Use in Schools*.
509 Music: Oxford University Press.
510 Words and Music: © C. M. Kao.
512 Copyright © 1972 Maranatha! Music USA. Administered by CopyCare Ltd.
516 Words and Music: © C. Micklem.
517 Music: Oxford University Press.
518 Copyright © 1975 Thankyou Music.
519 Words: The Executors of H. E. Lewis.
520 Words: Stainer & Bell Ltd.
522 Copyright © 1983 Thankyou Music.
524 Words: United Reformed Church. Music: (*ii*) Novello & Co. Ltd.
525 Words: adapted from the final sentences in Albert Schweitzer: *The Quest of the Historical Jesus*, © S. Woytt. Versification Stainer & Bell Ltd. Music: Oxford University Press.
527 Words: © The Church Pension Fund, USA.
529 Words: © T. Dudley-Smith.
530 Words: © J. Jenkins. Music: Oxford University Press.
531 Words: Oxford University Press.
532 Words: Mrs J. Tyrrell. Music: Oxford University Press from the *BBC Hymn Book*.
533 Words: ©; owner untraced. Music: © United Reformed Church.
534 Words: Copyright © 1971 Faber Music Ltd., from the *New Catholic Hymnal*. Music: Executors of W. K. Stanton.
539 Words: Stainer & Bell Ltd.
540 Words: Tr. © E. Evans and S. Orchard.
542 Music: Oxford University Press.
544 Music: (*i*) Oxford University Press.
547 Words and Music: McCrimmon Publishing Co. Ltd. and Stainer & Bell Ltd.
548 Words: © C. P. Thompson. Music: Oxford University Press.
549 Words and Music: © Stainer & Bell Ltd.
553 Words: © Judith Fetter.
555 © 1984, Utryck, Sweden (Iona Community/Wild Goose Publications).
556 Words: Oxford University Press from *Enlarged Songs of Praise*.
557 Music: Oxford University Press from the *English Hymnal*.
558 Words: © Iona Community/Wild Goose Publications.
560 Music: Oxford University Press.
565 Copyright © 1977 Thankyou Music.
567 Music: The Public Trustee for the Executors of Basil Harwood.
568 Words and Music: Oxford University Press.
569 Words: Oxford University Press from *Planting Trees and Sowing Seeds*. Music: © G. L. Barnes.
570 Words: © Oxford University Press.
571 Words: Oxford University Press.
572 Copyright © 1974 Thankyou Music.
574 Words © Mrs M. Seddon/Jubilate Hymns Ltd. Music: © J. Barnard/Jubilate Hymns Ltd.
576 Words: adpt. from *New World* © 1967 Oxford University Press. Music: Copyright © 1969 Vanguard Music Company, New York NY 10019.
578 Words: The Executors of H. E. Lewis.
579 Words: © H. Sherlock. Music: Oxford University Press.
580 Words: Copyright © 1978 Hope Publishing Company; all rights reserved.
581 Words: © Stainer & Bell Ltd. Music: Oxford University Press.

582 Words: © C. Micklem.
583 Words: © 1963 W. L. Jenkins; from *Songs and Hymns for Primary Children*, Westminster/John Knox Press.
585 Words: Tr. © S. Orchard.
586 Music: (*ii*) Novello & Co. Ltd.
591 Words and Music: © Kevin Mayhew Ltd.
594 Words and Music: © Kevin Mayhew Ltd.
595 Music: (*ii*) Copyright © 1971 Carl Fischer Inc., New York. All rights reserved; international copyright secured.
599 Music: The Executors of E. Thiman.
600 Words: © Stainer & Bell Ltd.
601 Words: Oxford University Press from *Enlarged Songs of Praise*.
602 Words: © J. Quinn, by permission of Geoffrey Chapman (a division of Cassell plc).
603 Words: © T. Dudley-Smith. Music: © Michael Baughen/Jubilate Hymns.
604 Music: Arrangement Oxford University Press from the *Revised Church Hymnary*, 1927.
607 Words and Music: Oxford University Press from *New Songs of Praise 6*.
609 Words and Music: Stainer & Bell Ltd.
611 Words: © Stainer & Bell Ltd. Music: Oxford University Press.
612 Words: © Mrs. J. Arlott. Music: Oxford University Press from the *English Hymnal*.
614 Music: Oxford University Press.
615 Music: Oxford University Press for the Trustees of the Walford Davies Estate.
616 Words: © J. Quinn by permission of Geoffrey Chapman (a division of Cassell plc).
619 Words: © Stainer & Bell Ltd.
620 Words: © Stainer & Bell Ltd.
621 Words: United Reformed Church.
622 Paraphrase © C. Hodgetts.
624 Words: Oxford University Press. Music: The League of Nations Union.
625 Words: © 1992 Hope Publishing Company, Carol Stream, Illinois 60188, USA. All rights reserved.
627 Words: © Prayer for Peace, 70 Weymouth Road, Frome, Somerset BA11 1HJ. Music: © P. Bateman.
628 Music: © B. S. Massey.
629 Copyright © 1968 Franciscan Communications, Los Angeles, CA 90015.
630 Words: Copyright © 1984 Hope Publishing Company; all rights reserved.
632 Words: The Executors of R. B. Y. Scott. Music: © The Executors of J. Hopkirk.
633 Words and Music: © R. Courtney.
634 Words: © Stainer & Bell Ltd.
635 Words: Oxford University Press from *Planting Trees and Sowing Seeds*.
636 Words: © Stainer & Bell Ltd.
637 Words: © Iona Community/Wild Goose Publications.
639 Words and Music: Oxford University Press.
641 Words: © Stainer & Bell Ltd.
642 Words: © Stainer & Bell Ltd. Music: Oxford University Press.
645 Words: from the *Resource Collection of Hymns and Service Music for the Liturgy* © 1981, International Committee on English in the Liturgy, Inc.; all rights reserved.
646 Words: © Stainer & Bell Ltd. Music: © B. Stephenson.
648 Copyright © 1969 Hope Publishing Company; all rights reserved.
649 Words: © G. Gardner.
650 Words: © D. Fox. Music: Oxford University Press.
651 Words: Oxford University Press. Music: © C. Micklem.
652 Words: Oxford University Press from *Planting Trees and Sowing Seeds*.
653 Words: © Iona Community/Wild Goose Publications.
654 Words: © 1967 B. Feldman & Co: International Music Publications.

655 Words: Oxford University Press. Music: © Lady Dunbar of Hempriggs.
658 Music: Oxford University Press.
659 Words: © Stainer & Bell Ltd.
661 Music: Oxford University Press.
664 Music: © D. Williams.
669 Paraphrase: © 1976 Hinshaw Music Inc.
670 Antiphon: © A. G. Murray. Tone: © The Grail.
671 Words and Music: © Iona Community/Wild Goose Publications.
674 Words: © I. Pitt-Watson.
678 Antiphon: © A. G. Murray. Tone: © The Grail.
680 Antiphon I: © A. G. Murray. Tone and Antiphon II: © The Grail.
693 Antiphon: © A. G. Murray. Tone: © The Grail.
695 Words: © I. Pitt-Watson.
696 Music: Chant (*i*): J. M. Thalben-Ball.
698 Antiphon and Tone: © B. Stephenson.
699 Antiphon and Tone: © The Grail.
702 Antiphons I and II: © A. G. Murray. Tone: © The Grail.
708 Antiphon © B. Stephenson. Tone: © McCrimmon Publishing Co. Ltd.
709 Words: Copyright © 1974 Hope Publishing Company; all rights reserved.
711 Antiphon and Tone: © B. Stephenson.
713 Copyright © 1977, 1980 Thankyou Music.
714 Music: (*a*) and (*b*) Oxford University Press for the Trustees of the Walford Davies Estate.
716 Music: © C. Micklem.
718 Music: (*b*) © W. White.
720 © Concordia Publishing House, USA.
721 Music: Oxford University Press for the Trustees of the Walford Davies Estate.
725 Antiphon: © B. Stephenson. Tone: © McCrimmon Publishing Co. Ltd.
729 Antiphon: © B. Stephenson. Tone: © McCrimmon Publishing Co. Ltd.
731 Words: © I. Pitt-Watson. Music: ©; owner untraced.
733 (Second Version) Music: Antiphon © B. Stephenson. Tone © McCrimmon Publishing Co. Ltd.
739 Music: (*ii*) J. M. Thalben-Ball; (*iii*) Oxford University Press for the Trustees of the Walford Davies Estate.
740 Words: © T. Dudley-Smith. Music: Oxford University Press.
741 Words: (*RSV*) par. A. Luff, Oxford University Press. Music: © McCrimmon Publishing Co. Ltd.
742 (Second Version) Music: Antiphon and Tone © B. Stephenson.
743 Music: Oxford University Press.
745 Music: Arrangement from the *Australian Hymn Book*, 1977.
746 Words: Tr. Oxford University Press. Music: © 1957 Philippo/Combre Editions, Paris.
747 Words: The Compilers. Music: © McCrimmon Publishing Co. Ltd.
750 Words: © 1940, 1943, renewed 1971, the Church Pension Fund, USA. Music: © 1978 *Lutheran Book of Worship*, Augsburg Fortress, USA.
752 Music: McCrimmon Publishing Co. Ltd.
753 Music: Les Presses de Taizé, published by Wm. Collins Ltd.
754 Words: © J. B. O'Neill. Music: © B. Newport.
757 Words and Music: © Stainer & Bell Ltd.

Addresses of main copyright holders can be found on p. 1120 of the Full Music Edition.

INDEX OF FIRST LINES AND TITLES (WITH TUNES)

This index includes hymns, psalms, canticles, prayers, and liturgical items. Where titles differ from first lines they are shown in *italic*.

Some of the hymns in *Rejoice and Sing* have first lines which differ from those by which they were known in books previously used in the URC, and the earlier versions are shown in square brackets here. Where the difference arises from the use of an alternative or fresh translation, the symbol † is included.

A separate list of prayer responses can be found in the Index of Themes in the Full Music Edition.

Psalms are indexed by first line rather than by Psalm number. They can be found in numerical order in the Psalms and Canticles section, from no. 669 onwards in the main body of the book.

In the tunes column, where psalm chants and other musical items do not have tune names as such, their composers' names are shown in parentheses.

INDEX

INDEX

INDEX

INDEX

INDEX

INDEX

INDEX

INDEX

INDEX

INDEX

INDEX